ATOMIC BOMB CINEMA

ATOMIC BOMB CINEMA

The apocalyptic imagination on film

JEROME F. SHAPIRO

ROUTLEDGE

NEW YORK AND LONDON

Published in 2002 by
Routledge
29 West 35th Street
New York, NY 10001

Published in Great Britain by
Routledge
11 New Fetter Lane
London EC4P 4EE

Routledge is an imprint of the Taylor & Francis Group.

Cataloging-in-Publication Data is available from the Library of Congress.

ISBN 0–415–93659–4—ISBN 0–415–93660–8 (Pbk.)

To my beloved *uchi no kamisan*,
Tomoko "Tonia" Yabe,
and our two wonderful children,
Dixon Takashi and Sydney Kozue.
Daily they restore my fractured world
with love and laughter.

CONTENTS

ACKNOWLEDGMENTS

In my first year of college, I asked an art professor how long it took him to make a photograph. With the polished sarcasm of a Zen master he scoffed, "All my life." With that in mind, I would simply like to thank the world for my existence, and also thank everyone I have ever known. But that does not seem appropriate. So, let me begin by acknowledging that same art professor for so immeasurably enriching my life and without whom this book may never have been written. H. Arthur Taussig, my cherished friend, thank you. And, thanks to the members of my doctoral committee, who, way back when, believed in me when it seemed like few others did: Dickran Tashjian, Anne Friedberg, Joseph L. White, Masayasu Normura, and especially Peter Clecak, who encouraged me to pursue my scholarship as a creative, spiritual activity.

A few individuals deserve special recognition: Joanne Trautmann Banks, Allan Casebier, Hayao Kawai, Toshio Kawai, J. Brooks Maue, Rabbi Mel Silverman, Gerald Vizenor, Seth Ward, and especially Tomoko Yabe and Shin-ichi Anzai, for inspiring and helping me to complete this book; Takashi Akinami, for his lectures on Japanese theater and a gesture of friendship that I was too young to appreciate; Harue Yokoyama and Masaki Haramoto, for teaching me ikebana and so much more; Thomas Dabbs, for his extraordinary generosity and brilliance in showing me that I could both shorten and improve my manuscript; William Germano, my editor, of course, along with Matt Byrnie, Lisa Vecchione, Lai Moy, and everyone at Routledge deserve more thanks than I could possibly offer; and Mr. Mumma, of Castro Valley, California, for teaching me to read when no one else could.

Some of the scholars that I strongly challenge in this book have encouraged me in my research, and some are even my friends. James Berger, Mick Broderick, David Desser, Linda C. Ehrlich, Robert J. Lifton, Donald Richie, and most especially Paul Boyer, I thank you.

Many others deserve my thanks, including: Takao Aoki, Sakura Asoda, Bonnie Lee Berger, Brad and Nenelle Bunnin, Donna Chaban, Steve Cohen, Randy Davis, A. J. Dickinson, Peter Dusenbery, Yasuhiro Enno, Raoul Fernandez, Aaron Gerow, Mike Gonzales, Michael Gorman, Bernard Greenberg, Kimi

Honda, Tarow Indow, Helen Irlen, Kenji Iwamoto, Joseph G. Jorgensen, Eriko Kamata, Setsuo and Chizuko Kamimura, June Kurata, Judith Kimura, Jayne Loader, Kit Machado, Leo Maloy III, Lorne Marin, Howard and Amy Mass, Edna Mejia, Masaki Nishimura, Reiko Nitta, Masako Notoji, Patricia Jean Olynyk, Al Painter, Richard B. Parker, Susan Pavloska, Frank Pollick, Anne Saddington, Yasuo Sakakibara, Masaki Satō, Chris Schreiner, Masatoyo and Yumiko Sawada and family, Takao Shōhōji, Robert Sklar, Pam Steinle, Andrea Streit, Masanori Suiko, Takahiro Sumiya, Jane M. Sweeney, Brian Teaman, Blake Thatcher, Akira Tochigi, Kazuo Totani, John and Tomoko Traphagan, Michael Treanor, Tadashi Wakashima, Brad Warner, Holger Westmyer, Dale Write, Betty May Yang, Satoru Yoshimoto, and my many teachers and students in Japan and the United States.

I wish to also acknowledge the support of Orange Coast College, especially the Fine Arts Division and the English Department; California State University, Long Beach, Philosophy and Comparative Literature Departments, and California State University International Programs; Waseda University, International Division, and my friends in the Kendo and Rainbow clubs; University of California, Irvine, Program in Comparative Culture, Film Studies, and the School of Social Sciences; Kyoto University, Faculty of Integrated Human Studies and Faculty of Letters; my many colleagues in the Faculty of Integrated Arts and Sciences, Hiroshima University, and especially our departmental secretaries, Tomoko Takeda and Kazumi Okano; the Japanese Association for American Studies; the American Studies Association; the Society for Cinema Studies; the Japan American Literature Society; the Hiroshima Society for the Science of Arts; the Japan Society of Image Arts and Sciences; Kyoko Hirano and the Japan Society; Richard Landis and the Center for Millennial Studies; and particularly Leonard Greenspoon and Creighton University's Klutznick Symposium.

Last, but not least: Harry and Sue, my parents, and Steven and Beth, my siblings; my many relations branching out from the Shapiro, Chaban, Yabe, Nishijima, Jitsukata, and Kuriyama families; and my host family in Japan, the Asodas. Most importantly, my wife, Tomoko, and our children, Dixon Takashi and Sydney Kozue—they have contributed so much to my writing this book.

I thank you, one and all.

INTRODUCTION

Vexing questions,
and atomic bomb cinema

It is a strange but psychologically most interesting fact that almost
every critical period in history considers itself as the worst that has
ever existed and as the one that precedes the final doom of mankind.

Our time is truly disruptive. . . .

—Gerhard Adler, "Psychology and the Atom Bomb"[1]

As I sit before my computer putting the final touches on this study, writing the introduction, I can just barely see my reflection in the monitor. I imagine myself to be an actor in the Nō theater of Japan. Before going on stage the actor sits before a mirror, with mask in hand, and meditates. This creates a state of *ma* or emptiness within him, thus allowing the spirit of the character he plays to fill the vacuum created by the *ma*. Through the actor the tormented spirit can tell his story, achieve catharsis, then return to the other world and rest. But the actor, who has his own story, is not just a vehicle for the spirit.

My story begins in the late winter of 1984 when I fled West from an unusually cold Tokyo to thaw out. As with all good journeys, the most important moments occurred during the return trip. On my way home I stopped in Nagasaki, and then Hiroshima. In Hiroshima I was dumbstruck by the dark silhouette of a body on stone steps, the surrounding surface having been bleached by the light of an atomic bomb. I have been unable to excise this image from my memory. It sits on my mind like a third eye looking inward. After returning to California I began, without any conscious plan or goal, to collect images of the bomb, primarily films. As frequently happens when one is too close to a subject, it took a friend to suggest that I use the films and ideas I had already collected and write a book on the image of the bomb in films, or what I now call *atomic bomb cinema*.

After some time, past events began to fit into place. I rediscovered a book on Japanese fairy tales that, although not read for quite some time, had sat next to my bed. The book, given to me in my childhood, was a favorite.[2] And, I can clearly recall watching *Godzilla, King of the Monsters* (i.e., *Gojira*) on TV (see Figure 6). Apparently, both strongly impressed me. When I think back to my childhood, many of the films I saw were about the bomb. Then, in 1982, a girlfriend's father died of lymphoma. The family believes he contracted the cancer from exposure to nuclear-weapons tests while serving in the military.[3]

The year my friend's father was exposed to radiation, 1958, is one of the peak years for the release of bomb films; it is also the year I was born. My first trip to Japan was in *Shōwa* 58 (1983), or the fifty-eighth year of the Emperor Shōwa. I chose fifty-eight as the number for my Waseda University Kendo Club jacket. No matter how I interpret these events—ironic coincidence, synchronicity, divine guidance—these events have influenced my life. With all this in the background, watching several hundred bomb films has been both a pleasure and a trial.

Viewing these films has changed the way I see the world. At a dinner party with colleagues from various departments of an American university where I was conducting research, we all began to describe our current research projects. After describing mine, one individual very involved with Amnesty International, bemoaned the "fact" that "people" have ignored the bomb for fifty years. Many scholars, particularly those stridently opposed to nuclear weapons, such as Robert J. Lifton, Donald Richie, Susan Sontag, Paul Boyer, and most recently Gar Alperovitz, make this same argument, but I do not.[4] Oddly enough, the bomb is the one issue where if you disagree with someone, or if the other person is not an anti–nuclear weapons activist, then you accuse that other person of ignoring the issue altogether. I suggested to everyone then that because the bomb cuts across every gender, race, ethnicity, class, and cultural, ideological, and national boundary, atomic bomb cinema serves as the perfect model for understanding how the politically powerless respond to their situation. It was at that moment that I understood my own work more clearly than I ever had before.

In late 1991 I returned to Japan, first to Kyoto University, and then to Hiroshima University where I am now an associate professor. My tenure at Hiroshima University has given me the opportunity to complete this study. As usual, the motivation came from very unexpected sources. In my classes on film and culture I stress the idea that good scholarship is driven by a highly personal need to find answers to vexing questions. One graduate student assisting me with my research quite rightly asked me, then, why I am drawn to sensational monster films. Her question took me by surprise, and it compelled me to reconsider the meaning of Japanese bomb films. The penultimate chapter of this book consists of my responses to her question. Only after finishing this chapter did I realize that I had come full circle on a journey I had started nearly twenty years ago. I first came to Japan to study how Japanese films—particularly the works of Akira Kurosawa—explore philosophical issues. Although other films and other filmmakers now seem more important and more interesting, my chapter on Japanese bomb films ends, curiously, with a discussion of Kurosawa's three bomb films.

As the year 2000 approached and passed, and I finished revising this manuscript, themes that I was not fully aware of when I first started writing seemed to rise to the surface and become more apparent, in particular, the importance of ancient patterns of thought in everyday life. It is a cliché as well as an absurdity to say that Japanese culture has a particular relationship to nature in light of Japan's self-destructive obsession with modernity. But, to find that this relationship determines how the Japanese create films about the bomb—that is, how the Japanese make the bomb meaningful to themselves—indicates that this relationship to nature remains a living, vital part of everyday life. Likewise, every educated person knows that Judaism is a pillar of Western civilization. But, to find that an ancient Jewish way of viewing the world informs most American films about the bomb—that is, how Americans make the bomb meaningful to themselves—indicates that these patterns of thought are truly a living, vital part of everyday life in mainstream American culture. Bringing this manuscript to a close has brought to my consciousness an awareness of how personal are the themes that inform my professional interests; these include the struggle to make a place for myself in a foreign world and, especially, a childhood brush with death that engendered a lifelong struggle to come to terms with my own mortality. Once again, I compare the shifting perceptions of my writing to the Nō stage. A book is like a stage because it is a medium between two worlds. Like a

Nō theater performance, my work seems to have a life of its own beyond that of the individual performers. As a writer, I become like the Nō actor who need not be fully aware of the spirit, or spirits, that moves him. The spirit that fills the Nō actor also needs an audience to hear his story. For this, I am grateful to the reader.

Atomic Bomb Cinema

Some will argue that the bomb instantly caused a permanent rift between our own time and the Edenic past. Jacques Derrida, one of the luminaries of the critical theory movement, opines, "Unlike the other wars . . . nuclear war has no precedent."[5] This sudden departure from a familiar world has, it is often argued today, left many with a sense of loss and disorientation—and worse, denial or "psychic numbing." At the same time, Frederic Jameson's famous notion that "pastiche and schizophrenia" characterize "the postmodernist [i.e., the post-1960s] experience of space and time" has been extended by others to characterize the very fabric of existence since August 1945.[6] More importantly, critics and scholars, like Jonathan Schell, also tell us that the past is largely irrelevant to surviving this perilous new age, and we must embrace new ways of thinking.[7] The rift, however, is more apparent than real. As Frank Kermode astutely writes, "It seems doubtful that our crisis, our relations to the future and to the past, is one of the important differences between us and our predecessors."[8] That is to say, the rift is more apparent than real because the notion of the rift is, ironically, a traditional way of thinking about how history unfolds itself. This idea appears in various texts written in numerous cultures at different times. Thus, while the bomb was indeed a startling event, it only seems to have cut our ties to the past.

At the height of the cold war, when the production of films with images of the bomb was at a peak, the psychologist C. G. Jung posed a question that underscores the continuity between the past and the present:

[A]s early as the beginning of the eleventh century the belief arose that the devil, not God, had created the world. Thus the keynote was struck for the second half of the Christian aeon, after the myth of the fall of the angels had already explained that these fallen angels had taught men a dangerous knowledge of science and the arts. What would these old storytellers have to say about Hiroshima?[9]

Modern psychology was born on the cusp of the Western world's lurch toward modernity. Its early founders—Sigmund Freud, Alfred Adler, and Jung—were also born on this cusp. They were a peculiar group of scientists who were obsessed with the mysteries of the human psyche, and convinced that dreams and stories could actually help individuals and groups to resolve difficult problems. They argued that dreams and stories are the products of both specific historical events and universal patterns of human thought. Long ago, these events and patterns of thought were woven into recognizable narratives. Almost paradoxically, these ancient narratives seem to structure how we perceive the world; and yet, they lend themselves to alteration and revision by succeeding generations. Clearly, these narratives are vital to how both individuals and cultures respond to a changing world. Ironically, however, the founders of modern psychology seemed to demonstrate little interest in another institution that was developing at approximately the same time: the cinema. This lack of interest is ironic precisely because atomic bomb cinema represents the best contemporary example of how human beings use traditional narrative structures and imagery to understand unprecedented events.

But why should anyone be concerned about films with images of "the bomb"? There are several good reasons why. The cinema and the atomic bomb are two of the most significant technological innovations of the past century, and both are very important to the culture. Atomic bomb cinema, the point where these two technologies intersect, is a statistically important part of the American filmgoer's diet. And, in contrast to commonly held beliefs, atomic bomb cinema is undeniably part of a process that helps people to understand the threat of nuclear war. Therefore, at least in this instance, the cinema is one cultural institution that contributes to a healthy society. If these academic justifications fail to pique the reader's interest, then there is another simpler reason that supersedes the others: many bomb films are just good fun to watch. In this study I will illustrate how recurring themes and formal structures are used in bomb films, and therefore must be treated as a coherent body of films; identify historical, mythological, and contemporary motifs; and analyze these films from two points of view: interdisciplinary (including perspectives from history, politics, economics, sociology, and aesthetics) and cross-cultural (American, Japanese, British, German, and Australian). Most importantly, I will demonstrate that the essential element of atomic bomb cinema is the *apocalyptic imagination*; filmmakers use this to structure their narratives and explore a wide range of ideological issues. These films, moreover, express the Jewish apocalyptic tradition, which exhorts the restoration of a fractured world more than they express the dominant Messianic Christian tradition's focus on the hereafter. I will also show how Japanese films are structured by a different but related essential element, what I call *the restoration of balance and harmony through playfulness*. I will also argue that there is an important, perhaps essential, similarity between bomb films made in the United States, other Western societies, and Japan.

Early on, the strategic importance of the intersection between the cinema and the bomb was recognized by government policymakers in a crude way. It is now widely known that during World War II the U.S. government tried to censor any popular discussion of nuclear energy, particularly in films. Recently, film historians have brought to light the extent to which the Supreme Command of the Allied Powers (SCAP) censored references to Hiroshima and Nagasaki in films made during the Occupation years of Japan, and the extent to which the Japanese government itself also suppressed, and even now continues to suppress, culturally and historically important films about the atomic bombings.[10] Nevertheless, since 1945 nearly a thousand films, both domestic and foreign, with images of nuclear weapons have been released in the United States. Most of these films have been very popular, and yet they have, until recently, been virtually ignored by everyone but the filmgoing public. While scholars and critics do write about these films, there are no other in-depth studies that conceptualize these films as a coherent body of film texts. Thus, atomic bomb cinema remains an unmined resource of information about our culture. The question remains, most importantly, what do these films tell us about American life under the shadow of the bomb? The answer, quite simply, is that these films reveal how deeply concerned are Americans about the bomb and its impact on the struggle for survival, the individual's pursuit of spiritual or psychological rebirth, and the establishment of a just society.

The political, academic, and popular debate over the influence of these two technologies—the bomb and the cinema—on modern culture has been tremendous, and often the more civil expression of savage power struggles. For example, on the one hand, Paul Boyer argues that the bomb is a virtual Kantian category—an internal filter, so to speak, of the mind— that shapes our very understanding of the world: "It is as though the Bomb has become one of those categories of Being . . . that, according to Kant, are built into the very structure of our minds."[11] Robert Coles, on the other hand, argues that our understanding of the bomb is shaped by the social environment.[12] The struggle for knowledge and control of nuclear weapons has, in either case, engendered massive security agencies that while intended to protect the citizenry have, at times, destroyed careers and lives, and subverted the democratic process, disempowering all but a few. The cinema has inspired no less of a debate than the bomb. David Cook, the film historian, reminds us that in 1895 the first audience of the commercial cinema panicked and fled the theater when a train magically appeared before them.[13] Since then, many have argued that the cinema has the power to influence not only the audience's responses in the theater, but also the development of society and culture. Struggles for control over the film industry have been bitter, with many casualties. Robert Sklar, a noted cultural historian of American cinema, writes, "For much of their history . . . movies had been a site of struggle over cultural power."[14] They still are. In fact, more than any other body of films, atomic bomb cinema is the paradigmatic site of struggle over cultural power for our time, and, consequently, the locus of highly dubious theoretical and empirical assertions about the bomb, cinema, and culture.

For instance, Donald Richie, an authority on Japanese films, was the first to denounce popular monster movies because of their "very refusal to make a responsible statement" about the bomb.[15] Expanding on this idea, Susan Sontag both established science fiction films as a legitimate subject for scholars and derailed further critical inquiry with her now famous declaration that popular bomb films, Japanese bomb films in particular, are "above all the emblem of an *inadequate response*" [emphasis in original] and only a "sampling, stripped of sophistication, of the inadequacy of most people's responses to the unassimilable terrors" wrought by the nuclear arms race.[16] But what is a responsible or adequate response, except, by implication, that of the critics? Be that as it may, Robert J. Lifton provided a theoretical foundation to Richie and Sontag's argument by using the films as further evidence for global psychic numbing.[17] Daniel Patrick Moynihan's now infamous 1965 report for the U.S. Department of Labor, "The Negro Family: The Case for National Action," was not widely available until 1967, the same year Lifton's book, *Death in Life: Survivors of Hiroshima*, was published.[18] Still, the report's divisive impact was immediate and widespread. At best, the ensuing controversy forced individuals and institutions to reconsider their own assumptions about a plural America; at worst, it stifled some areas of legitimate research and public debate (a parallel situation exists in Japan vis-à-vis A-bomb victims and other minority groups). The fallout on both the academic and the general sociopolitical landscapes from the report itself—that is, the report's theorizing one segment of American society as pathological—has been corrosive.[19] One would expect, therefore, that subsequent scholars, particularly cultural critics and social psychologists, would be more cautious or at least less strident in claiming that entire populations, even global populations, suffer from a debilitating psychopathology. The appeal of theories of pathology, nevertheless, remains as widespread as ever, if not more so, among scholars.

Among critics of the bomb and culture, the pathological line of reasoning reached its zenith in 1985. In the otherwise sober history, *By the Bomb's Early Light*, Paul Boyer gives historical legitimacy to the psychopathology argument by asserting that "Hollywood contributed its bit" to what amounts to society's bipolar "cycles" between paranoia and denial.[20] Boyer's book is so influential that many lesser scholars have tried, usually unsuccessfully, to use Boyer's argument as a foundation for their own. Most recently, Joyce A. Evans, in *Celluloid Mushroom Clouds: Hollywood and the Atomic Bomb*, repeatedly criticizes fictional narrative films for "not realistically depict[ing]" the bomb; and, in one of the best studies of bomb films so far, *Film and the Nuclear Age: Representing Cultural Anxiety*, Toni A. Perrine throughout employs the "cyclical" argument, and judges films for their "seriousness" or "[in]adequacy" in representing "nuclear disaster."[21] Working from a different theoretical background, James Berger, in a fascinating study, *After the End: Representations of Post-Apocalypse*, similarly condemns most people for being numb to their own lives, and popular culture for being a numbing vehicle. Berger especially criticizes the cinema because its "ideological sutures . . . hide the damages and repetitions" caused by traumatizing historical events and the threat of nuclear annihilation.[22] At the farthest extreme is Kim Newman who, in *Apocalypse Movies: End of the World Cinema*, adopts the cyclical argument and is more concerned with plotting films along his "nexus between exploitation and art" than with analyzing a film's meaning.[23] Christian Metz refers to these sorts of commentary as "restoring a 'good' cinema"—that is, as a type of criticism that advocates a certain style or ideology while condemning others, rather than a type of criticism that reveals the metastructures that shape the film and our responses toward the film.[24]

Neither the scholarly literature nor any given author's work is, of course, monolithic. Mick Broderick, in *Nuclear Movies*, subscribes to theories of global psychic numbing, but intentionally problematizes his theoretical assumptions, opening them up to question.[25] H. Bruce Franklin, in *Countdown to Midnight*, an anthology of nuclear-war short stories, writes:

> Science fiction does give us some unique insights into the sources, dangers, and dimensions of the nuclear menace. And understanding a problem is certainly the first and biggest step toward a solution.[26]

Perrine skillfully elaborates on Franklin's ideas and hints at a dilemma in interpreting such narratives. She argues that in films "deal[ing] with postnuclear scenarios . . . humankind must survive if there is to be any story to show." Perinne, nevertheless, resolves this paradox through her own denial of atomic bomb cinema's complexity. She concludes that bomb films "primarily give voice to disavowal, denial or apathy," and create an "inertia" that is difficult for audiences to "overcome."[27] Most other scholars in the field, with exceptions like Peter Fitting, have taken the psychopathology argument for granted and repeat the phrases "inadequate response" and global "psychic numbing" (and "the Atomic Age") with mind-numbing regularity.[28] I see things somewhat differently. Rather than denial, both bomb films and the critical commentary suggest how different strata of the culture are struggling to come to terms with the bomb.

I too am deeply concerned about popular culture. However, having spent a large part of my life in Japan—not as a visiting scholar cloistered in the university but as an expatriate cut off from my own culture and struggling with the immigrant experience—my views have tempered. As a scholar, moreover, I am concerned only with what the bomb means in our imaginations, and thus strictly limit myself to film and cultural analysis. To me, a film is good or bad only to the extent that after repeated viewings it remains interesting or challenging to analyze—an admittedly subjective experience. Regarding the morals or ethics of nuclear technologies, I am stridently and unfashionably apolitical. Therefore, my approach to these films differs radically from the scholars I have cited and others. I do not follow the standard scholarly interpretative strategies of looking at these films as evidence of nuclearism, a vast break in public consciousness, or covert political and religious propaganda, and thus a distorted representation of some nuclear reality. Such arguments seem to me to leave little room for irony, ambiguity, ambivalence, comedy, and debate (or what Robert Warshow calls the "current[s] of opposition [in "mass culture"] . . . which optimism itself helps to create").[29] These arguments are also hopelessly

Manichaean, teleological, and tragic. They assume that people cognitively and emotionally experience and process events in the same way and at the same speed, and express themselves in the same "discursive" form (as opposed to the "presentational" form).[30] They exist as, or fuel, a violent, "activist" type of apocalyptic imagination from which I wish to distance myself. In the human imagination, moreover, the bomb has not been the only destroyer of worlds. There have also been the ram's horn, Cortés's cannons, mustard gas, the Final Solution, the Japanese Zero, Agent Orange, and other technologies of destruction. Thus, as Frank Kermode warns, it is "childish to argue, in a discussion of how people behave under eschatological threat, that nuclear bombs are more real and make one experience more authentic crisis-feelings than" any other perceived threat.[31] All this is to say that if anything structures our minds like a Kantian category, it is not the bomb (as Boyer believes) but the apocalypse. Thus, to paraphrase Melvin J. Lasky, I am proposing a *revolutionary* interpretation (i.e., to solve a current dilemma we must *revolve* around and back to an origin) of postwar culture.[32] Specifically, I am arguing that the vast body of films that I call atomic bomb cinema is the most recent manifestation of the ancient apocalyptic tradition of continuance.

By "atomic bomb cinema" I am referring to films where the bomb is an explicit part of the *mise-en-scène* (the set or environment), theme, context, and/or the narrative. Merely mentioning the bomb, however, as many films do, is not enough to warrant inclusion in this study. At the end of the very popular love story, *The Way We Were* (Sydney Pollack, 1973), for instance, Katie Morosky (Barbara Steisand) is passing out antinuclear leaflets, but this is just one of many liberal lost causes that she champions throughout the story; this film is not mentioned in the relevant literature, and it is at best tangential to my own study.[33] By "cinema" I am, for the most part, referring to what scholars call "classical," Hollywood-style, fictional, narrative films. The most distinguishing features of Hollywood style filmmaking are the seamless camera work and editing techniques that obscure the presence of the camera, and give the two-dimensional film medium an appearance of lifelike three dimensionality. These techniques are used to help the spectator become more emotionally involved in the narrative, and maybe even forget, however briefly, that he or she is watching a film.

The "classical" Hollywood style is, however, an imprecise concept.[34] The very term "Hollywood" is misleading. The Hollywood style, after all, is used widely outside that small part of California. Moreover,

"Hollywood" itself is not a monolithic institution. Raymond Williams points out that every institution is composed of what he calls "dominant," "residual," and "emergent" forces, all competing for control of the institution.[35] In other words, institutions are constantly changing because they are made up of individuals struggling to survive in, change, and/or maintain the institution. (Few scholars today would disagree with Williams and yet, curiously, many persist in describing Hollywood as monolithically malevolent.) At the same time, there are also external forces that influence the development of an institution. Like any society or institution, Hollywood can be described as a collection of different individuals who voluntarily band together for their own benefit; or, a homogeneous community where individual identity is derived from the group. On the one hand, all filmmakers are guided by a single principal: profitability and the perpetuation of the industry. But on the other hand, Hollywood is also made up of individuals all competing for scarce resources with which to realize their own creative potentials. This paradox, the philosophical problem of "the one or the many," need not be resolved here; rather, it should be provisionally accepted as the dynamic phenomenon engendered by the term "Hollywood" (and "American culture," for that matter). In any case, the notion of a classical Hollywood style has heuristic value, for it suggests everything that filmgoers throughout the world have come to expect from the commercial cinematic experience. This expectation of what films should be is so pervasive that, for example, other styles can be referred to as, simply, "alternative cinemas."

To understand atomic bomb cinema it is not necessary to judge the relative value of Hollywood or the classical Hollywood style. Suffice it to say that while Hollywood is frequently condemned for relying on sensationalism and marketing strategies, it has produced a number of films of artistic integrity and lasting cultural importance. Indeed, some bomb films have been acknowledged as exemplary, or even film art. Generally, however, in atomic bomb cinema there is little radical variation from the "classical" use of the cinematic apparatus. That is to say, bomb films are generally not marketed as consciousness-raising events or art, but entertainment; the bomb is frequently a vehicle for reworking standard and often ancient narrative structures; and, while bomb films must often devise unique filmic structures to tell their stories, as we will see in *On the Beach* (Stanley Kramer, 1959), there are only a few films that offer formal surprises. The surprises are found in the unique twists that the bomb gives to traditional imagery and narratives, and classical filmmaking techniques.

"The bomb" is manifested in Hollywood films in a variety of ways—nuclear weapons, fallout, toxic poisoning, terrorism—and the anxieties these induce. Images and references to the bomb are in turn found in almost every film genre, ranging from the obvious war and science fiction films to less expected genres, such as comedies, love stories, and westerns. There are even films that mix genres such as musical/comedy and science fiction. In virtually every film we can also see the impress of older storytelling traditions, and the sociohistorical environment in which the films are made. Thus, cinematic representations of the bomb are influenced by what one might cautiously call an "eclectic" gathering of filmic and storytelling modes, techniques, and social issues.

Atomic bomb cinema is not a genre like the western, but a unique category of films that crosses the boundaries of many genres. Atomic bomb cinema is bound together by distinct, recurring themes. For example, in *Silkwood* (Mike Nichols, 1983) and the Australian film *Ground Zero* (Michael Pattinson, 1987) the protagonists take mythological journeys of self-discovery. The protagonists develop inner understanding when faced with nuclear catastrophe. That is to say, they develop personally within the context of a raised nuclear consciousness and then become political threats to government and industry. At every step, corrupt officials try to prevent them from discovering the truth about past (and present) nuclear accidents and murders intended to "cover up" the accidents. Both films were based specifically on actual unresolved court cases; however, in other bomb films, fictional protagonists follow the same mythological pattern, one in which a pugnacious and unrelenting David learns to survive and, sometimes, even defeat the nuclear Goliath.

Although many themes in atomic bomb cinema are pessimistic and express anxiety about America's future, not all bomb films or themes are negative. Admittedly, a fair number of films forecast a dystopic future, but only a very few describe complete annihilation. In *The Terminator* (James Cameron, 1984), a quintessential bomb film, social institutions bring about a nuclear holocaust, but humanity survives and learns from its mistakes. Again, to make the point clear, universal to bomb films the world over are the (generally hopeful) themes of survival and achieving individual and social rebirth in an oppressive environment.

These themes and modes of storytelling are not, of course, unique to atomic bomb cinema. There are films about the apocalypse that are not also about the bomb, most obviously films made before 1945. There are also post-1945 apocalyptic films, including Michael Tolkin's *The*

Rapture (1991), that are not about the bomb. As Mick Broderick puts it, "The cinema of apocalypse has a rich tradition."[36] There are also the modern "disaster movies," beginning perhaps with Alfred Hitchcock's *The Birds* (1963), about catastrophic events that nearly destroy whole communities—and this may be synecdochical for something more universal—or nearly annihilate humanity, such as *When Worlds Collide* (Rudolph Maté, 1951). Catastrophe, however, is not a synonym for either apocalypse or global nuclear annihilation. And, as Stanley Cavell has so eloquently argued, even screwball comedy and melodrama can be "read" as expressions of the abiding human concern for the conditions under which spiritual rebirth is possible, and as aesthetic responses to philosophical dilemmas, particularly skepticism.[37] Indeed, at both the level of the text and an anagogic level, a great many Hollywood-type films, for example, Jonathan Demme's *Silence of the Lambs* (1991), concern themselves with these issues, and thus atomic bomb cinema has a great deal in common with the entirety of classical cinema. But the subject of this study, to put it simply, is films about the bomb, which, coincidentally, have received little scholarly attention.

Many scholars claim that we live in "the atomic age." I find this to be a dubious claim because other influences have a greater daily impact on most people's lives. Americans, at least, are far more dependent on fossil fuel and computers than nuclear technologies, and many developing countries are still struggling to maintain adequate sanitation let alone build nuclear reactors. It is telling that, while the devastating environmental and genetic legacy of the Vietnam War may prove to have been far worse than that of Hiroshima and Nagasaki, no one, of whom I am aware, has ever professed that we live in the "Agent Orange Age." It might be more accurate to say that most people's experience of the world, including many Americans, takes place in the "Hunger and Famine Age."[38]

I do not aim to argue how influential the bomb has been on the American psyche—that is, whether it ranks first, second, or third in importance. Suffice it to say that the bomb is extraordinarily vital to our society. Fear of the bomb has, for many years, been an integral influence on our social consciousness; however, the bomb is not the only factor that determines its character. Many scholars also assert that recurrent anxiety about the bomb is cyclical, that is, people feel anxious about it only when there is a new technological development, or when conflicts appear to escalate toward nuclear war. The anxiety quickly subsides, however.[39] Paul Boyer pioneered this argument, and scholars ranging from H. Bruce Franklin to Joyce A. Evans have adopted it, either in whole or in part. Such arguments, again, are not new. As Seth Ward points out, "Long ago, Jewish sages . . . argued for cyclical periods in history."[40] The large number and constant production of bomb films, moreover, suggest that these cycles of anxiety express, more accurately, an unyielding concern over nuclear issues that is widespread and profound. Although there has been neither enough time nor enough data to formulate any specific conclusions about current trends in what is now called the post–cold war era, concern over nuclear issues has, clearly, not abated. Many bomb films have been produced and released over the past few years, and television stations and video rental shops are still doing a brisk business in bomb films.

So far, studies of "the atomic age" have been dominated by discussion of the print media, to which film is a mere footnote. Similarly, film scholars typically fail to describe the great diversity in atomic bomb cinema and instead focus on just a few representative films, often subordinating them to literature. My statistical analyses of atomic bomb cinema, however, reveal that Bomb films have been enormously popular with both filmmakers and filmgoers. Indeed, film is perhaps the most significant medium in our culture for expressing how the Bomb affects our lives. In the thirty-one years between 1914 and 1944, 20 films depicting a nuclear technology were released. From the destruction of Hiroshima and Nagasaki in August, 1945 to the end of 1949, an average of 5.8 bomb films were released each year. Since 1950 the average number of annual releases increased. The modal year is 1966 with 41 films, followed by 1985 with 34 films, and the eighth highest ranked year is 1958, with 27 films. The lowest ranked post-war year is 1949, with 3 films. After 1950, the lowest ranked years are 1972 and 1981, with 7 films each. From 1945 to 1999, bomb films account for roughly 4 percent of each year's releases in the United States, or 17.57 films per year. Four percent, or 17.57 films, may seem insignificant, especially when compared to broader categories of movies such as love stories, war stories, or teen-exploitation films; yet the average teenager sees only 12 films per year and the average adult sees a mere 3 films.[41] After 1946 the film industry fell into a prolonged decline; and yet, since 1950, the annual number of bomb films released has dropped below 12 only fifteen times. Atomic bomb cinema, moreover, is larger than other categories of films studied by film scholars. The number of bomb films that I include in this study, for example, is three times greater than the number of films listed in Silver and Ward's book on film noir.[42]

The statistical and thematic features of atomic bomb cinema that I have described thus far suggest something very different from what other scholars have concluded. H. Bruce Franklin, for instance, describes 1958 as the year of calm before the periods of tumultuous arms race and arms control; what he fails to consider, however, is that 1958 was part of a plateau that followed the end of a long period of stable increases in the number of bomb films, followed by a period of stable decreases in production.[43] This observation alone should cause us to question the accuracy of the cyclical theory. Popular culture's concern with nuclear issues is chronic, not merely cyclical or a case of acute "paranoia." Moreover, the bomb has not created a new Kantian category, but given new energy to ancient ways of speculating about the human condition.

"Culture" is another imprecise concept, and its definition lies beyond the scope of this study. What is important to keep in mind in our exploration of atomic bomb cinema is that the ideas that constitute a culture also constitute practices. Dipesh Chakrabarty reminds us that ideas "work not simply because they persuade through their logic; they are also capable, through a long and heterogeneous history of the cultural training of the senses, of making connections with our glands and muscles and neuronal networks." Just as bowing or moving one's hands while talking on the phone seem like unnecessary practices and for some outside the culture extremely difficult to imitate but to someone inside the culture second nature, so too filmmaking, filmgoing, and film criticism, in all their various modes, constitute related sets of practices.[44] As conscious beings, we practice at becoming aware of our senses; that is, through our awareness of experience we can critique the ideas and practices that experience evokes.

While cinematic experience is highly evocative, no fictional film can actually *represent* the human condition or even the nuclear condition, especially not in its entirety. Likewise, no single theoretical or methodological approach can represent the entirety of atomic bomb cinema. The dominant schools of thought in cinema theory tend to characterize film as either a mere reflection of what the culture thinks about itself, what it wants to think about itself, or as a vehicle that reproduces ideology by manipulating the subjectivity of the viewer. Such approaches are too reductive; at the very least, every film is going to be influenced by competing forces, and these theories tend to dehumanize both filmmakers and filmgoers, conceptualizing them as either passive to their own conditions or dangerous manipulators of social consciousness. To me, films are like stained glass windows or the carved wooden transom windows in Buddhist-influenced Japanese architecture that are known as ranma. (Though I am not here to argue that the light that passes through film is necessarily the same illuminating light of God that passes through stained glass, or the light and wind of Buddha that pass through ranma, we cannot completely rule out this possibility.) Like stained glass and ranma windows, films are designed to appeal to and inspire people regardless of sociocultural background, but especially the lay viewer. Both windows and films are viewed in a variety of architectural spaces—with others or in solitude, accompanied by music and voice or relative silence, and in a variety of affective and cognitive states. Not all windows and films have an obvious narrative, but most do tell a story and are especially dependent on symbol, using a variety of images, texts, icons, and more, all of which have familiar, obscure, specific, and contextual meanings. That is to say, in order to understand this story of windows and films, we must attempt interpretation.

In some ways film is similar to what we now call "traditional" theater. Japanese scholar Takao Aoki argues that premodern forms of popular or elite entertainment, such as Nō, Kabuki, and Bunraku—in which dance, chant, and music, as well as dialogue, are equally important elements— do not fit the paradigm of the hegemonic Western "written dialogue drama." Unlike the text of the Western dialogue drama, the text, for example, of a Nō play does not lend itself to the same kind of intensive study; that is, the experience of the performance, not the text, is essential.[45] Although classical cinema is highly dependent on the screenplay, it is not the only essential element; a film cannot be reduced to its written dialogue and effectively studied. Like a Nō performance, a film must be understood through the experience of the performance. All this is to say that the cinema, like stained glass or ranma windows and premodern theater, demands acknowledgment of our own idiosyncratic responses, or what Robert Warshow calls the "immediate experience."[46] I do not think we need to worry too much about the possibility of completely incommensurate understandings of the same film. As Donald Davidson has theorized, unless there are some shared understandings, any communication—even disagreement about the meaning of a film—would be impossible.[47] What we do have to worry about is that when one theory, method, or approach dominates interpretation, that is, analytical criticism, it can make us more susceptible to dogma and numb our desire for further inquiry. Our goal is to enliven our appreciation and our desire to review or reinterpret a film.

John Locke warns us against *enthusiasm*.[48] If my own journey as a disenfranchised, migrant Jewish-American expatriate living, teaching, writing, marrying, and raising a family in Japan has taught me anything, it is that a strict allegiance to any unyielding point of view (except the preciousness of life), theory, or methodology, is, to borrow Gerald Vizenor's phrase, a "terminal creed."[49] Trying to live without one's creeds, I have learned, is far more difficult than it at first seems—and in the extreme becomes yet another terminal creed. This study is, therefore, partly an attempt to tease out a more nuanced, even *playful*, approach to film analysis, an approach that allows the freest possible expression to the many voices that speak from within when I respond to any given film. Thus, in my analyses, I strive to be as interdisciplinary and cross-cultural as possible. And yet, as Cavell writes, "a complete interpretation . . . is not a matter of providing *all* interpretations but a matter of seeing one of them *through*" [emphasis in original].[50]

Atomic bomb cinema is a large, cumbersome, and often confusing subject that resists exegesis in subtle ways. However, because there are so many films and so many film genres, it is impossible to treat adequately the many different subcategories. Therefore, I am limiting the scope of this study to the essentials, to those themes that join seemingly disparate films into a coherent body. This study will look at the heart of atomic bomb cinema: the questions of death and rebirth, annihilation and salvation, and the individual and community. These questions are the essential elements of the *apocalyptic imagination*.

In the chapters that follow I will analyze key apocalyptic bomb films. These films will highlight the development of atomic bomb cinema and Americans' attitudes toward the bomb, changes in the culture, and the plurality of visions of America. I will also compare these key films to several important Japanese films, and consider problems in cross-cultural film analysis. Though this study's primary concern is American film and culture, comparisons to Japanese films will provide fresh perspectives on vexing questions.*

The apocalyptic imagination continues to influence American culture, in particular, how Americans think about the bomb. (For example, the fiery end of the Branch Davidians in Texas in 1993 reenacted the countless violent confrontations between established power structures and millennial cults that began before the birth of Jesus of Nazareth.) Over the centuries, many authors, often respected intellectuals, have chosen to work in the apocalyptic narrative tradition. The narrative tradition is used by both religious and secular authors; for, in the tradition, authors can easily combine past historical events, visions of the future, and other narrative traditions into moving stories that appeal to a broad audience. More importantly, the apocalyptic narrative tradition affords authors the ability to covertly criticize contemporary sociocultural, cosmological, and anagogic "crises." Atomic bomb cinema is, first and foremost, the latest innovation in the apocalyptic narrative tradition. Thus, analyzing these films means also speculating on more general philosophical questions; that is, what role do these films play in the development of culture, and what do they tell us about the human condition in the late twentieth and very early twenty-first centuries?

*Two Preliminary Notes to the Reader

First, a note on <www.atomicbombcinema.com>. In order to make supplementary information not included in this book easily available and at no cost to the reader, I have established this website. The site includes statistical data, graphs, my collection of film stills, images from scenes for which there are no extant stills, bomb-related curiosities, other relevant information, and links to other sites. The reader may also contact me through this website.

Second, a note on the romanization of the Japanese language in this book. Japanese is a very complex language, with four different writing systems: *kanji*, an ideographic system adopted from China, and three different syllabaries, *hiragana*, *katakana*, and *rōmaji* (i.e., the Roman alphabet), each with a different function in the language. While a syllabary can indicate how a word is pronounced, it can never express the full range of meanings evoked by a kanji; therefore, there is an unavoidable degree of arbitrariness in translating Japanese. For instance, Japanese people clearly distinguish between long and short vowels, but "Hepburn," the current official system for romanizing, does not. For consistency and simplicity I have chosen to follow *The Chicago Manual of Style* and indicate long vowels with macrons; for example, *kaijū* or *sensō*.[51] (The exceptions are very familiar words, such as Tokyo or Kyoto, because adding macrons could create confusion.) Since most kanji can be pronounced in several different ways, they are usually accompanied by *furigana* or *rubi*, a superscript or subscript, usually in katakana, that indicates pronunciation. The title for one Japanese bomb film is usually romanized as *Junai Monogatari* (*A Story of Pure Love*, Tadashi Imai, 1957). Without foreknowledge, no Japanese person can accurately comprehend this romanization, for they would perceive the syllables of the first word to be ju/na/i, where as, the rubi clearly indicates it to be ju/n/a/i. I have chosen to render this word as *Jun'ai*. According to *The Chicago Manual of Style*, when romanizing Japanese titles only the first word and proper nouns are capitalized; thus, I render the above film title as *Jun'ai monogatari*. In recent years, "Vs." and now "X" are used in film titles to indicate "versus," but, following the rubi, I romanize these as *tai*. Some authors will change an "n" before a consonant into an "m," or a "k" after a consonant into a "g," but I avoid these changes; for example, *genbaku* and *Kegonkyō*. Finally, in the Japanese name order surnames are followed by given names, but I have chosen to order names according to the Western convention because it is less confusing and more practical for readers who are unfamiliar with the Japanese language; for readers familiar with the Japanese language there should be no practical difference. These are just a few of the many problems in romanizing the Japanese language. I have made every effort to cross-check names and titles in English language references with Japanese language references. There may, however, be errors and omissions. I beg the reader's indulgence.

1
1895 to 1945
Prototypical bomb films

What counts is not so much the statistically measurable popularity of films as the popularity of their pictorial and narrative motifs. Persistent reiteration of these motifs marks them as outward projections of inner urges. And they obviously carry most symptomatic weight when they occur in both popular and unpopular films, in grade B pictures as well as in superproductions.

—Siegfried Kracauer, *From Caligari to Hitler*[1]

The development, use, and buildup of nuclear weapons has created a fertile environment for the proliferation of apocalyptic stories. And yet, when we think of apocalyptic narratives, we generally think of The Revelation to John in the New Testament, and not popular films. In *When Time Shall Be No More*, Paul Boyer shows that for many contemporary Americans, geopolitical events, not the least of which is the development of the bomb, are understood through a fundamentalist Christian teleology that ends with a scourging of the earth, establishment of a heaven on earth, the passing of judgments, and the salvation of the righteous.[2] This is an apocalyptic teleology. However, if we look closely at mainstream popular American culture, we can also see that the apocalyptic narrative tradition continues to shape the stories we tell, even if the stories do not adhere to fundamentalist doctrine. This is especially true of atomic bomb cinema. The apocalyptic narrative tradition, needless to say, is not the only influence on bomb films, nor are these influences limited to popular culture. To understand the development of atomic bomb cinema we must not only familiarize ourselves with the apocalyptic literary tradition but also with the nascent apocalyptic elements prevalent in early science fiction and horror films, as well as with some important critical tools. This chapter will begin with an explanation of how several seemingly disparate strands of thought and cultural tradition—the concept of the psychological "crisis," the "apocalyptic imagination," and, equally important, the influence of the apocalyptic imagination—weaves together popular and elite culture.

A Cultural Pattern: Monks Exhorting the People to Righteousness

It is a curious thing in the West that, during times of intense social change and cultural anxiety, maverick intellectuals with great charisma leave the monastery to exhort the laity and their own peers with spectacular eschatologies. We have seen this throughout history in diverse groups ranging from Jews during the Babylonian and Hellenistic diasporas to early and Medieval Christians. In our own time, however, we tend to overlook mainstream intellectuals and associate millennial movements with extremist groups that include Maria Devi Khristos, the Branch Davidians, Hamas, AUM Shinrikyō (or the Sect of Supreme Truth, which has recently changed its name to Aleph), suicide cults like Solar Temple and Heaven's Gate, and even Ronald Reagan, who captivated the world with fiery speeches about evil empires and utopias protected by space-based, nuclear umbrellas. Frank Kermode, moreover, has observed that in our time "[e]ven the scholar who studies crisis as a recurrent, if not perpetual, historical phenomenon, tends to single out ours as the major instance."[3] I would argue that this is not "even" but *especially* true of scholars who write about the bomb.

Some of our most respected intellectuals have aggressively stepped forward over the issue of the bomb, particularly the issue of its depiction in films. They have come from all disciplines: the humanities, the social and behavioral sciences, the natural sciences, and—since the bomb is often conceptualized as a modern plague—from clinical medicine. For instance, Dr. Helen Caldicott—a pediatrician who, in the 1970s, left her post at Harvard University to resuscitate Physicians for Social Responsibility (PSR)[4]—has announced that "[t]he World is on the brink of disaster." More to the point of this study, she adds that we should "[n]ever underestimate the subliminal and overt power of film and television!"[5] That chemist-with-a-conscience, Linus Pauling, agrees. At the preview of Stanley Kramer's 1959 film *On the Beach*, Pauling proclaimed: "It may be that . . . *On the Beach* is the movie that saved the world."[6] The cultural historian Paul Boyer specifically equates nuclear annihilation with "Armageddon"; and, like Caldicott, decries Hollywood while exhorting the reader to join the ranks of the righteously antinuclear to help in "driving back the shadow of global death" and destroy the "destroyer."[7] Historian and social critic Christopher Lasch similarly lays much of the blame for the ills of the "nuclear age" on the "world of flickering images."[8] Psychologist Robert J. Lifton—who writes about the so-called inadequacies of popular bomb films—uses a distinctly New Testament, evangelical style in his writings and speeches to cast himself in the role of the gentle shepherd, spreading "the good news" that will give us, the living dead who worship at the alter of nuclearism, salvation from our psychically numbed lives.[9] Although Michael Ortiz Hill, the depth psychologist, also hints at psychic numbing and waxes apocalyptic, he is the only cultural critic I know of who recognizes the grip of the apocalyptic imagination on himself, and then consciously embraces it as a necessary part of human experience.[10] Of all the intellectuals writing about the bomb, however, the most exemplary is the antinuclear philosopher Jonathan Schell. Evoking Sunday school lessons about choosing between good and evil, he writes, "Two paths lie before us." Even though insects are common images in apocalypses, I sometimes wonder if Schell was not inspired by the giant ants in the seminal apocalyptic bomb film *Them!* (Gordon Douglas, 1954); for, in his exhortation to antinuclear righteousness, he masterfully combines apocalyptic narrative structure, Manichaean rhetoric, Paschal imagery, and 1950s-style Hollywood science fiction into visions of postnuclear plagues of "insects and grass."[11]

Out of context, the scholarly commentary seems atavistic or comical, even irrational, but it is not. Rather, it exemplifies a common pattern of nuclear text and imagery that can be seen in all segments of American society. The scholarly literature is, in other words, an example of how the culture responds to and represents events that induce anxiety. My own writing, no doubt, is imbued with this power—that is, the power of the apocalyptic imagination. If I speak passionately against other scholars, however, it is not because I think they are evil or bad, nor even wholly wrong; it is because I think it is erroneous and dangerous to condemn entire societies as being pathological. Regardless of my commitments vis-à-vis the bomb, Judaism, or anything else, I have no desire to add to the world's grief by using my scholarship as a vehicle to insinuate myself into other people's psyches and advance my own self-righteous, utopian fantasies. My primary interests are in explaining to my own satisfaction what these films mean, contributing to the scholarly debate, and, I would hope, to provide some answers to several vexing questions that will help others to reach their own conclusions about the world they inhabit. In other words, rather than quicken the apocalypse, I prefer working to repair the world. And yet, as Michael Tolkin, the filmmaker, says, those of us who are "nourished and delighted by this sub-category of intellectual porn . . . don't mourn the end of the world, we want a sky box. The millennium is our entertainment and vocation."[12] Indeed, if there is to be an apocalyptic reckoning, then in my fantasies it begins here—in academe, which is as much or more in need of divine retribution than anywhere else. If you as the reader are not yet convinced of the importance and ubiquity of this patterned response to contemporary intellectual discourse, you will be by the end of this chapter.

The Apocalyptic Imagination before the Bomb

Jacques Derrida is well known for having written that "[t]he 'reality' of the nuclear age and the fable of nuclear war are perhaps distinct, but they are not two separate things."[13] Yet, no fictional feature film that I can think of is truly concerned with the technological, strategic, or geopolitical "reality" of nuclear war. Nor are they the emblems of nuclearism, global psychopathology, or mass schizophrenia. After watching hundreds of bomb films it seems to me that the best psychological metaphor for understanding what the bomb means comes from psychoanalyst Erik H. Erikson's suggestion that the bomb constitutes a "crisis." In *Identity: Youth and Crisis*, Erikson clearly defines this concept:

> [I]t may be a good thing that the word "crisis" no longer connotes impending catastrophe, which at one time seemed to be an obstacle to understanding the term. It is now being accepted as designating a necessary turning point, a crucial moment, when development must move one way or another, marshaling resources of growth, recovery and further differentiation. This proves applicable to many situations: a crisis in individual development or in the emergence of a new elite, in the therapy of an individual or in the tensions of rapid historical change.[14]

Conceptualizing the bomb as an Eriksonian crisis that must be resolved works well because it does not insist on a normative or single possible outcome, only that resolution of the crisis is necessary to future development. His definition of crisis has the additional advantage of allowing for substantial political, cultural, and personal differences over how a crisis should be resolved. Crises that arise from the physiological, psychological, and anagogic effects of nuclear war or nuclear-related disasters are common themes in atomic bomb cinema. In bomb films, these crises are typically expressed through the vital, ancient, narrative tradition that John J. Collins labels "the Jewish matrix of Christianity," that is, the *apocalyptic imagination*.[15]

At this juncture a caveat is in order. My phrase "the Jewish apocalyptic imagination" (and perhaps even Collins's phrase, "the Jewish matrix of Christianity") may give the misleading impression that the ideas that I am trying to develop here are highbrow, obscure, and arcane. One colleague felt compelled to point out to me that "the germ of the idea . . . is obvious in the 'High Holy Day services' and 'the most popular Jewish practices.'"[16] Indeed, but the Jewish apocalyptic narrative tradition is, in my mind, at least, the clearest formulation of these ideas; its influence extends far beyond Judaism, and it is the key to understanding atomic bomb cinema.

Apocalypse, as bomb films attest, never lies very far from the imagination. This is because the conceptual structure of its generic framework, as derived from Jewish tradition, is the foundation of the Christian worldview. The term "apocalypse" has generally been misused, or misunderstood, to denote an end rather than a continuum. Hal Foster, in his highly influential book *The Anti-Aesthetic: Essays on Postmodern Culture*, seems to have confused for a generation of scholars the apocalypse with "the end of ideology" and the end of history.[17] Kim Newman, again at the furthest extreme, blithely announces that having read a dictionary, he knows all he needs to know about the specific meanings of "millennium," "apocalypse," and other terms, then reduces these terms to denoting only literal representations of "world-ending or -changing catastrophes."[18] In other contexts, thoughtful scholars use the term too thoughtlessly. Stephen Prince, for example, several times refers to Akira Kurosawa's films as "apocalyptic," but provides no sense of what an apocalypse is in either Western or Japanese cultures.[19] Furthermore, apocalypse is frequently confused with other narrative traditions. Most notably, Susan Sontag, in her essay "The Imagination of Disaster," confuses apocalypse with disaster and later Jewish messianic prophecy, while Robert Torry, in his analysis "Apocalypse Then: Benefits of the Bomb in Fifties Science

Fiction Films," confuses it with Biblical testaments and deluges.[20] In addition, Christopher Lasch astutely recognizes that "the apocalyptic vision of the future affirms the possibility of human survival and transformation." And yet, Lasch sees the "modern secular form" of the apocalypse as evidence of the "minimal or narcissistic self" embodied in "[r]ootless men and women who take no more interest in the future than they take in the past."[21] In other words, the very word "apocalyptic" has also come to be misused as a term denoting a kind of mass psychopathology, as well as disaster and destruction. Thus, the word has lost its currency, and needs to be revitalized by returning to its root meanings.

In Greek, the word *apokalypsis* means "revelation."[22] The psychological connotation of the word, David Miller tells us, is to disclose or uncover, "especially as in a dream or vision, like the lifting of the veil for Ezekiel or John, writer of the Book of Revelation."[23] John J. Collins, in his seminal study *The Apocalyptic Imagination*, notes that since the late first century, the word "apocalypse" has been used primarily as a genre label for Christian narratives in which the central character takes a spatial or temporal journey, a cosmological plan is revealed to the character, and the character returns to exhort others to live in accord with the plan. The origins of the genre, however, can be traced back to at least the twelfth century B.C.E., but flourished in the hands of pre-Christian Jews. (According to Richard Freund, the Rabbis did not concern themselves with the apocalypse until the Hellenic period.)[24] The genre has not only survived the centuries, but also proven adaptable to many social situations. This is because, in part, a fundamental characteristic of the apocalyptic generic tradition is the assimilation of other literary traditions by authors trying to reach a broader audience.[25]

There are, of course, strong parallels between not only apocalyptic narratives and testaments and deluges, but also, for example, Hasidic and Jewish mystical storytelling traditions. In these stories, the central character, usually a rabbi, has a vision or his soul ascends to heaven, often without knowing or having a clear understanding of the existing crisis. Through this experience the rabbi learns that his community is threatened, he is then able to return to his community to teach. The rabbi's vision or revelation itself may thwart the threat, but the revelation remains an important ethical message. Little emphasis is placed on actually describing the hereafter, or the rewards received in the hereafter; rather, the emphasis is placed on just living in the here and now. The parallels between these Jewish narratives, Jewish apocalyptic narratives, and apocalyptic bomb films, such as *The Beginning or the End* (Norman Taurog, 1947) and even *The Time Machine* (George Pal, 1960), are striking.

Another characteristic of the apocalyptic tradition, and its relevance to atomic bomb cinema, is its ability to survive within what seem to be completely new generic traditions. For example, in *Film and the Nuclear Age*, Toni A. Perrine argues that time travel and travel between worlds as "narrative motif[s]" are "supremely cinematic." More importantly, citing Paul Coates, Perrine argues that the "emergence" of travel to other times and other worlds as new "literary theme[s]" are "linked to the simultaneous emergence of cinema" in the nineteenth century.[26] Travel in time and to other worlds, however, are not new narrative motifs at all, as Perrine suggests, but familiar features to readers of apocalyptic narratives.

In the apocalyptic worldview, humans are bound to a world in which the forces of good and evil struggle and are caught up in a preordained history that concludes with eschatological judgment. Collins states that the "genre is not constituted by one or more distinctive themes but by a distinctive combination of elements, all of which are also found elsewhere," as in, for example, testaments and oracles. The most important elements of this genre are familiar: visions, the development of history, otherworldly journeys (in time or space), cosmological speculation, revelations, the interpretation of revelations by supernatural beings, "'predictions' of past events, or *ex eventu prophecy*," pseudonymity, persecution, eschatological upheavals, final judgments, and mystical knowledge. These elements are woven into recognizable narrative patterns of journey, revelation, and exhortation. Citing Alastair Fowler, Collins suggests that the genre also develops in overlapping stages, or "phases." These stages are the assembly of the formal type, followed by the extensive use of the form, and finally "the secondary use of the form—for example, by ironic inversion or by subordinating it to a new context."[27] (Collins's ideas about patterns in the development of narrative traditions appear to be influenced by not just Fowler, but Northrop Frye as well.)[28] As Collins demonstrates, once we understand the formal framework of the genre, then we can begin to explore its sociological, literary, or psychological contexts and functions.

In *Narrative and the Self*, Anthony Paul Kerby writes that "narratives are a primary embodiment of our understanding of the world, of experience, and ultimately of ourselves," and that they are "the privileged medium for understanding human experience, an experience that is paradigmatically a temporal and hence historical reality."[29] It is through storytelling, in other words, that we come to understand our experiences and ourselves. Apocalyptic narratives, Collins explains, address experiences such as persecution, culture shock, political powerlessness, social change, "the dismal fate of humanity," and death. The cosmological and "mystical component," however, "is an integral factor in all apocalyptic literature." The language, therefore, is "expressive rather than referential, symbolic rather than factual." Thus, apocalyptic narratives are poetic and articulate a "sense or feeling about the world"—just as do bomb films.[30] Central to Collins's understanding is that apocalyptic narratives flourish during times of severe stress. He often refers to real or perceived crises in apocalyptic literature. This is particularly relevant to our own time, for arguments over "real" versus "perceived" nuclear "crises" are also central to the discourse of the nuclear weapons debate.[31] These real and perceived threats of nuclear war, as defined by nuclear strategists, who are themselves no doubt unconcerned with their own narrative traditions, fueled the massive investments in nuclear weapons, delivery, and defense, during the cold war era.

Atomic bomb cinema is also linked to earlier texts by a notion of revolution that is, paradoxically, both radical and conservative at the same time. Early apocalyptic texts are driven by a linear, progressive teleology; and yet, at the end of history is the recovery of an earlier state of being or grace. Likewise, many bomb films portray situations radically different from our own, yet these changes usually entail a return, or the longing for a return, to an earlier pristine or Edenic period. This should not be too surprising, for, as Melvin J. Lasky in *Utopia and Revolution* points out, our very notion of the political "revolution" is a metaphor derived from the Copernican idea that the celestial bodies return to their origins as they revolve through the universe.[32]

The key theme that connects atomic bomb cinema to the apocalyptic tradition, and what concerns us here, is the promise of not merely surviving the current oppressive conditions, but "rebirth." The apocalypse does not bring about the end of the world, but a crisis-like period of intense suffering that cleanses the world of evil. What was good or pure in the previous era survives to be reborn in the new era, and a just community or heaven on earth flourishes. That is to say, the apocalyptic tradition and atomic bomb cinema are inherently hopeful. This point, though it may seem tangential, bears some further explanation.

Collins demonstrates that early Jewish apocalyptic texts remain a vital force because they shaped the dominant Christian worldview. But it would be a mistake to infer from Collins's argument that it is only through the Christian worldview that the Jewish apocalyptic tradition influences atomic bomb cinema, or that the apocalypse also constitutes the matrix of Judaism. Harris Lenowitz, on the one hand, compellingly argues, for example, that "The millennium is an event whose direct relevance to religious Judaism cannot be understressed."[33] Richard Freund, on the other hand, shows us that "[d]espite efforts by non-messianic/apocalyptic Rabbinic teachers and writers to the contrary, wide divergences are found in a variety of periods . . . with echoes in denominational positions developed by Reform, Conservative, and Orthodox Judaisms in the modern period."[34] While the apocalypse and the millennium are not central religious events in Judaism, at least not to the same extent as in Christianity, historically the apocalypse has been and continues to be an important part of mainstream Jewish thought and culture. In a variety of ways Jews, myself included, do perpetuate the narrative tradition. The apocalypses associated with New Testament or Fundamentalist Christianity, particularly in America, are but one variation and not the dominant model in atomic bomb cinema. In other words, while the Jewish apocalypse forms the matrix of Christianity, the apocalypse has not become a distinctly Christian narrative tradition. Rather, in atomic bomb cinema the Jewish apocalyptic worldview seems to have a retained its broad appeal.

This is not because Hollywood is dominated by Jews, or because Fundamentalist Christians have no voice in Hollywood, or any other such cliché nonsense, but because of the inherent strengths, as already defined, of the Jewish apocalyptic worldview and narrative tradition. In Judaism, moreover, there is an essential hopefulness that is different from the transcendental salvation and accession to the Heavenly Kingdom in Christian theology. Often in Jewish storytelling, when a character does ascend to heaven it is not the end of the story, or a self-evident moral, but the starting place for moralizing and commenting on this world (not the world hereafter), our human perception of things, and the need to live better. Jewish tradition teaches *Tikkun Olam*, which is a commitment to repairing or restoring the world. Between Talmudic times and our own, the idea of Tikkun Olam has undergone considerable development. In general, however, we can say that Tikkun Olam teaches a groundedness in this world; and, it can be likened to the restoration of balance and harmony found in Japanese films, which I will discuss in detail in a later chapter. Tikkun Olam is found throughout Jewish thought and practice, and is, for example, the foundation of the Jewish wedding ceremony. The breaking of the wine glass in the wedding ceremony, almost paradoxically, symbolically expresses a commitment to repairing a fractured world. The breaking of the glass seals the wedding vow that brings together not merely two individuals but two families, which is the basis of society, in order to give future generations a chance to fulfill this commitment.[35]

In Genesis 9:11, God promises to never again flood the earth. "And I will establish My covenant with you; neither shall all flesh be cut off any more by the waters of the flood; neither shall there any more be a flood to destroy the earth."[36] Jewish tradition has interpreted this as being a self-imposed contract that allows God to punish individual sinners, even communities, but never again the whole world; and, humanity is hereafter responsible for the world's maintenance. Within this context, the bomb is a tactical weapon. Christian tradition looks for loopholes in the contract and then waits, more or less, for the end. Within this context, the bomb is a strategic weapon. Very few bomb films describe the strategic annihilation of humanity. Usually, wicked communities are destroyed and good communities survive to repair and restore a broken world; furthermore, savior figures do not work to bring a broken world to its final conclusion; rather, they help to repair the broken world. Consider French filmmaker Luc Besson's delightfully bizarre 1997 hit film, *The Fifth Element*. Some two hundred years in the future, "pure evil," we are told, will destroy the world in forty-eight hours. Leeloo (Milla Jovovich)— "the fifth element," "perfect," and "supreme being" who is nevertheless quite human in her vulnerabilities—is sent to earth to stop evil. But first she undertakes a quick video course in earth history, which focuses primarily on war and suffering, and culminates in spectacular images of thermonuclear blasts. Overwhelmed, she can find no reason to save the world, until Korben Dallas (Bruce Willis) reminds her that love, including their love for one another, makes saving the world worthwhile. In other words, unlike in Christian narratives, Leeloo does not martyr herself in the name of love or the salvation of the world, and she forestalls the conclusion to the Christian teleology in order to preserve the possibility of redemptive earthly love no matter how impossible the task; that is, her ultimate commitment is to Tikkun Olam. Of course, one could argue that in bomb films we see a secular, "Hollywood" version of the dominant Christian apocalypse; that is, a version in which the distinctly Christian elements have been carefully left out so as to appeal to the broadest possible audience. Such versions do not include an overtly supernatural messiah; evil is not forever destroyed; and the righteous do not ascend directly to heaven. Of course, this brings us back to the very point that I am trying to make: Atomic bomb cinema bears a greater resemblance to the Jewish apocalyptic narrative tradition than to that of the Christian tradition.

Many bomb films are uproariously funny. Atomic bomb cinema is enriched by America—a land diverse in the humorous traditions of many immigrant, impoverished, and dispossessed peoples; and yet, what appears to be a powerful, maybe even dominant, voice in atomic bomb cinema is what may be broadly called "Jewish humor." Steve Lipman, in *Laughter in Hell: The Use of Humor during the Holocaust*, points out that the Old Testament, the Talmud, and the writings of Jewish sages are "seasoned with dashes of irony." And, in a 1941 Nazi camp, Rabbi Erich Weiner observed that Jews' subversive humor "strengthened their will to survive as well as infused their power to resist."[37] Jewish humor, in other words, is filled with the spirit of Tikkun Olam. The will to resist and to survive is, ultimately, the will to repair and restore one's world.

One more Jewish tradition bears mentioning, and that is the importance of tradition itself. In his explanation of "the most important verse of the [Passover] Seder," the response to the "fourth son," Elie Wiesel asks the reader "What is the meaning of tradition?" Wiesel tells us that "The Hebrew word *masorah* comes from the word *limsor*—to communicate." More importantly,

A Jew must communicate a tradition. Not to do so is to mutilate it. As a Jew it is my duty to tell my child not only my story, but also the story of my story, which is also my child's story. . . ."[38]

This story—this tradition—is the telling of survival and self-actualization under oppressive conditions, and, ultimately, the repairing of a wounded world. I believe the Jewish apocalyptic narrative tradition is informed by humor, the very notion of "tradition," Genesis 9:11, and Tikkun Olam. These in turn are significant sources of hopefulness in atomic bomb cinema.

Hollywood filmmakers, for their part, are always looking for sources of hopeful, uplifting—which is not to say simple—narratives to exploit. That is their forte. For more than fifty years the apocalyptic narrative tradition has served them well. The hopefulness of atomic bomb cinema is, therefore, a testament to the continuing vitality of Judaism in the shaping of the contemporary corporate consciousness. Daniel Boyarin, an Orthodox Jew and a scholar at the University of California, Berkeley, has written most eloquently about the modern ghettoization of Jewish thought, and the importance of a plurality of voices, including a Jewish voice, in the discussion of contemporary society and culture. In his discussion of the Jewish *Midrash* tradition of textual interpretation, Boyarin argues that "[t]he liberal term 'Judaeo-Christian' masks a suppression of that which is distinctly Jewish. It means 'Christian,' and by not even acknowledging that much, renders the suppression of Jewish discourse even more complete." The term "Judaeo-Christianity," in other words, implies that Judaism is an anachronism, something antecedent to or understood only through Christianity. But, Boyarin adds, "recent theoretical writing about literature, which searches for a richer, more nuanced understanding of reading" has engendered a "revoicing of a Jewish discourse in the discourse of the West."[39] To Boyarin, this means that Jewish scholars and scholars of Judaism are no longer limited to the discourse of Jewish studies, but have regained a direct voice in the broader discourse of the West. (I would like to take Boyarin's point a step further: there needs to be a revoicing of Jewish discourse in the discourse of the *world*.) A *revoicing* of Jewish voices in the discourse of the West suggests, of course, that the suppression of Judaism has never been complete. Atomic bomb cinema is, again, a testament to Jewish "survivance" and the vitality of the Jewish apocalyptic narrative tradition.[40] Be that as it may, while the Jewish tradition may be the most important element in atomic bomb cinema, in keeping with the apocalyptic narrative tradition, it is not the only source of inspiration for filmmakers.

Like authors working in the apocalyptic tradition, filmmakers are highly adaptive, frequently incorporating—consciously and unconsciously— elements from other traditions. That is to say, atomic bomb cinema is a unique category of films, and it overlaps with other categories, particularly the more frequently discussed category of science fiction films. Some early fantasy, horror, and, especially, science fiction films, as we will soon see, have been particularly important to the development of atomic bomb cinema, and deserve more recognition than they have so far received. Granted, science fiction films do receive a great deal of scholarly attention; and yet bomb films, a specific type of science fiction film, have been largely misunderstood—when not completely ignored. Susan Sontag begins her seminal 1965 essay "The Imagination of Disaster" by praising some science fiction films about the bomb. Sontag then asserts that the science fiction film . . . is concerned with the aesthetics of destruction, with the peculiar beauties to be found in wreaking havoc, making a mess. And it is in the imagery of destruction that the core of a good science fiction film lies.[41]

While Sontag is a brilliant and incisive cultural critic, her observation here is, to put it simply, wrong. At their core, science fiction films are concerned with not just havoc, but with the physical and psychological rebirth that follows destruction. Since Sontag is wrong about science fiction films, she is, therefore, most certainly wrong about atomic bomb cinema. Only a very few bomb films describe complete and final annihilation. Sontag's essay blurs important distinctions by conflating the imagination of disaster with the apocalyptic imagination, and mundane catastrophe with anagogic crisis; for, in apocalypses, destruction is the catalyst for the rebirth of the old into something new and better. Sontag also compares these films to a seventeenth-century Jewish apocalypse, and to the state of Berliners at the end of the Second World War. She fails, however, to recognize important connections with the foundations of the generic tradition that would undermine her thesis. Sontag's analysis has, nevertheless, influenced most students of the cinema and especially those scholars writing about the bomb and culture.[42] Sontag's influence is even evident in the work of those who challenge her thesis.

In "Apocalypse Then," for example, Robert Torry carefully takes Sontag to task in order to illustrate that these films are critical. Referencing a small sample of bomb films, Torry specifically argues that the apocalypse is used exclusively to inculcate a beneficent reactionary ideology. Torry, however, goes so far in the other direction from Sontag that he ultimately comes full circle. Not only does Torry read these films as numbing propaganda, he finally argues that "an ultimately beneficent" apocalypse is found in only a few films, and that by 1953 the beneficent apocalypse "became very rare indeed."[43] But faith in a beneficent outcome, as numerous authorities on apocalyptic and millennial thought have pointed out, is essential to the philosophical, psychological, theological, and generic structure of all apocalyptic narratives.

Both Sontag and Torry miss the mark when it comes to the matter of science fiction films. Some science fictions films may, as Sontag asserts, "serve to allay" as well as "reflect world-wide anxieties," but they do not "inculcate a strange apathy" concerning nuclear-related fears.[44] Bomb films are, by and large, apocalyptic and therefore have nothing to do with public apathy (quite the opposite). Moreover, despite Torry's assertion that most are not beneficent, all bomb films are, at the very least, cathartic and thus therapeutic in much the same sense as the religious narratives of past epochs; and, at their best, many popular bomb films challenge the status quo, provide alternative visions of the future, and offer hope. This is a fundamental feature of the apocalyptic narrative structure, as many scholars in the fields of biblical studies, literature, and psychology have argued, and as Collins makes abundantly clear.[45]

While Collins clearly provides a sound intellectual foundation for understanding atomic bomb cinema, bomb films do not exactly resemble the most familiar biblical apocalypses, nor, for that matter, the more obscure ones that only scholars cite. The narrative and symbolic structures that constitute many bomb films, nevertheless, are both consistent with the apocalyptic literary tradition (although often in subtle ways) and meaningful to modern audiences. Consider Tony Scott's 1995 film *Crimson Tide*, which is about a U.S. submarine that is cut off from the chain of command just as it is receiving orders on how to respond to nationalist rebels in the former Soviet Union who are threatening world stability.

The ship's captain, played by Gene Hackman, and the executive officer, played by Denzel Washington, disagree over how to interpret their incomplete orders. The captain, out of hubris, orders nuclear missiles launched, but the executive officer refuses to confirm the launch order, and this begins a frightening conflict between the two men over what could either start or prevent World War Three. The racial issues that are less obvious in the early part of the film, moreover, take on major importance as their conflict reaches its ugly climax. The conflict ends with the white captain realizing that his black executive officer is right. In the film's final scene, at a tribunal after the military conflict has subsided, the captain shows that he has reached some inner self-awareness, and that he was wrong both in giving his order to launch and in his racist treatment of his executive officer. Submarines are often synecdochical for the broader social context; thus, the film suggests that subtle but revolutionary changes are taking place in American society.

On initial viewing, *Crimson Tide* does not seem to be influenced at all by the apocalyptic imagination because, other than concluding with a tribunal that passes judgment on the two men, it lacks clear development of the generic elements most commonly associated with apocalyptic narratives. And yet, the eternal dilemma within apocalyptic stories is the correct interpretation of signs, symbols, and events: Is this the real, final conflict or merely a prelude; does one initiate the final conflict without an unequivocal sign from God or delay and risk not only having made a tactical error in the war-to-end-all-wars but also having usurped God's will? This dilemma, according to Moshe Lazar, a scholar of apocalyptic literature and art, acts as a kind of internal governor in the engine of the apocalyptic imagination.[46] That is, the dilemma creates a dynamic, and dramatic, tension that keeps apocalyptic concerns running high but not high enough to reach a climax that would then dissipate interest in the apocalypse. It does this by keeping the apocalypse forever on the foreseeable horizon of human history. This apocalyptic dilemma structures *Crimson Tide* and makes the film a significant part of atomic bomb cinema. As in *Crimson Tide*, bomb films also, frequently, focus on characters who exist under very oppressive conditions or are suffering in some way. Also, though not as clearly seen in *Crimson Tide* as in other bomb films, atomic bomb cinema, more importantly, focuses on the premise that oppressive conditions or suffering can be eased, yes, through political empowerment or changing social conditions, but especially through mystical experience. In other words, atomic bomb cinema is primarily about *individual, and communal, survival and self-actualization under oppressive conditions.*

The hopefulness of atomic bomb cinema will, in following chapters, become increasingly clear, as will the symbols and metaphors for apocalyptic revolution. To more fully appreciate them, however, we must begin with antecedent silent and early sound films. In them we will find features that recur throughout atomic bomb cinema, including the utopic promise of science and technology, the psychosexual crisis of creature films, and the desire for a salvational apocalypse.

Trace Elements of the Apocalypse in Early Science Fiction Films

Because the apocalyptic imagination is such an integral part of the Christian and, to a lesser extent, the Jewish worldviews, even when the production of apocalyptic literature seems to be at an ebb, elements of the framework continue to fascinate us. Thus, many of the narrative structures, icons, symbols, and references in atomic bomb cinema can be found in the developing genres of the silent and early sound eras, especially science fiction and horror films. Consider the bullet-shaped spaceship that is fired out of a canon in Georges Méliès's film *Le voyage dans la lune/A Trip to the Moon* (France, 1902), a loose adaptation of the Jules Verne novel.[47] A group of astronomers build a rocket ship and travel to the moon, where they are captured, battle with the indigenous moon people, and then escape. At the end of *A Trip to the Moon*, the leader of the expedition and a moon person ride the outside of the bullet/ship as it descends to the earth and splashes into the ocean. Twenty-seven years later, in 1929, the German filmmaker Fritz Lang directed what is possibly the first feature length film based on *A Trip to the Moon*, *Die Frau im Mond*, which is known variously as *By Rocket to the Moon*, *The Girl in the Moon*, and *The Woman on the Moon*.[48] Thirty-four years after Méliès's film, William Cameron Menzies used an art deco version of Méliès's bullet/ship and canon in his film *Things to Come* (Britain, 1936). Sixty-two years after *A Trip to the Moon*, Major Kong rides a nuclear missile to Russian soil in Stanley Kubrick's film *Dr. Strangelove or: How I Learned to Stop Worrying and Love the Bomb* (Britain, 1964), a film that, however much a product of the prevailing Cold War angst, is clearly indebted to pre–World War II science fiction films. Finally, an homage to Méliès's *A Trip to the Moon* appears eighty-seven years later in yet another important bomb film: Terry Gilliam's *The Adventures of Baron Munchausen* (Britain, 1989).

Certainly *A Trip to the Moon* is not the only film or media with travel to nearby planets, nor is it the only possible source from which later films draw inspiration. But *A Trip to the Moon* is given a special place in film histories. Méliès's film is longer than most produced by his major competitors, and it reached near-international distribution, including Japan, within the first year of its release.[49] And in atomic bomb cinema the Ur- or seminal film is certainly Georges Méliès's *A Trip to the Moon*, for it has both an otherworldly journey and a vision and uses technology to create a fantastical element. These three elements deserve a closer, second look.

After arriving on the moon, there is a dream sequence with visions of a comet, followed by the Pleiades, and then Saturn, the Moon, and the Gemini twins. The most elaborate of these seven visions is the image of the Pleiades—Atlas's seven daughters turned into a group of stars. The Pleiades are not merely anthropomorphized, as are other images, but also transmogrified. As the travelers sleep, the comet passes overhead, followed by the Pleiades that pause above them, and then a woman's head pops out of the center of each star. The Pleiades then "dissolve" (or "lap dissolve," a film-editing term describing an effect in which a scene or part of a scene simultaneously "fades out" as another "fades in," and both scenes are momentarily visible on the screen superimposed on one another) into the last three celestial bodies.[50] As a symbol, the Pleiades are intricately woven with theological, cosmological, and metaphysical notions about the world. The importance of the Pleiades to the Jewish and Christian traditions should not be underestimated, for, as J. E. Cirlot writes, "The Jewish Cabbala provides a link between the mythological deities, in so far as they are creative and beneficent, and the seven celestial hierarchies." Included in this celestial septenary are the angels of destruction, and hope and dreams.[51] Inasmuch as apocalyptic literature is about destruction, hope, and dreams, *A Trip to the Moon*, with its symbolic otherworldly reflections on human emotions, has many of the generic elements that will be used in atomic bomb cinema; however, it lacks the mystical and eschatological elements. That is to say, although there is some criticism of the current world situation (which seems to only make French colonialism more attractive), *A Trip to the Moon* lacks the complete generic framework of the apocalyptic narrative, for there is no revelation, and no hortatory.

One prototypical bomb film that does incorporate the essential generic framework of the apocalyptic genre is director Fritz Lang's and screenwriter Thea von Harbou's *Metropolis* (Germany, 1927).[52] The film has an aura of frantic urgency to it, as though it were trying to understand the First World War and prevent the Second. The film also confronts class conflict, alienation, eschatological events, and rebirth. *Metropolis* is particularly important to this study because it addresses contemporaneous social issues through a fantasy about the future. These are, of course, important features of modern science fiction, but especially characteristic of the volatile issues dealt with in bomb films. The narrative of *Metropolis* is set one hundred years in the future, twenty-six years after the end of the second millennium, C.E.

The city of *Metropolis* has upper and lower worlds that divide and separate the classes; thus, the worlds of the upper and lower classes are as literal as they are iconic and symbolic. The central character is Freder. He is the son of Metropolis's ruler Jon Fredersen, and a prince among the elite. Freder is in the Eternal Garden of Pleasure when Maria, a worker's daughter, appears with the children she teaches. Freder is moved by her presence and so follows her into the underground city of the lower classes. Frightened by what he sees there, Freder returns to his father and asks why the workers must live such desolate lives. Fredersen's answer offers little comfort: It is the only life for which they are fit. The prince then returns to the underground world where he changes identities with a pauper, takes the pauper's job, and then attends one of

Maria's sermons. Catherine Wessinger defines two basic and very different types of millennial cults. "In catastrophic millennialism, society and humans are seen as being so evil that they must be destroyed before the millennial kingdom can be constructed." Conversely, "Progressive millennialism asserts that humans working in cooperation with the divine or superhuman will can create the millennial kingdom noncatastrohically."[53] Maria, like most characters in bomb films (even the psychotic General Jack D. Ripper in *Dr. Strangelove*), is a progressive millenarian. In her sermon she tells the story of Babel, she preaches peace and patience, and says the workers must wait for a "mediator": the "heart" who will join the "hands" and the "mind" together.

Fredersen employs the master wizard Rotwang to kidnap Maria and give her appearance to Rotwang's robot (which, Rotwang says, is in need of a soul). Fredersen hopes to strengthen his control over the workers through the new Maria, but through its actions he loses control over the events that he set into motion. The robot inspires the upper classes to new levels of debauchery and the workers to riot (a common motif in, for example, mythology and Wagner's operas). In a frenzy, the workers attack the power plant. Failing to heed their foreman's warning, the workers inadvertently flood their own city. Only Maria, Freder, and Freder's lower-class friend Josephat are aware of the disaster and can save the children. When the workers realize their folly, they track down the celebrating robot and burn her. Meanwhile, Rotwang chases the real Maria into a cathedral, followed by Freder. As Freder and Rotwang fight atop the cathedral, Fredersen kneels; helpless and paralyzed with fear, Fredersen can only watch. Rotwang falls from the cathedral to his death. All the main characters meet at the entrance of the cathedral. There, Maria encourages Freder to join the hands of the workers' foreman and his father.

Metropolis ostensibly reflects the class anxieties typical of German cinema and intellectual thought during the depressed 1920s; and the scholarly literature tends to approach the film only as political allegory. Siegfried Kracauer, in his classic study of early German cinema, *From Caligari to Hitler*, argues, "On the surface, it seems that Freder has converted his father; in reality, the industrialist has outwitted his son." According to Kracauer, a charismatic leader who betrays the workers yet keeps their confidence is a recurring sub-rosa motif in German film. This is because, he says, German politics has never had a true revolution.[54] Be this as it may, Kracauer is concerned with neither the symbolic and theological elements of the film nor the polysemous nature of the iconography that allows for multiple readings of the film text. For Kracauer the religious or deep psychological subtexts in the film are secondary to the politics. In the struggle for social justice that the film depicts, however, there resonates an ancient apocalyptic theme that cannot be ignored; that is, it acknowledges secular, humanist society's fallibility while simultaneously affirming the possibility of revelation and individual and social rebirth. These ideas recur again and again in atomic bomb cinema, but let us examine them more closely in *Metropolis*.

At the symbolic level, *Metropolis* is similar to the millenarian movements of the Middle Ages. The medieval millennial movements that Norman Cohn describes in *The Pursuit of the Millennium* were not lower-class revolutions. Rather, he argues, these movements were attempts to restore the status quo of accepted social relations that were being disrupted by rapid socioeconomic change and technological development. These violent, even self-destructive, movements were commonly led by charismatic personalities, often times maverick ecclesiastics, who promised the agitated peasants that they could bring about the end of evil, restore order in the world, and earn heavenly salvation. Frequently, these millennial movements were brutally suppressed. In other words, millennial movements are usually not revolutionary in the modern political sense.[55] Likewise, the workers' rebellion in *Metropolis* is not a true class revolution. Led by the charismatic robot, the workers act without forethought or political agenda and almost destroy themselves in their frenzied attack on the upper world. In the end, order is restored without any real redistribution of political power. What is implied at the end of the film is that communication is established between the heart and the hands. That is to say, the workers are brought under control and the masters realize their responsibilities to the workers. In a word, it is a kinder, gentler metropolis—built on the narrative foundation of the apocalypse.

The religious symbolism of the final scene is heavy-handed and hard to avoid. Maria brings about the transformation of Freder as the "mediator" between heaven above and earth below. This is obviously the quaternary of the Father, Son, Holy Ghost, and the Virgin Mary. The name "Fredersen" means son of Freder, and at the conclusion of *Metropolis* the son teaches the father. Likewise, in Christian ideology, the Son transforms the jealous Old Testament God into the New Testament God of Love. An even more obvious biblical allusion than this final scene is Freder's crucifixion on the arms of the giant clock at which he works. Just as

Christ descended into hell and took on the world's sins, Freder descends into the workers' city and takes on the job of a worker. As Freder hangs on the arms of the clock, he looks up and, echoing Christ's own pleading with his Father, asks out loud, "Father, will these ten hours never end?" In a later scene Freder, like Christ, is betrayed by the workers, and they try to kill him. He survives, but one of his followers is stabbed in the side and mortally wounded—just as Christ was pierced in the side by a Roman lance. Following the destruction of the power plant, the underground city is purged by a flood, and the lights go out in the city above ground. Freder reappears and brings about a transformation of the father, a union of opposites, and the resurrection of the masses. S. S. Prawer, in his book *Caligari's Children*, calls the flood in *Metropolis* a "man-made Armageddon," the site of the final battle between good and evil in the Revelation of St. John, and rhetorically asks, "What would . . . 'Armageddon' films [be] without science fiction?"[56]

On the door of Rotwang's laboratory is a pentacle, or five-pointed star—popularly associated with Christ as well as with both good and evil magic. In John's apocalypse, the false prophet (the devil) reigns for a period of time before he and his servant are thrown to their doom and burned in a lake of fire. Likewise, Rotwang and his servant rule for a short time before one is burned and the other is thrown to his doom from the house of God. At the end of the film the workers are united with the masters in the upper world. In both John's Apocalypse and Lang's *Metropolis*, a period of trials and tribulations is followed by the return of the Messiah and ascension of all souls to heaven, where they are joined with God forever.

Along with its political and religious themes, *Metropolis* is a mythological journey of self-discovery. As a young man, Lang had traveled extensively, including in Asia, and, as a member of Europe's literati of the time, was undoubtedly familiar with Asian thought and culture. The influence of Asia or the East can be seen in several of his films. Like the Buddha, Freder, a prince, suddenly and unexpectedly witnesses poverty. Further, what he observes is something from the lower levels, from his unconscious. Shocked, he begins a spiritual quest for self-knowledge and understanding of the world in which he lives. The prince's journey to the lower levels initiates a conflict between the two worlds. The conflict escalates until the proverbial flood purifies the land and brings about a new beginning. This mounting conflict, the moment of greatest dramatic tension, becomes a cusp between destruction and salvation, in psychological terms, a "crisis."

At the conclusion of *Metropolis*, Freder successfully brings the lower or unconscious elements to the upper level or consciousness. There he forces his father/consciousness to recognize and accept the needs and rights of the workers/unconsciousness. Conscious acceptance of the unconscious or spiritual needs is, as we will see in later chapters, concomitant with the rebirth that follows a psychological crisis. By 1927 many of Europe's literati were subjects of analysis or reading the works of Freud and his disciples, particularly the Christian mystic Jung. Harbou and Lang were surely at least familiar with modern psychology. Following closely with then contemporary intellectual thought, the film text of *Metropolis* ties together modern industrial and technological society both to ancient narratives of revolution and to modern notions of psychological development.

Metropolis is, undoubtedly, an apocalyptic drama. Virtually every aspect of the genre is used, including theological and mystical allusions to ancient narratives of transcendence. It has the iconography, the messiah, Jung's mystical quaternity of completeness, the "Maria," and the elements of epic self-discovery that are given to the character Freder. He takes a journey to another world, has several visions, and the unfolding of history is revealed to him and interpreted by Maria. The film begins with Freder swooning at the sight of Maria, and then leaving the Edenic "Eternal Garden of Pleasure"—presumably forever. He enters the underground world were he witnesses an explosion that kills many workers, then has a vision in which the dead workers become live human sacrifices to a pagan god. He meets Maria and they talk. It is through Maria that Freder realizes what he must do. To Freder, Maria is the mediating supernatural being that Collins describes in *The Apocalyptic Imagination*. Collins writes that "the constant element is the presence of an angel who interprets the vision or serves as guide on the otherworldly journey."[57]

While early apocalyptic literature depicted the oppression of a people by foreign or colonial powers, *Metropolis* depicts what has since come to be known, in Marx's terms, as class oppression, or perhaps "internal colonialism."[58] In both cases, conflict leads to crisis, and an eventual rebirth of the society. The film's optimism, and the retention of power by Fredersen, is an acceptable conclusion in the apocalyptic narrative tradition.

Metropolis is an important example of how filmmakers rework, for the screen, the narrative framework of the apocalyptic imagination. It developed a way of expressing Jewish and Christian revelations with the generic elements of epic struggle and self-discovery, but in a way acceptable and meaningful to modern secular audiences. And, like most apocalyptic texts, *Metropolis* comments on the social conditions of the day while concentrating on the traditionally powerful and consuming mystical dimensions of the conflict.

Pictorial and narrative elements of *Metropolis* can be seen in apocalyptic films ranging from William Cameron Menzies' *Things to Come* (Britain, 1936) to Paul Verhoeven's *Total Recall* (1990). Menzies's film, which H. G. Wells helped to adapt from his own story, has a final war, a period of tribulations, the return of the messiah, judgments, and the establishment of a *Metropolis*-like utopian city. Verhoeven's bomb film (which I will discuss in more detail in a later chapter) is based on Phillip K. Dick's short story "We Can Remember It for You Wholesale," and is a clever reworking of Harbou and Lang's narrative. The plot follows an elaborate machination to destroy a group of rebels. The brutal ruler of a mining colony on Mars sends his protégé and spy, to whom he is emotionally attached, down to Earth. On Earth, the spy is a "lowly construction worker." The spy eventually returns to Mars where images from his own mind reveal to him a possible future of salvation. The spy then deposes his brutal mentor and frees the lower classes. This entire narrative, the film suggests in its mind-boggling final moments, might, after all, just be the central character's artificially induced dream of action and adventure. This dream, if it is a dream, awaits revelation—by both the dreamer, if he can wake up, and by the audience (us).

Other aspects of apocalyptic bomb films can be traced to early silent films. Consider the monsters, or mysterious creatures (*kaijyū*) as the Japanese call them, commonly seen in bomb films. From which sources are they influenced? (Japan, of course, also has its own influential traditions and early, silent monster films, which I will discuss later.) One possible influence is Méliès's *A Trip to the Moon*, which includes a fight with the Selenites—the fantastic moon people who explode when hit with an umbrella. And, in Méliès's film *A la Conquete du pole/The Conquest of the Pole* (France, 1912), there is a maneating monster akin to a yeti, or abominable snowman.

Though the terrifying monsters and creatures that populate apocalyptic literature and art are not unique to the genre, they do form one more link between the apocalyptic imagination and atomic bomb cinema; moreover, recognized apocalyptic texts (e.g., the books of Daniel and John) are not the only Jewish or Christian sources for the monstrous or the apocalyptic in atomic bomb cinema. The paintings of Hieronymus Bosch (Dutch, 1450–1516) and engravings of Albrecht Dürer (German, 1471–1528) are now common icons of the apocalyptic imagination.[59] More specifically, S. S. Prawer traces the origins of terror, horror, and science fiction films from the Gothic horror genre of the eighteenth century to the films of Méliès and other early filmmakers. Prawer says, "These early productions . . . are the beginnings of a wave whose crest is reached in the silent German cinema."[60] The importance of German cinema, as we have already seen, cannot be underestimated. Early German cinema, especially German expressionism, is particularly important because it helped to establish a mode of filmmaking whereby the external world or film style, mise-en-scène, camera work, and editing all function as symbolic systems or indexes to the character's internal experience—including the experiences of characters on otherworldly journeys in apocalyptic bomb films.

Also fundamental to the development of horror films is the Jewish legend of the Golem. In 1580 Rabbi Judah Loew creates a humanoid creature, the Golem, to protect the Jewish community of Prague from anti-Semitic pogroms; but there are unintended consequences: the creature becomes more human than expected, falls in love, and suffers a tragic demise. A subtext of the story, thus, is the philosophical exploration of the very notion of man creating life artificially, that is, the definition of humanity or life itself. (A detailed comparison of the rich Golem legends and scholarly literature is tempting, but beyond the scope of this study.) The first Golem film, *Der Golem*, was made in 1914 by the German filmmakers Paul Wegener and Henrik Galeen. Wegener also cowrote, codirected, and acted in two other versions. By the late 1970s several more silent and sound versions had been made.[61] To the list of Golems we may want to add the robot in Lang's *Metropolis*, and numerous synthetic beings in atomic bomb cinema.

Obviously, Jewish and Christian traditions are not the only sources for fantastic monsters and creatures in apocalyptic bomb films. Nor are all monsters humanoid. Mutated insects and "prehistoric" or mythical monsters of all kinds populate atomic bomb cinema. These other creatures also have predecessors in the silent and early sound eras. Surely, the prototypical monster is Méliès's yeti, and many creatures, such as the giant ants in the apocalyptic bomb film *Them!* (Gordon Douglas, 1954), take inspiration from the Teutonic dragon Fafnir in Fritz Lang's eschatological film *Die Nibelungen* (Germany, 1924).[62]

The indisputable prototype for bomb film monsters, however, is the early sound film *King Kong* (Merian C. Cooper and Earnest B. Schoedsack, 1933). King Kong is a combination of Golem and Fafnir—with the ethnocentricity and paternalism of an Edgar Rice Burroughs novel. While two white men vie for different reasons for the same white woman on an isolated tropical island, the dark-skinned natives kidnap the woman and offer her to the giant gorilla they worship: King Kong. Never having seen a white woman before, the prehistoric Kong goes ape for Ann Darrow (Fay Wray)—whose name alludes to Clarence Darrow, defense attorney at the Scopes Monkey Trial of 1925. Just as the Golem did before him, Kong pursues a woman up a tower—the Empire State Building to be exact—where he falls to his death. Standing before the dead Kong, fictional filmmaker Carl Denham exclaims, "It was beauty that killed the beast." Of course, not every creature falls to its death. Nevertheless, the movement from high to low places is very important in bomb films, especially in *The Beast From 20,000 Fathoms* (Eugene Lourie, 1953) and *Gojira/ Godzilla, King of the Monsters,* (Inoshirō Honda, 1954).

The influence of *King Kong* has not and should not be underestimated. Ray Harryhausen, special effects director on many award-winning films including the seminal American bomb films *The Beast from 20,000 Fathoms* and *It Came from Beneath the Sea* (Robert Gordon, 1955), has acknowledged the importance of *King Kong* in his work.[63] In an interview with Inoshirō Honda and his wife Kimi a few years before his death, the director told me that *King Kong* was an important inspiration in his career, especially to his seminal film *Gojira*.[64] A few other bomb-related monster films include: *The Day the World Ended* (Roger Corman, 1956), *Monster on Campus* (Jack Arnold, 1958), *The Amazing Colossal Man* (Bert I. Gordon, 1957), *Frankenstein—1970* (Howard W. Koch, 1958), the bomb/Golem film *It* (Herbert J. Leder, 1967), and even *The Toxic Avenger* (Michael Herz and Samuel Weil, 1985). Psychosexual crisis serves as one of the subplots in each of these films.

While most of us would agree that even adults are not immune to typically "developmental" crises, adolescence seems to be a stage in life marked by the drama of psychosexual crisis. In a refinement of Erikson's crisis concept, Joseph L. White uses the term "troubled adolescent" to describe the large number of young people whose psychological development resembles neither textbook cases of normal nor abnormal psychology. "The important question," says White, "is how adolescents cope with conflict."[65] Avoiding social isolation by being involved in various extracurricular activities is one important coping strategy. And in a classic use/value theory text, *Movies as Social Criticism: Aspects of Their Social Psychology*, Ian Jarvie makes a compelling case for seeing the cinema as a key social event in the lives of young people. Since young people (those in their teens and early twenties) make up the single largest film audience, filmmakers have a strong impetus to create characters at psychological stages of development with which youth can easily identify, yet complex enough to draw older audiences as well.[66] We have all seen abundant examples of films where scientists (and their creations) are often troubled by psychosexual crises. Indeed, many bomb films feature "troubled" characters enduring the classical developmental crisis.

Consider two of the most famous: *Them!* (Gordon Douglas, 1954), which makes overt references to Biblical eschatology, and *Gojira*, which is not apocalyptic in the Western sense but depicts an eschatological crisis. In both films the creature suffers from and symbolizes a psychosexual crisis. In *Them!* we find ants nearing maturity, a near-pubescent girl, and a heroine and hero who argue over gender roles. The argument is resolved in the heroine's favor when she asserts her identity as being both female and scientist. The psychosexual crisis in *Gojira* is more ambiguous. Nevertheless, it can be argued that as the heroine of the story struggles through the crisis that Gojira represents, she also struggles through a psychosexual crisis: the dilemma of choosing between the man she loves and the man to whom she is engaged—another troubled scientist.

The troubled scientist figures significantly in atomic bomb cinema, and the prototypes for these scientists can be traced back to important early films and literature. Consider, for example, James Whale's 1933 film of H. G. Wells' story *The Invisible Man*, and the many other film versions that followed; or, the countless versions of Robert Lewis Stevenson's *The Strange Case of Dr. Jekyll and Mr. Hyde*, beginning with Selig Polyscope Company's 1908 *The Modern Dr. Jekyll*, or Mary Shelley's *Frankenstein, or, the Modern Prometheus*, which has been the basis, of course, for innumerable films, beginning with James Whale's 1931 *Frankenstein*. In such films there is usually a scientist who postpones marriage to devote himself to scientific experiments that usurp the laws of nature. These experiments, moreover, are elaborate alchemic metaphors for the scientists' psychosexual-social crises; and, these stories remind us that not all crises are resolved successfully, or are, at least, tragic. H. G. Wells's story, *The Island of Dr. Moreau*, has inspired at least four films; the first is Erle C. Kenton's 1933 film *The Island of Lost Souls*, and the most recent is

John Frankenheimer's 1996 *The Island of Dr. Moreau*. James B. Twitchell argues that two important themes that feature in films based on this story are what he refers to as "the physical conjunction of man and beast" and the totalitarian political oppression by a ruthless and maniacal scientist.[67] The screen adaptations of these literary masterpieces, or their motifs, have been reworked into a variety of bomb films, including: *Dr. Cyclops* (Ernest Schoedsack, 1940), *Tarantula* (Jack Arnold, 1955), *The Amazing Colossal Man* (Bert I. Gordon, 1957), *I Was a Teenage Werewolf* (Gene Fowler, 1957), *Frankenstein—1970* (Howard W. Koch, 1958), *Attack of the 50 Ft. Woman* (Nathan Juran, 1958), and the series of films beginning with *Planet of the Apes* (Franklin J. Schafner, 1968). Most importantly, let's not forget the demented scientist in Kubrick's 1964 film, *Dr. Strangelove*, whose very name denotes a widespread psychosexual crisis that ends in nuclear war and virtual universal annihilation.

Of course, silent films and early films that introduced sound are not the only mass media that later filmmakers use as a source of raw materials for bomb films. There are, for instance, many similarities between two of the original *Superman* cartoons, "Arctic Giant" (Dave Fleischer, 1942) and "The Underground World" (1943), and *The Beast from 20,000 Fathoms* and *Unknown World*, respectively (Terrell O. Morse, 1951). However, the conduit between creature and horror films and apocalyptic bomb films is *Metropolis*; Lang's film made available to atomic bomb cinema a wide range of icons, symbols, and narrative patterns by combining the apocalyptic literary genre's use of otherworldly journeys, visions, and eschatological upheavals; science fiction's technologically created utopias and dystopias; and horror's psychosexual crises.

To understand *Metropolis*'s influence on science fiction, let us take another look at Rotwang and his robot. Rotwang is referred to as a wizard. Thus, he uses his science as a kind of magic, or perhaps we should say alchemy, just as the learned Rabbi Loew used magic to create the Golem. The scientist/wizard's unstable psychology has obvious roots in other horror films, such as the 1908 and 1909 adaptations of *Dr. Jekyll and Mr. Hyde*, and Wegener's famous 1912 *Der Student von Prag/The Student of Prague*.[68]

As for the Golem, Harbou and Lang cleverly distribute its attributes to several characters. Wegener's Golem is mystically transformed by love, just as in the myth of Pygmalion. Love makes the Golem human. And, as in *Homunculus* and *Der Golem*, Rotwang's robot is used to control the masses.[69] But in *Metropolis*, it is Freder who is transformed by love; and it is Rotwang himself, not his Golem-like creation, who is driven to his doom by unrequited love.

Rotwang still pines after Hel, who died giving birth to Freder. At the end of *Metropolis*, the demented Rotwang mistakes Maria for Hel. He pursues the frightened Maria to the top of the cathedral where, just like all good Golems, he falls to his death. Additionally, Maria is like the women in *Der Golem, Frankenstein, King Kong,* and, to a lesser extent, *Gojira*: not only is she is threatened by a monster, but she is also the apex of a love triangle between the man she loves and a Golem who loves her. In later chapters I will show that as important as Maria is in *Metropolis*, heroines become even more important in atomic bomb cinema.

Robots that are out of control or cause others to lose control have become routine, and the most clichéd form of robot is now a computer, as for example, in the popular bomb film, *Colossus: The Forbin Project* (Joseph Sargent, 1970).[70] Rotwang's robot, however, has been resurrected most effectively in the characters of three bomb films: the science officer in Ridley Scott's *Alien* (1979), and the cyborg in James Cameron's *The Terminator* (1984) and *Terminator 2: Judgment Day* (1991). In each of these films a robot is able to deceive people with its human form until its true nature is revealed. Furthermore, the robots are set on fire and perish. In *The Terminator*, the fire actually reveals the cyborg's true identity. And in *Alien*, for example, the central character confronts the robot in a womb-like computer referred to as "Mother." The robot tries to suffocate her by placing a rolled-up pornographic magazine into her mouth. Might this have been a scant suggestion of a psychosexual crisis? Like Rotwang's robot before them, these robots all violate Isaac Asimov's famous "laws of robotics"; that is, they represent a threat to human life.[71]

Harbou and Lang made apocalyptic scenarios accessible to audiences of horror and science fiction films through *Metropolis*. Though their influence on horror is somewhat obscure, Prawer has identified in James Whales's 1933 film, *Frankenstein*, visual allusions not just to *Der Golem* but to *Metropolis* as well.[72] Thus, it is Harbou's and Lang's mixing of apocalyptic religious symbolism with horror and science fiction genres that made the development of bomb-related, apocalyptic creature films possible. And in bomb films, as in *Metropolis*, the Golem-like synthetic beings, or sentient robots, ancient creatures, mutants, and aliens, serve the same function: a subtextual exploration of the meaning of our humanity.

Clearly, films such as *Gojira, The Terminator, and Them!* are the product of a world poised on the brink of nuclear annihilation. Paul Boyer writes that the bomb has radically changed consciousness.[73] There is indeed truth to this, but only to the extent that it has made us more aware of the world in which we live, not less, as Boyer and others have argued. The change, however, is not so radical that older forms of thought, feeling, and experience no longer make sense. In fact, quite the opposite is true.

Just how influential have these prototypical apocalyptic films been on the various strata of American society and culture? In a 1994 essay commemorating the twenty-fifth anniversary of the first landing on the moon, Arthur Schlesinger, the celebrated historian who was a special assistant to Presidents Kennedy and Johnson, writes about the dream of space travel. He begins by describing the amazing similarities between Jules Verne's *From Earth to the Moon* and the Apollo missions. Then he adds,

> For those of us who as children read Verne and H. G. Wells ("The First Men in the Moon") and saw movies such as Fritz Lang's 1929 "By Rocket to the Moon," the realization of this dream in 1969 seemed something unimaginable. It had never occurred to me that such an event would happen in my lifetime. In 1969, fantasy becomes fact.

Schlesinger begins to wax apocalyptic in his interpretations of what has been revealed to humanity through otherworldly space travel. He claims that "[o]ne result" of landing on the moon "may be to give earthlings a more vivid sense of what they hold in common." The return trip, he asserts, allowed the astronauts to see "through superficial conflicts to the ultimate unity in which fate has enveloped us." Schlesinger argues that to not continue space exploration "would surely be a betrayal of man's innermost nature." Then, quoting the creator of the television program *Star Trek* and other futuristic programs, Gene Roddenberry, he adds,

> "Our prime obligation to ourselves," Roddenberry has said, "is to make the unknown known. We are on a journey to keep an appointment with whatever we are."[74]

Are these not revelations? Caught in some sort of science fiction time loop, the apocalyptic imagination influences both scholarly and popular media, which in turn influence even the most sophisticated spectators, as well as the musings of the cultural elite, who in turn recycle the apocalyptic worldview in later works of criticism, literature, television, and especially film. Consider, also, the title of the Smithsonian Institution's abortive controversial exhibit for the fiftieth anniversary of the bombing of Hiroshima and Nagasaki: *The Last Act: The Atomic Bomb and the End of World War II*.[75] Is this not an *ex eventu prophecy*, the restructuring of a past event into an apocalyptic narrative with a penultimate battle?

Thus, earlier storytelling and filmmaking traditions provided the raw materials for understanding the bomb. The utopic promise of science and technology, the psychosexual crisis of creature films, and the desire for a salvational apocalypse are each present in silent and early sound films. After 1945, filmmakers began to use these films as the raw materials for the apocalyptic bomb film subcategory, some subversively. After all, is not the benevolent cyborg with one gloved hand in James' Cameron's 1991 film *Terminator 2: Judgment Day* an homage to Kubrick's crazed scientist Dr. Strangelove? And, is not Fritz Lang's crazed wizard with one gloved hand and a strange love for a dead woman later resurrected as the one-gloved, physically and psychosexually demented scientist in Kubrick's 1964 black comedy, *Dr. Strangelove or: How I Learned to Stop Worrying and Love the Bomb*?

2

1945 to 1949

The initial elation after Hiroshima and Nagasaki

Maintaining the secrecy essential to carry out the bombing of Hiroshima was a feat in itself.

—Colonel Murry Green, USAF-Ret., *The Retired Officer*[1]

The need for ostentatious secrecy is of vital importance on the primitive level, for the shared secret serves as cement binding the tribe together. The need for such a secret is in many cases so compelling that the individual finds himself involved in ideas and actions for which he is no longer responsible.

—C. G. Jung, *Memories, Dreams, Reflections*[2]

Secrets are about all that Americans had in the years between 1945 to 1949 (see figure 1). In June 1946, according to historian Richard Rhodes, "the U.S. nuclear weapons stockpile consisted of only nine Fat Man bombs, of which no more than seven could be made operational for lack of initiators." By mid-1947 the number had increased to only thirteen bombs. Little Boy, used on Hiroshima on August 6, had a yield equivalent to 12.5 kilotons of TNT. Estimates for those killed immediately approximate 120,000; over the next five years an additional 80,000 persons are reported as having succumbed to Little Boy–related injuries and illnesses. Fat Man, dropped on Nagasaki on August 9, had a yield estimated at 22 kilotons, yet by the end of 1945 only 70,000 deaths were attributed to Fat Man; over the next five years an additional 70,000 persons are reported as have succumbed to Fat Man–related injuries and illnesses. (Topographic and sociological factors account for these wide differences.) The death rate in both cities was about 54 percent.[3] As astonishing as these numbers are, they make sense only in the context of modern warfare and modern life. Compared to other military operations and to other mortality statistics, the total numbers of persons killed and the total geographic area destroyed (a few square miles in each case) remains relatively small. "The Strategic Bombing Survey," writes Rhodes, "estimates that 'probably more persons lost their lives by fire at Tokyo in a 6-hour period than at any [equivalent period of] time in the history of man'"; more than 100,000 died. And, counting only the wounded, Hitler's failed invasion of the Soviet Union alone cost Germany 1.2 million troops.[4] Estimates for Soviet lives lost during the war generally run around 20 million. Indeed, humanity does not need nuclear weapons to destroy itself. According to recent figures, each year in the United States there are more than 100,000 alcohol-related deaths, and "168,000 premature cancer deaths" related to cigarettes alone.[5] In one small region of Japan, the government has recognized 12,615 surviving claims out of 17,000 applications "for certification as Minamata disease [mercury poisoning] victims."[6] Finally, considering the size of the Soviet military at the end of the war (1.6 million Soviet troops were prepared to invade Japan alone!) it is unlikely that, even under the best conditions, nuclear weapons could have decided a war with the former Soviet Union.[7] One top secret evaluation of the Strategic Air Offensive, dated May 11, 1949, notes that an "atomic offensive would not, per se" win a war on Soviet territory.[8] The secret was therefore even more important.

As early as 1943, the Danish physicist Niels Bohr, who, writes Rhodes, advocated an "open world modeled in some sense on the republic of science" (which is itself an optimistic assessment of academic science), warned that it was futile to try and monopolize nuclear weapons technology. Of course not everyone agreed with Bohr's point of view, and opinions differed considerably. Estimates for the Soviet's ability to achieve nuclear capability ranged from within a few years to never. Vannevar Bush and James B. Conant, members of Roosevelt's Top Policy Group for the Manhattan Project, warned that the monopoly would be broken within five years. The official British estimate was 1957 to 1958, and the official American estimate was purposely pessimistic: 1952 to 1953.[9] According to journalist and historian Godfrey Hodgson, when

Secretary of War Stimson informed newly appointed president Harry Truman of the fission device, he added, "It is practically certain that we could not remain in this position [of monopoly] indefinitely."[10] Despite these warnings, the Truman administration attempted to maintain its monopoly on nuclear weapons. And, says Rhodes, Winston Churchill championed this policy of keeping our nuclear technology secret from the world in general and the Soviets in particular. The physicist Edward Teller, a fervent anti-Soviet and the primary advocate of the "Super," or thermonuclear fusion device, was also surprised when President Truman announced the Soviet's successful detonation of their first atom bomb, Joe I, on September 23, 1949.[11] As it turned out, even Bush and Conant underestimated the Soviet's ability to build a fission device.

From August 1945 through 1950 the United States did its damnedest to *convince* itself that it possessed a secret, and this secret made the country feel unique and more secure. Almost paradoxically, the considerable effort required to maintain the nation's "secret" and security seemed to enflame latent fears of insecurity and jeopardize individual identity and personal freedoms. According to Hodgson, "The House Un-American Activities Committee [or HUAC] was set up in 1938, and from the start devoted about four-fifths of its attention to investigating the Left."[12] In 1947, well before Joe I or Joseph McCarthy, HUAC began looking for communists in Hollywood—neither the first nor the last such crucible for Hollywood. In 1948 the Hollywood Ten were fined and imprisoned, and many others had their careers and lives ruined by an actual blacklist. And yet, conversely, most scholars and left-leaning critics still typically condemn Hollywood for being a tool of the political right. Again, the general opinion of contemporary scholars of the bomb and popular culture is that Hollywood has numbed Americans' awareness to nuclear issues. Considering these vastly different caricatures of Hollywood, it is, therefore, imperative that we take a fresh look at the films themselves.

In this chapter I will discuss the history and development of bomb films and their cultural context between the years 1945 to 1950. Specifically, I will discuss *Above and Beyond*, *Notorious*, and *D.O.A.*, and analyze two films in greater depth: *First Yank into Tokyo*, and *The Beginning or the End*. This chapter is organized along the following three key issues: the legacy of racism, colonialism, and nationalism following the war; the secret; and, the surfacing of an apocalyptic consciousness, in bomb films. This consciousness facilitates both the probing and the propagandizing of the morality and ideology of having used nuclear weapons; that is, the difficult question of our *responsibility*. The last part of the chapter is devoted to analyzing the film *The Beginning or the End*, through which I will show how these different issues are inextricably connected to one another. Interwoven throughout the chapter, as elsewhere, are challenges to the often seemingly deliberate misreadings (from the political left and right) of the films, and to assumptions that lead to gross mischaracterization of America's relationship to the bomb.

The Legacy of Racism, Colonialism, and Nationalism

Only a handful of bomb films even mention Japan or the Japanese people. There are a number of possible reasons why, including the diminished importance of Japan as the cold war began (important from a military perspective only as a base for "containing" Soviet expansionism), and guilt. Paul Boyer, in *By the Bomb's Early Light*, is partly correct in stating that "Hollywood contributed its bit to the larger cultural process by which Hiroshima and Nagasaki gradually sank, unconfronted and unresolved, into the deeper recesses of American awareness."[13] "Unresolved," yes. "Unconfronted," absolutely not! Beginning in the 1950s, the numbers of bomb films increased dramatically, and stayed relatively high for more than a decade. This suggests that Americans have confronted these issues in symbolic and metaphoric ways; for which Hollywood is contemptuously condemned by certain exacting academics who prefer more blatant, less ambiguous forms of discourse and criticism.

The Second World War did not begin with the surprise bombing of Pearl Harbor, nor did it end with the destruction of Hiroshima and Nagasaki. For many in Japan, and in other nations as well, World War II is the result of Western imperialism and colonialism. The American use of military strength to forcibly open Japan in the late nineteenth century to trade and outside influences was a defining moment in world history that has bred hatred and distrust. (It is also an ambiguous moment, for internal political factions also took advantage of the Americans' presence to seize power.) The destructive enmity that characterized World War II did not dissipate with either the war's end or the end of the cold war. Consider two mid-1990s events: the acrimonious responses, from both Americans and Japanese, to the Smithsonian Institution's scrapped plans for exhibiting the Enola Gay; and, the predictably bitter exchanges following President Clinton's refusal to apologize for the destruction of Hiroshima and Nagasaki. To this we might add the frequent scandals caused by Japanese officialdom's unwillingness to apologize for, take responsibility for, or even acknowledge, Japan's actions during the war; also, Japan's frequent flirtations with anti-Semitism, anti-African-American sentiments, and general foreigner bashing (some of which I experience in my university and daily life). At the very least, many who were personally touched by the war still have not resolved their feelings about who is responsible for what. An unusual mutual misunderstanding and enmity consequently continues between these two closely tied "friendly" countries. The conspicuous absence of Japan and the Japanese from American films about the bomb, therefore, demands more than just a cursory dismissal of Hollywood.

The first film to contain actual images of a nuclear explosion is *First Yank into Tokyo* (Gordon Douglas, 1945). It is the story of one soldier's suicide mission to rescue an American held in a Japanese prisoner-of-war (POW) camp. Unbeknownst to the Japanese, the POW is an important physicist. Beyond this reference and the nuclear explosions in the final scenes, the film concerns itself with the racist propaganda that dominated both sides in the Pacific theater of war. In fact, the narrative of the film seems to be more influenced by the film *Casablanca* (Michael Curtiz, 1942) than by the development, use, or aftermath of the atomic bomb. The physicist and the atomic bomb are mere plot devices around which the ideology of the film is spun.

Though more blatant than most films, the message of *First Yank into Tokyo* is typical of how the Japanese enemy was demonized. The Japanese antagonist (Richard Loo) is described as highly intelligent and clever, but depraved: he lusts after white women (as did the villainous Burmese, played by Sessue Hayakawa, in Cecil B. De Mille's 1915 film *The Cheat*). In the end, he is defeated by the equally intelligent American protagonist (Tom Neal). More importantly, the American is especially chaste and with no complementary miscegenational inclinations. While the hero does not overtly break any taboos against interracial sex or love, the hero's inevitable death nevertheless indicates xenophobia, fear of miscegenation, and a latent homophobia. The hero, for instance, speaks the Japanese language (albeit extraordinarily badly), has undergone irreversible plastic surgery to look Japanese, and, more importantly, was roommates with the Japanese villain in college. The hero has, therefore, become too Japanese, too contaminated, so to speak, to be comfortably reassimilated by his own kind—an implicitly white America. Thus, the film's narrative structure seems to borrow much from familiar colonial narratives about those held captive or who otherwise had too much contact with Native Americans.[14] All this clearly foreshadows the hero's doom. The hero lives long enough to help the physicist and the heroine escape, and the scientist delivers "final and terrible retribution" to the Japanese, thereby guaranteeing that no more soldiers will die in war.

We should not delude ourselves into believing that racial thinking was, or is, only a limited or extremist phenomenon. In Alfred Hitchcock's highly praised 1940 film *Foreign Correspondent*, Stephen Fisher (Herbert Marshal) is a German-born Englishman who spies for the Nazis and sabotages the European peace movement. His savagery is repellent even to himself, but just before his demise, he justifies himself to his English-born daughter, telling her that though he resisted at first, "I used my country's methods because I was born with them." Racial thinking was a factor in every dimension of WWII. Nevertheless, in *War without Mercy: Race and Power in the Pacific War*, John W. Dower documents the racism in the media and propaganda of both Japan and the Allies, and shows that racism was a far more important factor in the Pacific theater of war than in the European theater of war. (Dower even notes that the racial conflict was put into apocalyptic terms, but never develops this idea.) Dower claims that anti-Asian racism was present before the bombing of Pearl Harbor—and that it continues to influence many Americans' attitudes and official policies.[15] (Indeed, in fall 2000, the espionage case against Wen Ho Lee for handing over nuclear weapons secrets to China seemed to blow up in the Justice Department's face amid angry charges of "racial profiling"; some critics are now claiming that, just as with capital punishment crimes, a disproportionate number of minorities are the targets of national security investigations and punishment).[16] We can easily find support for Dower's thesis in the popular media of the time. For instance, of the original *Superman* cartoons (1941 to 1943) five episodes have war-related plots. Three take place within the United States, one in South America, and one in Japan. One of these five cartoons is about Nazi sabotage in the United States, another is about Nazi soldiers in South America, and a third is about unidentified Caucasian saboteurs in an American munitions company. In still another, Superman sabotages a Yokohama shipyard and rescues Lois Lane, and, finally, Japanese saboteurs try to disrupt the American war effort. This last cartoon is the only one with an obvious racial slur; the episode's title is "Japoteurs."[17] Over the years, anti-Asian and anti-Japanese sentiment has obviously not disappeared from the United

States, and yet many Americans today would be offended by the racial logic of *First Yank into Tokyo*. The irony of *First Yank into Tokyo*, however, is that many Japanese today would find this racial logic quite reasonable, even legal. In 1997, Ashikawa University successfully fired Professor Gwendolyn Gallagher after thirteen years of satisfactory employment. The university claimed it needed "'fresh foreigners' (*furesshu na gaikokujin*)," because Gallagher had become "over-'Japanized' (*nipponaizu*)." A cornerstone to the university's defense was that Professor Gallagher married and had children with a Japanese national. On February 1, 2000, Ashikawa District Court Chief Judge Norio Saiki ruled that the university's dismissal of Gallagher was "objective and rational."[18] Stories of systematic discrimination abound among minority groups in Japan, and few such cases ever make it into the courts, but, occasionally, courts do rule in favor of plaintiffs. Irrespective of how the courts rule, according to this racial logic, culture is biological but can be transmitted through the exchange of bodily fluids.

When the Japanese are mentioned in atomic bomb cinema, Euro-American racism and sexism frequently, but not always, emerge. There have been two semibiographical films about Lieutenant Colonel Paul Tibbets Jr., who led the 393 and 509 Bomber Squadrons and piloted the Enola Gay (named after his mother), which dropped Little Boy on Hiroshima. *Above and Beyond* (Melvin Frank and Norman Panama) was released in 1952; *The Enola Gay: The Men, the Mission, the Atomic Bomb* (David Lowell Rich), a made-for-television film, was broadcast in 1980. The second film is particularly instructive.

In *The Enola Gay*, women are generally perceived as disruptive influences on men fighting the war. And, by neatly mixing issues of race and gender, this film describes the Japanese as, at best, incompetent. In one particularly significant scene, women working for the military decide Tibbets's lone B-29 poses no threat, and so do not pass on an early warning to Hiroshima, thereby shifting responsibility or guilt to the Japanese, who have only themselves to blame for the unexpectedly high number of casualties. (At 8:15 A.M., most civilians, including most children, were outdoors and unprotected, and on military-related work details or going to work or school.) Any moral questions about the American male character are easily assuaged in an earlier scene. Base security tries to arrest one soldier because he is a wanted criminal. Tibbets, however, is able to use his military authority to shelter the man. Thus, the film smoothes over a difficult moral dilemma, and concludes that even the worst

American is morally fit to serve in the country's military, fight its wars, and kill its enemies.

Again, the question is, Why should the Japanese be so conspicuously absent from atomic bomb cinema? Again, the answer is that the Japanese are only ostensibly absent. *The Heroes of Telemark* (Britain, 1965), a bomb film directed by the American filmmaker Anthony Mann and starring American actor Kirk Douglas, clearly agonizes over the moral dilemma of civilian deaths ("collateral casualties" in the current vernacular) in modern war. Through a story about the Norwegian Resistance's own bloody attempts to stop the Nazi production of deuterium oxide, this film most certainly debates the morality of bombing Hiroshima and Nagasaki. Significantly, the film admits that there is no clear answer. While *The Heroes of Telemark* may be exceptional in its clear treatment of the issue of civilian casualties vis-à-vis nuclear war, it is not by any means unusual.

In the fifteen years or more since I first saw *First Yank into Tokyo*, my own responses have evolved in ways I could not have anticipated. I now identify with the doomed American protagonist more than I ever expected I could. As an expatriate living in Japan, married to a Japanese woman, and raising two mixed-blood children, I have experienced first hand the xenophobia that shapes the ideology of *First Yank into Tokyo*. Some of my colleagues—both American and Japanese—have made it clear that they eye me with suspicion because I have stayed too long in Japan. Others have been very supportive. Dower is indeed correct that the legacy of trans-Pacific racial prejudices continues; and yet, the scholarly voice, even Dower's, cannot help but simplify. As the poetry of the apocalyptic imagination and other bomb films teach, life between two worlds is a bittersweet blessing.

The Secret

Until 1950 the United States had a monopoly on functional nuclear weapons, yet very few—only thirty-four—bomb films were made. Of course, there is always a production lag time, and films begun in the late 1940s may not have appeared until the early 1950s. Many bomb films, however, have very low production values and were made in short order, or modified at the last minute, to exploit sensational events. More importantly, there was no immediate nuclear threat to the American people. Only after Joe I did Hollywood begin to produce a great number of bomb films, and only then do we begin to see images of America truly at risk or under attack. Bomb films made between 1945 and 1950 do, of course, express concerns about future nuclear wars, and some even describe attempted nuclear attacks (these attempts are always thwarted and the secret remains safe). Two well-known films that are often referred to in the scholarly literature, *The Best Years of Our Lives* (William Wyler, 1946) and *The Lady from Shanghai* (Orson Welles, 1948), for example, indeed make telling references to the bomb. Other, more important issues, however, overshadow the bomb in these films, and make these films tangential, at best, to atomic bomb cinema. *The Best Years of Our Lives* is more concerned with the reintegration of veterans into mainstream America, and *The Lady from Shanghai* is really about the type of tragic character that always concerns Welles. Most films of this early era are, in any case, ostensibly concerned with maintaining the American nuclear monopoly.

The most popular and most critically acclaimed bomb film of the immediate postwar era is Alfred Hitchcock's *Notorious* (1946). In the first edition to *The Art of Alfred Hitchcock: Fifty Years of His Motion Pictures*, historian and critic Donald Spoto argues that not only is *Notorious* one of Hitchcock's twelve best films and his finest of this period, but that it also depicts "a depth and humanity manifested by few films of that era."[19] More important to our concerns, in the second edition Spoto adds, "Right after watching it, you may tend to forget its plot about Nazis working with uranium ore in Brazil, in a race to develop the bomb at the end of World War II."[20] Evans, Newman, and Perrine use *Notorious* as evidence for the usual theories of pathology derived from the leading scholars—none of whom mention the film—but I believe *Notorious* is an excellent counterexample to these standard arguments.[21]

Ostensibly, *Notorious* is about Alicia Huberman (Ingrid Bergman), the daughter of a convicted spy, and T. R. Devlin (Cary Grant), a federal agent, who recruits Alicia to infiltrate a Nazi cabal in Rio de Janeiro with whom her father was associated. In order to ingratiate herself, Alicia marries the leader, Alex Sebastian (Claude Rains). Eventually she and Devlin discover that the Nazis are smuggling uranium ore in wine bottles. (According to Spoto, the ore is for nuclear weapons, but the film offers no clear explanation of its intended use.)[22] After realizing Alicia is a spy, Sebastian and his mother who opposed the marriage (Leopoldine Konstantin) poison Alicia. Finally, Devlin rescues Alicia and they acknowledge their love for each other.

Spoto calls it "Hitchcock's most famous MacGuffin: the uranium in the wine bottles."[23] Hitchcock himself introduced the term *MacGuffin*, a plot device that moves the narrative along by sweeping the characters and the film's spectators into events beyond their control, while by the end of the film the device appears to be relatively unimportant. At the level of the text, the MacGuffin often functions as a sort of wild goose chase or snipe hunt (used to initiate or train neophytes) that lures the hero. Spoto explains the MacGuffin as "some object which appears to be of importance to the characters" but has little significance to the film.[24] The stolen money in *Psycho* (1960) is another excellent example. The MacGuffin is a defining feature of Hitchcock's films, and his films help to define the "Hollywood" film—which includes, as we will see in the next chapter, important bomb films such as *On the Beach* (1959). At the subtextual level, the MacGuffin allows for the exploration of the metaphysical dimensions of the events and the psychological dimensions of the central characters. Another defining feature of Hitchcock's films are men who have mother fixations, and men who are unable to make commitments to the women they love. In *Notorious* the wine bottles could have contained anything nefarious. Thus, the story is about spies and bombs only to the extent that we can extrapolate from these characters the personality of spies or those involved with nuclear weapons; in this case, hardly at all. Spoto writes,

> Although *Notorious* seems to be a spy melodrama, in fact it is not. The espionage activities are really Hitchcock's MacGuffin, his ubiquitous pretext for more serious, abstract issues. Here, the serious issue is one of common humanity—the possibility of love and trust redeeming two lives from fear, guilt and meaninglessness. . . . Spies and uranium provide the dramatic context. They get us into the theater in the first place and keep us entertained as a deeper moral fable unfolds.[25]

In later films, Hitchcock similarly uses the cold war as a background for exploring character development.

Notorious is about the neuroses of two characters and is only peripherally concerned with the bomb. At most, *Notorious* directly highlights the American obsession with secrets, and its (deleterious) effect on men and women. Thus, we could say that *Notorious* and Hitchcock's other cold war films are about the effects of the government's paranoia and secretiveness on individuals, but this would disregard the more important themes that concerned Hitchcock throughout his career. In most of his films, Hitchcock shows disdain for institutions and authority. More to the point, *Notorious*, if anything, indirectly highlights the absence of a real fear of nuclear annihilation in films prior to 1950. The threat of a nuclear attack on the United States is never even considered.

Paul Boyer claims that following the bombing of Hiroshima, "[i]n Hollywood, writers rushed to incorporate the atomic bomb into their movie scripts," and offers *The House on 92nd Street* (Henry Hathaway, September 1945) as his example.[26] This is the first post-Hiroshima bomb film, and, according to Leonard Maltin, is loosely based on accounts of a Nazi spy network that operated in New York City during the war.[27] Mick Broderick, on the one hand, notes that the director "experimented with a documentary approach . . . to evoke a heightened sense of realism and immediacy," and this would seem to add validity to Boyer's argument.[28] Pam Cook, on the other hand, points out that just after World War II, 20th Century Fox, the studio where the film was produced, "embarked on a series of 'serious,' 'realistic' crime films employing semi-documentary devices and often including newsreel footage." Cook also points out that the producer of *The House on 92nd Street*, Louis De Roche, "launched and supervised" Fox's famous *March of Time* newsreel series.[29] In other words, *The House on 92nd Street* is more than a knee-jerk response to the bomb, and it is part of a broader pattern of experimentation with genre and filmmaking. I think Boyer is, again, overstating his case on the basis of one film or, to be generous, several such films.

At first, few early popular and critically acclaimed films exploited nuclear anxiety. Rudolph Maté's classic film noir, *D.O.A.* (1950), was completed about two months after Joe I, and about three months after McCarthy first spoke about communists working in the federal government—the producers had time to alter the film to make it more topical. In *D.O.A.* radioactive material is used by a common, crooked businessman to poison the central character. The killer's motivation? Good-old-fashioned American greed and lust. *D.O.A.* is one film that could have—even at the last minute—capitalized more on cold war fears, but it did not. Both *Notorious* and *D.O.A.* were popular when released and continue to be popular among film enthusiasts and scholars. Both films are considered important film noir, and both are commonly seen in revival houses, on late night TV, or on cable movie channels.[30] Both films also feature radioactive materials as the MacGuffin, yet *D.O.A.* tries less to keep "the secret" than does *Notorious*. The poison could well have been the arsenic that Alex and

Mother used to poison Alicia in *Notorious*. No connection to the bomb, national security, or espionage is established.

The Surfacing of an Apocalyptic Consciousness

From 1945 to 1950 a singularly important film stands out for its apocalyptic treatment of the bomb: *The Beginning or the End* (Norman Taurog, 1947). This Oscar-winning film is a pseudodocumentary that dramatizes the building and use of the first nuclear weapons. Many who made contributions to building the two bombs are portrayed and named, and the title of the film is, according to a 1946 *Science Illustrated* article on the then forthcoming film, taken "from President Truman's memorable speech on atomic energy."[31] It is surprising, in our time, to see how familiar the public was with the leading scientists of the day, or at least interested in seeing these people represented on the silver screen. Physicists or "rocket scientists" were once popular heroes. Still, J. Robert Oppenheimer (Hume Cronyn) gets sixth billing, following General Groves (Brian Donlevy), two fictitious heroes (Robert Walker as Jeff Nixon, and Tom Drake as Matt Cochran) and their love interests (Beverly Tyler as Ann "Shorty" Cochran, and Audrey Totter as Jean O'Leary, the future Mrs. Nixon) (see cover photograph). The film begins in 1946 with the dedication of a time capsule for the twenty-fifth century. It is announced that a print of the film is included in the time capsule; that it is included is a testament to the glowing optimism people had toward the bomb. This is to say, the filmmakers believed that 1945 was not the end and that humanity would survive the nuclear dilemma for at least another five hundred years. Let us look at this film carefully, beginning with a plot summary, then an overview of how the film has been received, and finally an analysis of some key elements: racism and revenge, progress and technology, crisis and the apocalyptic narrative structure.

Oppenheimer is our guide to the secret world of the Manhattan Project, and narrates the opening scenes. The film, however, centers on two young men. The first is Matt Cochran, a graduate student who is obnoxiously omnipresent. He works on every key experiment and participates in every decision. The film even places the fictional Matt Cochran at a real event, the famous meeting between Einstein and President Roosevelt, that was prompted by a group of scientists who convinced Einstein to warn the former president that the Germans might build a nuclear weapon. Throughout the entire picture Matt struggles with his conscience. On the one hand he is a "dreamer," committed to the peaceful use of science, and on the other hand he sees how the bombs can help end the war quickly. The second young man is Colonel Jeff Nixon, an intelligence and security officer (one can only speculate about a reference to Richard M. Nixon). Jeff also appears everywhere, and so the two men become the best of friends. Jeff is sympathetic to Matt's struggles with his conscience, but finds his path is clearer.

Toward the end of the film, Matt and Jeff are on Tinian Island, where the 509th will launch its attack. Matt, still a graduate student, makes final preparations on the bomb. Exhausted, he briefly swoons while working and accidentally knocks several small bricks of fissionable material into the bomb casing. A chain reaction begins, threatening the entire island. (Such an accident could cause only a minor but "dirty" explosion.) Realizing that he has put the entire island at risk, Matt retrieves the bricks with an unprotected hand. Heroically he saves the lives of many men, and the project, but at the cost of his own life. Within a few minutes radiation sickness sets in and we never see Matt again—at least not alive.

This particular death is fiction. Since the 1934 death of Marie Sklodowska Curie, radiation has claimed the lives of many, including at least one Manhattan Project scientist.[32] But nothing like Matt's unbelievably quick death from radiation sickness is mentioned in the histories I have read. The remake of *The Beginning or the End*, called *Fat Man and Little Boy* (Roland Joffé, 1989), also depicts a young man who dies from radiation sickness with similar rapidity. The two actors even look alike! The latter film, however, acknowledges the addition of this fictional character. And, in the 1946 film, this fictional character is more central than either Oppenheimer or Groves (who jointly directed the Manhattan Project).

Following the destruction of Hiroshima, Jeff returns to Washington D.C. where he is met at the airport by his fiancée and Matt's wife. At the Lincoln Memorial, with the Washington Monument in the background, Jeff hands Matt's last letter to Mrs. Cochran. As Mrs. Cochran reads the last paragraphs of the letter, a ghostlike image of Matt appears and speaks the words that she reads. This monologue describes events that have occurred and explains events that will happen; in other words, a critique of human and cosmological events. In essence, Matt has become the supernatural being that interprets the revelation for the uncomprehending human. The revealed cosmological changes, in the final part of Matt's long, concluding monologue, make this film a modern, secular, *apokalypsis*:

In the past, man sought useless war. Hunger and pain has often been vial. Yet stubbornly he has stumbled out of the chaos, lifted his eyes and gone on to make a better world. Now in the gravest hour of life on earth he has found the *secret* of the power of the universe. You, the giver of a new life, must know that what we've unleashed is not the end. With all my love I tell you this, Shorty, men will learn to use this knowledge well. They won't fail. For this is the timeless moment that gives us all a chance to prove that human beings are made in the image and likeness of God (emphasis added).

Unintentionally, this film invites the viewer to speculate on whether the victims of Hiroshima and Nagasaki, Dresden and Hamburg, Pearl Harbor, Singapore, Auschwitz, or the victims of any other conflict were also made in the image of God.

What has been written about *The Beginning or the End* is important because it reveals the complex and varied responses Americans have had toward the bomb. Most significantly, everyone ignores the narrative structures and symbolic content, and instead focuses on how accurately the film represents, or misrepresents, what he or she perceives to be the reality of nuclear technologies. The 1946 *Science Illustrated* article, for example, is largely about the new, cozy relationship between scientists and Hollywood, and particularly how this film was inspired by a letter from a one-time Oak Ridge scientist to his former student, actress Donna Reed.[33] In a 1947 review in the *United Nations World*, Ruth Rivkin, a sharper critic than most, condemns the film for "almost a ritual sacrifice" of the scientists, while the military continues their "undisturbed lives."[34]

Likewise, the focus of scholarly writing on *The Beginning or the End*, and most other bomb films, has, regrettably, been mostly concerned with verisimilitude. Mick Broderick, for instance, accurately, if simplistically, calls it "official propaganda riddled with inaccuracies and half-truths."[35] Scholarship on *The Beginning or the End* has, furthermore, been flawed by the tendency of scholars to value secondary sources—that is, other scholars' texts—more than the films themselves. This has led to a great deal of confusion and misreading of the film. In Jack G. Shaheen and Richard Taylor's essay in Shaheen's stridently antinuclear anthology *Nuclear Films*, after the accident Matt is misquoted as tragically realizing, too late, "That's what I get for building this thing."[36] One after another—Paul Boyer in 1985, then film historian Garth S. Jowett in 1988, and most recently Joyce A. Evans in 1998—repeat this misquote, and bend it to their own particular ideological positions (ranging from that the film is dangerously pronuclear to hysterically antiscience). Evans even misquotes the film's title.[37] What Matt actually says is an ambiguous rhetorical question: "*Maybe this is* what I get for *helping build the* thing?" (emphasis added). Furthermore, only Boyer, who places so much emphasis on Matt's deathbed comment, acknowledges the ambiguities that make the film difficult to interpret.[38]

Robert Jay Lifton and Greg Mitchell, in their 1995 book *Hiroshima in America*, do correctly quote Matt's lines, but their entire discussion of bomb films is so ideologically driven that it again distorts the lines out of all proportion. The authors claim that *The Beginning or the End* is the first of only three American films that directly address the making and use of nuclear weapons in Japan, and that all three support what they call "the official narrative."[39] This is a straw-man argument. Mick Broderick's well-known 1991 filmography *Nuclear Movies* clearly identifies a number of films that make overt and metaphoric references to Hiroshima and Nagasaki. Some of these films are very critical of the use of nuclear weapons—for example, *Time of the Heathen* (Peter Kass, 1962), in which an Enola Gay crewmember goes crazy from guilt.[40] Lifton and Mitchell also criticize the three films for being "artistic failure[s]" (as opposed to their endless praise of European "art" films), and for their inaccurate representations of Hiroshima, Nagasaki, and all nuclear war. They are particularly critical of the "logical inconsistency" of *The Beginning or the End*. History is important, as are the facts of nuclear weapons. Nevertheless, it is curious, to say that least, that Lifton, an "eminent psychiatrist" and "Distinguished Professor of Psychiatry and Psychology," and Mitchell, a respected author and editor, should be so obsessed with the literal manifest content and so numb to the symbolic latent or subtextual content of "Hollywood"-style fictional narrative films.[41] To understand what Matt's deathbed comment means we must, as Boyer suggests, look to the film itself (and not to any external "reality") to see how this confusing message is resolved.

The Beginning or the End offers many justifications for the use of nuclear weapons, including racism, revenge, progress, and theology. John Dower, again, shows that Americans feared and hated the "Japanese" more than the "Nazis," and that this racism continues today.[42] Indeed, *The Beginning or the End* acknowledges that Americans began building the bomb because they were afraid the Nazis would develop one first, yet used the weapon against the Japanese. In an unintended bit of ironic dialog, the film portrays President Truman as saying, "Thank God we've got the bomb and not the Japs—They'd use it." More importantly, military intelligence disparagingly reports that the "Japs will fight to the last woman and child." But is that not an

American virtue, do we not endlessly repeat the words of Patrick Henry, "Give me liberty or give me death"? Sam Keen's book *Faces of the Enemy* demonstrates that the process of enmity ascribes to ourselves all the attributes that we value, but projects onto the enemy the attributes that we hate in ourselves.[43] As *The Beginning or the End* demonstrates, the same attribute can be both a racial slur and a racial virtue, depending on whether we attribute it to the enemy or ourselves. The Japanese, thus, came to embody our own potential for zealous destructiveness.

Revenge also motivates *The Beginning or the End*. On the Enola Gay, Jeff notes that "250,000 people, in one second" have been "wiped off the map." Crewmember Parsons then, incorrectly, claims the Japanese people were warned, "ten days of leaflets, that's ten more days warning than they gave Pearl Harbor." In the minds of many Americans, particularly these filmmakers, the war must have begun on December 7, 1941, for the film sweeps aside a history of the European and American intimidation, extortion, intervention, and brutal colonialism in Japan and Asia that fueled Japan's own aggressive racial and colonial policies, and the war. There were plenty of warnings before Pearl Harbor, but few wanted to read the signs.

Progress also justifies the bomb. The film does not treat lightly the destruction of two cities and the loss of many lives, but there is little doubt, in *The Beginning or the End*, that Western technology will bring about a new age for all humanity. Matt foretells a glorious future that is reminiscent of the future foretold by the British proto–bomb film *Things to Come* (William Cameron Menzies, 1936); Matt's future, however, is a less romantic and more suburban version. The grandness of social progress is reinforced by developments in the personal lives of the central characters. Just before Matt and Jeff leave for Tinian Island, Jeff proposes to his girlfriend. Then, as the two men board the plane that will carry them and their surprises for the Japanese, Fat Man and Little Boy, Ann confides in Jean that she is carrying a surprise for Matt. This is to say, she is pregnant. In addition, as the Enola Gay carries out its mission, a general on Tinian Island compares waiting for the mission to being a father, for it is "worse than having a baby—and I've had six." Thus the film creates an inescapable parallel between the bomb and the birth, or the beginning, of a new age.

The metaphor of birth is important in atomic bomb cinema, and I discuss it in detail later in this book. What is important for us now is to recall

Melvin J. Lasky's thesis that in the West, "[w]hat is new is quickly taken to be unique; what is hopeful or meliorative, in the modest way of complex human affairs, is greeted as a sign of final things; and what may be good or important or encouraging must needs be elevated to a place in some cosmic scenario."[44] In keeping with the apocalyptic tradition, in *The Beginning or the End* the bomb brings about a new golden age for man. Matt's apocryphal vision of the future does not describe an entirely new human race, but a world reborn into a Garden of Eden of unlimited material abundance. Thus, the bomb is not the product of a patriarchal, technoindustrial society's ability to mobilize its resources toward a single goal, nor the feminine, generative power to create. Matt reveals to us that atomic energy *is* the hand of God extended to his chosen people.

Any fear of nuclear weapons is assuaged by the discovery of a desert tortoise that survived the first blast in Alamogordo, New Mexico. The tortoise demonstrates the bomb's ability to discriminate and kill only the enemy (a theme repeated in Dick Powell's *Split Second*, 1953). In J. E. Cirlot's *A Dictionary of Symbols* there is only an entry for the turtle. The turtle appears as a symbol in many different cultures, with many different meanings. Cirlot writes that "These disparate senses have, nevertheless, one thing in common: in every case, the turtle is a symbol of material existence and not of any aspect of transcendence." He goes on to write, "In view of its slowness, it might be said to symbolize natural evolution as opposed to spiritual evolution which is rapid or discontinuous to a degree."[45] Thus, the bomb is a "natural" evolutionary step forward in science and technology, and we Americans, being the first to evolve, are destined to survive as the fittest of the species (a conceit that the eminent scholar and psychologist Hayao Kawai, among others, has aptly criticized).[46] And, according to the logic of the Protestant work ethic, our technological developments are sure signs of God's blessings. Therefore, it is no longer through divine intervention or miracles that God makes himself known, but through natural, explainable developments. The reduction of God to an unseen clockmaker who values enterprise and favors Americans is an important theme in contemporary American culture, and I will return to it in my discussion of George Pal and Byron Haskin's *War of the Worlds* (1953).

These complex theological justifications are very important. In Matt Cochran's monologue, the comparison of atomic energy to fire combines theological and historical materialist explanations of human development. What makes life worth living in this film is not a transcendent value such as work, community, or spiritual commitment, but an ever-increasing standard of living extended to an ever-increasing number of people. (Ironically, the enemy in 1947, that is, the communists, would probably have agreed with Matt.) The bomb is depicted as a great move forward in man's mastery of the universe—as ordained by God and described by Erikson.[47] Thus, as in post-Deuteronomic apocalypses, right or wrong, the victimization of those living in Hiroshima and Nagasaki is regrettable, but nonetheless determined or preordained. God has given the atom to man, and man has used it to struggle against poverty. The Japanese were not victims of the bomb so much as victims of Western romantic ideology: the Promethean struggle to know, and to take from nature all that it has and bend it to man's will. Unable to keep up with the pace of events set by the Americans, the Japanese are unfortunate collateral casualties to divine progress.[48]

In addition to its faith in technological solutions to world problems, *The Beginning or the End* (and, *Fat Man and Little Boy*) expresses a faith in the ability of current social institutions to muster the men and materials necessary to solve the problem, and keep the rest of us safe from any threat. The government employs the most talented men and acquires the most expensive equipment to build the bombs. Moreover, the wartime government knew how and when to use the bombs.

There is, however, a price to pay for this golden age. There is a certain amount of guilt and shock at the wound we inflicted on the Japanese people. Robert Jay Lifton describes this as near universal "psychic numbing," but this may be merely a projection of his own psychological defense mechanism.[49] Some, certainly, felt a sense of guilt and numbness immediately after the announcement of the bombing of Hiroshima. Oppenheimer, who had a gift for finding poetic language to sum up immediate experience, has described himself, scientists, and "the Gadget" in many ways. At one point he referred to the bomb as the Greek plague of Thebes and as the Indian God who says "I am become Death, the destroyer of Worlds," and, more simply, that scientists had "known sin."[50] Many others, such as infantryman Paul Fussell, were elated by the use of the bomb, and have vigorously defended its use.[51] Humans, in other words, are complex and capable of mixed feelings. Reductive arguments that describe or prescribe one response ignore the human capacity for ambivalence. ("Psychic numbing," is, after all, a classic "catch-22," for denial of psychic numbing is considered proof of psychic numbing.) *The Beginning or the End* expresses this ambivalence and resolves it through religious metaphor.

Matt Cochran's death functions in two ways toward alleviating any guilt the viewer may experience. Through Matt's death the film suggests "See, we also lost good men to the bomb; Americans are also victims." Further, Cochran's sacrifice or martyrdom to the bomb parallels his namesake's martyrdom for his beliefs; thus, *The Beginning or the End* becomes a homily for faith in technology, and the bomb is the "path" to a meaningful life. According to John J. Delaney's *Dictionary of Saints*, in the first century, Matthew was a Jewish

> publican tax collector (Matt. 9:9–13; 10:3) at Capharnaum when Christ
> called him to follow him (Mark 2:14; Luke 5:27–32), and he became one
> of the twelve apostles. . . . He was the author of the first Gospel. . . .
> According to tradition, Matthew preached in Judea and then went to the
> East, where he suffered martyrdom in Ethiopia, according to the Roman
> Martyrology; in Persia, according to another legend.[52]

Matt Cochran is similarly called to a new faith, and then travels to the East, where he is martyred. Before his death, Matt also writes an apocryphal text (with apocalyptic elements), a gospel so to speak, about the kingdom to come in the post-Hiroshima world. *The Beginning or the End* is a testament to faith in the religion of technology.

In his monologue, Matt Cochran describes a crisis that has taken place, and explains that man has passed the ultimate test. Matt says, "In the gravest hour of life on Earth he [mankind] has found the secret of the power of the universe." In the secular society, however, the "secret" power is not esoteric, mystical, or spiritual knowledge, but a national secret controlled by the soon-to-be Atomic Energy Commission. For American men (no women were included in this decision), having chosen rightly, the utopic future is now a foregone conclusion: Man will learn to use the power for good and establish a heaven on earth.

Though *The Beginning or the End* depicts the bomb as an auspicious event, it is not a fully developed apocalyptic bomb film. Elements of the apocalyptic genre are present, but obscured by the unquestioning commitment to the bomb. There is, for example, an unfolding of history; past events are described—that is, predicted (*vaticinia ex eventu*)—by a participant as though they were in the present or future; a cosmological crisis causes a crisis in an individual who is then reborn; there is a journey; mystical knowledge is gained; and a future in which all people are united is foretold. Most importantly, there is the revelation. After his death, Matt reappears as a supernatural being and interprets the events of Hiroshima and Nagasaki. (Lifton might describe this development differently, possibly calling it a form of the "pseudo mastery of the death encounter" that is central to psychic numbing.)[53] Yet, absent from the film is a sense of impending crisis, a final battle that looms ominously in the future. Rather than exhorting the spectator to action, or even pious inaction, *The Beginning or the End* reassures us that the battle has been won—abundance is imminent.

The liberal and romantic ideology of *The Beginning or the End* continues to be part of atomic bomb cinema. One recent example is the film's remake, *Fat Man and Little Boy*. This film is an apotheosis to two historical geniuses and their relationship: the scientist and so-called father of the atom bomb, J. Robert Oppenheimer, and General Leslie R. Groves, military administrator of both the Pentagon's and the bomb's development. (Presumably Fat Man refers to Groves, who had a healthy girth, and Little Man refers to the slim Oppenheimer.) The film is romantic because it erroneously equates these two men's relationship with that of Faust and Mephistopheles—as if politics never influenced either man's decisions, only some unspoken drive to build the bomb.[54] The film obscures the ideological conflicts these two men had and reduces every issue to personality. The film is liberal because the crisis is successfully resolved through technological progress and existing social institutions. Thus, the film's portrait of the world is overwhelmingly liberal: After all, everyone is on the same side, and reasonable people operate in the middle, strive for consensus and progress, while avoiding extremist political entanglements. It is the liberals' misperception that because they strive for a middle path they are apolitical. All problems are personal and resolved through analysis, not debate.

The most important scene in *Fat Man and Little Boy* is a party that takes place in the Oppenheimer home at the Los Alamos base. Oppenheimer (Dwight Schultz) discovers his son is up past his bedtime, watching the adults. As Groves (Paul Newman) looks on, Oppenheimer tucks his son into bed and tells him that if he wants to go horseback riding the next day he must go to sleep. Of course, the child pleads to stay up. Oppenheimer explains that sometimes we must be willing to do things that we do not like if we are to get the things we really want—clearly, an analogy for the bomb. Through his sermon to the son it is clear that the father has come to accept the bomb as a bitter but necessary pill that will bring world peace. In this film, out of the crisis of World War II comes the bomb, itself a crisis of conscience, which brings about the next stage in man's endless struggle for perfection. Because *Fat Man and Little Boy* is so uncompromisingly liberal and romantic, there is no room for an apocalyptic vision. In liberal and romantic ideology, "man" is at the center of "his" world and does not need God to justify "his" actions. "Man" pays the price for progress and reaps the benefits. Similar assessments of Oppenheimer can also be found in academic literature. Lifton, in particular, tries to draw our attention to the important "relationship between the 'bomb secret' and the secrets of childhood." Here, Lifton focuses in on the important psychological characteristics of what he calls "nuclearism" and "nuclearists."[55]

Reducing Oppenheimer's adult behavior to childhood experience depoliticizes both the person and the context in which the behavior takes place, thus drawing a one-dimensional portrait. (Sam Keen's argument in *Faces of the Enemy* is similarly flawed.) Oppenheimer was anything but one-dimensional. Lifton's argument is also Manichaean. While the "good guys" (antinuclear activists) exhibit unusual intellectual and emotional free will, the actions of the "bad guys" (the "nuclearists") are determined by some psychopathology. The psychology of enmity that Keen describes is a definite if subtle force in Lifton's understanding of the world.

Few films express the giddy optimism of *The Beginning or the End*. This does not mean that subsequent films are pessimistic, for the apocalyptic genre is inherently optimistic. For the most part, the film is a celebration of the new age begun when America "found the secret of the power of the universe." Shaheen and Taylor correctly point out, but only in passing, that the publicity still for the film (figure 1) depicts the bomb, but a sign that reads "Censored" obscures the bomb.[56] Thus, *The Beginning or the End* attempts to create a cohesive tribal identity, based on imminent abundance, through inviting us to share an ostentatious secret. By sharing this secret we become members of the new American utopia.

The Beginning or the End is an apocalyptic bomb film. Yet, because the crisis has passed, the cosmological consequences seem minimized, and paradise is just around the corner. Thus, the drama is bled out of the apocalyptic vision. *The Beginning or the End* is important historically and sociologically because it is the first apocalyptic bomb film, and because it illustrates a society at the end of an apocalyptic era; but, it is only a minor example of the genre's full potential. This potential, Alastair Fowler's second phase of generic development, is reached only after nuclear war becomes a real possibility; that is, only when nuclear Armageddon, a final conflict between good and evil, becomes possible, as it does in the 1950s, when the crisis is no longer an experience of the past but of the future.[57] Only then does the apocalyptic imagination become truly meaningful to modern filmmakers and audiences.

3 1950 to 1963 PART 1

A complex growth industry

We no longer live on what we have, but on promises, no longer in the light of the present day, but in the darkness of the future, which, we expect, will at last bring the proper sunrise. We refuse to recognize that everything better is purchased at the price of something worse; that, for example, the hope of greater freedom is canceled out by increased enslavement to the state, not to speak of the terrible perils to which the most brilliant discoveries of science expose us.

It is the psychic primal night which is the same today as it has been for countless millions of years. The longing for light is the longing for consciousness.

—C. G. Jung, *Memories, Dreams, Reflections*[1]

Following the Soviet's successful detonation of Joe I, nuclear war became a real possibility, and the production of all types of bomb films by all types of filmmakers increased. After 1949 the formal and ideological structures of bomb films also became increasingly complex. Nevertheless, during the period of 1950 to 1963, bomb films remained overwhelmingly optimistic. Even antinuclear films expressed confidence in humanity's ability to overcome the temptation to use the new weapons, or at least the confidence that a better world could be built following a full-scale nuclear war. Thus, because of the complexity and the large number of films produced in the fifties and early sixties, it is necessary to cover this period in two chapters. This first chapter will introduce some lesser-known films along with some well-known films, yet all clearly evoke the ideological issues that preoccupied atomic bomb cinema during this period. In the second chapter we will primarily look at the seminal apocalyptic bomb films from the fifties and early sixties, ones that explore more sociological and personal issues. Again, in this first chapter I will establish the ideological issues in atomic bomb cinema of the fifties, roughly speaking, through brief analyses of the following seven films: *Five*; *The World, The Flesh, and the Devil*; *Red Planet Mars*; *The Day the Earth Stood Still*; *Split Second*: *War of the Worlds*; and *On the Beach*.

There are, in the academic literature, two basic schools of thought about the 1950s. One school argues that it was a period of mindless conformity and naive optimism, while the other school argues that, in fact, it was a period of social fragmentation and intense—if repressed—anxiety. Most scholars consider only the observable cycles of public anxiety that correspond to specific nuclear threats. My own research, however, indicates that these cycles are just the tip of the iceberg, and beneath the surface of these flare-ups in corporate consciousness flows a healthy, ongoing process of assimilation and evaluation to which film contributes. Actually, the fifties can be characterized by all this and everything in between. The same audiences that stayed home in 1955 to watch *Father Knows Best* or a Disney program on television also went to movie theaters to see films like Nicholas Ray's *Rebel without a Cause*—which, incidentally, Mick Broderick considers to be a bomb film.[2]

For each social issue of the fifties (and all other periods for that matter), such as family, religion, gender roles, and race, there were radical, reactionary, liberal, and conservative bomb films made. An important characteristic of this period is that films that appeared liberal or progressive frequently had a seemingly backward outlook on social ideology, while ostensibly conservative films appeared often surprisingly visionary and had a progressive outlook on social ideology. Arch Oboler's 1951 film *Five*, for instance, at first describes the nuclear holocaust as a catalyst for achieving the liberal dream—establishing a community in which all peoples can live together in peace and harmony; but, slowly, the narrative undermines this dream. *Five*, moreover, is not only a prototypical post-apocalyptic survival narrative (which developed more fully in the 1970s and 1980s), but is also an exploration of the volatile topics of gender and race that were surfacing in American society at that time. That is to say, *Five* is indicative of the cold war–era liberal movement. Oboler's *Five* was so effective that the basic narrative became a formula for a number of other filmmakers, including Roger Corman (*The Day the World Ended*, 1956, and *The Last Woman on Earth*, 1960).[3]

The story is simple. Shortly after the nuclear war, Michael (William Phipps), the main character, wanders into a type of new Eden. He invites four others to share in his labors of building and farming the new kingdom. (Labor is an important issue in this film.) But not all of the characters are prepared to live in his new holy land and so perish as a result. Mr. Barnstaple (Earl Lee), who is old and senile, succumbs to what may be radiation poisoning; Eric (James Anderson), a self-serving, Cain-like egotist, murders Charles out of racial hatred and kidnaps the only woman, Roseanne (Susan Douglas), leaving the compound for the city where he contracts radiation poisoning; and, while Charles (Charles Lampkin) is considered an admirable character he is, however, black—and thus disadvantaged in a new world order that is again franchised by the white male. Roseanne, legitimately pregnant from before the war, gives birth to a baby whom she refuses to name until she discovers the fate of her husband. Once she finds her husband's corpse the baby dies. This is, indeed, a tragic occurrence that leaves her desperate but, nonetheless, pure of purpose. Roseanne then returns to the new kingdom, prepared to live under Michael's dominion.

At first the film seems to forward a progressive view of the modern agrarian utopia. But the narrative demands that only two survive, and the film regresses to xenophobia, racism, and a hostility toward modernity through its justification of the elimination of Mr. Barnstaple, Charles, and Eric. Michael, named after the archangel who drove Adam and Eve out of Eden, accepts everyone as his equal and even defends Charles against Eric. At the same time, however, he demands that everyone obey the law. Michael insists that everyone help to build and work the fields even though there are plenty of supplies in the local stores. He refuses to allow anyone to return to the cities, which he believes are the cause and locus of a decadent world that destroyed itself, and which contain the highest concentrations of radiation, something that threatens to contaminate their sacred sanctuary. All those who die fail, in some way, to adapt to Michael's utopian vision.

The first to die is the elderly Mr. Barnstaple, a banker who always dreamed of going to sea. Shocked by seeing his world destroyed, Mr.

Barnstaple slips into fantasy. He believes he is merely taking a few days' vacation from work, and speaks endlessly about returning to his responsibilities at the bank. His physical and mental health deteriorate, and one day he demands that he be taken to the seashore, so Michael and the others journey to the ocean. There, they rescue Eric, who has been washed ashore. He tells them of his harrowing journey from Mt. Everest to America. Moments after Eric has told his story, Mr. Barnstaple dies.

Eric speaks with an accent, and acts with the European effeteness that is antithetical to the myth of American egalitarianism and rugged individualism. From the moment this character is introduced, we know he is going to be trouble. To the worldly Eric, Michael's utopia seems provincial and manly in a crass way, so it at first appears that their conflict is one of personality. But there is also an ideological dimension to this conflict. Eric openly disdains Michael's "return to primitive agriculturalism," and wants everyone to return instead to the city, where he believes exists other survivors who can be organized into a community to repopulate the city—of course, with himself as leader. Eric also espouses a heretical evolutionary philosophy—that is, the five survived because they developed a special immunity. He explains to the others that as in Europe during the plagues, there must be enough select survivors to maintain civilization. At this point, he also deems Charles a mistake who should leave this new Aryan nation. Although he eventually apologizes to everyone, claiming his behavior was due to a great deal of stress, Eric still refuses to contribute his labor, and even sabotages the crops. Thus, Michael demands that Eric leave the new Eden. At this point, Eric tricks Roseanne into going to the city with him, where she will become more of a sexual slave than a companion, and kills Charles, who discovers his plot. (Eric cowardly attacks and stabs Charles from behind.) Once in the city, Eric contracts radiation poisoning and runs away mad, the baby dies, and only Roseanne survives to return to Michael.

While at first the film appears to treat Charles with dignity and compassion, without obvious racial stereotypes, the latent bigotry and sexism of the film become more obvious in its depiction of the division of labor in the new Eden. Tzvetan Todorov, in *The Conquest of America: The Question of the Other*, argues convincingly that in Eurocentric, colonial ideology, those considered racially inferior are often equated with women or children (who are inherently perceived as inferior), and are therefore given the same social roles.[4] This ideology seems to have survived in *Five*. For instance, Charles and Roseanne seem, at certain points, retained only as domestics. They cook and clean the dishes. Of the five, only Charles and Roseanne wash the laundry. Thus, while the Edenic myth (in the patriarchal form of Genesis 2:5–25, not Genesis 1:26–32) demands that only one man and woman survive to repopulate the world, it is Anglo-American ethnocentricity that demands that they be white, manly, American pioneer types. Simply, while Mr. Barnstaple is too old, Eric and Charles are redundant and unnecessary for different but crucial reasons. Roseanne is not a fully enfranchised member of the new order but a biological necessity. Thus, this film has much more to do with the vision that the fifties had of itself than with the forwarding of a distinct postapocalyptic vision—that is, unless one can argue that the fifties culture *in general* represents a type of postapocalyptic vision. At the same time, however, while both Mr. Barnstaple and Eric die because of character flaws or psychological predispositions that prevent them from surviving the crisis and making the transition to the postapocalyptic world, Charles has no such flaw, nor is his death tragic; this makes his death all the more difficult to reconcile with the film's ostensive liberalism. *Five* is an example of a reactionary apocalyptic film, one in which the "vision" consists of rugged white individualism applied to social maintenance. Thus, typical of the 1950s, beneath the wholesome, optimistic liberalism, which resides on the surface of the film's text, is a great deal of angst about the changes liberalism brings.

What is possibly the most radical film of the 1950s is also an apocalyptic bomb film. Ranald MacDougall's 1959 film *The World, the Flesh, and the Devil* provides a much more profound view of race, gender, and postapocalyptic survival than *Five*, and it is even oracular in an old-world sense; yet it too is so preoccupied with the social issues of the 1950s that it is difficult to call the film truly visionary. The film has only three characters: one black man, one white woman, and one white man. The singer Harry Belafonte, who plays Ralph Burton, is given top billing, followed by Inger Stevens and Mel Ferrer, who play Sara Crandall and Benson Thacker. The three characters are the only persons in North America to survive a nuclear war that devastates the planet. Left alone, the three are forced to evaluate their racial and gender assumptions. Significantly, it is the woman who is the most progressive, most able to overcome her prejudices, and adapt to the new environment. The strongest character, the character who undergoes the most change and leads the others, is Sara.

The World, the Flesh, and the Devil begins with mining engineer Ralph Burton alone and trapped deep inside an underground mine. When the sounds of rescue die out, Ralph decides to dig his own way out of the tunnel. The symbolism here is obvious: trapped in a cave, Ralph is still psychologically and politically repressed by his social position. Unlike Plato's disillusioned masses, however, Ralph realizes that if he is to be saved, he must physically do it himself; later, he learns that saving himself also means having the courage to be part of the larger community. Symbolically, he is reborn and empowered by surviving the crisis.

After leaving the cave, Ralph discovers that everyone died from radiation with a very short half-life (a protoneutron bomb perhaps?). He journeys to Manhattan, establishes a home in an apartment there, and spends his time saving books from the deteriorating library, rewiring his apartment building, and broadcasting SOS signals. Thinking he is alone, Burton becomes increasingly neurotic. For example, he brings home many mannequins and dresses them as guests for some rather swell fifties dinner parties. Then one evening, in a seemingly insane and self-destructive gesture, he hurtles one of the mannequins off his apartment building. Sara Crandall is already living in the Big Apple when Ralph arrives, but is too traumatized to approach him, so she watches him from a safe distance. When Burton throws a mannequin off his apartment building, Sara mistakenly thinks he has jumped to his death, and screams in horror; and so, finally, the two meet. Eventually the two share dinners and companionship.

Sara expresses her increasing fondness for Ralph, and struggles to tear down the racial boundaries between them. Ralph, however, struggles to maintain his distance. For instance, one night Ralph prepares a fancy birthday party for Sara. When she asks him to dance with her, Ralph refuses, coldly saying that the help is not allowed to dance with the patrons. Sara is understandably enraged.

Later, a white man, Benson, arrives to the city barely alive. Ralph nurses Benson back to health. After Benson regains consciousness he demands that Sara make a choice between him and Ralph. When Sara refuses, the two men begin to quarrel. Sara becomes enraged at the two men for fighting over her as though she were an object to be possessed. Nevertheless, Benson threatens Ralph and the two men arm themselves with guns and chase each other through the city. Eventually, Ralph throws down his gun, refusing to be drawn into a war. Conspicuous in a fifties film, it is the black man who takes the difficult path and turns the other cheek, but not because he is defenseless. Frustrated and defeated by Ralph's refusal to give him the satisfaction and legitimacy of having resolved the problem through what he could call a manly, fair fight,

Benson begins to leave the city. Sara, however, manages to intervene and reconcile the two men. In the end, she takes both men by the hand, and together they walk into the dawn of a new morning.

Frank W. Oglesbee, writing in 1978, agrees with Hollis Alpert, who argues in a 1959 film review that *The World, the Flesh, and the Devil* is a racist film, pandering to white fears of miscegenation: "Segregationist Southerners and the South African government will be heartened to know that even in a relatively empty world the race problem continues."[5] These critics, however, offer little insight into the film. Only two relevant scholars have commented on this film. H. Bruce Franklin, on the one hand, correctly points out that the film concludes with the three walking "arm in arm to start civilization over again with neither racism nor monogamy." Spencer R. Weart, on the other hand, says, "Nuclear weapons brought nothing new to the theme" of postcataclysmic survival.[6] Weart is only half right. The apocalyptic theme and the science fiction genre change little because they are vehicles with which we criticize ideology and social conditions, and envision the future. And clearly, *The World, the Flesh, and the Devil* speculates about the world and the changes that need to be instituted. The point missed (or avoided) by critics is that the solutions the film proposes are revolutionary to both ancient apocalyptic narrative, and to contemporary Western culture: matriarchal exogamic polygamy. Though not part of a markedly experimental period in filmmaking, *The World, the Flesh, and the Devil* succeeds in giving the bomb narrative a new, more fully rounded shape. It is worth noting here that the film appears on television occasionally, and remains popular in cult film circles, and that it was remade, sans bomb, by a New Zealand filmmaker as *The Quiet Earth* (Geoff Murphy, 1985).

Religion is an important topic in the atomic bomb cinema of the 1950s, particularly in John Hoare Balderston's film adaptation of his own play *Red Planet*, called *Red Planet Mars* (Harry Horner, 1952). The solution to the nuclear crisis that this film offers is a reactionary Christian revolution. Radio contact is made with the people of Mars, and ultimately it is revealed that because the Martians accept Christ as their savior they therefore live in a technologically and morally advanced world. These revelations completely destabilize the Soviet Union, and out of the chaos a Russian or Greek Orthodox theocracy takes power. The United States also verges on the edge of chaos, but the president recalls his father's devout wisdom and decides to do away with any separation of the Christian church and state. In contrast to the chaotic former Soviet

Union, this peaceful transition to an absolute Christian state suggests that the Heavenly Father prefers democratic capitalism to totalitarian communism. Redemption, in any case, is not found in progress per se, but in correcting the mistakes of the past—an orthodox acceptance of our Puritan forefathers' wisdom and not the modern liberal state. An increased standard of living is the reward for the righteous. Russell Kirk, in his introduction to *The Portable Conservative Reader*, notes,

> In Ambrose Bierce's *Devil's Dictionary* one encounters this: "Conservatives, *n*. A statesman who is enamored of existing evils, as distinguished from the Liberal, who wishes to replace them with others."[7]

The world, according to *Red Planet Mars*, turned its back on existing evils and set about to create new ones, culminating in a crisis: the threat of the bomb. Now the bomb forces us to contemplate what brought us to the brink of disaster. In accord with a Christian worldview and the apocalyptic imagination, the Martian transmissions *reveal* a heavenly kingdom for the faithful, and destruction for the wicked. In the end, humanity finally recognizes that the promises of a liberal, progressive society are only distractions from the truth.

Red Planet Mars highlights the etiological proximity of radical and reactionary politics. Melvin J. Lasky, in *Utopia and Revolution*, tells us that "revolution" was originally a term that astronomers used to describe the return of heavenly bodies to their place of origin. This notion of "revolution," bringing the world back to its original pristine state, influences both radical and reactionary utopian visionaries.[8] The reactionary revolution in *Red Planet Mars*, however, is out of keeping, really, with traditional Christian apocalyptic narrative because it relies so heavily on technological revelations; but it is a revolution that coincides perfectly with the then currently growing need to link old-time religion with new-world democratic technocracy. Though this idea may seem out of place, it lies at the heart of what atomic bomb cinema is really all about and it looks ahead more than it looks behind. That is to say, *Red Plant Mars* describes technocratic developments as necessary to the fulfillment of a preordained teleology, at least here on Earth.

A more liberal film that also describes a Biblical solution to the nuclear crisis is the very popular *The Day the Earth Stood Still* (Robert Wise, 1951), which is loosely based on the 1940 science fiction novelette *Farewell to the Master*, by Harry Bates.[9] A flying saucer lands in Washington, D.C. and Klaatu, a representative of an intergalactic government, demands to address the world's leaders. When this cannot be arranged, Klaatu (Michael Rennie) assumes an Earthling's identity: John Carpenter. The Biblical allusion is inescapable. The initials J. C., stamped on the travel bag he carries, stand for "Jesus Christ," who was a carpenter. Carpenter contacts Dr. Barnhardt (Sam Jaffé), the world's foremost scientist. Barnhardt looks remarkably like Albert Einstein—again, pseudonymity adds authority to apocalyptic texts. Klaatu tells Barnhardt to assemble scientific representatives from all the nations. Then, as Carpenter makes his way to the meeting he is killed by the military. After Carpenter is miraculously resurrected he reveals to the scientific wise men and women, who have traveled very far to meet him, this warning: If the people of Earth use nuclear weapons to threaten the intergalactic stability he will destroy the planet. Carpenter then boards his space ship and ascends to the heavens.

Scholars often refer to *The Day the Earth Stood Still* as an example of apocalyptic filmmaking. I believe, however, that it has much more in common with biblical testaments. Genres do, nevertheless, overlap, and this film does have a structure that falls in line not only with ancient apocalyptic narratives but also with what became in the fifties commonplace in bomb films. That is to say, films employing traditional narrative structures most often use these structures only when they can be embedded beneath the details of technology. Technology is not taking over but surfacing; it is being made feasible and ever-present within these ancient narratives' structures. For instance, we might consider Dr. Barnhardt the genre's character who receives a revelation that he cannot understand. Instead of a dream, the revelation comes in the form of a scientific problem that Barnhardt is working on but cannot solve. Klaatu/Carpenter is the supernatural being who interprets the revelation. He literally enters the scientist's office and corrects an incomplete formula written on a blackboard, and interprets its meaning. Klaatu/Carpenter is the supernatural messenger who delivers a reevaluation to Barnhardt and his fellow scientists, and they, in turn, become his earthly representatives charged with warning the heretical. While wise old men who receive a revelation and then become charged with warning transgressors of the law is an important element in the apocalyptic genre, it is not until the 1950s that these wise old men were expected to understand astrophysics.

The physicist Niels Bohr hoped that the bomb would force human beings to live together more peacefully by modeling society on his idealized city on the hill, what Michael Polanyi called "the republic of science"; only this republic of science could "answer the challenge of the bomb."[10] In *The Day the Earth Stood Still* the fulfillment of Biblical messianic prophecy starts within the liberal republic of science and then spreads to the larger society, just as Bohr had hoped it would. But in retrospect, Bohr's worldview seems naive and limited. Indeed, it may be that *Red Planet Mars*, with its overt reactionary religious message, may be more visionary than *The Day the Earth Stood Still*, with its progressivist vision.

In Psalms, John J. Collins points out, the messiah not only delivers the people from Roman occupation (2:25), but also punishes Jerusalem because "From the chief of them to the least of them the people were in complete sinfulness" (17:20).[11] Thus, Psalms suggests that the Jews' sufferings are indeed caused by oppressive external power; but, more importantly, their sufferings are caused by the general decay of morality within the society, for which everyone is responsible. Likewise, in *The Day the Earth Stood Still* the cold war, the bomb, paranoia, distrust, and wickedness are all a product of worldwide sinfulness for which everyone (sage scientists excepted) is responsible. But in *The Day the Earth Stood Still*, salvation does not come through the power of the individual to find the inner path to God, as was expected of the oppressed Jews of antiquity. That is to say, however reflective of the Old or New Testament the narrative may seem, the film forwards the message that salvation is gained through the power of the liberal institutions of science and technology, or, at the least, the power of scientists to lead us into a world of righteous living. The film also denies difference (political, cultural, or otherwise), something old narratives allow in the notion of sin; difference, however, is something irreconcilable in the new, liberal politics of power via technology.

In this era, 1950 to 1963, many Americans promised and many Americans believed that the liberal establishment and the power of its scientific and technological engines (as symbolized by the bomb) would solve the world's "problems" in the abstract, not sins as they are related to specific individuals, and produce a utopia. Later films, however, increasingly challenge this vision of the present and the future, and as the technological euphoria passes, we find many collateral casualties. It is instructive to examine one such casualty: Dick Powell's 1953 directorial debut, *Split Second*—a film virtually ignored in the scholarly literature.

Similar to Archie Mayo's well-known film *The Petrified Forest* (1936), *Split Second* centers on an escaped psychopathic criminal (played by Stephen McNally) who is yet another psychological casualty of war. But although he is a veteran of World War II, and therefore a victim, he is too brutal to earn our sympathies or redemption. He and his two henchmen hold several people hostage in an abandoned mining town called Lost Hope City, Nevada. The hostages include a newspaper reporter, a Las Vegas dancer with a heart of gold, an adulteress, her lover, the husband, and an old prospector. Since the city is now part of a nuclear weapons testing facility, the bad guys think it is an ideal temporary hideout. However, the criminals are unprepared when the warning signal is sounded an hour earlier than expected and are killed in the explosion. Only the reporter, the dancer, the husband, and the prospector survive both the sociopaths and the bomb. They escape the blast by hiding in a cave—an already familiar symbol of rebirth. Inside the cave the husband (now the widower) says to the others: "Let's take a look at the world of tomorrow."

Split Second justifies its use of the bomb by putting it within the context of an apocalyptic event that—like famine, flood, and God's other scourges—punishes the wicked and rewards the righteous; otherwise, the (test) bomb would be morally suspect. Again, a common motif in atomic bomb cinema, especially in the fifties, is the (attempted) coupling of traditional religious myth with liberal or progressive views of technology. Other issues aside, by incorporating the blast, which is in sync with the personal morality of the characters, the film exhibits a strong faith in the power of technology to bring about a better world.

One year after the film's release, while directing *The Conqueror*, in which John Wayne stars as Genghis Khan, the dawn Dick Powell created in *Split Second* became a halting reality. It is alleged that in the summer of 1954, when the company was filming on location near St. George, Utah, exposure to radiation from nearby centers conducting nuclear weapons tests caused a high incidence of cancer and related deaths in residents and the film's cast and crew.[12] If this is indeed the case, then it is truly a sad irony that *Split Second*'s (and Powell's) moral and political conservatism, progressivist vision of technology, and unquestioning faith in the bomb should prove so disastrous when filmic fantasy became manifest in reality.

One Englishman and two Hungarian émigrés (both of whom fled the Nazis) played especially significant roles in the development of early atomic bomb cinema. Émigré Leo Szilard, a theoretical physicist, was the first person to consider atomic bombs seriously and should be considered the true father of the bomb—ironic because he later stridently opposed it. Six-time Oscar-winning émigré George Pal produced four bomb films, and the first three are easily ranked among America's most important science fiction films: *Destination Moon* (Irving Pichel, 1950), *The War of the Worlds* (Byron Haskin, 1953), *The Time Machine* (Pal, 1960), and *Atlantis, the Lost Continent* (Pal, 1961). Both Szilard and Pal were influenced by the English writer H. G. Wells. Szilard and Wells were friends, and Szilard claims it was Wells's stories that inspired his ideas.[13] Pal's first bomb film is based on a book by the respected science fiction writer Robert A. Heinlein, who also cowrote the screenplay; today the film is known mostly by serious science fiction fans. Pal's fourth film is based on a play by Gerald Hargreaves, now mostly forgotten, and not considered a good film. Pal's second and third films, however, remain quite popular with audiences and critics, and both are adaptations of Wells's novels. Wells conceived the bomb, Szilard gave the bomb idea physical existence, and Pal gave the bomb filmic form.

The War of the Worlds is about a Martian invasion of Earth. It was first serialized in *The Cosmopolitan* from April to December 1897. The following year it was published as a book. In 1938 Orson Welles broadcast his famous radio version of the story, which changed the locale from England to New Jersey and New York City. Welles's central character is a reporter who, for the first half of the story, gives us a live, real time, accounting of the invasion. In Pal's version the central character is Clayton Forester, Ph.D., the leading scientist in "astro and nuclear physics." Clayton heads the Pacific Institute of Technology, or "Pacific Tech" (an homage to "Cal-Tech," located very near to Hollywood and to J. Robert Oppenheimer).[14] Today, the characters seem dated and thin, and politically incorrect role models. The film's images, however, are startling, the tale is gripping, and it remains one of the most popular films ever made.[15]

Clayton and colleagues are on a fishing trip in the mountains of Riverside, California, when a meteor falls nearby. Clayton is asked to investigate. The next day at the meteor site Clayton meets Sylvia Van Buren and her uncle, Pastor Matthew Collins. Later that night, fantastic Martian spaceships arise out of the meteor. Pastor Collins extends the hand of human friendship but the invaders turn their heat ray on him. The military tries to stop the invaders, but their weapons have no effect. General Mann even orders a nuclear weapon to be used, but it too is useless. More meteors and more spaceships arrive on Earth, and it seems that nothing will stop the invaders from conquering the world. Inside a church Clayton and Sylvia hold each other for what appears to be the last moment of their lives when, unexpectedly, the spaceships begin to crash.

The narrator explains that the Martians had no immunity to the bacteria that God, in his wisdom, created to defend humanity.

Pal pushes the film's narrative into a surprising direction that makes it, in the end, far different from Wells's novel or Welles's radio play, in which the Martians are not absolutely indestructible. At the same time, Pal pushes the film's symbolism into an equally surprising, if heavy-handed, direction. Indeed, the film seems to present the Martians as a backdrop to human characters who, in the post-Hiroshima environment, have lost touch with nature and must recognize that their powers may be rendered useless by greater powers. This symbolism is important to our discussion for it is closely tied to the film's ideology.

In the opening scenes there is a dissolve (see chapter 1) from the still flaming meteor to Clayton's campfire.[16] That is to say, for a few moments the campfire is superimposed onto the meteor. This composite image draws a parallel between Clayton and the Martians. All are on a journey for renewal, and all are headed toward disaster. Eventually these fires will burn out of control in the film, perhaps, symbolizing Clayton's burning psychological urges that go beyond his science.

The Martians, we are told, have left their dying planet in search of a fertile world. While the Martian technology is superior, they cannot get their most basic biological needs met on their planet, so they journey to the mountains of California. In addition, the audience is told, the Martians are biologically primitive compared to humans. These scientific facts help explain the alien invaders' function within the film. They are mirrors, symbolic expressions, or psychological projections, of Clayton. After all, Clayton is the most advanced human, yet he, like the Martians, cannot satisfy his most basic, primitive requirements at home. Likewise, Clayton has left the sterile laboratory for recreation in the more robust but primitive mountains. That is to say, Clayton, again like the Martians, goes to the mountains of California in search of something.

At the meteor site Clayton meets librarian Sylvia Van Buren. The two make a perfect 1950s B-movie couple: Clayton (Gene Barry) has the jaw only true heroes are born with, and Sylvia (Ann Robinson) is a combination of *Playboy*'s girl next door and Disney's Sleeping Beauty, with an Eiffel Tower bra. Still, their mutual attraction is not immediate. Sylvia asks Clayton for a match to light her cigarette, but he does not smoke. Smoking was such an accepted practice and common filmic symbol in this period of history, unlike our own time, that this scene can easily be interpreted as suggesting Clayton's repressed burning desire for basic pleasures.

As their conversation continues, Sylvia reveals that she wrote her master's thesis on the scientist who made the cover of *Time* magazine. When Clayton introduces himself as said scientist, Sylvia says that she did not recognize Clayton because he is wearing glasses. Clayton comments that he only wears the glasses to see things far away; he then takes off his glasses to eye the attractive and appreciative Sylvia. Thus, his vision, and his life, needs to be refocused.

That night Clayton and Sylvia go to the square dance in town. As they dance, in the mountains above, a spectacular spacecraft emerges from the meteor and is joined by other crafts in their own dance formation. Thus, not only do the spaceships mirror the human beings' communion, they also represent a primitive force that arises out of the *forest*—symbolizing the primitive forces that arise in Clayton *Forester* as he becomes increasing interested in Sylvia.

Once the Martians make their presence known, the military goes into action. At the forward base Clayton advises, Sylvia serves coffee and doughnuts, and her uncle, Pastor Matthew Collins, provides moral support. Before the army engages the enemy, Pastor Collins tells Sylvia how much he likes Clayton, then marches off to meet the Martians. With Bible and cross in outstretched hands, Collins recites Psalm 23—until the Martians, not in a mood for Christian salvation, fry him with their heat ray. This pitiful scene is important, for it establishes that the fall of man and God's plans really have nothing to do with Martians; that is, they have science and technology, but are without religion. The notion that there are some places without religion surely creates an extraordinarily eerie feeling in audiences, particularly in the Christian-dominated American society of the 1950s. Since the Martians are a Godless evil force, the ensuing war is "just," according to the Christian definition; so, extreme actions, even the use of a nuclear weapon, are acceptable.[17] The enemy, however, is not only the alien Martians, but also the enemy within. The external reality of the pastor's death now gives Clayton license to begin removing his own internal demons.

After the pastor is killed, human technology fails, the Martians rout the military, and even Clayton and Sylvia must escape in a small plane. When the plane crashes, they find refuge in a farmhouse, but are discovered by the enemy. A Martian ship lowers a television camera into the house, which Clayton chops off with an ax—a strikingly primitive instrument that works temporarily to save the two. Having lost their optical device that helps them see things far away, one Martian enters the house for a closer look. This time, Clayton uses the ax to dispatch the alien. But let us not forget Clayton's similarity to the Martians.

After returning to the institute, one of the elder scientists connects the alien camera to their video equipment, and then he drags Sylvia in front of the camera in a seemingly superfluous scene. After looking at Sylvia's projected image, as Clayton eyes Sylvia directly, the scientist says he is not surprised that the Martians took a special interest in her. Again, the Martian's behavior is shown to mirror and foreshadow Clayton's in a scene that, in its own inane departure from the plot, seems to suggest the inanity of science in a time of true crisis. But the scene is really necessary on the symbolic level that Pal pushes with such determination. Just as Clayton had to remove his glasses to take a better look at Sylvia, so too must the Martians. The parallel is firm. The destructive Martians are only bringing man's problems with technology to the forefront. Indeed, these problems existed before the Martians arrived, and the problems would still be there if the Martians had never come at all.

General Mann, having lost one pastor and one battle, calls in the Flying Wing, the latest aeronautical wonder, to drop a nuclear weapon on the Martians. The bomb, however, is ineffective and the scientists are forced to flee as the military futilely continues to fight. In the chaos that follows the Martians' attack on Los Angeles, Clayton and Sylvia are separated. He fights with looters—human aggression proves as menacing as the Martins, and Clayton loses his glasses. Here and through the rest of the film the symbolism is thickly spread. Without his glasses, Clayton can now truly see his solution: Sylvia. From a story Sylvia told about her childhood, he knows that he will find her in a church, so he searches the churches of Los Angeles, and in the process, he finally searches his own soul. After looking in several churches Clayton finds her in a church whose minister is wearing approachable, secular attire and not the traditional clerical uniform of Pastor Collins. As Clayton and Sylvia embrace, the Godless but God-bashing Martians shatter a stained glass window of Christ. Then there is silence. Clayton and Sylvia go outside and discover that all the ships have crashed and all the Martians are dying. The narrator announces that God, in his "infinite wisdom," made human beings immune to the bacteria and viruses of the earth, but not the Martians.

How are we to interpret this failure of (General) "Mann's" secular world of science and technology? Are his demons—the Martians—truly exorcised? The alien invasion and destruction of civilization certainly makes Clayton Forester's journey seem otherworldly, but does his journey end in a significant revelation about his place in God's universe? And is Clayton's faith in God, for that matter, truly reborn? To answer these questions, we must place the film in its historical and sociocultural context.

Despite the closed American frontier, *The War of the Worlds* repeats a familiar American myth: the East is a place of thought, knowledge, and authority while the West is a place of action (absent is the usual antipathy between rural and urban dwellers). Washington, D.C., coordinates the world's defenses against the invaders, and it is the president who gives permission to drop the bomb on the Martians. Of course, the action takes place in the most Western continental state, in California, where the Martians first arrived. Also, everyone is a consummate professional. And except for those few loiterers and looters that are heavy-handed plot devices, the civilians evacuate the city in a more-or-less orderly fashion (unlike the chaos that takes place in Japanese films, which is even more frightening to a society that stresses order above all else). The system functions as it should. All this helps justify the technology and social institutions. Though these institutions are morally and ethically justified, they are finally ineffective at purging the threat. Just as the technological and social systems that Sizard and Pal fled failed to prevent the Holocaust (and, in fact, sent people to the gas chambers in an efficient, orderly fashion), so too does the technology and social systems of the 1950s fail Earth. It would seem, therefore, that the more cosmological the battle the more "Mann's" or "Man's" secular institutions and technologies become increasingly powerless. And so we must turn to another power. But what is the exact nature of this power?

Oppenheimer thought it was the redemptive power of God. Inspired by the poetry of John Donne, he named the first test of a nuclear weapon "Trinity," after a well-known Donne poem that seeks to vivify abstract liturgical concepts.[18] To Oppenheimer, the Holy Trinity probably expressed Bohr's theory of "complementarity."[19]

The crisis of the bomb evoked in Oppenheimer the fantastical but structured worldview of John Donne; in *The War of the Worlds* it evokes the urbane but brooding reflections of Matthew Arnold. The call of Arnold's poem *Dover Beach*, "Ah, love, let us be true to one another," overrules the traditional view of salvation (and even overrules the fates of countless of hundreds of "ignorant armies clashing by night") as Clayton's search for Sylvia is elevated, indeed, to being the most important thing in the world. *The War of the Worlds* exemplifies a liberal bourgeois, secular vision of religion. Clayton does not seek God in the churches, but rather to spend his last moments with Sylvia. Furthermore, God no longer intervenes for the righteous, but waits passively, revealed to an individual as the individual is revealed unto himself.[20]

In the final analysis, the crisis of the Martian invasion is a metaphor for personal rebirth and spiritual union—within the confines of postwar humanist values. The Martians are escaping a dead planet. They burn with desire for a new life. Likewise, Clayton has escaped the dead life of the university to the forest, but he does not understand his desire for a new life until after he meets Sylvia. Once he is joined with Sylvia in the church, the crisis subsides. Their union is sanctified in a church of moderate passion where the minister is dressed in secular cloth. Thus, Clayton's journey brings him back into the fold of liberal bourgeois respectability. His new suburban life with his "sylvan" lover is secure.

Some films seem to depict only the catastrophic events of the apocalypse, the illness, suffering and death, and not the genre's paradigmatic morality of rebirth and continuance—until, that is, we carefully examine the films' narrative and cinematic structures. One such film is Stanley Kramer's 1959 film *On the Beach*, which has often been oxymoronically praised as an apocalyptic bomb film about the annihilation of humanity. Based on the best-selling 1957 novel by Anglo-Australian Nevil Shute, the film describes, in what was for many at that time a shocking way, the effects of radiation on humans beings and the powerlessness of the republic of science to preserve life on earth. *On the Beach* is exemplary of 1950s films that make a pretense at a broad kind of social criticism, because finger-pointing destabilizes the liberal notion of consensus, but devolves into facile character analysis that diffuses personal or collective responsibility. *On the Beach* is perhaps the most famous bomb film that clearly demonstrates the inability to fix blame for the nuclear holocaust.

The first scene begins in deep waters, beneath the surface of the ocean. The film soon reveals that there has been a brief nuclear war, and radiation is spreading from the northern hemisphere to the south, killing everyone and everything. With everyone in North America dead, a U.S. nuclear submarine, the *Sawfish*, finds its way to Australia, where the people wait to die. A romance develops between the ship's captain, Dwight (Gregory Peck), and Moira (Ava Gardner), a local woman. The captain, however, elects to return with his crew to the United States to die alongside his already dead wife and children. After the other main characters have died or taken their suicide pills, Moira watches as Dwight sails into the horizon. The camera cuts back and forth between their gazes. We watch from Moira's point of view (POV) as the submarine dives beneath the surface. The camera seems to follow the ship down, and then resurfaces in the heart of an evidently lifeless city. In a clever piece of editing, the water becomes a piece of paper that is blowing down the streets of Melbourne. The camera travels through the city, resting, as the film ends, on a large banner that warns us that "THERE IS STILL TIME BROTHER." The film's true shock value, however, comes not from the spectator's identification with all that is (or can be) dead, but through identifying with Moira and the camera. With this in mind, an in-depth analysis of *On the Beach* will help to demonstrate the subtle importance of the apocalyptic imagination to atomic bomb cinema.

Everyone suffers in this film. But the source of this suffering has little to do with imminent global nuclear annihilation, and more to do with the nature of desire in a patriarchal society. The bomb, while fearfully important in *On the Beach*, is what Alfred Hitchcock calls a "MacGuffin" (see chapter 2), the storytelling device that obscures the true source of everyone's suffering. The theme that runs through all the different relationships in this film is the lost opportunity for love and marriage. Most notably, Moira (named after the Greek goddess of fate) confesses to her former suitor Julian (Fred Astaire) that she was foolish for rejecting his love and the chance for happiness through matrimony, and Julian confesses to another character his envy of the bliss of matrimony and fatherhood that the other character has enjoyed. Later, Julian asphyxiates himself in his Ferrari—a sublimation for his unrequited love.

Almost the only deaths or preparations for death that we do not see are Moira's and Dwight's. Clearly, Moira suffers considerably because her life lacks the fulfillment that comes with marriage. In contrast, once Dwight decides to return home to his wife and family, he accepts his fate and faces his death with courage. However, we can hardly say that Dwight gains some mystical insight through recognizing his impending death. Nor can we say that the film reveals any mystical knowledge. Thus, the question of explaining why the film is so moving remains. To resolve this question, let us look at the use of the cinematic apparatus—that is, how the film itself, not the narrative, is constructed.

While the narrative suggests that everyone dies (which is antithetical to the apocalyptic imagination), where there is a camera, there is a camera operator and a narrative that continues. In the penultimate scenes, the camera records Moira's gaze, or POV. In a sense, the camera continues to record Moira's POV through the final moments of the film—that is, she, at least, survives to repent and pine for her unrequited love. Thus, it is through her eyes that we see the warning that there is still time. But time for what? *On the Beach* has all the elements common to the genre of 1940s women's films known as "weepies," including what Mary Ann Doane says are women who desire to desire.[21] Like so many other women in weepy films, Moira remains permanently outside bourgeois acceptability and is therefore doomed forever to desire from afar others' fulfillment. Once the camera dips beneath the waves, however, the audiences may identify not simply with Moira's gaze, but with the camera's POV itself; that is, through editing techniques that obscure the camera's presence, the audience experiences the film as though they were walking the streets of Melbourne.

This film has the ostensive effect of an antinuclear consciousness-raising event. But, whether one identifies with Moira's gaze or the camera itself, the spectators experience continuance because moral exempla beg for rejuvenation (like catharsis in Greek tragedy). That is to say, from a narrative that ends in universal annihilation, the cinematic structure of *On the Beach* recovers the apocalyptic promise of continuance beyond the nuclear holocaust. The cinematic structure reassures the audience that surviving a nuclear war is possible.

While *On the Beach* does not describe an otherworldly journey or a revelation, in accord with the nature of the apocalyptic imagination, the film fulfills the audience's need or desire for the experience of having survived nuclear annihilation. The film also exhorts the audience to righteousness through its treatment of Moira; and, like Horatio at the end of *Hamlet*, the camera survives to carry the warning message. (As we will see in a later chapter, were this a Japanese bomb film, it might well have been Moira's spirit that returns to tell us of her tragic, unfulfilled longing.) With the narrative pulling the audience in one direction, toward annihilation with no hope of fulfillment (unless, possibly, one is married), and the cinematic apparatus pulling the audience in another direction, toward surviving the unsurvivable, it is little wonder that audiences feel emotionally drained and shocked. The success of *On the Beach* established, furthermore, a formula of *nuclear bathos* that later films have also used successfully, such as the two 1983 TV movies (TVMs): *Testament* and *The Day After*. Like *On the Beach*, both TVMs also received considerable critical praise for their supposed realism and humanism. The bomb is a MacGuffin. Again, some bomb films see only the apocalyptic condition and not its spiritual dimension. *On the Beach* is one such film. It is, in the end, the 1950s classroom instructional film gone arty.

Kramer's penchant for classroom morality lessons on the one hand, and an inability to fix moral responsibility on the other can be seen in the film's explanations for how the world destroyed itself. At a morbid house party held in the captain's honor, one of the guests accusingly asks Julian to explain the war and justify the role scientists played. Julian says that the war "was carefully planned down to the tiniest mechanical and emotional detail. But it was a mistake." The world, he says, "was gloriously destroyed by a handful of vacuum tubes and transistors. Probably faulty." As for the scientists, "Every man who worked on this thing told you what would happen. The scientists signed petition after petition, but no one would listen." But, if the scientists knew this would happen, why did they build the systems? Later, on board Dwight's submarine during a scientific reconnaissance mission, Julian is again questioned. One of the officers asks, simply, "Who started it?" Julian retorts: "Albert Einstein." He continues by saying,

> The war started when people accepted the idiotic principle that peace could be maintained by organizing to defend themselves with weapons they couldn't possibly use without committing suicide. . . . Somewhere, some poor bloke probably looked at a radar screen and thought he saw something, and knew that if he hesitated 1/1000 of a second his own country would be wiped off the map, so, so, he pushed the button and the world went crazy, and, and, . . . [unable to finish, Julian leaves the room].

Most of us would agree with Julian; we are all responsible for the world's survival. Yet, his answers gives the impression that there is no social world of political conflict, only a strangely distorted personal world, and there are no bad people who do wrong, only good people who make mistakes. Not only does the film gloss over the genuine political issues that are likely to initiate a nuclear war, it also ignores the secrecy, deception, and lack of democratic control that surrounds nuclear weapons. *On the Beach* is a sentimental and simplistic explanation of a complex world. There is no clearly defined battle between good and evil, or even competing superpowers. The nuclear war was merely an accident, not even a teleologically determined cosmological battle. In its negativity, *On the Beach* is not as radical as it pretends. In my view, the continual reflections of hollow char-

acters, the obvious directorial machinations (such as Peck being photographed in the shadow of the *Sawfish*), make this film the perfect
"made for liberals who want to think they are radicals" art flick. However,
as much as it succeeds as an art film, it fails not only as a statement of radical thinking but also as lasting entertainment.

At the time of its release this film created quite a stir, and was quite a
shock to audiences, particularly to educated liberal audiences. The scientist
Linus Pauling, after seeing the film, proclaimed, "It may be that . . . *On the
Beach* is the movie that saved the world."[22] For Paul Boyer, the historian of
"the Atomic Age," the film remains an important node in the formation of
his own "nuclear consciousness"; twenty-six years after the event, Boyer can
clearly recall "[c]oming out of a Times Square movie theater at midnight
on New Year's Eve, 1959, having just seen the end of the world in *On the
Beach*, overwhelmed by the sheer *aliveness* of the raucous celebrators"
(emphasis in original).[23] (Boyer never explains his motivations, but it does
seem unfair to impugn others for not marking the New Year through intellectual self-flagellation.) Saving the world is no meager achievement, even
for the gods, let alone a magic lantern. But what sort of world is being
saved, how, and by whom? The film says it is a world where impotent scientists express their powerlessness by signing petitions, but at the same
time, accept research grants for weapons development.

The usually favorable reviews that scholars have given the film are
indicative of the generally moribund and powerless state of the academic
humanities and left-leaning intellectuals, especially those who are alienated from and disparaging of "popular culture." Since the 1930s most
American intellectuals, as Robert Warshow astutely argues in *The
Immediate Experience*, have had an ambivalent relationship to popular
culture, condemning it for misleading the masses, yet still believing it
might be used to educate, if not lead, them.[24] Peter Clecak shows that by
1945 the "Old Left" in America had been neutralized; faith in capitalism,
albeit a substantially different capitalism, had been restored, and the
masses abandoned the radical's call to arms; New Deal economics was fast
becoming a casualty of the cold war; and, radicals were forced into
abeyance by the threat of censure, imprisonment, deportation, and death.
With little social space within which to maneuver, left-leaning cultural
critics have, consequently, tended to rally around particular bomb films,
such as *On the Beach*, when it serves their specific social agenda, but generally attack what I call atomic bomb cinema as merely the modern
numbing opiate of the masses.[25]

By 1954, when Oppenheimer was stripped of his security clearance, scientists had also lost favor with the public. This was in part due to internal disputes within the republic of science and in part due to being expedient political scapegoats. The end result was the same: both social critics and scientists were forced to acquiesce their right to lead the world to a new tomorrow. In effect, as many cultural critics have indicated, the intellectual Left in America had become increasingly immobilized by bitterness and resentment.[26] The moribund elements of *On the Beach*, and to an extent *The War of the Worlds*, is reflective of a type of nihilism surfacing on the left more than a direct statement on the bomb, and an expression of just one trend within atomic bomb cinema. As we will see in the following chapter, the more "conservative" films, ironically, are less nihilistic and more inclined toward progressivism.

4 1950 to 1963 PART II

Cold war fantasies

Perhaps the most fruitful distinction with which the sociological imagination works is between "the personal troubles of milieu" and "the public issues of social structure." This distinction is an essential tool of the sociological imagination and a feature of all classic work in social science.

—C. Wright Mills, *The Sociological Imagination*[1]

In the previous chapter we analyzed a few films that typified the ideological concerns found in bomb films of the 1950s and early 1960s. A few of these films had unexpectedly radical ideals about social relations. Others, however, seemed to put forward a progressive ideology; yet, beneath the surface of the text we found countercurrents that undermined the films' liberal pretenses. Regardless of how we judge these films, ideology was relatively uneasy ground on which to stand during the 1950s. In this chapter we take a second look at the same era, but in a more comfortable domain for atomic bomb cinema—the fantastic. Rather than push the audience toward liberal or conservative enlightenment, the films in this chapter explore the sociological and personal angst in the years 1950 to 1963.

Six films stand out as seminal in the development of the apocalyptic bomb film subcategory in atomic bomb cinema during these years. In chronological order, they are: *Rocketship X-M* (Kurt Neumann, 1950;

a.k.a. *Rocket Ship X-M*), *Unknown World* (Terrell O. Morse, 1951), *Them!* (Gordon Douglas, 1954), *The Story of Mankind* (Irwin Allen, 1957), *The Incredible Shrinking Man* (Jack Arnold, 1957), and *The Time Machine* (George Pal, 1960). Analyses of these films will form the core of this chapter. In addition, we will briefly examine the very important films *Godzilla, King of the Monsters* (Inoshirō Honda and Terry Morse, 1956), *The Amazing Colossal Man* (Bert I. Gordon, 1957), and some rather unlikely, lesser-known bomb films from this period.

H. Bruce Franklin argues, in *War Stars*, that "the first two movies against the arms race [*The Day the Earth Stood Still* and *Five*] both appeared in 1951," but his estimate is off by at least a year or more. The lesser-known *Rocketship X-M*, released in 1950, is clearly antinuclear, and is perhaps also the first postnuclear holocaust film.[2] It is the story of an experimental ("X") rocket ship ("R") on its first voyage to the Moon ("M"). Foreshadowing the film's theme, *RXM* is launched from the United States Proving Grounds, White Sands, New Mexico. The *RXM* crew journeys to the Moon for scientific or nontraditional reasons, but also because the expedition might lead to the establishment of a lunar base that can enforce peace on Earth; this is a common theme during this era, and one that is remarkably similar to ancient journey narratives. The ship, however, accidentally goes off course, and the crew lands on another "M" planet, Mars. There the crew discovers the ruins and mutant survivors of a civilization that destroyed itself in a nuclear war. The leader of the expedition, in one of many early cinematic foreshadowings of antinuclear discourse in the 1980s, says Mars went "from atomic age to stone age." The inhabitants kill two of the crew. Three return to the ship; one is wounded and unconscious. The survivors return to Earth but without enough fuel to land; they are doomed to crash and destroy themselves. As the ship hurtles toward Earth, the romantic leads, Colonel Floyd Graham (Lloyd Bridges) and Lisa Van Horne, Ph.D. (Osa Massen), reconcile their differences and acknowledge their mutual love. The two find meaning in their deaths by informing humanity of what they learned on Mars. Following the crash of the *RXM*, the space program's director defends the project. He says Dr. Van Horne "supplied us with information that may well mean the salvation of our world." "Salvation" is an unexpected word. It implies something beyond merely saving the world from self-destruction. It suggests that transcendental knowledge has been gained. Within the subtext of the film, does the word "salvation" make sense? I think so.

Though cloaked in the language of science fiction space travel, the film is remarkably similar to other apocalyptic revelations. Briefly, the film involves an otherworldly journey and a revelation unfolding history. And the wisdom gained by the travelers is interpreted for the edification of all. In apocalyptic literature, revelations frequently direct the journeyer to warn heretics and transgressors.

Rocketship X-M is probably the first bomb film to have a space journey that leads to a revelation and warning about nuclear technology. It also deserves credit for establishing another first: a progressive attitude toward the status of women, and, to a lesser extent, non-Anglo white cultures (later films also extend this attitude to nonwhites). Throughout the flight Dr. Lisa Van Horne, the only character with an obvious accent, is either patronized for being too feminine or criticized for not being feminine enough. Yet, while Van Horne has her own lessons to learn, in each critical conflict the film takes Van Horne's side.

Feminist film criticism has taught us that films often portray women as incomplete without a stronger man, and force intelligent women into romantic relationships where they lose their independence. And indeed, throughout the *RXM*'s journey, Graham aggressively tries to woo Van Horne, but she is understandably indifferent to Graham's advances. This film is, in fact, critical of masculine single-mindedness. It is, for example, the senior scientist's own blunders, his repression of emotions, and his unwillingness to listen to the "feminine," that imperils the entire trip. And, on the return trip Graham and Van Horne must rely on only each other, so they learn to respect the other's abilities, which seems like a more reasonable foundation for a mature relationship. If anything, the film warns women not to sacrifice their emotions and intellect in order to advance their careers.

One of the chief virtues of *Rocketship X-M* is that both Van Horne and Graham are reformed. At the start Graham is an abusive male chauvinist pig. He ridicules Van Horne for her apparent lack of "feminine" feelings. Yet at the end of the film Graham learns respect for Van Horne. He says she changed, but Van Horne insists that it is not she but Graham who has changed. Graham recognizes this and says he has come to love Van Horne without wanting to change her. Graham has grown from a womanizer into an accepting and caring lover. Van Horne also changes. In contrast to the senior scientist, she discovers a balance between "feminine emotions" and "masculine logic." Together, Graham and Van Horne send the message, yet it is, tellingly, the voice of the feminine that speaks the words of salvation to a masculine-dominated world—a theme that appears more strongly in Japanese films.

Otherworldly space journeys that lead to the salvation of Earth—in, for example, *Beyond the Time Barrier* (Edgar G. Ulmer, 1960)—are a staple of atomic bomb cinema. But space is not the only location to which men and women, usually scientists, journey. The year after Robert L. Lippert Pictures released *Rocketship X-M*, it released *Unknown World* (1951), which is even more explicitly about the threat of nuclear weapons. The basic plot of *Unknown World* is identical to *Rocketship X-M*, yet the characters are less developed, less three-dimensional. Audiences, by this point, were probably already familiar with the formula, so any gaps in explaining characters' motivations or plot developments was not then, and certainly not now, a problem in understanding the narrative. *Unknown World* focuses more on developing the apocalyptic subtext, the ideology, and the artistic pretense of the film. The first few minutes of *Unknown World*, are, for example, a clear homage to *Citizen Kane* (Orson Welles, 1941). The film begins with a newsreel that describes a larger-than-life figure (a scientist) and his attempt to lead the world toward peace. The newsreel, however, is a film within a film, and segues into a scene in which the newsreel is being watched by the very persons it portrays, and when the lights come on in the screening room, one reporter describes what everyone just saw.

In addition to allusions to other films, *Unknown World* blends elements of the apocalyptic genre, such as the development of history and pseudonymity, and other biblical genres, in clever ways. The newsreel itself describes, in no uncertain terms, the history of nuclear weapons, the growing threat of global thermonuclear annihilation, and how a group of longhair scientists are trying to save humanity from extinction. The leader of this group is Professor Jeremiah Morley (Victor Kilian). The biblical Jeremiah, a prophet and scholar, spends a great deal of time lamenting and warning people and communities over breaking their covenant with God, and prophesying future events in which transgressors are destroyed and the just are redeemed. Professor Jeremiah Morley, likewise, spends his time telling audiences all across America that unless something is done, humanity will soon destroy itself with nuclear weapons. Jeremiah, therefore, forms The Society to Save Civilization. The society, made up of scientists and engineers, proposes to journey to the center of the earth to find a safe haven from nuclear war. The very reporter who was introduced in the first scenes pays for the project in exchange for passage on the journey. In another tip of the hat to Welles, the young reporter is in fact the jaded son of a wealthy San Francisco newspaper publisher.

True to the American utopian tradition, they build a craft, the Cyclotram, to escape the decline of an older civilization and germinate the flower of the older civilization in a new world. As though going down into Dante's inferno, they stop in four different places, each a deeper level beneath the surface. They call these places Hades, the Valley of the Shadows, the Promised Land, and the Haven for the Dead. Only four of the seven crew members survive the first three levels, to find in the fourth level that it is impossible to reproduce in their new haven. The four vote on whether to remain and live their lives in peace and harmony, but with no future, or to return to the surface. Only one, Dr. Morley, chooses to stay, saying, "You're young, you don't know. I've lived through the terror of two great wars. I've had enough!" At that instant there is a fantastic cataclysm: lightning, thunder, floods, and volcanic eruptions. The three make it to their craft, while Morley, acting more like Moses unable to cross into the promised land, allows himself to be swept away by the storm. The Cyclotram is carried away in the storm, and eventually it rises, looking somewhat like a giant whale, back up through their hellish journey to the surface of the sea. They, like Jonah, have survived a crisis, and so rise through the primeval underground sea, and like Jonah are reborn from the ocean with a renewed commitment to fight for the survival of humanity.

When they reach the surface and look out from their craft, the three see a tropical paradise. The film ends as the character Max Bauer (Otto Waldis) sighs, "The Universe is in harmony," scientist Joan Lindsey (Marilyn Nash) joyously observes that they have found civilization and people, and reporter Wright Thompson (Bruce Kellogg) proclaims, "I feel like I will live for ever." Max, a scientist, fled the Nazis and has been fleeing ever since. Joan, like her namesake, is a crusader, an award-winning physician, and "an ardent feminist" who has fled the male-dominated world because she is "afraid of living." She, like Sylvia in *The War of the Worlds,* is one of the few heroines in films of this period who smokes. Wright is spoiled, "afraid of death," and in a sense is the prodigal son.

What makes *Unknown World* and other films like it interesting, is that it expresses what C. Wright Mills calls the "sociological imagination"; that is to say, an appreciation for the distinctions and connections between "the personal troubles of milieù" and "the public issues of social structure."[3]

This is expressed, most poignantly, through the characters Wright and Joan. While everyone else is selfless in his or her pursuit of a haven for humanity, Wright is on the journey only for meaningless adventure. In order to survive, however, he learns that he must be part of the group, and work for the benefit of all, not just himself. He also learns to appreciate the magnitude of what the scientists are trying to accomplish. As in *Rocketship X-M*, Wright also learns to appreciate Joan for her scientific abilities, as well as her feminine attractiveness. Through Wright's transformation into a caring, responsible person, Joan learns to stop distrusting men, and falls in love. Unlike *Rocketship X-M*, the motivation for Joan's change of heart or for falling in love are not clearly explained. What is clear is that for all three of the survivors, the crisis of their own personal troubles are resolved through the journey. While the resolution of personal troubles through bourgeois love may, in our time, seem trite and ideologically suspect, there is a more important sociological dimension. All three proclaim that through their journey they have come to realize that they cannot escape the public issues of social structure—that is, the arms race— and even gender, but must return to the surface and work for the survival of all of humanity.

Hollywood is frequently attacked as a monolithic, ideologically uniform industry, and is often held responsible for the repressiveness of the 1950s. While *Rocketship X-M* and *Unknown World* are not masterpieces of enlightened, liberal film art, they do stand in direct contrast to the films that scholars use as evidence for the reactionary politics that supposedly dominated Hollywood in the 1950s. These two films have surprisingly optimistic and progressivist visions of humanity learning to overcome a crisis that threatens all. While some may condemn the films' obligatory love stories, it cannot be denied that the men undergo considerable consciousness-raising before they are ready for the responsibilities of saving the world or a commitment to another person. Compared to films like *On the Beach*, the characterizations of the women in these science fictional films, needless to say, stand out for their independence and intelligence in a world that is hostile to competent women. Remarkably, such enlightened films as *Rocketship X-M* and *Unknown World* may in fact be the norm in atomic bomb cinema.

At the far right of the spectrum of bomb films that give women a central place in the narrative is Nathan Juran's *Attack of the 50 Ft. Woman* (1958). In it a wealthy woman is married to and desperately in love with a philanderer whose only interest in his wife is her money and her "Star of India" diamond. The woman encounters a strange alien whose only interest in the woman is, like the husband's, her diamond. This very close encounter with an alien exposes her to radiation, and she grows to fifty feet tall. Her doctors chain and sedate her. She breaks loose and goes looking for her two-timing husband, finds him with his gold-digging girl-friend, and kills them both. The sheriff then shoots and kills the fifty-foot woman. Again, the bomb is a MacGuffin, a device used to explore other issues, in this case gender relations and biology. Throughout the film, all the other characters, from the sheriff to the woman's doctors, are sympathetic and loyal, if patronizing, to the jilted woman. The ending thus comes as somewhat of a surprise; rather than remaining sympathetic to woman, the film blames her. The sheriff comments, after shooting the woman, that mother nature makes women overreact. *Attack of the 50 Ft. Woman* is an interesting but odd film. It is both sympathetic to women yet, by our standards, demeaning in its representation of them as either passive victims or out of control. It is tempting to dismiss this film because of its reactionary ending. But it is more productive to see this film for what it is: a cheap, quickly made exploitation film that sits uncomfortably on the cusp of the tremendous social crises that were just taking form in the United States. It is just one of many voices in atomic bomb cinema.

It Came from Beneath the Sea (Robert Gordon, 1955, with special effects by Ray Harryhausen and Charles H. Schneer) is a more innovative, popular, mainstream science fiction film, and so a more representative bomb film. Here again the bomb is a MacGuffin, in the guise of a radioactive octopus. The film openly discusses the changing roles of women, criticizes macho and patronizing men, and encourages women not only to demand careers but also relationships on their own terms. At the end of the film, the woman scientist turns down the submarine commander's marriage proposal, and, instead, proposes that he leave his career for her career. She then puts her hand under his chin and gives him a big kiss, after which the commander acknowledges the attractions of this "new breed of woman." A disturbingly unresolved, and radical ending for a "Hollywood" film of this period. These four films suggest that film historians need to revise the standard or received notions about Hollywood's portrayal of life in the 1950s, particularly in films about the bomb, but not only these four films. Progressive cultural politics and extraordinary visions of the future can also be seen in the better-known films of the 1950s, such as *Them!*

Them! (1954) was not the first creature film to include the bomb, but it is one of the era's most important and most popular, and the clearest expression of the apocalyptic imagination. What makes *Them!* so fascinating is that it expresses concern about many different levels of human experience. This complexity, however, makes it one of the most difficult films to analyze in this study.

The location is the desert of New Mexico, not far from Jornada del Muerto (Journey of Death) where just before dawn on July 16, 1945, at 0529:45 hours, the Trinity test took place; that is, the first nuclear weapon was exploded.[4] The action of the film begins just before dawn, magic hour in cinematography. A somnambulistic young girl (Sandy Descher), dressed for bed, is wandering through the desert. She carries the hollow head of a doll (an image repeated in James Cameron's 1986 bomb film *Aliens*). Two state policemen, Sergeant Ben Petersen (James Whitmore) and Officer Ed Blackburn (Chris Drake) rescue her. Eventually they come upon the girl's family's travel trailer. The trailer has been torn apart, and there are no signs of her vacationing family. Later the two policemen find a small store that has been similarly destroyed, the owner dead, presumably murdered. Ed stays behind to investigate and is killed—off screen. FBI agent Robert "Bob" Graham (James Arness, who played the murderous alien carrot in Christian Nyby's 1951 bomb film *The Thing from Another World*) joins Ben in his investigation. Bob sends castings from strange animal tracks that are found near the trailer to the Department of Agriculture. Doctors Harold and Patricia Medford (Edmund Gwenn and Joan Weldon) are sent to investigate. This father and daughter team of myrmecologists (insect specialists) from the USDA leads the investigation to the discovery of giant ants, mutated by exposure to radiation.

With the help of the military, under the strictest secrecy, they locate and gas the giant ants' nest. Patricia then leads Ben and Robert on a reconnaissance mission into the nest. The doctors conclude that two queen ants and their consorts had already left the nest to start other colonies. One colony hatches on board a cargo vessel at sea, and the Navy is forced to sink the ship. A bizarre police report about a badly mutilated man, Mr. Lodge, and his two missing sons leads the authorities to another colony in the sewers of Los Angeles. Martial law is declared and the police and military enter the sewers. Patricia, Ben, and Robert lead the troops. In a battle to rescue the two boys, an ant kills Ben. However, the boys are saved. After making certain that none of the newly hatched queen ants have escaped, they set fire to the ants. Despite the successful resolution of the plot and the budding relationship between Patricia and Robert, the film ends with a note of uncertainty about the future. The elder Dr. Medford's frequent references to biblical apocalypses adds to this air of anxiety and foreboding.

The Bible is a real and living part of many Americans' lives, especially for intellectual conservatives. And we must consider this tradition in our assessment of atomic bomb cinema, particularly because apocalypticism is typically a conservative movement, though, as we have seen, it is co-opted by liberal, reactionary, and radical factions. All of these ideologies are seen in 1950s films, sometimes as competing elements and sometimes as complementary elements. *Them!* mixes issues of social relationships, such as gender roles, with a great deal of concern for biblical prophecy. Yet, in their analyses of the film, almost none of the critics or scholars seriously consider Dr. Medford's biblical references, let alone acknowledge the references' literal meanings. Following Richie's, Sontag's, and Lifton's leads, these pundits, instead, busy themselves looking for signs of an "inadequate response," "psychic numbing," reactionary politics, and religious palliatives. This is, as Peter Clecak describes it in *America's Quest for the Ideal Self*, part of a general pattern in the Left's antagonism toward religion, particularly evangelical and neo-Pentecostal religions.[5] Be that as it may, in order to appreciate the political and sociological subtexts in *Them!* we must seriously consider the story before looking for thin political polemics.

Expertise is an important theme in *Them!* Everyone, from the night watchman to the mother, from the scientist to the soldier, is a professional; and, professional affiliation is the *locus* of an individual's power. The respect that each person earns depends on his or her ability to carry out a job. Competency, moreover, is considered more important than gender. For example, when Robert objects to a woman entering the anthill, Patricia forces him to recognize that she is the only person with both the expertise and physical ability to enter the caves and determine the operation's success. She demands that he treat her as a professional first and a woman second. And, as in *The War of the Worlds*, occupation, type, and *source* of authority is correlative to *location*. Intellectuals comes from the East. Doers come from the West.

Yet, the individual's expertise or competency is not enough. The somnambulistic young girl's father, Allan Helenson, was an FBI agent. The storekeeper is described as the proverbial crafty old codger, the American rugged individualist, who lived in the desert longer than anyone else and knew the dangers. Likewise, Ed Blackburn is an experienced police officer familiar with the desert. Mr. Lodge, whose mutilated body and missing sons lead to the discovery of the third ant colony, is described as the ideal father who would never jeopardize the safety of his children and so took them to play in only places that he knew well. Yet, all these people were killed by the ants. Ben, too, despite his familiarity with the mutant ants, is killed.

All the victims succumb when separated from the community or special system. The ants have brought about a change where mere expertise in one's own field is no longer enough. The individual must now function within the system and be a team player. This signals a definite change in American culture. At best, individualism in this film, and similarly in other bomb films of the period, is giving way to cooperation and community. At worst, this indicates the trend in postwar culture that William H. Whyte Jr., has dubbed "organization man" behavior.[6] Organization men and women subordinate their own values to the needs of the institution or system, and sublimate political impotence with harmless personal enrichment activities. In any case, *Them!* is a structural-functionalist's (one brand of anthropology) ideal world.[7]

Each person has an expertise or function within a highly structured society, and each person's job is important and respected. There are no rivalries between professionals, governmental agencies, or even corporations, which are so common to later creature-bomb films like *Alien* (Ridley Scott, 1979) or *Aliens* (James Cameron, 1986). When there is a crisis, all the appropriate arms of the government are mobilized, and everyone cooperates to accomplish the desired goals. Similarly, in *The War of the Worlds*, everyone pulls together for the good of the community. But unlike *The War of the Worlds*, the secular institutions and technologies not only function correctly, they successfully resolve the crisis. The system, not a bourgeois God, saves the day.

The loner, the rugged individualist of the Old West, no longer has a place in the post-Hiroshima world of *Them!* The bomb, in this film, has made even the nuclear family, the corner stone of fifties and neo-fifties ideology, a nonviable institution. Only the group can guarantee survival of the community and safety for the individual. To leave the group for even a moment is to risk death. Patricia walks off into the desert alone and is attacked by the ants. Ben knowingly separates himself from the others and is killed by the ants. Finally, when a sewer roof collapses,

Robert is cut off from the others and attacked by the ants. Only the effort of the group saves him. Even a general pitches in and dirties his hands trying to rescue Robert.

To claim, as H. Bruce Franklin and Nora Sayre do, that the ants represent the communist threat to American society is to make a mountain out of an anthill.[8] Clearly, the very social structure that makes "them" so dangerous is the very social structure that saves the world: one must "out ant" the ants. It is the social structure the film celebrates. Because the film is far more concerned with internal changes, any xenophobia or paranoia in *Them!* is of secondary importance. That is to say, in *Them!* good Americans, some old-fashioned some *nouveau*, struggle to overcome a crisis and come to terms with rapid social changes. This victory requires traditional, old-world communal bonding (at the expense of some individualism) as well as new-world scientific specialization.

Them! is frequently described by scholars and critics as somehow exemplary of fifties gender roles. Peter Biskind, for instance, claims that while a few men are sacrificed to the women's movement, the rest of the film works to constrain women in traditional roles. Biskind also calls the ant society matriarchal or communist, which is fallacious anthropomorphizing and not consistent with the narrative.[9] Many, possibly even most, women and men did aspire, ascribe, subscribe, and prescribe to the orderly sexual roles and family life that Elaine Tyler May, for example, describes in her history of cold war era American families and radical feminism, *Homeward Bound*.[10] However, this way of life was neither uncontested nor uniformly expressed in the media of popular culture. Clearly, Patricia Medford stands out as an expression of some women's dissatisfaction with the "traditionally" exclusive roles of wife, lover, and mother. As I interpret this film, *Them!* acknowledges and supports the broadening spectrum of gender roles that emerged after World War II.

At one end of this spectrum is Ben Peterson who is perfectly capable of giving tender care to a young child who is not his own. When the young girl is shocked out of her somnambulistic state, she runs to Ben for comfort, and not a woman or any other man. Clearly, this is not the emotionally repressed man that is said to typify 1950s culture. Nor are the women emotionless, or incapable of giving the love that Ben offers. At the other end of this spectrum is Mrs. Lodge. The ants kill her husband and trap her two young boys, so she is understandably distraught; but, she is by no means "hysterical," out of control, or overly emotional simply because she is a woman. Mrs. Lodge remains helpless, passive to the events around her. She is the "traditional" mother. Her role is to maintain hearth and home. Because she is not the professional soldier or scientist fighting at the front lines of social change, her behavior seems perfectly reasonable within the context of a highly structured society.

What adds dimensionality to this spectrum are the unwed agent Robert Graham and Dr. Patricia Medford. Graham is the traditional single man, protective, caring, but patronizing toward Patricia, to whom he is attracted. Patricia is portrayed as charming, attractive, and likewise attracted to FBI agent Graham. What most clearly distinguishes Patricia from Mrs. Lodge, however, are their sources of power. We have seen that there is a relationship between location (East or West) and locus (USDA or FBI), and expertise, authority, and power. There is also a source of power and authority. One woman's source of power is science, and the other woman's source is motherhood—two powers with which we must reckon. In this film motherhood does not seem to mean simply reproducing, but also being a good parent, like Mrs. Lodge. More to the point, Patricia's source of power or identity is not merely her gender or sex, but her professionalism and ability to contribute to society in ways normally reserved for men.

Patricia is first introduced when she and her father, Dr. Harold Medford, arrive in New Mexico on board a military plane. Patricia's skirt gets caught on the ladder as she climbs out of the plane—as though "stuck" on the outward trappings of American womanhood. Apparently, these trappings are more important to others than to Patricia, for she declines help and frees herself. That same day she wanders off into the desert alone, and is attacked by an ant. She screams, runs, trips in her heels, and falls down. The three men run to her rescue, and under the direction of the elder Dr. Medford, Robert and Ben kill the ant.

Is the frail, dependent woman betraying and undermining the scientist? Hardly. In a later scene that parallels Patricia's encounter with the ant, Robert is alone when he is attacked. He too lets out a high-pitched scream and runs away before being rescued. Again the issue here is not gender, but the individual's vulnerability when separated from the group. Following Patricia's experience in the desert she exchanges her skirt and heels for a desert explorer's attire, just as her father changes out of his suit. Both scientists return to more formal wear during meetings. But when Patricia enters the Los Angeles sewers with the troops she is in army fatigues. Her elderly father, however, remains in his suit. Surely, Patricia is an admirable character. She is intelligent, attractive in many ways, and, most importantly, able to adapt and overcome challenges where others cannot.

The ants are not a metaphor for the dangers of matriarchal or communist societies. Organized insects posing a threat to humanity is an ancient narrative device. Giant ants work because they are scary to us, the audience. They are intelligent but hostile and dispassionate. In giant form they are as otherworldly as the Martians that are revealed to us, finally, in *The War of the Worlds*. In aspect, they are cold and mechanical, a fearful techno-alien threat. The scariness of the ants themselves dwarf any critical parallel of communist communities run by liberated women. Yet, because they have little other than their antlike characteristics, it is easy for the spectator, critic, and scholar to project their own fears onto the giant ants.

In *Them!* the ants kill the Helenson family, and Mr. Lodge as he and his two boys play just outside the sewers. Like the young girl, these boys are robbed of their protector/s at a very vulnerable age. The girl enters a somnambulistic coma, and begins wandering through the desert. The boys, however, instead of running away from the ants (the logical thing to do), follow their instincts and hide inside the sewers—now the ants' nest—where they are trapped, to be consumed. The sewers, thus, suggest a potent psychological idea: the symbolic womb, or the unconscious. According to Erik H. Erikson, the transition from childhood to adulthood is experienced as a crisis. It is now recognized that throughout a person's life there is the potential for many other transitions and crises, such as the completion of a woman's maternal responsibilities to her children, and menopause; and, for men, the infamous midlife crisis. Some try to resist crisis and transition. This is called "identity foreclosure," and it is psychologically dangerous. Clearly, this story warns women, in particular, against foreclosure or identifying the self exclusively with any one role; and, instead, provides a range of role models at different stages of life: the young girl, Patricia, Mrs. Lodge, and the child psychologist who attends the little girl. Likewise, the film also warns men against foreclosure, and provides some unexpected role models. Ben, again, takes a paternal responsibility for all the children, and is uncannily gentle for a 1950s macho kind of guy; yet it is to him that the frightened girl runs when she wakes from her coma—not her aunt, the doctor, or any of the other women in the room. The film also demonstrates how men, Robert especially, should not try try to impose rigid gender roles on women.

In addition to warning women against identity foreclosure, the film also warns men against the exclusive identification of *woman* as *mother*. The loss of a parent is a painful experience that must be confronted, an all too-common reality for the children of the many American soldiers who died in World War II and in Korea. But the pain cannot be dealt with by resisting the transition to adulthood, that is, remaining in a dependent and undifferentiated state by hiding in the psychic womb. The wounded child must be rescued from the nest and brought back into the light of consciousness.

If the ants in *Them!* are anything other than mutated ants, then they surely are a projection of Robert's internal crisis. The psychologist and scholar Hayao Kawai points out that someone who is stuck in identity foreclosure is likely to literally wither away and die; conversely, at the other extreme, a society, family, or individual that exclusively equates woman with mother runs the risk of turning women—even women who identify themselves exclusively with the mother figure—into vengeful, devouring, predatory beasts.[11] And understandably so! A subplot of *Them!* is the budding but rocky relationship between Robert and Patricia. What lies between them is Robert's inability to see Patricia as anything other than *woman*. Patricia challenges Robert's image of woman and demands that he change. At the interpersonal, psychosocial level, this change is difficult. But Robert tries hard. At the levels of identity and psychosexual development, the change is experienced as a crisis in which the individual, or an image that person carries, must be destroyed. Like the phoenix, from the debris of the old forms arises a new psychic formation. The individual is reborn. Thus, for Robert, rescuing and destroying his childish image of woman as mother is the crisis he must overcome before he can begin a healthy relationship with Patricia. His image of woman, which has become an image of a devouring mother, is symbolically destroyed with the burning of the ants in the final scene. Like the phoenix, the burning of Robert's image of woman gives rise to a new, fuller image of woman that can lead to a successful, mature (dare we say modern?) relationship with Patricia.

The question that remains is, What impact has the bomb had on the complicated 1950s world in which these characters exist? Not everyone greeted the advent of the bomb as if it were humanity's coming-out party. Films like Taurog's *The Beginning or the End* hail the bomb as a harbinger of a golden age. Other films like *Them!* question the auguries of pronuclear prophets. Apparently, for many people during this period the bomb demarcates man's passage into a strange and perilous time. Some films of this period, such as *The Beginning of the End* (Bert I. Gordon, 1957) depict the development of nuclear weapons as the beginning of the crisis—not the end. Others, like *The Story of Mankind* (Irwin Allen, 1957) depict the bomb as responsible for a future crisis. One of a few, *Beyond the Time Barrier* (Edgar G. Ulmer, 1960) for instance, hints that we may not survive the crisis; that is, Hiroshima and Nagasaki marked the beginning of our decline into anarchy, barbarism, chaos, and possible annihilation.

Them! paints a foreboding portrait of what the bomb has delivered unto us. Standing next to the carcass of a ten-foot-long ant, the elder Dr. Medford says "we may be witness to a biblical prophesy come true: 'And there shall be destruction and darkness come upon creation and the Beasts shall reign over the Earth.'" While this prophecy is not from any specific biblical passage, the general tone suggests Daniel, and the Revelations of John. In the absence of clear associations between mythical elements and historical persons, such as those for which Collins argues, I think it safe to assume that the beasts refer to that which the bomb has engendered; or, at the metaphoric level, the beast within, which Robert must subdue if he—each of us, in fact—is to survive this crisis.

Likewise, the ants are also a parallel for the young girl's development, and by extension, humanity's. Patricia points out that the ants have not only mutated in size but also in developmental patterns. The ants hatch directly from the eggs into adulthood, bypassing the larval and pupal stages. Both the girl and the ants are traumatized by an early end to their childhoods; it is little wonder that the girl is catatonic and the ants turn against human beings. Clearly, *Them!* suggests that our collective childhood and our innocence have been pushed aside by an utterly mature metabolic catastrophe. Humanity has, grudgingly, passed through a crisis and there is no turning back from the "new age." The elder Dr. Medford speaks of this new age with apprehension and a longing for the simplicity of a bygone era. Like the sword of Saint Michael, the bomb has driven humanity out of a Garden of Eden; an old story in new and completely poignant trappings.

Them! mourns the loss not only of humanity's childhood, but also of the individualistic childhood of American society. This loss is experienced as an early waking from childhood that is manifest in the somatic experience of the young girl and the two boys, the changed developmental patterns of the ants, and the adults Patricia and Robert. As mentioned, the film begins with the young girl wandering in a somnambulistic state. She has been wandering alone since the early morning ant attack that killed her sleeping family. Eventually she is brought out of this state and into the reality of her orphaned condition—being an orphan is a common occurrence in American society, and the "feeling" of lost childhood in this film hits the viewer strongly. The bomb that has roused us from the pleasant dreamlike state of childhood too early. At first we are in a state of shock. Now we must face the reality of what has happened.

The image of the child itself, as I have suggested, does not indicate a regression toward some unresolved trauma, but signals the possibility of positive, new developments. In a superior term paper, Caleb Bendix, a foreign exchange student in my class on atomic bomb cinema at Hiroshima University, draws on Freud, Jung, and Hayao Kawai to sum up the image of the child:

> Through many different roles, active or inactive, the child plays an important part in the synthesis of the hero. Serving as healer, link to the unconscious mind, and as object of value the child serves as a catalyzing element for the atomic bomb movies. Their playful nature and innocence allow for probing into sensitive areas of the unconscious. Put into flux by the presence of the atomic bomb, the hero is aided by the child.[12]

Jung puts it this way: In "the psychology of the individual" the symbolic appearance (in dreams or creative works) of "the 'child' paves the way for a future change of personality." Jung also notes that the "child motif not infrequently occurs in the field of psychopathology," especially among women. Indeed, in a number of bomb films the "child motif" appears alongside heroines who are struggling through a crisis. Perhaps the best example is *Aliens* (James Cameron, 1986); the "director's cut" version, released somewhat later, makes this connection quite explicit. Conversely, in *On the Beach* (see chapter 3), Moira's literal and psychological distance from any child might be interpreted as foreshadowing her tragic inability to resolve her crisis. But, in *Them!* we see that the child motif foreshadows Robert's, more than anyone else's, imminent personality change; that is, in bomb films the child motif is equally or more important to male characters. While Bendix's paper focused on films of the 1990s, and thus failed to realize the full import of his own discovery, the child motif appears throughout atomic bomb cinema, including many of the American and Japanese films that I will be discussing. As important as the child motif is, a full exploration of each appearance in a film that I discuss is, unfortunately, beyond the scope of this study. One final point, therefore, needs to be made here in order to make clear the relevance of Bendix's argument to the main theme of this book. Jung writes that the "'child' is all that is abandoned and exposed and at the same time divinely powerful; the insignificant, dubious beginning, and the triumphal end."[13] I would put it this way: In bomb films the "child" is typically a harbinger of crisis and the apocalypse.

What makes *Them!* so important to atomic bomb cinema, thus, is its use of the apocalyptic imagination to express real concerns about nuclear proliferation and consequent changes in the cosmological and mundane levels of life. The filmmakers reworked the generic elements into a narrative that is rich in symbolic associations, yet the symbols are neither simplistic nor inaccessible to the viewer. Though the etiology of the symbols may be arcane and lost to the average spectator of this film, they are nonetheless alive to the culture. That is to say, the film arranges known symbolic images in a way that is oblique yet meaningful and powerfully moving for the spectator. For instance, the first image we see is of a Joshua tree.[14] The tree frames the right and upper sides of the screen, a common framing device in landscape photography. Joshua was Moses's successor and military leader of the Jews who captured Jericho and Canaan. In Christian art, the Archangel Michael often accompanies Joshua, and the destruction of Jericho prefigures the Last Judgment.[15] According to J. E. Cirlot, the Joshua tree is, moreover, the Tree of Life.[16] Most importantly, the film is an example of Alastair Fowler's second phase of genre development.[17] *Them!* uses apocalypses that are familiar to audiences, and consciously works them into the narrative to create an evocative critique of contemporary events.

Them! is hardly the centrist or reactionary film that some critics want it to be. Rather, it is an apocalyptic narrative that plays on the fears of audiences on a number of levels. Fear of insects, fear of the bomb, fear of the apocalypse. The film's first concern is fear—not politics—because fear is fun.

If any film is an indication of sociological and personal angst in the years 1950 to 1963, however, it is the American film *Godzilla, King of the Monsters*. In 1954 Inoshirō Honda's *Gojira* was released, and apparently it had a very limited showing in the United States. American studios became interested in the film, and Toho eventually sold it to Embassy Pictures.[18] Under the direction of Terry Morse, the film was re-edited, in order to make it more coherent for English-speaking audiences of the day, and rereleased in 1956 as *Godzilla, King of the Monsters.* Although significantly altered, the 1956 film remains faithful to the spirit of the original 1954 release; if anything, for American audiences, it makes certain issues even more obvious. In a later chapter I will discuss the Japanese *Gojira* in greater detail; here I will focus, albeit very briefly, on only the American rerelease.

The 1956 film creates a narrator, Steve Martin (Raymond Burr), an American newspaper reporter with considerable experience in Japan, many friends, and a deep sympathy for the country; and so, he is invited back to cover a breaking story. The film reveals that nuclear weapons tests in the Pacific have woken and given radioactive powers to a dormant monster. This creature, Godzilla, then wreaks havoc on Japan. Martin witnesses all this for our benefit, and is himself injured. Martin's reporting of these events seems patterned after Orson Welles's reporter in his 1938 radio version of *The War of the Worlds*, thereby giving an apocalyptic structure to the film. In other words, the reporter goes on an otherworldly journey, an eschatological event is revealed, *ex eventu*, and the reporter interprets that event as a warning. It cannot be overemphasized that while the apocalyptic imagination is not completely foreign to Japan, there is no hint of it in Honda's 1954 film; that is, the apocalyptic imagination structures how some Americans interpreted and re-edited this film for American audiences. The warning, nevertheless, directly identities profound concerns for Americans that are developed more fully in later American films. And, as the level of destruction increases, Martin gives voice to the persistent and growing unease that many Americans had with their place in history: as having an ambivalent relationship with Japan; as the first to develop and use nuclear weapons; and, as a superpower rushing, perhaps foolishly, to develop and deploy even more powerful, thermonuclear, weapons.

The development and testing of hydrogen bombs by the superpowers during the mid-1950s further energized the apocalyptic element in atomic bomb cinema. Irwin Allen's 1957 bomb film *The Story of Mankind* is an adaptation of Hendrik Willem Van Loon's 1921 award-winning, bestselling history by the same title.[19] The film, with the then fashionable "cast of thousands," depicts a cosmological tribunal, the "High Tribunal of Outer Space," where the devil (Vincent Price) and the spirit of man (Ronald Colman) travel through history debating the merits of humanity. At question is whether or not the tribunal should allow mankind to destroy itself with the "super H-bomb." The film ends with the High Judge (Cedric Hardwicke) announcing, "This court will soon convene again to determine finally whether mankind will continue or be destroyed by the super H-bomb." The High Judge then stares directly into the camera, that is, at the film audience, and warns us that "this choice is entirely up to you." *The Story of Mankind* uses many apocalyptic elements, including the development of history, revelations, and judgments, to exhort humanity into living righteously. In fact, I would say that it is the single most literal example of a traditional apocalyptic narrative being worked into a bomb film that exhorts the audience. As the most obvious example of the use of apocalyptic narrative elements it is also the clearest example of Fowler's second phase of generic development. Thus, *The Story of Mankind* is very important to atomic bomb cinema, but it is so literal, so obvious at the surface of the text, never reworking apocalyptic narrative elements in the subtext, that it contributes little to the development of the apocalyptic genre, and is an all but forgotten film.

As we move from the animal world to the human world, the mutagenic power of the bomb takes on new proportions. There are several bomb films about people being shrunk or enlarged by radiation or exposure to nuclear weapons test: *Dr. Cyclops* (Ernest Schoedsack, 1940), *The Amazing Colossal Man* (Bert I Gordon, 1957), *The Cyclops* (Bert I. Gordon, 1957), *Attack of the 50 Ft. Woman* (Nathan Juran, 1958), and more. The most important of these films is Jack Arnold's 1957 film *The Incredible Shrinking Man*. Not at all incidentally, Jack Arnold is one of the most prolific and imaginative directors of bomb films. *The Incredible Shrinking Man* is the second of his five bomb films, one of his more commercially successful films, and probably his most recognized film.

The Incredible Shrinking Man is a film that looks at both the social and the spiritual conditions of life under the shadow of the bomb. And its approach to the mystical dimensions of the apocalyptic crisis is highly inventive. In the scholarly literature, however, this film is commonly used as evidence for widespread fears about the medical effects of nuclear weapons, atmospheric radiation, and even the appearance of deadly strontium 90 in milk and human bones and teeth. Boyer remarks that the film "had obvious psychological roots in the fear of genetic damage from radiation."[20] Indeed, Boyer accurately assesses the ostensible text, which foregrounds radiation's effects on the body, and the illness and suffering the bomb causes. Such interpretations, however, miss the more important subtextual issues about the central character's existential condition.

The central characters are Robert Scott Carey (Grant Williams) and Louise Carey (Randy Stuart). The two are on vacation on his brother's yacht. The film begins with white titles, images of a growing fog, and a shrinking man, all against a black background. As in *Split Second*, the horizonless opening shot suggests stasis. The camera, however, moves from the waves of the Pacific Ocean to the horizon, and then to the sky. There is a dissolve from the sky to a crane shot of the ocean and a boat. Like *On the Beach*, this film also begins in deep waters, but on the surface. In a voice-over, the hero says, "This strange almost unbelievable story of Robert Scott Carey began on a very ordinary summer day." But we, the audience, know better. A boat on the ocean is a clue that a journey has already begun. The camera moves in on the couple, the two flirt, and Scott announces that they will sail to the Philippines to find adventure. Louise gently reminds him that he must return to both home and work at the end of the week. After Louise goes below deck, a strange, amorphous fog momentarily envelops the boat and Scott. (Strange mists, clouds, rains, and the actual black rain following the bombing of Hiroshima and Nagasaki are a common part of bomb imagery.) The scene dissolves into an ordinary suburban home. Again in a voice over, Scott says, "But then on an equally ordinary day six months later" he is accidentally sprayed with insecticide.

Scott beings to shrink. His doctor concludes that radiation from the mysterious fog combined with the insecticide, caused Scott to shrink (a fundamental point that is elided in the scholarly literature).[21] Scott's case is leaked to the press, contributing to his morose feelings of isolation and difference. Eventually he gets so small that he takes up residence in a dollhouse. When Scott's brother takes Louise shopping, their pet cat attacks Scott. Louise returns home to find a bloodied piece of cloth and thinks the cat ate her husband. Actually, Scott is trapped in the basement where he resolves that "as man had dominated the world of the sun, so I would dominate my world."

Scott must survive many adventures while in his basement. Foreshadowed in the first scene is Scott's desire for adventure on the high seas. He gets more than he wished for when the water heater bursts and the miniature Scott, like Odysseus, is drawn into Charybdis (the whirlpool) and nearly drowned. (The film's foreshadowing and use of symbols from myth makes sense, for a widespread belief about personality and the apocalypse is that no crisis can be forever avoided.) Scott's greatest triumph is his battle with a giant spider (insects, or in this case arachnids, again) that guards a piece of stale cake (see figure 2). Prior to the battle, he sees a bird, a common symbol of the human soul, thought, imagination, and the spiritual process.[22] After killing the spider, Scott is covered with blood. Wearily, he drags himself to the cake and breaks off a piece. He looks up and sees the dawn through a vent, then passes out. It is night when he wakes up. Scott climbs through the vent and into the garden. In another voice-over Scott exhorts us that, though still shrinking, he is at ease with his place in the universe because he has discovered a mystical meaning to his bizarre, otherworldly heroic journey.

The screen in the vent that Scott climbs through, casts shadows, on the wall behind him, that take on the appearance of crucifixes. Scott is even wearing tattered robes. But I will not argue that he is an explicit Christ figure; rather, the Christlike figure is yet one more element in an elaborate symbology used to evoke in the audience even more profound ideas.

This whole final part of the film, from the battle to the exhortation, is a true blood ritual, a communion of the blood and the cake *qua* flesh (the Eucharist, so to speak). This blood ritual, in turn, is a symbolic integration of what the spider represents. J. E. Cirlot tells us that the spider is a symbol for the center of both the universe and the psyche.[23] All this makes sense when we recall that Scott's relationship to the spider was clearly foreshadowed, by insecticide, early in the film. Thus, Scott cannot avoid the spider if he is to survive his crisis; it is through his struggle with the spider that Scott gains his mystical understanding of his place in the universe.

Arnold's *The Incredible Shrinking Man*, a significantly altered version of Richard Matheson's novel *The Shrinking Man*, was released in 1957.[24] Both Matheson's novel and William Whyte's influential study *The Organization Man* were published in 1956.[25] All three describe the problems and anomie of the rapidly changing postwar environment. Significantly, after leaving the navy, Robert Scott Carey becomes an organization man in his brother's firm. Scott is stuck in a job in which he finds little fulfillment, and his wife good-naturedly dissuades him from fantasies of more than his yearly two weeks' vacation. Vacations are safer than journeys but have less opportunity for individual growth or change.

Scott's shrinking is a somatic symptom or symbolic expression of an even deeper anagogic crisis. This is the crisis of a veteran trying to adjust to civilian life, and a reluctant organization man who lives without the hope of adventure and heroism or a future with fulfillment. Later, the media's intrusive attention only further diminishes Scott's sense of personhood. His doctors, likewise, can see only the illness and not the patient's anagogic experience, his hopelessness. For many theologians, philosophers, physicians, and prophets of the apocalypse, hope is, as noted medical humanist Eric J. Cassell puts it, "one of the necessary traits of a successful life." Hope, and, as Cassell writes, the perception that suffering can be an "enlarging" experience, an "*engine that drives* [one] *toward enrichment*—toward fulfillment in dimensions of the human condition other than those closed by the illness or toward attainment of some transcendental goal" (emphasis in original), are what helps us to understand or give meaning to, and overcome, oppressive conditions.[26]

In the light of this film, it is indeed ironic that Cassell, in his influential study *The Nature of Suffering and the Goals of Medicine*, writes that "Persons are able to enlarge themselves in response to damage, so that rather than being reduced by injury, they may indeed grow."[27] Midway through the film, before being trapped in the basement, Scott meets a female midget who works as a circus freak, and she helps him find the hope and courage to rebuild his future. But this is just the beginning of healing, and Scott's crisis can only be resolved by his encounter with the spider. Journeys, especially journeys to other worlds, and battles, especially battles with strange creatures, are frequent metaphors for crisis and psychological transformation. Scott's shrinking and confrontation with the spider in his basement are, in other words, his heroic journey. The awakening or *growth* of Scott's spiritual life—in response to the diminution of his physical or mundane life—takes the form of a revelation, and that is what completes the apocalyptic nature of this bomb film. At the end of the film, Scott crawls out of the confines of his own basement and into the limitless potential of his garden. He looks up into the skies and comes to a profound understanding of his place in the universe. For the first time since the film began, Scott seems exuberant about his future:

> What was I, still a human being, or was I the man of the future? If there were other bursts of radiation, other clouds drifting across seas and continents, would other beings follow me into this vast new world? . . . [Now small enough, Scott crawls through the screen in a vent to the garden.] I looked up as if somehow I would grasp the heavens, the universe, worlds beyond number, God's silver tapestry spread across the night. . . . My fears melted away, and in their place came acceptance. All this vast majesty of creation [the camera cranes up from the insect-sized Scott in a jungle of grass, and dissolves into the stars], it had to mean something. And then I

meant something too. Yes, smaller than the smallest, I meant something too. To God there is no zero. I still exist [the camera focuses on Jupiter and we hear the music that ends the film].

The possibility of a community of others like Scott, a just world, and fulfillment expresses Peter Clecak's American quest for the ideal self. The images, visual and verbal, used to describe this quest are also religious, alchemical, and mythological symbols of psychic transformation.[28]

At the end of Scott's journey he has gained a mystical understanding of the ultimate reality of things, and he communes with God. This is a common feature of the apocalyptic genre. While it might be possible to describe these experiences objectively, such descriptions fail to evoke the experience. Logic and descriptive language is an inadequate vehicle for mystical experience. Communicating these experiences is the job of the expressive forms of culture: ritual, poetry, and the visual and performing arts. In atomic bomb cinema, *The Incredible Shrinking Man* is one of the finest examples of the evocative symbolic expression of mystical experience.

Jack Arnold is one of the most prolific and imaginative directors of bomb films; and, although his films avoid happily-ever-after endings, they are usually hopeful. Most of his films take a strong position against nuclear weapons. *The Incredible Shrinking Man*, however, is an odd film, for the benefits of the bomb clearly outweigh the costs. This is, moreover, a revolutionary film in many ways. The narrative, for instance, can be read as a radical departure from generic tradition. The crisis that Robert Scott Carey experiences brings him back into harmony with nature, and it brings about his understanding of humanity's place in the universe. This understanding, expressed in his final soliloquy, is filled with the consciousness-disrupting contradictions that one finds in a Zen Buddhist *koan* (e.g., a paradoxical question or story). Also, Scott never really goes anywhere geographically, instead remaining in his own home during most of the film, and in the end he spiritually enters and becomes one with the universe. This Buddhist, or Buddhist-like, conception of human experience, and the narrative resolution, is probably unique in Western atomic bomb cinema. It is ironic, considering that the bomb has helped engender this new consciousness in America; and yet, this drawing from other generic, symbolic, and cultural traditions is in keeping with the apocalyptic narrative tradition. That is to say that in contradistinction to *Them!* this film is more concerned with the individual than the community—the bomb brings about a progressive change in Scott's consciousness, and all that he gains from his diminution is summed up in the final images: because Scott survives the crisis and learns humility he is allowed to reenter, or revolve back into, his Garden of Eden.

Scott takes an otherworldly journey in which he sees many strange things. Of course, at first he does not understand their meaning. Traditionally, a supernatural being would interpret or reveal their meanings to the traveler. But there is no such being. Most apocalyptic texts, furthermore, use an eminent historical person as the central character. Scott is an ordinary suburban dweller. The absence of a supernatural being and an eminent person at first seems to confound my thesis that *The Incredible Shrinking Man* is an apocalyptic narrative. However, the apocalyptic genre freely draws on many different sources and traditions. Fairy tales, myths, and legends often feature ordinary characters, or characters who do not know their supraordinary status, or who go on incredible adventures. Prior to battling with the spider, Scott sees a bird in his garden. Cirlot says birds are generally associated with the human soul, thought, imagination, and the spiritual process; and according to George Ferguson, in Christian tradition it can represent the spiritual, the Holy Ghost, and the Annunciation to Mary. Thus, the presence of a supernatural being is evoked by the otherwise insignificant presence of the bird (the word of God in Christian symbology). But Scott is separated from both the bird and the garden, and does not understand their significance.[29] After killing the spider Scott is covered in its blood. Exhausted, he falls asleep. When Scott wakes, he goes through the vent to the garden and gives voice to his new understanding of the universe. These scenes and symbols form an elaborate symbol for rebirth. However, the revelation takes place in a modern suburban town. What is important here is that in *The Incredible Shrinking Man* all the major elements of an apocalypse are expressed as symbols that form a revelation, and this revelation is retold or interpreted by the traveler to his audience in a way that exhorts others to follow his path.

While Boyer is substantially correct in pointing out the fear of atmospheric testing that drives this film, he misses the subtextual mark by saying that the film's roots lay in the fear of genetic mutation.[30] Other scholars not only miss the mark, they cannot even find the target. Sayre claims that in science fiction films of the 1950s, including *The Incredible Shrinking Man*, "the future—once an exhilarating concept—grew more ominous: there was no longer any assurance that one had any place in it, that continuity could be counted on." Robert Scott Carey, she writes, "becomes a pathetic homunculus."[31] Sayre's assertions are completely antithetical to what Carey says in his final soliloquy, and what the film suggests through symbols and the use of the cinematic apparatus. *The Incredible Shrinking Man* does hold out the promise or assurance of salvation and transcendence from the trials and tribulations of this world, through the gaining of mystical knowledge and the possibility of community. H. Bruce Franklin writes that "Perhaps the metaphor that most eloquently expresses a common sublimated self-image of the individual in a nuclear world is the 1957 movie *The Incredible Shrinking Man*; after passing through a radioactive cloud, the protagonist becomes smaller and smaller, more and more insignificant, until he disappears."[32] What Franklin, like many other theory-driven scholars, fails to recognize is the enantiomorphic nature of symbols; that is, that every symbol contains its opposite. If we are to take Franklin's thesis seriously, are we also to believe that the increased size of the ants in *Them!* is a metaphor for their increased political significance and a new self-image? Hardly. Scott's monologue clearly points out that he is cosmologically and theologically very significant. Furthermore, in Scott's world there are no isolated events. His transformation is synecdochical for changes in the culture. Anagogic transformation may not be important in historical-materialist analysis. But it is important to the culture.

All this is in keeping with the narrative tradition of the apocalyptic imagination. In apocalyptic texts, mystical knowledge empowers the powerless by teaching how to transcend oppressive conditions and thus prevail over evil. Mystical knowledge, more importantly, empowers us to overcome our individual sufferings because we see them as part of a transcendental plan ordained by God. Just as in *On the Beach*, the bomb or radiation is an important issue in the film. But the bomb itself is a MacGuffin used to explore the deeper meanings of contemporary society and culture within the context of a world faced with the threat of nuclear annihilation. Here again, the apocalyptic imagination, crisis, and the American quest, along with Cassell's ideas on the experience of suffering and transcendence, dovetail rather nicely.

One final, important point about Robert Scott Carey remains to be explored: his status as a war veteran. The war veteran plays a prominent role in atomic bomb cinema in such films as *Split Second* (1953), *Escape from New York* (John Carpenter, 1981) and its sequel *John Carpenter's Escape from L.A.* (John Carpenter, 1996), *The Terminator* (James Cameron, 1984), *Steel Dawn* (Lance Hool, 1987), among many others.

So, rather than limit our analysis of the veteran to the character of Robert Scott Carey, I would prefer to look at a bomb film that more fully explores the existential condition of the war veteran.

Of all these characters in atomic bomb cinema, none is more poignant than Colonel Glenn Manning (Glenn Langan), the hero of Bert I. Gordon's 1957 film *The Amazing Colossal Man* (and his 1958 sequel, *War of the Colossal Beast*). This low-budget film is one of the best-known 1950s bomb films, yet it too has received only scant attention in the scholarly literature. This is not surprising, for the text and the subtext seem to be at odds. The film, on the one hand, fits easily into the nuclear paranoia rubric. To some extent Colonel Manning does symbolize or represent a 1950s America traumatized by nuclear fears. The insignia for an army colonel, the "full bird," is, after all, an American bald eagle, the official totemic animal of the United States.[33] Also, *The Amazing Colossal Man* depicts only the catastrophic events of the apocalypse, the illness and suffering and death, and not the apocalyptic genre's paradigmatic morality of rebirth and continuance. The exhortation of the audience, on the other hand, is very unclear and buried deep in the subtext. Indeed, while the film does explore the hero's existential condition, he does not survive and nothing is revealed to him; this is exactly what makes Manning's suffering so poignant. And yet, the very complex and multivalent subtext indicates there is a lot more to this film than mere psychic numbing and nuclearism. Thus, what makes *The Amazing Colossal Man* so illuminating, in our discussion of the apocalyptic imagination in atomic bomb cinema, is that, to some extent, it is a counterexample to the typical bomb film narrative.

At five A.M., that magic time between night and day, between dreams and reality, when anything can happen, Colonel Glenn Manning is crouched in a trench somewhere on a nuclear test site in Nevada. It is a very special day, for a plutonium bomb will be detonated for the first time. And following the test, Manning is supposed to marry his fiancée. A small, private aircraft strays into the restricted airspace, stalls, and crashes. Manning disobeys orders to stay in the relative safety of his trench. As he runs to the aid of the pilot, Manning looks up at the bomb sitting atop its tower, and is dumbstruck at the sight. Just then, the bomb detonates. Manning covers his eyes as he is struck by the powerful blast. Just before the scene dissolves, we see a now bald, nearly naked Manning standing alone in the dark. It is a striking image.

Manning's skin has been literally burned away. Miraculously, though, Manning grows new skin overnight, but remains bald. H. Arthur Taussig says that hair, or what he calls "displaced hair," is a frequent symbol that alerts us, at least unconsciously, to villainy or a character who is in some way not what he or she seems to be. Depending on the culture, this can be too much or not enough hair on some part of the body.[34] Not only does Manning grow new skin, he continues to grow larger, eventually towering over Las Vegas casinos, and he becomes demented. Eventually, in a reenactment of *King Kong*'s final scene, he puts down the woman he loves so the army can get a clear shot at him, and then he falls into the waters below Hoover Dam. Throughout this film there is an intense questioning, by all the characters, of why this strange event should happen, yet no clear answer—the type of reassuring, narrative-closing answer that we have come to expect from B-grade science fiction films—is ever given.

Clearly, too much is going on in this film for it to be merely about nuclear-induced paranoia, but the subtext does not easily open itself to interpretation. The film, furthermore, appears to be a confusion of many unrelated symbols: the bomb; enormous growth; baldness; a giant, phallus-like syringe; a failed attempted at injecting a lifesaving serum into the marrow of Manning's calf bone; and Manning's use of the syringe to impale one of his doctors. Still, there are some clues that can help us resolve some of the film's enigmas.

Toward the end of the film, as the colossal Manning slips further into dementia, he rhetorically asks Carol Forest (Cathy Downs), his fiancée, "What sin can a man commit in a single lifetime to bring this upon himself?" Unlike Oedipus, Manning is never able to answer the question, and thus never learns the truth of his own identity. Carol reassuringly tells him there is still hope that the doctors can "bring you back to normal," but Manning retorts, "You don't really believe that! They'll never find a cure for me." The argument causes him sudden heart pain, and before leaving to sulk in his tent he tells Carol: "I'm all right, I'm all right. I just don't want to grow any more. I don't want to grow any more." For Manning, the doctor explains in graphic detail, the problem is not that he is growing, but that his heart is not keeping pace with the rest of his body. What Cassell would call the "personhood" of Glenn Manning is, metaphorically, beginning to disintegrate. This metaphor of growth is strikingly similar to what we find in the scholarly literature and daily discourse, where it is common to hear people say—with great anxiety in their voices—that the nuclear dilemma demonstrates how humanity's moral development has not kept pace with its technological development. Also, Manning's refusal to grow, when taken as a psychological metaphor, is a determination to die. Despite the doctors' promises of a cure, Manning, unlike Robert Scott Carey, is unable to find hope, which Cassell considers so necessary to "a successful life." But what could change such a gentle and altruistic man into this cruel and self-destructive monster? The answer lies in Manning's repressed memories seen in a dream, an important part of the film never talked about in the scholarly literature.

Following his injury from the bomb blast, Manning is in a coma, but is awoken by a distressing dream. The dream begins with the newspaper headlines "U.S. Enters Korean War." At a picnic, Carol is upset that Manning, a reservist who at first did not wait to be called up, actually enlisted. He tells her that he is thinking about "the future," especially theirs, and then they kiss. The scene dissolves into newsreels of the Korean War. Then we see Manning in hand-to-hand combat, killing two enemy soldiers, and blasting one in the face with his weapon. Unlike Manning, the North Korean soldier does not cover his face in time—an important symbol suggesting that though Manning survives he has seen too much. He survives but his buddy does not. Manning is visibly stunned by the gruesome carnage he has made of another human being, and the shock of a friend dying in his arms. A dissolve to a hero's welcome home, another picnic, and then the fateful bomb test that changed him forever. At this point, Glenn Manning awakens from his coma, deeply troubled, and to the shock that he has become a "freak." In this dream lies the answer to Manning's troubling question: What sin did I commit to justify this suffering?

Glenn Manning is no Job; his sins are obvious. Though the cause may have been just, his sin is, still, the killing of another human being. Worse than the sin itself, Manning has not expiated his sins by taking the journey to hell that other soldiers, like Odysseus and Robert Scott Carey, take following a war. *The Amazing Colossal Man* is more than a film of nuclear fear; it is one of many films made about war veterans that follow every war. The excellent *Wings* (William Wellman, 1929) and the more famous *All Quiet on the Western Front* (Lewis Milestone, 1930) stand out as early examples. More recently, there is the plethora of Vietnam films, which includes the obvious *Platoon* (Oliver Stone, 1986), the not-so-obvious *Cool Hand Luke* (Stuart Rosenberg, 1967), and the relatively obscure but very important *House* (Steve Miner, 1986). There is also Clint Eastwood's 1986 film that spans Korea, Vietnam, and Grenada: *Heartbreak Ridge*. And, of course, there is the ultimate Korean War veteran's film, *The Manchurian Candidate* (John Frankenheimer, 1962). But in marked contrast to other wars, there has been very little public discussion about the war in Korea, and, I suspect, Korean War films are relatively rare. *The Amazing Colossal Man*, in a desperately quiet way, tells us the story of one Korean War veteran—who could be the veteran of any war—suffering from shell shock, or what is now called "posttraumatic stress disorder."

In *Memories, Dreams, Reflections*, C. G. Jung notes that psychologically healthy "soldiers in the field dreamt far less of war than of their homes." Conversely, "Military psychiatrists considered it a basic principle that a man should be pulled out of the front lines when he started dreaming too much of war scenes, for that meant he no longer possessed any psychic defenses against the impressions from outside."[35] Manning has gone to war and done things no one ready to marry and start a family expects to see or do (much as my own father did during the Korean War). Then, out of altruistic motives, he comes face-to-face with the awful destructive power of the bomb. These are life-changing experiences; we might even say experiences that can bring about personal growth and a deeper understanding of the human condition. But they can also bring about a most profound personal *crisis*. Manning, however, internalizes but cannot assimilate these experiences; he dreams more of war and horror than of home and happiness. Finally, he cannot *rebuild* himself, as Cassell puts it, by focusing his energy toward self-understanding and positive new goals.[36] Rather than trying to come to terms with his crisis, Manning says only, "I just don't want to grow any more." He has, in psychological jargon, "foreclosed" his identity to the possibility of growth beyond the crisis. Adding to this, his experiences have made him an outcast, and his doctors treat the illness while coldly neglecting the person. At this point, the film offers no more clues as to why Glenn Manning should not survive his crisis. When Carol pleadingly asks why such a bad thing should happen to such a nice guy, a sympathetic reporter can only say that "Things like this just happen, there doesn't have to be a reason."

The bomb, while important in this film, is, again, a MacGuffin. It adds a narrative device that makes this fantastic story about a giant acceptable to audiences of the late twentieth century, but it is only part of the hero's anagogic experiences. The bomb, moreover, is merely the last of many hardships that Manning experiences, the proverbial last straw. *The Amazing Colossal Man* is, in a word, the moving story of one victim of posttraumatic stress disorder who does not survive. The film does have a rather disturbing message, that the human heart has not yet developed enough to solve the nuclear dilemma. This film, however, is not a tragedy, for Manning, sadly, learns nothing from his experiences. He is simply destroyed by them. *The Amazing Colossal Man* is, as stated above, a bomb film but seems to be only a marginal *apocalyptic* narrative; for, while the hero goes on several otherworldly journeys, no salvational, transcendental reality is revealed. In an ambiguous, perhaps poetic, way, the film nevertheless exhorts the audience against the perils of war, rapid social and technological change, and, especially, turning away from a crisis. *The Amazing Colossal Man* is, thus, one of the exceptions that, as we will see in the next film, makes the rule all the more interesting.

Perhaps the quintessential bomb film of the period from 1950 to 1963, if not the entire postwar era, is the 1960 film *The Time Machine*, produced and directed by George Pal. H. G. Wells first published *The Time Machine* in 1895. His central character is known simply as the Time Traveler, and the story is told by a second person. The film, however, uses a first-person narrative flashback in which the central character describes his own story, and the central character is none other than H. G. Wells himself. The film is a story within a story. Wells travels to the future, returns to the present to recount his adventure to his friends, which takes up the majority of the film text, then travels back to the future. It takes Wells approximately ninety minutes to tell his story, roughly the length of the film. The film, moreover, seems simple but is surprisingly rich and multifaceted, demanding a more careful and nuanced reading than it has received in the relevant scholarly literature.

The story takes place when the British are at war in South Africa. However, images of the First and Second World Wars, allusions to subsequent and future wars, and, most importantly, images of the bomb, bring the narrative up-to-date. These specific historical events, as well as the hopes and fears that gripped people fifteen years after the bombing of Hiroshima and Nagasaki, are structured as a historical revelation in a secular apocalypse.

The film begins with sundials, clocks, and the Big Ben clock tower floating against a dark background (this image is repeated in Nicolas Roeg's 1985 bomb film *Insignificance*), followed by an explosion and fireball. As the fireball rises it illuminates the title and author's name. The story itself begins on January 5, 1900, at 8 P.M. Four friends have gathered for dinner at the home of inventor H. George Wells (Rod Taylor). Their host is conspicuously absent. Suddenly Wells enters the room and collapses in his guests' arms. Though disheveled and exhausted, Wells insists on telling his story while the details are still fresh in his mind. His best friend, David Filby (Alan Young), tells him to relax: "You've got all the time in the world."

As Wells begins his story the scene dissolves into December 31, 1899, when they witnessed Wells's latest invention: a miniature time travel machine. Wells announces his intention to travel to the future, and to prove he has the means, he sends the miniature prototype into the future. His incredulous friends, however, dismiss his invention as mere parlor magic. So, a dejected Wells climbs into a full-scale time machine and travels forward in time. At each stop he witnesses war. On August 18, 1966 Wells witnesses a nuclear war and the consequent volcanic destruction of the world. He barely escapes a fiery death, but he cannot stop moving forward in time until October 12, 802701, when his time machine stops beneath an odd cave with a sphinx overlooking the entrance. There he finds a post-nuclear-holocaust Edenic world. This world is inhabited by two peoples. There are the childlike Eloi, and the technologically advanced mutant Morlocks that feed, clothe, and then cannibalize the Eloi. Wells falls in love with an Eloi, Weena (Yvette Mimieux), who is later taken by the Morlocks to be eaten. Wells rescues Weena and destroys the Morlocks' caverns. The surviving Morlocks set a trap for him, but he escapes by returning to his own time—just in time for his dinner party. A dissolve concludes the flashback. Wells then shows his friends a flower, given to him by Weena, that Filby says is unknown to any scientist. Yet, his friends still remain incredulous. So, Wells returns to the Eloi and Weena. The only things Wells takes with him on his return trip are three unidentified books, with which to help him rebuild civilization. The spectator is left wondering which books. The housekeeper, Mrs. Watchett, asks Filby, "Do you think he will ever return?" Filby's reply brings us back full circle to the very beginning of the film: "One cannot but wonder. You see, he has all the time in the world."

The characterization of H. G. Wells at first seems confused. He is withdrawn from the social world at home but highly involved in the events of the future. This, however, is in keeping with the complex nature of American politics and culture in the 1950s and 1960s; that is, the many competing aspects of American culture are condensed into the character of H. George Wells. He is highly critical of the world in which he lives, saying "I don't much care for the time I was born into. It seems people aren't dying fast enough these days, they call upon science to invent new, more efficient weapons to depopulate the earth." And yet, Wells never challenges the status quo. Instead, he flees to the future.

Once in the future, Wells comes into conflict with another technological society. He and the Morlocks compete for influence (or hegemony) over the Eloi. In other words, Wells's battle with the Morlocks is analogous to the American policy of "containing" the Soviet threat of world dominance while fulfilling the American manifest destiny. Like so many Americans during the 1950s and early '60s, Wells avoids political conflict at home but takes the lead in the future. Wells does for/to the Eloi what the Occupation did for/to the Japanese, what the Marshall Plan did for/to Europe, and what the Peace Corps has done for/to many other peoples. In this way, the central character paints a typical portrait of the middle-class, Anglo-American man: frightened of the bomb, yet confident that science and technology, governed by liberal social institutions, will eventually build a paradise. Politics is, however, a minor theme in this film.

The Time Machine is, above all else, the story of a hero's journey or quest for mystical knowledge, or in the psychological vernacular, self-actualization. Yet, it is a journey that is structured by a particularly American conception of the individual in relationship to society. When Wells first announces his intention to travel in time, one of his friends inquires if this won't affect the course of history. Wells says he is prepared to take that risk. Another friend objects to the very notion. "The future," he says, "is irrevocable." Wells responds pensively:

> I wonder. You know, that is the most important question to which I hope to find an answer: can man control his destiny, can he change the shape of things to come?

(*The Shape of Things to Come* is the title of another Wells novel, published in 1933 and made into the proto–bomb film *Things to Come* in 1936, directed by William Cameron Menzies.) Like most heroic journeys, this one starts out with a riddle. There is even the sphinx-like statue overlooking the entrance to the Morlocks' caverns.

Ostensibly, Wells seeks answers to the social injustices of his own time. He travels to the future in search of hope, even solutions, and especially some way to prevent wars. However, he comes away with answers to questions he did not anticipate. What Wells discovers is a society of which he can feel a part, people to whom he can commit himself, and a community for which he is willing to fight. Previously, Wells stood aloof from society, condemned the wars, and hid himself in his laboratory. Now, in the land of the Eloi, he becomes an active participant. He even risks his own life and kills to protect his adopted home. Wells discovers something in addition to social commitment: personal satisfaction through love. What Wells discovers is something that Peter Clecak argues in his book *America's Quest for the Ideal Self: Dissent and Fulfillment in the '60s and '70s*, is essential to the American character.

Clecak shows that America is driven by three themes, or what he calls Quests. These are the Quests for Social Justice, a Community of Like-Minded Others, and Personal Fulfillment. Furthermore, these Quests coalesced during the 1960s into "The Movement," and then began to fragment in the 1970s, drawing different people to different Quests.[37] While it might take a stretch of the imagination to label *The Time Machine* a movement or counterculture film when compared to, for example, the self-indulgent road film *Easy Rider* (Dennis Hopper, 1969) · or the contentious bomb film *Silent Running* (Douglas Trumbull, 1971), it does express similar concerns. In a sense, then, we see in *The Time Machine* the very pattern of sociocultural development that Clecak later defines. Again, Wells has a revulsion to war; he is motivated by the Quest for Social Justice; he adopts a Community of Like-Minded Others; and he finds Personal Fulfillment through love. Once he reports to his friends the answers he has found, Wells retreats to the Community of Like-Minded others where he pursues self-fulfillment through love and work.

Clearly, Wells is going through an identity crisis—a crisis which, according to Erikson, can lead to a new identity formation. And, from the very beginning of the film it is clear that Wells is in search of community, identity, and especially a meaningful normative relationship. The only woman he has contact with is his aged, asexual, and unchanging Mrs. Watchett. His relationship to her is one of dependency, like a child to a mother. Filby, moreover, invites Wells to spend New Year's eve with his wife and child. And though Wells is visibly pleased by the idea, he declines. Wells needs his own home, not a surrogate. Filby, however, remains worried, and extracts from Wells a promise that he will not leave his front door until morning.

The door, a symbolic portal into another psychological state, is a major motif in the film. The further Wells travels into the future, the farther through the doorway he can pass. Once Wells moves into the near future he can cross his own doorway. Further into the future, Wells twice approaches Filby's home, but stops at the stairs. Once he is even invited inside, but declines. On Filby's door we see a Red Cross poster of a nun offering succor to all who are in need. The home is the hearth and haven from the heartless world. Yet Wells cannot ascend the stairs because he is not at home. He prefers his trip into the distant future, a trip he takes while remaining completely at home; that is, the time machine only travels through time, he never takes it outside the space that is his workshop, although others later move it for him just beyond his door.

The first thing Wells sees in the future new world is a sphinx. These images, the sphinx, Wells's murder of the Morlocks, and his desire to possess Weena at first seem to suggest that there is an ego conflict in the subtext of *The Time Machine*, and that a Freudian reading is required. Robert J. Lifton, the leading scholar in the humanistic study of persons exposed to atomic bombs, and a social psychologist in the psychoanalytic tradition, however, warns us that the Oedipal desire to kill one's father and sleep with one's mother may in fact symbolize other psychosocial experiences.[38] Therefore, we must be sensitive to other symbolic interpretations.

The image of this particular sphinx at first suggests the effects of time, that great civilizations wane, that knowledge and organization fall into chaos. As a symbol, however, the sphinx is quite heterogeneous, referring to the mother-image, nature symbolism, and the multiplicity of the cosmos, enigma, and, says Cirlot, an ultimate meaning to the cosmos that is "forever beyond the understanding of man."[39] The sphinx is also emblematic of Wells's quest to discover if man can control his destiny and shape things to come. After seeing the sphinx, Wells comes to the communal hall of the Eloi, and to a doorway that he can, at last, cross—into the hall, a portal into a new world. The hall is laid out in the shape of a mandala. The mandala symbolizes the desire for completeness, centeredness, and order.[40] Thus, when Wells enters the hall, where he eats from a rich harvest of fruit, he is symbolically approaching the goal of his journey in all its sociocultural, political, and psychological ramifications.

After entering the hall, Wells goes to the river where he finds the Eloi. There, as the Eloi stand idly by, he saves Weena from drowning. The Eloi are a reflection of his own political indifference, psychological alienation, and emotional distance from women. The river is an ambiguous symbol. "On the one hand," Cirlot writes, "it signifies fertility and the progressive irrigation of the soil; and on the other hand it stands for the irreversible passage of time and, in consequence, for a sense of loss and oblivion." More commonly, making contact with water signals a regeneration or rebirth of the individual, as in the baptism.[41] Thus, Wells is at risk of forever losing contact with women in general as he sees Weena drawn into the rapids of the river. So, he acts quickly, instinctively, to rescue Weena. In so doing, Wells is irrigated with the redemptive powers of instinct, saved from the muddle of experimental science that marks his normal life. Indeed, just like Clayton Forester in Pal's earlier production, *The War of the Worlds* (1953), Wells saves himself by saving another (Weena). But *The Time Machine* goes beyond the shallowness of the individual saving himself through love, and criticizes the construction of the masculine identity in patriarchal Western society.

Later in the story, the Morlocks take Weena to their caverns for dinner, and Wells saves her a second time (see figure 3). Caverns are mysterious, one might say even womblike, or the contained world of the unconscious. The caverns are also heavily allusive. Hades, of course, is where mythological characters frequently travel. Orpheus, a good example of a lover in the underworld, travels there to retrieve his beloved Eurydice. The "Journey into Hell," Cirlot writes, "symbolizes the descent into the unconscious, or the awareness of all the potentialities of being—cosmic and psychological—that are needed in order to reach the Paradisiac heights."[42] Strong words, but nonetheless a mythic pattern that drives this futuristic bomb film. In the Morlocks' caverns Wells destroys yet another aspect of his former self. As Madonna Kolbenschlag suggests in *Lost in the Land of Oz*, by fixating on logic, competition, and production, men turn into cannibals of women.[43] In the bifurcated new world the Morlocks are the manifestation of this destructive potential in Western men. Likewise, should the scientist and inventor H. George Wells fail to survive the journey, his crisis, he would become a Morlock. Thus, just as in *Them!* where Robert enters a sewer to destroy his monsters, Wells enters the caverns to destroy the Morlocks and symbolically save himself and Weena from his own potential for misogynistic cannibalism. Wells's adventure in the Morlocks' cavern also symbolizes his psychological maturation into a person capable of healthy relationships with women. However, despite all that Wells achieves, his journey of psychological rebirth is not over. Wells confesses to feeling "trapped in a world in which I don't belong." So he must take what he has learned and return to his own time.

What follows Wells's return to his own time is a familiar feature of popular, bourgeois films. Frequently the last few minutes of the film form a coda, which, according to H. Arthur Taussig, can either subvert any radical message and reassert the status quo or subvert the status quo and assert a radical message.[44] In 1960s mainstream American culture it was not enough for Wells to return to his own time with the potential for a healthy relationship. The potential must be consummated. Boy must get girl. Yet, it is too late in the narrative to introduce a new character, and for Wells to have brought Weena back to his time would reopen another narrative, one involving what happens when new-world natives are brought back to the old world (an idea that Gerald Vizenor confronts directly in his novel *The Heirs of Columbus*).[45] Therefore, at the last moment, Wells has no choice but to, in the words of Mrs. Watchett, return to Weena "right where he left her."

So far we have examined the sociopolitical and psychosocial aspects of Wells's journey into the future. What we have yet to discuss is the importance of the Edenic myth to American culture, why the destruction of the Morlocks is necessary to Wells's successful resolution of his crisis, and the peculiarity of American violence. On the one hand, violence can express psychological processes. Myths and fairy tales throughout the world depict violent transformations. Violence can, on the other hand, express sociological and psychological realities. Richard Slotkin, in his seminal book *Regeneration through Violence: The Mythology of the American Frontier, 1600–1860*, argues, simply, that "[t]he first colonists saw in America an opportunity to regenerate their fortunes, their spirits, and the power of their church and nation; but the means to that regeneration ultimately became the means of violence, and the myth of regeneration though violence became the structuring metaphor of the American Experience."[46] Slotkin concentrates on narratives about the colonists' struggles against the Native Americans, but also draws parallels to other episodes of extreme violence in American history, including the war in Vietnam.

The Native Americans, in particular, provided the colonists with a paradox. The resolution of the paradox inevitably led to violence. If the New World was the land of chaos then its inhabitants must be subdued. If, however, the New World was *Arcadia*, or in fact Eden, the "Indians" were either despoilers or those who had not experienced a fall from grace and therefore could not experience God's forgiveness and redemption. In any case, Puritan values demanded that something be done. This amounted to either killing them or saving them through captivity, indoctrination, and baptism. More frequently than not, the latter led to the former. But the colonists were not only reclaiming Eden and saving the savages, they were also redeeming themselves. Through their own hardships, including capture, torture, and the battles they fought with the Indians, the Puritans emulated the redemptive sufferings of Christ and performed God's work.

Likewise, Wells's course of action is clear and determined by axiomatic precepts about the nature of the world. He must save the Eloi from the Morlocks. Thus, Wells acts out the myth of reclaiming the new-world Eden from the wilderness, settling the wild American frontier, bringing salvation to the good Eloi, and destroying the degenerate Morlocks. Like the colonists before him, Wells experiences regeneration through ritualistic bloodletting. Furthermore, for the hero of *The Time Machine* there is no ambiguity. It is perfectly obvious who are the despoilers of Eden and who are the primitives in need of salvation. Eden had been clearly bifurcated into the evil Morlocks and the good but simple Eloi. Such a Manichaean vision gives the hero moral impunity and ensures there are no mistakes; or, in the modern vernacular, no collateral casualties. *The Time Machine* is the product of an Anglo writer, an immigrant European filmmaker who redeemed himself in America and 1960s Hollywood; the expression of regeneration through violence seems, in retrospect, obvious.

The Time Machine is a complicated film, and the character of H. George Wells is not determined by only the myths established during the colonial era. Wells is also typical of how modern scientists are portrayed in atomic bomb cinema of this period, 1950 to 1963. Since American cultural mythology is based on external deeds as evidence of internal character, the culture's heroes are extroverts, which is a problem for the stereotypical introverted scientist. Fictional scientists of this period frequently encounter events that force a change in their psychological dispositions, and they move from being introverts to extroverts. There are, of course, parallel figures in other genres that foreshadow the Wells character. However, in this case Oppenheimer, the brilliant but introverted young scientist turned public figure, did much to establish the mythology of the scientist in the 1950s and '60s.

Oppenheimer is most often characterized as a solemn, pensive person who tried to remain aloof from people, preferring poetry to politics. However, after being recruited by the military and made director of the Manhattan Project, an astonishing transformation occurred. He became the consummate personnel director. He was deft at handling personal and professional differences, and he motivated people when things seemed impossible. John Else's well-known 1981 documentary, *The Day after Trinity*, for instance, portrays Oppenheimer as an almost mythical, larger-than-life figure; it celebrates his transformation from aloof scientist to personable leader, and mourns the tragedy of his transformation back to scientist and poet. Indeed, Oppenheimer was near universally respected and trusted as both a leader and as a scientist. This is an unusual accomplishment for one so introverted. Once the war was over, Oppenheimer's persona began to change back into that of an introvert. His answers to official inquires became more poetic and elliptical. In public he frequently quoted obscure and arcane texts. It is little wonder that the military and the Atomic Energy Commission stripped him of his security clearance. To military minds, anyone who looks inside him- or herself for answers, as introverts do, instead of looking to the chain of command, is a threat to the entire organization. In the end, Oppenheimer was not the "organization man."

In Pal's *The War of the Worlds*, Clayton Forester is clearly modeled after J. Robert Oppenheimer. In the course of the film he changes from the introverted bookworm scientist into the heroic man of action and the lover. Likewise, in *The Time Machine* H. George Wells starts out as a solitary introvert who prefers his laboratory, then becomes a leader of men, a hero, and a lover. This psychological movement is evoked, symbolically, by the slight spatial movement of the time machine in and out of George's workshop. While the combination of poet and scientist reaches its apotheosis in atomic bomb cinema, it has a long tradition in Anglo-American literature.

At the end of *The Time Machine* there are three books missing from Wells's library. Is this an allusion to Prospero's twenty-four unnamed books in Shakespeare's *The Tempest*? Possibly, but it is not important. What is important is the clear differences and similarities between the characters of Prospero and Wells. While both are introverts, Prospero's exile is imposed on him, but Wells's exile is self-imposed. Prospero returns home after learning that he no longer wants to live his life in his self-fashioned new world, and that he must re-enter the world from which he came. Contrarily, Wells abandons his laboratory—but to rule over the Eloi. The clearest difference, however, is that though both claim to be concerned with the ultimate reality of the universe, one is a scientist and the other a magician, the Renaissance equivalent of the master scientist. Prospero learns that the effort to control nature through magic works for only a period, but Wells brings his books with him to the land of the Eloi because he is more convinced than ever that he can control nature through science. Thus, as in Pal's *The War of the Worlds*, the ideology of the film remains euphorically secular and liberal, the walk into the sunset that pales the eminent disaster waiting for the utopian. In terms of psychological narrative, Wells, in the end, has not yet reached the point where Prospero's story virtually begins.

Before considering the apocalyptic dimension of this film we need to examine an image that has hitherto been conspicuously absent from our discussion of *The Time Machine*. Specifically, what are the Morlocks, and why are they so frightening? The Morlocks are, perhaps, an allusion to Moloch in Milton's *Paradise Lost*. The film, however, explains that the Morlocks are the descendants of those humans forced to live underground following the nuclear holocaust. Over the centuries they transmogrified into technologically advanced cannibals. Thus, what makes them so scary is that, in Western ideology, they exhibit both the best and worst characteristics of humanity. Compared to the "primitive" Eloi, the Morlocks are the height of human achievement: they have reason, technology, social structure, culture, and they can plan for the future. It is the Morlocks who insured the survival of all humanity, including the Eloi. Yet in spite of all their achievements, the Morlocks are what Euro-American culture fears most about itself: a savage, inhuman disposition for cannibalizing one another. This answer, however, begs another question.

Why is it that such frightening creatures populate so many science fiction films, especially apocalyptic bomb films? To understand the relationship between the monstrous and the future, we must again look to the past. In a superior study, *The Monstrous Races in Medieval Art and Thought*, John Block Friedman writes about accounts of incredible peoples told by returning European explorers. These stories inspired a great body of literature and art. Friedman demonstrates that the concept of a "primitive" people was not part of the medieval worldview. Rather, to the European explorers, "exotic peoples were often seen as degenerate or fallen from an earlier state of grace in the Judeo-Christian tradition." Friedman also shows that the literature justified European conquest and colonization through the transmogrification of other peoples into monsters.[47] Likewise, the Morlocks are, as the film so clearly establishes, degenerate and therefore evil. Thus, the ideology that allowed the Europeans to subjugate other peoples (and the Nazis to deracinate a range of "degenerates") also allows Wells to destroy the Morlocks with little moral reservation.

The importance of the monstrous to the apocalyptic bomb film sub-category cannot be underestimated. Consider the similarity of the monsters in bomb films to the medieval monsters illustrated in Friedman's book. For example, compare the Martians in *The War of the Worlds* to an eleventh-century Blemmyae (see figure 4); the resemblance is uncanny. (Also, the eyes of the Martians and their camera equipment are compared to television—which posed a monstrous economic threat to the film industry at this time.) The Morlocks in *The Time Machine* and the monster in *The Day the World Ended* (Roger Corman, 1956), also bear a strong resemblance to this Blemmyae, and an even greater resemblance to other medieval monsters in Friedman's book. Both the Martians and the Morlocks are intellectually advanced but biologically degenerate. More importantly, in both *The Time Machine* and *The Day the World Ended* the monsters were once human. In *The Time Machine* the Morlocks escape the postholocaust environment by living in deep caverns—only to mutate into monsters. In *The Day the World Ended* those human beings who are caught in the radioactive mist after a nuclear war become the degenerate race that medieval travelers described. And in both films these monsters must be destroyed if Eden is to be reclaimed.

There is another important, if quite unexpected, similarity that we must now consider. In Japan's 1966 television season, the thirteenth episode of *Ultra Q* (i.e., the first Ultraman series) introduced the monster Jamila (a.k.a. Jamira or Jamilar).[48] In this episode, a rocket ship is lost in deep space and lands on a distant planet. Only the captain, Jamila, is able to adapt and survive, but, for reasons unknown, he transmogrifies into a monster. Embittered, Jamila returns to earth to seek his revenge. Ultraman wrestles, of course, with Jamila but he cannot easily defeat the monster, which is perhaps typical. Rather, just as in *The Day the World Ended,* where rain destroys the monster and purifies the earth, Ultraman uses water to destroy Jamila. Neither monster is bad because they are tragically transmogrified human beings, and therefore quite pathetic. The power of water, a primordial substance, to correct these tragic mistakes, and cleanse and restore the earth, is perhaps universal. This symbolism, and the pathos of the monsters, is certainly in keeping with the motifs of other Japanese "mysterious creature films," and we will return to these ideas in a later chapter. The point here is that the episode's outlook is very dark; although Jamila is a threat that must be subdued, the heroes of the program are quite remorseful and erect a memorial plaque to the heroic captain. It is fairly certain that Jamila's creator, Eiji Tsuburaya, at least knew of Pal's and Corman's films. It is very possible that Tsuburaya studied images of monsters from other times and cultures and knew of the Blemmyae. But it is difficult to say whether Jamila is the direct descendant of these foreign monsters, indigenous Japanese or Asian monsters, or simply the product of Tsuburaya's own unique genius. What is certain, and more important to us, however, is that Jamila looks remarkably like the medieval Blemmyae, as well as Pal's and Corman's monsters, and that Jamila, like these other creatures, is in some way degenerate. Such monsters almost never lose their currency in the culture. Jamila remains quite popular even today, and in 1995 the JR Nishi-Nihon company (or, Japan Railway West) used Jamila (a curious choice) in a poster to promote good manners on its trains.

Jamila is not a product of the bomb. And, for that matter, only the monster in *The Day the World Ended* is a direct product of the bomb, while Jamila, the Morlocks, and the Martians are products of their environments. Whether or not these modern monsters are the direct product of the bomb, or identical to medieval monsters, or even each other, is of secondary importance. What is of primary importance to us is that they all serve the same function. Just as Friedman's medieval monsters helped the people of their time to formulate a meaningful definition of being human, so too do the monsters of our time help us in our struggle to formulate a meaningful definition of *human*. The question is, Have Hiroshima and Nagasaki, Nazi concentration camps, or even American internment camps, and now space travel, changed the definition of human, and if so, how?

The search for a meaningful definition of humanity following the bombing of Hiroshima and Nagasaki is universal. This search, however, is not strictly the product of the bomb, American culture, or even of the Western apocalyptic imagination. The apocalypse is merely a formal strategy used to evoke and explore the question. The search for a meaningful definition of humanity is found in Japanese bomb films, for example, *Gojira* and Akira Kurosawa's *Dreams* (1990), as well as American bomb films. As in the medieval literature that Friedman cites, the monsters in all of these films create a dialectic from which we can determine our humanity—before and after the bomb, and before and after the apocalypse.

Now that we have identified many of the different levels at which *The Time Machine* functions, and many of the different issues it evokes, we are left with the final question: Is *The Time Machine* an apocalyptic bomb film, and if so, what is its contribution to atomic bomb cinema? As I pointed out earlier, George Pal saw firsthand the perversion of Western heroic ideals and reason in the First and Second World Wars. After arriving in America, his animation and feature films often showed a concern for the threat of antidemocratic militarist movements, and more importantly, the desire for a redemptive utopia. Several of his feature films, especially *The War of the Worlds* and *The Time Machine*, link his political and utopic concerns with apocalyptic themes.

The destruction and purification of the world by nuclear weapons, the smiting of the Morlocks, Wells's reclaiming of paradise, and his enlightened rule are all part of the modern apocalyptic imagination. Apocalyptic texts frequently exhort and proselytize. Through fear of punishment and the promise of reward, they exhort backsliders to follow the law while seeking to persuade Gentiles of the one true God. *The Time Machine* is such an exhortative and missionary text. On the one hand, it condemns as heretics and backsliders those who have lost the true Enlightenment faith. Reason was not supposed to enslave and kill, but free humanity from want and toil. The film exhorts members of the "civilized" world to be just, and warns those who would misuse science that they will reap only sorrow from their own misdeeds. At the same time, it foretells a promised land for the righteous. On the other hand, *The Time Machine* also entices the Gentiles to become members of the Enlightenment community by holding out the promise of a better life through science and technology. This is to say, the apocalypse brings about the purification of Earth, a redemptive promised land, and an Enlightenment utopia in which reason and science govern both man and nature. Again, the Morlocks are the heretical users of science and technology, they are doomed by the word of God; though the Eloi are not waiting for anyone or anything, they are the oppressed righteous who are in need of salvation. To the Eloi, Wells is Daniel's "the One Like the Son of Man," a supernatural heavenly savior who redeems the Jews from the oppressive rule of the Gentiles, and to whom the kingdom is given.

From Wells's perspective, he is the traveler who is taken on an otherworldly journey and to whom the unfolding of history is revealed—by, for example, talking rings and futuristic history books that explain why the Morlocks' ancestors descended below the surface while the Eloi's ancestors remained above. Through his otherworldly journey Wells finds the answer to his question, "Can man change the shape of things to come?" (This is, needless to say, a question often asked in apocalyptic literature, and is a source of much contention among theologians: Are our destinies determined by God even before we are born, or do we have free will to determine our own actions?) After the journey it is Wells's mission to recount his revelation to those who will listen and heed the revelation.

From the perspective of Wells's friends, particularly Filby, Wells is the righteous man who has been taken on an otherworldly journey and seen the unfolding of history. Wells returns and recounts his story to a select group of followers who are the foundation for a community. Filby is a believer, the most important disciple, to whom Wells reveals the content and meaning of the revelation, and is entrusted with the sacred objects: the flower that Weena gave to Wells. As a disciple, it is Filby's responsibility to maintain the revelation. Within the narrative it is established that Filby is the executor of Wells's estate. This job is inherited by Filby's son James. Inheritance of sacred trusts is a common feature in Jewish narrative traditions.

From the spectator's perspective, Wells is both the traveler and the supernatural being who interprets the revelation. That is to say, Wells takes the journey and through his own narration interprets the meaning of the revelation. Thus, if we identify with the third-person perspective, the hidden-observer status of the camera, then we are part of the community to whom Wells reveals the events and meaning of the journey. In this way, we are invited to share the film's ideological commitments. Furthermore, the film gives itself credibility by using two techniques typical to the apocalyptic genre. First, it uses *vaticinia ex eventu*, or the telling of past events as though they were in the future and are foretold by the central character. Second, the use of pseudonymity, or the adoption of an important historical persona as the central character, adds authority to the story. The original author, H. G. Wells, referred to the central character only as the Time Traveler. Pal, however, adopts the original author's name for the Time Traveler.

The film, however, also invites the audience to share in Wells's journey. The dissolve into past events is one formal strategy that helps us see events from the hero's perspective. In this way, the film becomes a first-person narrative; and, the audience becomes the first-person narrator, while Wells becomes the supernatural being who interprets the meaning of the revelation. Thus, the audience experiences humanity's greatest crisis and rebirth following the nuclear apocalypse. The audience walks away from the theater somewhat harried from the experience, but confident that they have survived and will survive other such experiences.

Convincing audiences that they can survive is the most important function of the apocalyptic genre, and very important to filmgoers of the 1950s and 1960s. Early apocalypses exhorted and warned the people of future trials and tribulations. But they also foretold a promised land and redemption after the apocalypse. Apocalyptic bomb films function in the same way. The possibility of nuclear war is real and frightening. Even the most optimistic or pronuclear bomb films depict nuclear war as a devastating and radical change. In this day and age everyone is aware of the trials and tribulations that will follow a nuclear war—that is, if we survive at all. In the apocalyptic tradition all other ideological concerns are secondary to the promise of crisis and rebirth. *The Time Machine*, like all apocalyptic bomb films, promises hope and survival. As Cassell reminds us, without hope a "successful life" is impossible; likewise, without confidence in humanity's survival after the apocalypse, politics is an academic exercise.

Wells discovers that he cannot change the world from which he comes. And yet, he can change his own life by traveling to another time where he can build a new community. (Establishing new communities for the righteous is, again, a common theme found in ancient apocalyptic literature and elsewhere, most obviously in the expressive forms of culture in the United States.) Thus, *The Time Machine* indicates to us that political empowerment is out of reach and we have no hope of making a change in our time. It does say, however, that we can change the course of our own lives. In addition, the film is clearly antinuclear, for it condemns the bomb as a dangerous misuse of science. Nevertheless, it does hold out for us the promise of surviving a global nuclear crisis, and the hope of psychological transformation and personal salvation. While the film's politics is pessimistic, its psychology is optimistic. And, in the final analysis, *The Time Machine* is the penultimate American bomb film, for it promises social justice, a community of like-minded others, and self-fulfillment in a time beyond the apocalyptic crisis of nuclear weapons; "penultimate" because it is unlikely there can be an ultimate apocalyptic bomb film, for that would entail the death of the genre.

To summarize this chapter, the films I have described show a sophisticated use of apocalyptic and postapocalyptic themes. This indicates that between 1950 and 1963 atomic bomb cinema had reached the second phase in Fowler's theory of generic development. Collins says Fowler's theory explains developments in early apocalyptic texts, and so far

Fowler's theory explains developments in atomic bomb cinema as well. Collins also claims that apocalyptic texts draw on a wide variety of sources, including sociological, theological, and mythical traditions. The apocalyptic text is quite malleable to local exigencies. And we have seen this to be true in apocalyptic bomb films. In particular, supernatural beings who interpret revelations are no longer credible to the culture, so filmmakers have developed strategies to diffuse or incorporate that function into other characters, the narrative, the image, or the cinematic apparatus. Nevertheless, the essential features of the apocalyptic genre remain. These films exhort the righteous and condemn the heretical, they criticize current oppressive conditions, and, lastly, they promise rebirth following a future crisis.

Faith in technology and current social institutions is almost universal in the atomic bomb cinema of this era. For a while, conservatives, liberals, radicals, and reactionaries alike by and large expressed this faith. Then, as danger to the environment became more apparent, and the social institutions could no longer keep pace with demand, doubt began to creep into atomic bomb cinema. Concomitant with doubt is the development of Fowler's third phase of generic development in the apocalyptic bomb film subcategory. In the next chapter we will examine some films for their ideological content and generic developments.

5 1964 to 1979
Losing faith in social institutions

A smell of death and corruption pervades the place, ranging from the
ordinary carrion smell to somewhat subtler stenches with strong overtones of ammonia (decomposing nitrogenous matter, I suppose). The
general impression, which transcends those derived from the evidence
of our physical senses, is one of deadness, the absolute essence of
death in the sense of finality without hope of resurrection. And all this is
not localized. It's everywhere, and nothing has escaped its touch. In
most ruined cities you can bury the dead, clean up the rubble, rebuild
the houses and have a living city again. One feels that it is not so here.
Like the ancient Sodom and Gomorrah, its site has been sown with salt
and ichabod ["The glory is departed"] is written over its gates.

—William C. Bryson, Captain, USN,
Nagasaki, September 14, 1945, in a letter to his wife.[1]

Much has been written about this
era, and again it is Paul Boyer
who has done the most to shape our understanding of these years vis-à-
vis the bomb. For him, the years 1959 to 1963 are a reprise of the vital
years 1945 to 1947. Boyer writes, "This second period of nuclear fear and
activism ended abruptly in 1963" when the three nuclear superpowers
signed a treaty banning atmospheric tests. He goes on to argue that following the treaty there was "a sharp decline in culturally expressed
engagement with the issue." Consequently, he has dubbed the period of

1963 to 1980 (after which Ronald Reagan became president and initiated the SDI program) "the years of the Big Sleep."[2] Statistical analysis of atomic bomb cinema, however, suggests a very different phenomenon than what Boyer describes.

The average number of bomb films per year for the years 1945 through 1999 is 17.89. For Boyer's first historical epoch, roughly 1945 to 1949, the average is 5.8 films per year. After 1950, however, the averages for each of Boyer's specific historical periods, or cycles, never varies from the overall average by more than 29 percent (or 5.14 films). In "the years of the Big Sleep," 1963 through 1979, the average does decline to 16.88 films per year; but that's only a statistical difference of less than 6 percent, or just one film, from the overall average. In the next chapter we will take a second, more detailed look at what these numbers mean. For now let us grant that Boyer's history occasionally corresponds with the numbers of films released in some years. But no matter how we statistically massage the numbers, the overall distribution of films does not bear out Boyer's thesis of, what amounts to, bipolar episodes of paranoia and psychic numbing that are cycling inextricably toward a final confrontation.

When looked at over the entire postwar period, the numbers and characteristics of bomb film narratives suggest that there is not one issue but many. Also, "culturally expressed engagement with the issue," *qua* atomic bomb cinema's engagement with the issues, is influenced by many factors other than just the arms race. On the one hand, fluctuations in the number of films released each year suggest that atomic bomb cinema responds to the demands of the industry and history. Audiences tire quickly, so there is constant experimentation with generic formula and historical events. On the other hand, the relatively constant release of bomb films over the entire period suggests that there is a basal rate at which the culture is engaging in these issues. The basal rate, and recurring themes, fads, and fashions, all suggest that genres and formulas have a life span independent of the actual events or films that inspire them. The culture is not, as Boyer argues, suffering from "cycles" of acute anxiety and activism, nor is it suffering from "Hollywood" manipulations to help keep the issues surrounding nuclear weapons "unconfronted and unresolved."[3] Rather, the culture processes information at a generally constant rate that has led to qualitative changes in our understanding of the issues; at the same time, there are occasional events that prompt some to take action based on the information already processed. Again, as insightful as Boyer is, he, like other cultural critics, grossly oversimplifies Hollywood's role in whatever problems he sees in American culture.

In this chapter I will analyze Stanley Kubrick's 1964 film, *Dr. Strangelove or: How I Learned to Stop Worrying and Love the bomb*, in great depth because of its exceptional presence during a time when atomic bomb cinema appears, to some, to have disappeared. We will also look at three films that were influenced by *Dr. Strangelove*: George A. Romero's *Night of the Living Dead* (1968), John Carpenter's *Dark Star* (1974), and L. Q. Jones's *A Boy and His Dog* (1975)—all of which are exceptional (albeit quirky) films that bring fresh ideas to atomic bomb cinema and perhaps reflect some of the idiosyncrasies of the period in which they were produced. So, let us begin with one of the most important of all bomb films, *Dr. Strangelove or: How I Learned to Stop Worrying and Love the bomb*.

Kubrick, Terry Southern, and Peter George adapted George's novel *Red Alert* for the screenplay of *Dr. Strangelove*. The film is tightly scripted and highly economical; nothing is superfluous. There are just a few actors and one actress, only five sets, and several exterior shots of an air force base and planes in flight.[4] Basically, there are three locations: General Ripper's office in Burpleson Air Force Base, the War Room, and the inside of one B-52 bomber en route to its target in the Soviet Union. Additionally, one scene takes place in General Turgidson's bedroom, with its all important adjoining toilet room that remains off camera.

The narrative structure of *Dr. Strangelove* is unusually sophisticated for a bomb film. As the narrative progresses the pace quickens, events unfold more rapidly, and crosscutting among the War Room, the B-52, and Burpleson Air Force Base increases. *Dr. Strangelove* begins with one action that cascades into three separate, but causally related, lines of narrative action. These stories and the lives of several characters are then interwoven through crosscutting.

The plot is amazingly simple. In the film's introduction we are shown cloud-shrouded mountains, and a narrator informs us of rumors about a Soviet "doomsday device." Next, we are shown two planes in flight, one refueling the other. The background soundtrack is the song "Try a Little Tenderness." Then, the first line of action begins when General Jack D. Ripper (Sterling Hayden), the insane Base Commander of Burpleson Air Force Base (the fictional 843rd Bomber Wing of the all too real Strategic Air Command), orders the thirty-four planes under his command to attack the Soviet Union. Ripper, fearing a "commie"-led conspiracy to "sap and impurify" his manliness, hopes to create "Peace on Earth" by leaving the United States no alternative but to initiate a preemptive strike. General Buck Turgidson (George C. Scott) is alerted to Ripper's actions, and he informs Washington of this break in the chain of command. President Merkin Muffley (Peter Sellers) invites the Soviet Ambassador into the Pentagon's top-secret War Room—a clear breach of security—to observe and assist as he orders American troops to attack Burpleson AFB and force Ripper to recall the planes. Muffley also assists the Soviets in shooting down the American bombers. After Ripper commits suicide, his assistant, Group Captain Lionel Mandrake (Sellers), a British officer on loan to the Americans through an officer-exchange program, deduces the recall code and relays the code to Washington. Several planes are shot down, most return to base. But the radio on one B-52, piloted by Major T. J. Kong (Slim Pickens), is damaged by a Soviet missile and cannot receive the recall code. Despite all odds, Kong demonstrates American ingenuity and drops a thermonuclear warhead on an Inter-Continental Ballistic Missile (ICBM) complex, thus triggering the Soviet's secret doomsday device that virtually destroys the world. However, Dr. Strangelove (Sellers), the president's special advisor, proposes that the most important men could be quickly assembled to survive in underground caverns. He says that at a ratio of ten women to each man, the country's gross national product would be back to normal in one hundred years. Everyone, the Soviet ambassador included, gets very excited over Strangelove's ideas. Turgidson, however, warns against Soviet expansionist policies, and encourages action to prevent "a mine-shaft gap!" The film's climax is a series of spectacular and elegant thermonuclear explosions. The background soundtrack to the explosions is a particularly cheery version of the song "We'll Meet Again," which was used to conclude nightly BBC radio broadcasts during the Second World War.

Dr. Strangelove pushes the edge of believability—almost to the point where we can dismiss the film as too fantastic, but not quite. On the one hand, the film is a burlesque; all the characters and institutions are lampooned. One source of humor is that each character is familiar, a cliché, a stereotype taken to the point of unbelievable exaggeration. On the other hand, the characters are so tightly constructed that they are credible, real. We can identify them or even with them. Thus, behind the humor lies an intense seriousness: the characters and events are not real but the neuroses seem plausible. Kubrick, Southern, and George, built their screenplay on a foundation of Freudian psychology. To make their ideas more entertaining, they embellish and exaggerate with sexual and scatological humor. It is this dynamic tension between seriousness and satire that makes *Dr. Strangelove* a compelling drama that never loses its appeal. Existing on a border, as it does, *Dr. Strangelove* both invites and frustrates analysis.[5]

The visual puns, double entendres, and hyperboles in *Dr. Strangelove* are by now well known, so let us just review a few of the jokes used in the film. There are visual jokes, such as the bomber being refueled in midair at the beginning of the film. From the way the scene is photographed, combined with the song "Try a Little Tenderness" playing in the background, the planes appear to be copulating. And, toward the end of the film, Major Kong is sitting on top of one of the bombs when the doors open beneath him, he rides the bomb as it plummets toward the target. That is to say, the bomb's latent phallic imagery becomes manifest or obvious when it protrudes from between Kong's legs as he rides toward the perfect union of Freud's bipolar drives: Eros and Thanatos. This "strange" anthropomorphic sexualization of weapons, moreover, brings about a climax of a different sort. These are just two examples of the frequent references to sex and warfare. Each of these images point to the demented nature of the characters and their more than professional relationships to weapons technology.

There are also ironic jokes. When Turgidson and Soviet Ambassador de Sadesky brawl, the president testily tells them, "You can't fight in the War Room." Also, there are intertextual jokes. Dr. Strangelove wears one black glove just like the demented wizard Rotwang in *Metropolis*. And, the name of misogynistic general, Jack D. Ripper, is an appellative pun that reminds us of the legendary Victorian serial killer of women. Perhaps to a lesser extent, Ripper also reminds us of the tragic belief that men can achieve power by forswearing love or physical contact with women. Alberich in *Das Ring de Nebulungan*, Richard Wagner's operatic reworking of myth and legend, renounces love in order to gain the magical Rhinegold and its power to rule the world. Both Alberich and Ripper, out of greed or dementia, set into motion a series of events that end in apocalyptic destruction of the world. Ironically, other filmmakers frequently use *Dr. Strangelove* as a source for intertextual jokes or homage, including *Naked Gun: 2½* and *Terminator 2: Judgment Day* (1991), which I will discuss in a later chapter.

Most importantly, the character's names are jokes. Merkin Muffley's name is highly suggestive, though obscure. *Muff*, of course, is a slang term for the female genitalia, or a term for prostitutes. *Merkin* has some similar meanings to muff, plus a merkin is a pubic wig.[6] One of the best jokes involves the introduction of General Buck Turgidson. In his first scene, Turgidson is sitting on a toilet, off camera, and as his name suggests, he is constipated. Similarly, Colonel "Bat" Guano's (Keenan Wynn) name means, simply, bat shit. Guano is an interesting character because he has no clue about what is happening. This is to say, like a bat, Guano is completely in the dark. This does not stop him from formulating conclusions, however. For Guano, at the root of every problem is a "deviated prevert" committing unspecified acts of "deviated preversions" (*sic*). The relationship of character to names comes to the foreground when Turgidson is told that Dr. Strangelove's real name is Merkwerdigichiliebe; to which, Turgidson says, "a Kraut by any other name." At the end of the film Strangelove proves Turgidson to be correct when, just as doomsday begins, he stands up from his wheelchair and proclaims, "Mein Führer, I can walk!"

Bertrand Russell, British philosopher and one time leader of antinuclear movements, has argued that the only true proper nouns are "this" and "that."[7] Persons' names are actually adjectives. As an adjective, Dr. Strangelove's name is an opaque neologism; its meaning rides on the surface and needs little clarification. Clearly, it is a *strange love*, which is mobilized by an imminent nuclear crisis that will send humanity deep into the mythological, perhaps Platonic, cave where all life can be hermetically controlled for its own good. The question is, why do the other characters find Strangelove's subterranean Utopia so acceptable, appealing even? Turgidson answers the question when he remarks that "a Kraut by any other name" is still a Kraut. Thus, the desire for world domination, no matter what the name, Nazism, British Colonialism, World Soviet Communism, or American Imperialism, is still the same repugnant thing: "deviated preversions," or in this case what Lifton, the social psychologist, would call *nuclearism*.

The literature on *Dr. Strangelove* is too voluminous and too varied to summarize adequately. However, three very different articles point to the range of critical opinions about the film. Peter Baxter's "The One Woman" (1984) typifies the dominant trends in current film scholarship: a combination of neopsychoanalytic, Lacanian linguistic, and Marxian theories, and especially the feminist film theory of Laura Mulvey, who argues that all Hollywood film is Oedipal in structure. Baxter syllogistically concludes that *Dr. Strangelove* is a typical Hollywood film.[8] Charles Maland's "Dr. Strangelove (1964): Nightmare Comedy and the Ideology of Liberal Consensus" (1979) is much more conventional, approaching film as though it were a literal text, to be read as though it were academic discourse. Specifically, Maland oxymoronically argues that *Dr. Strangelove* is quintessentially American, and that it demarks a "paradigm revolution" in American society.[9]

Lastly, George W. Linden's "'Dr. Strangelove' and Erotic Displacement" (1977) is very different from the other two. His starting place for analyzing *Dr. Strangelove* is not the film itself, but how his understanding of the film changed over the thirteen years since its release. In essence, then, Linden is following Robert Warshow's recommendation to start "with the simple acknowledgment of his own relation to the object he criticizes."[10] Linden says that in 1964 he and everyone else thought "the plot and theme were congruent and coextensive." That is to say that the film was really about humanity's self-destruction through subservience to a technology humanity created. Considering the general fear and technophobia of the time, "It is no wonder we had difficulty seeing the film as funny." Linden shows that the film is about the "erotic displacement" of love with death, for "while we snicker at the Victorians for repressing Eros and becoming neurotic, we fail to see that we are also repressed. We may be sexually free, but we have repressed death"—that is, Thanatos. Linden concludes that *Dr. Strangelove* is not just a film about nuclear war, "It is also an attack on our propensity to substitute violence for love." Linden concludes that the issues in *Dr. Strangelove* are deadly serious, yet the humor saves the film from the "blatant message-mongering of Stanley Kramer." In other words, the film does not offer the spectator a specific course of action. The sardonic humor, however, makes us sensitive to our own anxieties about the issues, and so, we would hope, act on them more effectively. While all three articles are provocative, to me Linden's article is the most convincing.[11]

In my opinion, *Dr. Strangelove* employs a type of 1960s revival of Freudian psychology to explore psychopathology, and criticizes our present political institutions and technoindustrial society. But the film is of course more than just the Oedipal conflict, sociocultural criticism, "erotic displacement," and other outgrowths of the free love movement. *Dr. Strangelove* is a warning. The filmmakers create a clearly hypothetical situation. The events are plausible, but not as imminently possible as they are in *On the Beach*, or *Fail Safe* (Sidney Lumet, 1964). The filmmakers never ask the spectator to believe that the events are real, only that they could be real. The spectator is warned, and then left to decide his or her own course of action.

Warning the world through fantastic narratives is what the apocalyptic genre does best. In the modern world at least, it is not necessary for the audience to accept the narrative as a literal revelation in order to be affected by the text. In *Dr. Strangelove* we are asked only to recognize the potential for such an outcome.

Dr. Strangelove reveals the unfolding of history. It describes a final confrontation, a battle of Armageddon, so to speak, between the forces of good and the forces of evil—though it is not clear which side is which. Leading up to this final battle are machinations and conspiracies. Cabals on each side try to outmaneuver the other. The very first scene of the film establishes these mysterious activities, as does the doomsday device itself. Both the device and the original bomb, which was called the "Gadget," are built in absolute secrecy. The device itself is jacketed with lethal Cabal Thorium G. The word "Cabal" suggests not only the secret societies that build these weapons, but the Jewish text of mystical knowledge and thaumaturgy, the *Cabala*.

While the film does not have a supernatural being, it does have Dr. Strangelove. Like Daniel of the Old Testament, he lives in a foreign land, and works for the king who conquered his people. Strangelove is President Muffley's most trusted advisor; it is his job to interpret what others cannot. In a sense, it is Strangelove who interprets Muffley's dreams and his chaotic visions of world destruction. Muffley and his advisors see the events as leading to inevitable doom. But Strangelove interprets these events differently. For Strangelove, in the ashes of nuclear war lies the possibility of glorious rebirth.

Kubrick's film represent no ordinary apocalypse. It is satirical and subversive, and it cleverly integrates ancient symbology with the "groovy" camp of the 1960s; that is to say, this film is a very serious stand-up routine. The events that unfold in *Dr. Strangelove* are the same events that destroy the world in *The Time Machine*: a world driven by greed and power uses science to win wars; a series of wars lead to a final confrontation and nuclear war; one group of people remains on the surface of the dead planet and another group descends deep into subterranean caverns. *The Time Machine* and *Dr. Strangelove* have virtually identical histories. The only difference is that in *Dr. Strangelove*, the Eloi never survive the war, and after one hundred years the Morlocks leave their caves to rule the world. Out of the ashes of nuclear war, a Fourth Reich is born. Therefore, it could not itself indicate a paradigm shift. Rather, the old order, the old paradigm, is reborn into a pristine, new, world.

Although not heavy-handed, Kubrick's film is subversive. *Dr. Strangelove* is guilty of "deviated preversions" against the frequent sanctimoniousness of atomic bomb cinema in its first two phases (assembly of the formal type, 1945 to 1949; and conscious use of the type, 1950 to 1963). The film satirizes the world's propensity for producing psychotic individuals and the possibility of putting them into positions of power. *Dr. Strangelove* also subverts the apocalyptic genre's usual orthodoxy by drawing attention to the apocalyptic myth itself and our proclivity for looking to the future for solutions to our problems. By using the genre to satirize our inclination to idealize the future, *Dr. Strangelove* moves atomic bomb cinema into Fowler's third phase of generic development—that of irony and subordination.[12] Having analyzed *Dr. Strangelove*, and its place within atomic bomb cinema, we can return to the question posed earlier: What of its social significance?

In the years following the release of *The Time Machine* (1960), many events contributed to changing the generally optimistic way Americans viewed their lives (see chapters 3 and 4). For Godfrey Hodgson, postwar American history is a tragedy of classical proportions: There are great achievements, hubris, and a climatic fall from grace that dispelled many of the myths that Americans held about themselves.[13] The loss of a myth is a crucial moment in the history of any people, for, as C. G. Jung notes, "A tribe's mythology is its living religion, whose loss is always and everywhere, even among the civilized [*sic*], a moral catastrophe."[14] This is, at least in part, because historical events that bring about the loss of myth are almost invariably seen as part of a larger cosmological drama. But drama is not always a part of a larger history. Atomic bomb cinema is one exception. What bridges history and drama is our experience and perception of events as crises. And, as we will see, such experiences inevitably engender new myths.

Although human consciousness cannot be summarized with newsprint, in this period of time five events stand out as particularly significant crises: the nascent development of "the movement," atmospheric testing of nuclear weapons, the Berlin Blockade, the Cuban Missile Crisis, and the assassination of John F. Kennedy. First, growing civil unrest dispelled the myth that a liberally governed industrial society was providing political and material equality to all Americans.

Exacerbated by our continual military involvements in Asia and Southeast Asia, the frustrations of the impoverished and disenfranchised eventually spread to other groups, thus the veneer of what Hodgson calls the Liberal Consensus began to chip and split. Second, nearly two decades of nuclear weapons tests made electromagnetic pulse (EMP) and strontium 90 household words. It had become common knowledge that EMP could cripple unshielded electrical equipment throughout a very large geographic area, and that strontium 90 was poisoning the food chain and showing up in mothers' milk. Third, when the Soviets blockaded Berlin, President Kennedy urged the country to prepare by building fallout shelters and by learning how to "duck-and-cover." Fourth, the Cuban Missile Crisis then shook American self-confidence to its core and dispelled the myth of American omnipotence, invulnerability, and isolation from an otherwise chaotic world. This crisis also dispelled the myth that we could and would guide the rest of the world into enlightened living.[15] Boyer refers to these years, 1959 to 1963, as the second period of anxiety and activity over nuclear weapons (the first period was 1945 to 1947).[16]

Fifth, the assassination of President Kennedy, like the wounding of the Fisher King Armfortes, brought an end to many national myths: (1) the myth of a country led by consensus; (2) the myth that anyone, especially a white, young, affluent, handsome, and charismatic president, can make a difference by being part of "the system" (thus filling the movement's ranks with the disaffected affluent who sought alternative paths to power and prestige); and (3) the assassination and subsequent botched investigations, rumors of conspiracy, and revelations of moral turpitude dispelled the myths that the "liberal establishment" was building a new Camelot that would last forever. ("Camelot," itself, is an appellative myth, created shortly after Kennedy's death.) As the decade progressed, all of these events contributed to the sense, often merely visceral, that America was in a slow decline from a period of material abundance to scarcity.

For our purposes the most important event of the era is the release of *Dr. Strangelove,* a significantly smaller event, indeed, but one perhaps more descriptive of deflated optimism. Yet *Dr. Strangelove* sparked people's imaginations; it was a lighting rod for the disaffected. (In fact, I am constantly amazed by the number of people older than myself who reverently refer to the film as an event that made them most aware of the nuclear threat). Stanley Kubrick put into words and images the country's not-so-latent fears. In so doing, his film worked further to dispel (or perhaps supersede) the myth that "the system," or the "establishment," was rational and working for everyone's benefit. More importantly, *Dr. Strangelove* worked strongly to evaporate the naive and romantic notions Americans had about the bomb.

Because *Dr. Strangelove* successfully combined black comedy with criticisms of "the establishment," it gained popularity with general audiences, the movement, and intellectuals. Equally or even more important is Kubrick's own status among the American literati. *Dr. Strangelove*'s comedic appeal, rich metaphoric associations, and antiestablishment sentiments make it the darling of students, intellectuals, and film scholars who keep it circulating on college campuses, in revival houses, and on TV. In essence, *Dr. Strangelove* gave media validation to an intellectual class, their sentiments, and their experiences in a way that few popular films before or since have been able to.

The influence of *Dr. Strangelove* was particularly strong on intellectuals sympathetic to the growing movement. Film scholar Allan Casebier describes the film in much the same way as Linden does: as a seminal experience for his generation of intellectuals.[17] Boyer, too, gives the film particular significance.[18] Kubrick, it would seem, expressively summed up what many thought and felt was wrong with the country's leadership. Kubrick's film became a symbol, the flag behind which many rallied. The clever dialogue and satirical inversions of military language provided a model for the subversion of what antinuclear activists call "nukespeak."[19] The film also provided a convenient *tabula rasa* onto which intellectuals could project their fears and anxieties. *Dr. Strangelove* remains a favorite source of ironic and satirical imagery to which public figures are derogatorily compared—particularly former secretary of state Dr. Henry Kissinger, who was already an important figure among nuclear warfare strategists.[20] Linden writes that

> [s]ince the logic of the film was the logic of our lives, it is no wonder we had difficulty separating one from the other. It is no wonder we had difficulty seeing the film as funny.[21]

Considering the intensity and rapid pace of events at the time, I think Linden nicely evokes what many must have felt about the film.

Dr. Strangelove, in addition, contributed much to the world's visual lexicon. At the very least, it changed atomic bomb cinema; that meant it changed the genre of films Americans see each year. Along with Kubrick's other films, such as *2001: A Space Odyssey* (1968), *Dr.*

Strangelove influenced a generation of filmmakers. This influence can be seen in John Carpenter and Dan O'Bannon's first film *Dark Star* (1974), and James Cameron and Gale Anne Hurd's films *The Terminator* (1984) and *Terminator 2: Judgment Day* (1991). References to *Dr. Strangelove*, and the copying of its scenes and images, can be found in many other films. In recent years, however, *Dr. Strangelove* has itself become an object of parody and satire. Since at least May 1998, Japan's NHK-BS2 TV station, the mouthpiece of the conservative government bureaucracy, which usually treats the bomb with affected seriousness, has been using short animation to introduce its late-night movie series. One work parodies Colonel Kong's ride on the missile that begins doomsday. And, in *Broken Arrow* (John Woo, 1996), a nuclear warhead momentarily appears as a phallic erection from Air Force Major Vic Deakins' (John Travolta's) crotch. *Dr. Strangelove* seems to have even entered the medical lexicon: According to the often apocryphal magazine, *Time*, doctors now further stigmatize their crippled patients by referring to an uncontrollable or "anarchic hand" as "the Dr. Strangelove Syndrome."[22] All this is to say that *Dr. Strangelove* has proven fertile material in the invention of new myths.

Most importantly, *Dr. Strangelove* refutes the notion that Americans are, or were, numb to the issues of nuclear war, or that Hollywood contributes to this numbing by presenting its monolithic images of the bomb. On the one hand, in 1964, when *Dr. Strangelove* was released, the second- and fifth-highest grossing films were *Goldfinger* (Guy Hamilton) and *From Russia with Love* (Terence Young).[23] Both are James Bond films, both star Sean Connery, and both are bomb films. Bond films have remained popular for nearly forty years, and, with slight variations in some recent films, the ideology of each Bond film is almost identical.[24] There is an extragovernmental organization, run by a megalomaniac, or a maverick who steps outside the normal chain of command, and threatens world security. The threat often involves the theft of Soviet, American, or British nuclear weapons. James Bond solves the problem and re-establishes the status quo. This is to say, the superpowers learn nothing and cynically return to normal cold war, or now post–cold war, relations. The bomb remains a necessary but dangerous evil. The authors of *Magill's Survey of Cinema*, whose primary ideological commitment is the success of the film industry, describe *Dr. Strangelove*'s profits as "respectable," especially for an inexpensive film. The review of the film adds, "The financial success of *Dr. Strangelove* is proof that the American public is not content solely with mindless comedies, romances, and thrillers."[25]

For nearly twenty years after the end of World War II, Americans in the mainstream generally thought they had reached, or nearly reached, a permanent state of material abundance and social harmony, which they hoped to share with the rest of the world. The great and tragic events occurring between 1960 and 1964 did much to end this glorious and optimistic period. In retrospect, it was an incremental and subtle change. When you talk to people who are old enough to remember the era, it is clear that at the time most did not fully understand the significance of these events. Nevertheless, the country slowly recognized that Camelot had come to an end. The round tables at which the Eloi sat and ate, at which H. G. Wells instructed them on philosophy, history, and science, have been displaced and are no more. Just as *Gojira/Godzilla* (1954) expresses the loss of glory, confusion, and ambivalence about the future that many Japanese feel even now, *Dr. Strangelove* similarly expresses what many Americans feel about their world. By 1964 the glory had also departed the United States.

Having analyzed *Dr. Strangelove* in some detail, it is now time to focus our attention on its influence on later films. To illustrate its influence, we will consider *Night of the Living Dead*, *Dark Star*, and *A Boy and His Dog*. The first of these three films might seem like an odd selection since it is, ostensibly, a horror film.

In 1968, George A. Romero's *Night of the Living Dead* was released— the first in a series of *Living Dead* films. In the summer of 1990 I showed this film to an undergraduate class, called The Image of Minorities in American Films, at an American university. Most of my students were not even born when Romero made his film, and in comparison to the films they grew up with—*Halloween* (John Carpenter, 1978), *Friday the 13th* (Sean S. Cunningham, 1980), and *Nightmare on Elm Street* (Wes Craven, 1984), all of which have become film series—*Night of the Living Dead* appears to be a tame, low-budget, low-tech, campy, cult film. Yet, even the vivid gore of disemboweled and flayed humans in *Predator* (John McTiernan, 1987) failed to disturb the students as much as Romero's *Night of the Living Dead*. S. S. Prawer, in his book *Caligari's Children: The Film As Tale of Terror*, writes that

> [w]hen we are startled by scenes that seem to go beyond our previous tol-
> erance-level, we must consider them in their context and ask ourselves
> whether the movement or thought and feeling of the whole work requires
> these scenes for the natural conclusion, in the way that the logic of *King
> Lear* needs the blinding of Gloucester. . . . When the context is realistic,
> as in Romero's *The Night of the living Dead* [*sic*], the action of which, but
> for its one central fantasy (the resurrection brought about by some

unknown radiation effect), takes place in a perfectly recognizable American setting, then we must ask ourselves whether the psychological and social action of the film makes sense, has a serious point, or completes a movement of thought and feeling; or whether it is a mere heaping-up of shock-effects for their own sake.[26]

Let us take a deeper look at this film and see why it continues to disturb us.

As in *Dr. Strangelove*, the plot is simple and the mise-en-scène economical; the focus of attention is on the events and the interaction of characters. The film begins with a serious sister and irreverent brother, Barbara (Judith O'Dea) and Johnny (Russell Streiner), visiting their father's grave in a semirural Pennsylvania cemetery. While Johnny tries to frighten Barbara with ghost stories, a zombie appears and attacks her. Johnny tries to help but is killed. The zombie and several of his companions pursue Barbara, but she escapes to a seemingly abandoned house. A few minutes later a black man arrives. The man, Ben (Duane Jones), begins to barricade the house from the zombies. Barbara is too frightened to help and remains in a state of shock throughout the film.

After Ben has made the house temporarily secure, two white couples, Harry and Helen Cooper and their adolescent daughter (Karl Hardman, Marilyn Eastman, Kyra Schon), and Tom and Judy (Keith Wayne, Judith Ridley), emerge from their hiding place in the cellar. Ben is angry because no one offered help when he and Barbara were fighting for their lives. Throughout the film Ben and Harry fight over who will lead them to safety. Ben discovers a television set, and a news report explains that a returning space probe carried back with it an unknown radiation that has brought the recent dead back to life. Also, a TV news reporter attempts to interview the government's military and scientific leaders about the crisis, but none are willing to answer the reporter's questions. This report shows "the establishment's" ineptitude and propensity for lying to the American public. Eventually, the trapped humans attempt an escape. Tom and Judy are killed, barbecued, and eaten. Harry locks Ben outside for the zombies to eat, but Ben breaks in and kills Harry. Next, the Coopers' daughter turns into a zombie and, as an homage to *Psycho* (Alfred Hitchcock, 1960), the young girl kills her mother with a cement trowel. The zombies attack the house en masse. Johnny, now a zombie, drags Barbara off for a family reunion of sorts. Ben escapes to Harry's hiding place in the cellar, and so he is the only one to survive the night. As morning dawns, he watches the locals shoot the zombies still lingering around the house. Ben peers through the window, and one of the locals shoots him through the head. The final moments of the film is a sequence of newspaper-quality still photographs that depict the black man riven with meat hooks and hauled off to be burned with the rest of the zombies.

Robin Wood, in *Hollywood from Vietnam to Reagan*, argues that *Night of the Living Dead* undermines many of the horror genre's conventions, and that Romero's film is really about the collapse of patriarchal consumer capitalism and the ideological norms of its participants. However, because the militia, or "posse" as he calls them, restores the status quo, all hope for a changed society is destroyed. Wood therefore calls *Night of the Living Dead* a completely negative film. Wood is an insightful scholar, and his use of psychoanalytic and Marxian theory is very revealing.[27] However, Wood's analyses are so theory driven that they become cumbersome and lose their explanatory powers; his approach ultimately obscures other equally important issues that came with the film's release, and that remain important today. What is needed here is Ockcham's razor. A simpler, more obvious approach will take us further toward understanding the film and the culture.

In 1968 and 1969 the contradictions in American society seemed to come to a head. On the one hand, the urban boundaries that protected middle America from the violence of civil unrest became more permeable; and on the other hand, the divisions in American society along race, class, gender, cultural, and ideological lines had never been more apparent. Romero's *Night of the Living Dead* addresses several of the issues that both divided and united the country.

The Coopers may very possibly represent that population in America who believe they can hide from the prevailing "zombies": war, a crumbling economy, tumultuous social conditions, and the flaws of the patriarchal family structure. Consequently, as Wood points out, all that they repress eventually consumes their family, and as a result, they also become zombies. The same is true of Barbara and Johnny. Tom and Judy, on the other hand, resist the zombies but are not strong enough to think for themselves and must be led either by Harry or Ben. Because they are weak characters they quickly become fodder for the zombies. It is these characters' own flaws that lead to their demise.

Wood strongly argues that the hero's color, that is, his racial status, is very important because it signifies his "otherness." And yet the audience is clearly intended to identify with him not as a victim but as a true American hero, albeit a tragic hero. Ben's fate disturbs us because it flies in the face of what mainstream Americans, at least, profess to hold most dear: the beliefs that we are all equal, everyone who works hard can make it to the top, and each person can make a difference. Ben achieves heroic proportions by surviving the night and attempting to help his fellow characters. In the end, though, he crumbles morally under the pressure and is unceremoniously shot because he looks too zombie-like.

Clearly, *Night of the Living Dead* expresses the frustrations and double standards that many groups have experienced in the United States—particularly people of color. Consider the newspaper-style photographs at the end of the film. One shows a close up of a meat hook in Ben's chest. Blood has oozed out of the hole, indicating to everyone, not just the spectator of the film, that Ben was human when killed. Yet, none of the militia shows any remorse over their mistake. Because we do identify with representations and with fictional narrative characters, anyone who is sensitive to brutality and indifference toward other human beings cannot help but be pained by the film's conclusion.

The zombies can represent many things. In particular, they provide a gruesome, unnatural confrontation with death. By 1968 American soldiers and the mentality that supported the war in Vietnam was giving in to stories about the grotesque and senseless circumstances of death. Also, Vietnam was noteworthy for the improved medical units that could "save" the horribly wounded from what would have been sure death in earlier wars. Indeed, many physical and mental zombies were returning from the swamps of Southeast Asia. The militiamen in the film are indifferent hicks, participants in a volunteer turkey-shoot. They are led by pot-bellied Sheriff Cannon MacLellen (uncredited), who is armed to the teeth and impatiently smokes his cigars as he barks out orders for the shooting and burning of the zombies. These men represent that violent part of American society that kills compulsively and recklessly, even savoring war and dehumanizing targets as an opportunity for what Richard Slotkin calls "regeneration through violence." Here we are not talking about just the Klan-like element or the new militant Right, but the potential for another My Lai massacre or even a Waco, Texas that seems so much a part of the American character.

In relation to the war in Vietnam, and American society in general, Ben also represents those groups or persons in the United States who resist what Wood calls the normal structuring of patriarchal, capitalist relationships, plus the violent traditions of American culture and the war. At first Ben shows great concern for everyone's welfare, including Harry Cooper's. But slowly he is drawn into the cycle of violence and hate that leads to his own moral downfall and eventually his death. Ironically, after killing Harry Cooper, Ben escapes the zombies by fleeing to the cellar, where he survives. Even though Ben's desire to fortify the house seemed the more reasonable course of action, and he the more reasonable person, it turns out that Ben was wrong and Harry correct. Therefore, it would seem that there is little middle ground between the zombies and the militia. Both are threats to human life.

Wood argues that *Night of the Living Dead* is "total negativity," and I agree, but for different reasons. Wood claims that because the old social order is restored, the apocalyptic nature of the film must be discounted. For Wood, apocalypses are very literal, political revolutions that must result in a new order, not the return to or reestablishment of an old order.[28] In other words, Wood's interpretation misses, for whatever reasons, the multiple perspectives that allow for a more sensitive and ironic reading. In my interpretation, the film starts with the zombies, the evil dead who oppress the just and establish a false order. Eventually there is a final battle between good and evil, and the sheriff's militia reestablishes the old social order. (Ben, who like Moses disobeyed the word of God, is morally flawed and is therefore not permitted into the promised land.) Thus, from the sheriff's perspective, rather than Wood's, there is a revolution, and the society returns to the old, just order.

However, through Ben's death a metaphor is established: the militiamen are like the zombies. Therefore, from the spectator's perspective the film is a satirical and ironic apocalypse. Like Kubrick, Romero subverts the apocalyptic genre for other purposes. To paraphrase a popular song by the Who, the new boss is the same as the old.[29] Though cynically and rightfully observed as changeless, a revolution has been made. Thus, atomic bomb cinema reflects a core concept of the apocalyptic imagination of the 1960s. In this sense the apocalypse does not prevent the old order from rising again; rather, it functions in quite the opposite manner.

Romero's apocalypse does not hold out the promise of a better world following the period of trials and tribulations, but a dystopic vision of a world in which the oppressed can expect nothing from the future but more oppression. The apocalypse leads to a revolution in which, once again, the Morlocks survive to rule the world, but there is no hero from the past to rescue the victims of the living dead and the Eloi all but disappear. For Wood, apparently, every apocalyptic text must end with a clearly stated new social order. Moreover, that new social order must be different from the patriarchal, consumer capitalist society, which he so detests. Because

Wood does not recognize the different uses and phases of the apocalyptic genre, because he does not see irony as one possible treatment of the apocalyptic scenario, he mistakenly concludes that Romero's film is not part of the apocalyptic genre. Through obvious allusions and a TV news report, moreover, the film links radiation (which generates the zombies) to the military-industrial complex, and in turn to the ruin of society. Thus, the film's obvious black humor, its ironic and satiric treatment of its themes, places Romero's *Night of the Living Dead* well within Fowler's third phase of atomic bomb cinema.

The black humor and satiric treatment of the bomb and social institutions that characterize *Dr. Strangelove* and *Night of the Living Dead* are also the foundation for another important cult film, *Dark Star* (1974). Originally a student film project made at the University of Southern California's School of Cinema and Television, this film started the careers of director John Carpenter and writer Dan O'Bannon. Carpenter, ironically, never finished his degree.[30] Trying to read *Dark Star* as an apocalyptic narrative, however, only obscures its greater importance to atomic bomb cinema. *Dark Star* evokes Americans' increasingly cynical view of their social institutions, and darkly parodies the very American science fiction film genre, especially the pristine, orderly, and idyllic worlds of Kubrick's *2001: A Space Odyssey* and Gene Roddenberry's TV series *Star Trek*.[31]

Dark Star is about the five-man crew of the spaceship *Dark Star*. Their mission is to seek out planets with intelligent life, and more importantly, to prepare areas of space for colonization by destroying unstable planets. At the start of the film, the crew has already spent twenty years in space, but each member has aged only three years. The crew includes Commander Powell (Joe Sanders), Lieutenant Doolittle (Brian Navelle), Sergeants Pinback (Dan O'Bannon), Boiler (Cal Kuniholm), and Talby (Dre Pahich), an alien, a computer with a female voice, and thermostellar devices—that is, bombs that talk.

Everything that can go wrong goes wrong. The preface to the actual mission includes the death of Commander Powell, who is killed by a short circuit in his chair; his body is then stored in a cryogenic freezer. Systems begin to deteriorate at a rapid rate. There are radiation leaks. The sleeping quarters are no longer habitable, and the storage bay, along with the ship's entire supply of toilet paper, self-destruct. Pinback is even bitten by his own pet alien (a beach ball with feet). Eventually we learn that Pinback is actually Bill Frueg, an idiot fuel maintenance technician who was mistaken for space jockey Pinback and put on board the *Dark Star*. Needless to say, morale is low, and the crew has become morose if not neurotic.

To add insult to injury, the crew receives a message from Earth. They are told that their last message, which took ten years for Earth to receive, was shown worldwide, during prime time, and they "got good reviews in the trades." Everywhere, flags were flown at half-mast, and a week of mourning for the death of Commander Powell was observed. The crew is also told that Congress has made cutbacks in the budget, so there isn't enough money to repair the *Dark Star*'s radiation shields or Powell's seat. But, the spokesman says, "you guys will make do. Keep up the good work."

After passing through an electromagnetic asteroid belt, a critical malfunction develops. Bomb #20 is twice activated, but each time, the computer convinces the bomb to return to the bay. The crew ignores the computer's warnings about the malfunction. Then, when the crew activates bomb #20 to destroy an unstable planet, the release mechanism fails and the bomb will not drop out of the bay—just as in *Dr. Strangelove*. Armed and ready to explode, Pinback (O'Bannon) tries to convince the bomb to disarm and return to the bay, but to no avail. (The voice of the bomb must be O'Bannon's, adding humor and irony to the argument.) The crew tries everything imaginable to disarm Thermostellar Device #20.

Unsure of what to do, Doolittle miraculously revives Commander Powell, who suggests teaching the bomb "phenomenology." So, instead of manually releasing the bomb as Colonel Kong in *Dr. Strangelove* does, Doolittle dons a spacesuit and tries to persuade bomb #20 that it cannot trust its own sensory impressions of the world. Convinced, the bomb returns to the bay to contemplate a meaningful existence. Deciding it is a god in an otherwise empty universe, bomb #20 announces, "let there be light." Only Talby and Doolittle survive the explosion. Talby is trapped by the Phoenix asteroid and spends eternity circling the galaxy. Doolittle, who is a surfer from Malibu, California, finds a piece of wreckage and surfs his last wave by riding the gravitational pull of the planet; eventually, he burns up in its atmosphere.

Carpenter's and O'Bannon's *Dark Star* is a subversive attack on the science fiction subgenre, space adventures, and the subgenre of American mythology: the liberal postindustrial society. In the world of *Dark Star*, encroaching civilization has made working in space just another job. The real threat to human survival is not intergalactic conspiracy or menacing alien creatures, but the routinization and monotony of modern living. To survive these dangers, we must learn to "make due" in a world of bureaucratic indifference, scarce resources, decaying social institutions, and, especially, lowered expectations. It is well worth keeping in mind that *Dark Star* was released just shortly before *Rocky* (John G. Avildsen, 1976), Sylvester Stallone's bicentennial salute to a post-Vietnam America of decidedly lowered expectations, an America where the audience can no longer expect the hero to defeat his opponent but rather to just barely survive until the final bell is rung. The irony of *Dr. Strangelove* is that the human element fails, but the technology exceeds even Buck Turgidson's expectations. The irony of *Dark Star* is that neither the human nor the technological elements work. Even the genre fails to meet our expectations. The film itself is ostentatiously low-budget. Gone is the glory of a high-tech American society.

From the misadventures of the spaceship *Dark Star*, we return to the postapocalyptic future here on Earth. In 1975, one year after the release of *Dark Star*, a new subgenre took full form: the post–nuclear holocaust survival film. Of course, no genre develops *ex nihilo*, from thin air. Post-holocaust survival films have much in common with earlier films that projected the Holocaust into the near or distant future and/or on another planet. This subcategory of atomic bomb cinema ranges from *Rocketship X-M* (1950) to *Planet of the Apes* (Franklin J. Schaffner, 1968), and many significant films of the 1980s and 1990s. Two post–nuclear holocaust survival films were released in 1975: Robert Clouse's *The Ultimate Warrior* and L. Q. Jones's *A Boy and His Dog*. The former (staring Yul Brynner and Max von Sydow) is a predictable drama that concludes with hopeful images of literal and metaphoric rebirth, and is evidence that different phases of generic development do overlap. *A Boy and His Dog*, however, is a darkly satirical and comic vision that pushes the edge between optimism and pessimism. Let us take a closer look at this subversive film.

A Boy and His Dog is an adaptation of one of Harlan Ellison's many award-winning novels. The story takes place in the year 2024 A.D., starting where *Dr. Strangelove* ends. It opens with a series of explosions and mushroom clouds, followed by a "crawl" or prologue explaining that World War Four took place in 2007 and lasted only five days. "Politicians had finally solved the problem of urban blight."

A Boy and His Dog follows the adventures of an eighteen-year-old boy named Vick (Don Johnson), or Albert as he is sometimes called, and his aging dog, Blood (Tiger). Together they survive the desolate, post-nuclear Phoenix, Arizona environment. After the war Blood loses his natural ability to hunt, but he gains the telepathic ability to communicate with Vick and locate food and people. Vick has only one thing on his mind: sex. The problem is women are few and far between due to their low survival rate. Vick and Blood do, however, discover one who has been gang raped and murdered. Vick bemoans her senseless death, claiming that she could "have been used" at least once more. Blood, aside from regular meals, has only one thing on his mind: finding "Over the Hill" (the future's equivalent of Boy's Town). Vick strikes a deal and offers, "—find me a broad and we'll go to the promised land." (Finding the promised paradise that lies just over the hill is a recurring theme in virtually all postnuclear holocaust survival films.) During their search for food and sex, Vick is watched by ominous men, but the camera only shows us their blue surgical booties and canes. Almost by accident, Blood finds a woman and they trap her in the dilapidated gym in the ruins of a high school. As it turns out, his victim, Quilla June Holmes (Susanne Benton) is actually pursuing Vick. She willingly makes love with him, runs away, and lures Vick "Down Under." Blood warns Vick that he is acting like a jealous juvenile and is being tricked by the girl. "God knows what they'll do to you [Down Under]." But Vick insists on pursuing the girl, so after a tearfully sentimental farewell, Vick descends deep into the earth, into the new Topeka.

Because they live beneath the surface, the people of Topeka occasionally need new blood, so to speak, to keep their gene pool healthy. Topeka, named after the city in Kansas, is a hyperbolic rending of middle-class utopia—something straight out of *The Music Man* (Morton Da Costa, 1962) but with Big Brother high technology. Topeka is run by the Committee, all of whom could have walked straight from the set of the TV program *Father Knows Best* (1954 to 1962, CBS/NBC) and changed their street shoes for leather boots (or surgical booties). The Committee consists of Mr. Craddock (Jason Robards), Doctor Moore (Alvy Moore), and Miss Mez (Helen Winston). Michael, their humanoid robot, enforces their rules. Vick is captured, scrubbed clean, dressed in fresh clothes, and then taken before the Committee. Vick is much pleased to learn that it is his honor to impregnate the town's eligible maidens. But Topeka is not given over to supporting carnal pleasures. Much to Vick's chagrin, he is gagged and tied to a hospital bed. A catheter connects him to a semen pump, thus preventing Vick's pleasure but providing his brides with vials of fresh semen. In order to maintain propriety, Vick is married to each of the women as he lies helpless and humiliated in his bed. And, since the town leaders fear that Quilla's success has made her a political threat, they order her to become one of Vick's brides. However, Quilla is in sum a bad, bossy woman, and has ideas of her own. She has lured Vick to Topeka with the intention of leading a coup that will place her in control. Dressed in her white wedding gown, Quilla rescues Vick. But the coup is brutally suppressed. Only Quilla and Vick escape to the surface, where Vick can get "back in the dirt so I can feel clean." It is night on the surface when Vick finds Blood. Because he waited too long for Vick to return, Blood is near death from hunger, dehydration, and wounds from their previous battle. As Vick kneels by the dying dog, Quilla coolly tells Vick that they are too late to save Blood, and they need to think about themselves. She looks into Vick's eyes and tells him that she loves him. At that moment an expression of decision spreads across Vick's face. The image dissolves into the final scene, a morning campfire. Blood thanks Vick for making such a sacrifice, and comments that Vick has not eaten anything. Vick replies that he is not hungry. As they walk toward the sunrise Vick says, "She said she loved me. It's not my fault she picked me to get all wet brained over." Blood sarcastically replies that she had "marvelous judgment, if not particularly good taste," and the two begin to laugh. With the sun on the horizon, Vick and Blood, the happy pair, begin their search for Over the Hill.

Let's overlook what seems to be some fairly overt sexism in this film and try to determine why it has such a cult following. *A Boy and His Dog* combines elements of the buddy film, the troubled-adolescent film, the postapocalyptic survival film, the hero's journey for self-knowledge, and other genres, in very unexpected ways. Blood and Vick are partners that complement and compensate for each other. Blood provides the brains, and Vick provides the brawn. When cornered, they fight side by side, and become closer through the regenerative ritual of violence. Still, Vick is an adolescent, and he must go through the problems that all young men face. Love, sex, and domesticity, however, only prove to be temporary distractions. In the end—as in some twisted or strange version of the *Lassie* films and TV programs—the boy returns to his dog. Like Peter Pan in a world turned inside out, Vick occasionally journeys to an inner fantasy world, yet he refuses to grow up, and thus he returns to his own world. The structure of relationships between the characters, and between the characters and their worlds is really quite interesting, and understanding this structure, though seemingly digressive, will help advance a broader analysis of the film and atomic bomb cinema. Let us observe the characters more closely.

In this film, as in many others, the subordinate characters are projections of the central character, Vick, or function as parts of his psychic structures—in this case, a very Freudian structure. The main characters are grouped into sets of three, or sets of two in need of a third member, which function as the id, superego, and the ego. The relationship or psychic function of each character, however, changes depending on the location: above ground or Down Under (Topeka); these psychic functions, moreover, are often inverted and subverted. Vick represents unrestrained libidinal desires. He refuses to plan for the future; he takes unnecessary risks; and he is driven by primal urges. He is not a very good middle-class boy, nor a good candidate for "organization man." Blood is the superego; he imposes both history and rules on Vick, as well as rewards and punishments. In Freudian psychology, the superego, which is an internalization of the father's law, develops before the ego. Thus, it is no coincidence that Blood is male. Topeka, in a sense, represents a competing superego, a false consciousness that is trying to draw Vick in via Quilla and his clearly articulated id. The third member of this triumvirate is Quilla, for she tries, if unsuccessfully, to negotiate between Vick and Blood. It is Quilla who tries to direct Vick's energies toward not merely the law, but the future, building, and domesticity. She offers him dreams of a home with a guest room for Blood. In a sense, in Quilla's vision of the future, designed to deceive Vick, the family is comprised of a father, a mother, and a male child—a thoroughly Freudian, or Oedipal, family.

In the Down Under the triumvirate changes somewhat, though the functions remain the same. The Committee, for instance, is another triad composed of two men and one woman, and Mr. Craddock clearly runs this committee. Topeka is most definitely a patriarchy, but more importantly, it is set up as Vicks's testing place, an inner suburban dream town, abundant yet a static nightmare. Once in Topeka, it is obvious that Vick's libidinal desires have gotten him into trouble with the superego, which seeks to restrain and control him, to make him a good citizen in a lobotomized town instead of being true to himself. Quilla, the ego, attempts to rescue Vick, direct his energies, and establish herself as the head of the Committee and the psychic triad. Once Quilla rescues Vick, functions are again reversed. Quilla becomes the id; it is she who desires to possess Vick and to overthrow the law of the superego, while Vick/ego is more interested in survival. Vick tries to negotiate his way through the traps set for him by both the Committee/superego and Quilla/id. Once Vick and Quilla make their way back to the surface these relationships again shift.

This film wants its cake (in this case Quilla) and to eat it too; that is, it both uses and subverts Freudian psychology, as well as American ideology. For instance, to the extent that Quilla is the id she must be brought to the surface. Once exposed to the light of analysis, the id can be acknowledged and the somatization, or psychosomatic symptoms, of repressed desire disappears: Blood is healed. To the extent that Vick is the id, *A Boy and His Dog* rejects Freud's belief that only through some repression of the id can civilized man survive.[32] In the end, the film returns to the beginning: women are a scarce resource and only after being completely used should they be discarded. By choosing Blood over Quilla, Vick rejects the ego, rejects romantic love, rejects the desire to procreate, rejects women, and rejects Freud's vision of civilization in favor of sex and violence, or Eros and Thanatos. And Vick feels better off for having done so, not worse, as Freud would have us believe. This film, though, is not quite that simple.

Clearly, dressing Blood's wounds with Quilla's wedding gown and then feasting on her suggests that a marriage between the id and the superego has been consummated. In another inversion, it is female Quilla who is the Christlike ego, sacrificed for the salvation of man. But Blood, not Vick, consumes the Eucharist that brings about communion between God/superego and Man/id. Nevertheless, all that has taken place is in the service of the id. The communion brings about a change in Vick. What remains to be seen is whether in Vick's next stage of development he will consume and integrate Blood's psychic function—yet another inversion of psychoanalytic theory.

Freud's ideas are frequently used as the structure for organizing characters and narratives. Equally frequent is the lampooning of those ideas. In my opinion, *A Boy and His Dog* does not use and subvert the Freudian motif as successfully or coherently as other films, and its rendering of womanhood proper as conspiratorial is unfair. But whether the film's ambiguities are intentional or unintentional, good or bad, is not important. What is important is that *A Boy and His Dog* has an ending into which the spectator can project many different interpretations: feelings of repression or oppression; rebellious longing for a world without the complications of women, saviors, and/or egos; or the desire for transformative experience. To my mind, the third interpretation seems the most compatible with the other two, and is therefore the most complete and the most plausible. Now let us turn our attention to the type of civilization that is represented in *A Boy and His Dog*.

A Boy and His Dog openly mocks the sacred cows of American history: the Kennedy family, the cold war, social planning, and urban renewal are all attacked at the beginning of the film. These social institutions are maintained Down Under in Topeka. Topeka is a combination of George Orwell's vision of a Big Brother society in *1984*, but dressed in Walt Disney's vision of Main Street, U.S.A. According to the "Elder's Proclamation," the underground was built in God's image. Everyone wears painted-on happy faces. It is a world of endless picnics of white bread and mayonnaise, Jell-O molds with canned fruit, homemade fruit pies—for which everyone gets first prize—and no ants. But conformity is scrupulously enforced. A loudspeaker incessantly regurgitates recipes and overly saccharine aphorisms: "We are never so happy as we imagine. Another helpful hint for living from the Committee's almanac." One recalcitrant couple is brought before the Committee for repeated "lack of respect, wrong attitude, failure to respect authority." Their punishment is "the Farm," a euphemism for the cemetery. But no one is executed in Topeka. Instead, the Committee orders heart attacks and memorial services at Lakeside Methodist. No one escapes the Committee's watchful eyes. Vick sees a lap dog and tries to communicate with the unwitting pup. Fearing the worst, the dog is interrogated by the Committee. Since the dog is unwilling to either confirm or deny telepathic communications with Vick, it too is sent to the Farm.

Only in the anarchy of the surface does our hero have a dignified fighting chance. Recalling a theme in *Dr. Strangelove*, the totalitarian society of Topeka will quite literally "sap and impurify our precious bodily fluids." Again, the gene pool needs replenishing and Vick is robbed of his semen in a most unmanly way.

In the world of *A Boy and His Dog*, World War Four is a blessing in disguise. Topeka, the inheritor of prewar society, is again the old regime renewed but eternal. On the surface, however, thanks to the war, men are once again real men, and women are barbecue. The American spirit of manly, violent, preindustrial rugged individualism is reborn in the postapocalyptic environment. The true *ancien régime* is restored.

Indeed, this is an apocalyptic bomb film that ironically subverts the utopic vision of films like George Pal's *The Time Machine* (1960). The final apocalypse purifies the earth of a decadent society and allows the rebirth of the righteous rugged individualist into a dystopic future. Like Huck Finn, the hero of *A Boy and His Dog* does not rebuild society but revels in his newfound freedom from the constraints of morbid and corrupt social institutions. Following a period of trials and tribulations, Vick and Blood search for Over the Hill. Finding Over the Hill is not important; what is important is that they remain independent.

There are other elements of the apocalyptic genre in *A Boy and His Dog*. In a sense, Blood has a supernatural gift. He uses his powers to reveal to Vick the meaning of past events and their portent for the future. Though worthy, Vick does not comprehend his lessons, and despite Blood's warnings is lured to Topeka. In this otherworldly journey he witnesses firsthand the fate that awaits the unrighteous. After returning from this journey in which the truth of civilization is revealed to Vick, he and Blood set out in search of the promised land.

It can be argued that these images are too distant from the images in earlier apocalyptic texts. I cannot accept this counterargument, for it would presuppose a single, original image. In *The Apocalyptic Imagination* Collins shows that pre-Christian Jews and early Christian writers have reworked even older traditions into the apocalyptic traditions. There is no single Ur- or seminal image. At the psychological level, narratives and symbols do not need to be identical in order for the influences of early texts to be apparent. Like many apocalyptic bomb films, *A Boy and His Dog* rearranges traditional narrative elements (e.g., the order of events) and uses modern, secular symbols to evoke in the spectator the ancient apocalyptic imagination. Yet, as we trudge through the dispossessed 1970s the images of secular apocalypse becomes just as twisted and incomprehensible as the decade itself.

Now that we have examined several films, it is time to return to the broader questions that I introduced at the beginning of this chapter. Specifically, what are the interrelationships among sociocultural change, popular attitudes toward nuclear technologies, and generic developments in atomic bomb cinema? After the release of *Dr. Strangelove*, four changes in atomic bomb cinema occur. First, a shift into Fowler's third phase occurs at the beginning of this period, but it is not a paradigm revolution; rather, it is indicative of a common pattern to how genres are reworked and developed over time. Second, images of nuclear technologies lose their pristine and idyllic edges. Third, films with pronuclear commitments seem to struggle to defend the technologies despite a growing body of evidence that the technologies were even more dangerous than generally believed, and that the nation's leadership was purposely misleading the public. And fourth, *Dr. Strangelove* unearths a previously little-known vein of cynicism in atomic bomb cinema.

Cynicism is nothing new to American culture. Theodore Dreiser's *Sister Carrie*, first published in 1900, for instance, is particularly cynical.[33] Kubrick's film noir contributions, *Killer's Kiss* (1955) and *The Killing* (1956), are particularly cynical. Film noir—one of the most cynical of film genres—began to develop in the United States well before 1945, peaked in 1950, and has never disappeared.[34] Of course, several bomb films have come out of this generic tradition. Early postwar optimism never completely eclipsed this dark streak in American consciousness; thus, rather than Boyer's years of the "Big Sleep," we might describe the 1960s as a renaissance of cynicism. Of course, it was not just frightening revelations about the bomb that brought on this renaissance, but rather, as Peter Clecak argues, there were several events that conspired to create uncertainty for Americans about their world:

> Between the middle sixties and the end of the seventies, Americans were pushed into a rediscovery of limits and limitations of all sorts. This rediscovery of limits was a haphazard affair, a piecemeal response to an accumulation of events and trends in evidence since the middle sixties. . . . Exploding the hope of an "American century," Vietnam ushered in an era in which America's global power seemed markedly limited and tawdry rather than limitless and beneficent.[35]

This climate of burgeoning doubt is expressed in many areas of American society, but is particularly eloquent in atomic bomb cinema. Paradoxical though it may sound, Kubrick's *Dr. Strangelove* is a pinnacle of cynicism that has influenced many younger filmmakers, and an important artifact of contemporary culture. Other bomb films have contributed to this climate of doubt by pushing the period of trials and tribulations to the foreground of popular consciousness while still holding out the promise of transcending our oppressive conditions. As we have seen, no matter how cynical atomic bomb cinema becomes, virtually no films violate the apocalyptic genre's promise of rebirth and salvation following a period of trials and tribulations. In other words, after 1960, when America's former glory seemed to slip away, Fowler's third phase of generic development began to emerge, and the apocalyptic imagination remained as strong as ever in atomic bomb cinema.

6 1980 to 1989
The Reagan era

[O]ur eye seems guided by the mysterious authority of the decade, by that fiction which identifies a change in sensibility—if not a scheduled apocalypse—every ten years.

—Harvey Gross, "The Problem of Style and the Poetry of the Sixties"[1]

Thus, by the end of the seventies American social and cultural critics questioned the central assumption of Enlightenment thought more thoroughly than ever.

—Peter Clecak, *America's Quest for the Ideal Self*[2]

Social and cultural critics were not the only ones to question Enlightenment thought. If anything, critics comprise the rear guard of a movement that had begun much earlier. But this is hardly surprising. Despite our self-aggrandizements, we academicians are as likely to follow cultural trends as to lead them—especially in the social sciences and humanities. In any case, Peter Clecak shows, and I think correctly, that the late sixties, the seventies, and the early eighties are far more complex than is generally believed, and that social critics have been unduly sour in their pronouncements. Indeed, much of the sociocultural criticism of these years is facile, and clouded by ideological agendas. This is particularly true in the criticism of bomb films.

Frances FitzGerald writes, in a brief 2000 essay, that President Reagan's saber rattling in the early 1980s provoked "the largest antinuclear movement in cold war history." But, FitzGerald claims, and perhaps rightly, that because Mr. Reagan offered to "share S.D.I. technology with the Soviets" and "promis[ed] the elimination of nuclear weapons," the "antinuclear movement, its rhetoric stolen, gradually faded away."[3] This would seem to support Paul Boyer's 1985 thesis of near bipolar "cycles" concerning the bomb. The picture that Boyer himself paints, however, is naturally far more complex. Boyer, the leading historian on America's relationship to the bomb, maintains that by the 1980s "the nexus of circumstances that had sustained the Big Sleep for some fifteen years was beginning to break up." Boyer cites many events that brought about the break up of this nexus. Two events, however, stand out. First, "The accession of Ronald Reagan . . . provided the final decisive push back toward antinuclear activism and revived cultural awareness."[4] It is interesting and telling that both Reagan and Boyer look "back toward" an idealized past—when they and the country were young—for models of how Americans should feel and behave toward the bomb, Reagan toward the 1950s and Boyer toward the late 1940s. Secondly, and more relevant to our concerns, Boyer claims that after many years of obscurity, local, grassroots American antinuclear movements "gained massive visibility in 1979 with the release of the Jane Fonda movie *China Syndrome* and the accident at Three Mile Island."

If antinuclear movements "gained visibility," then, as Boyer points out, they must have existed prior to 1979. Logically, this implies that many Americans are capable of long-term, focused attention to issues that are important to them. After analyzing public opinion polls from the 1950s to the 1980s, Spencer R. Weart concludes that "Most people had known all along that they were in danger [of "imminent nuclear war"], whether or not they chose to talk about it."[5] People were talking about it, but not in voices most scholars are accustomed to hearing.

Boyer clearly overstates the importance of *China Syndrome* (James Bridges). Though the film did receive much popular and critical attention, it is not the only antinuclear film, just one blatant and pedantic example. Furthermore, Fonda is both a star and a well-known activist, but Boyer confuses these two parts of her life when he says it is a "Jane Fonda movie."[6] Fonda worked on this film not as a filmmaker but as an actress playing an investigative reporter. In her career she has played a variety of characters including whores and sex kittens—unseemly in the eyes of the modern women's movement.[7] In short, she could hardly be considered the darling of the *Left* no matter how enthusiastically condemned she is on the *Right*. (Ironically, by the year 2000 Fonda has become a largely forgotten celebrity; her increasingly popular costar Michael Douglas has been appointed to the post of UN Ambassador on Nuclear Disarmament.)[8] In addition, Boyer includes the 1958 film *The H-Man* in a list of American films, without informing us that it is a Japanese film, directed by Inoshirō Honda.[9] This is important because the reader naturally assumes Boyer is referring to artifacts of American culture unless otherwise stated. My complaints may seem too pithy, but Boyer's errors are part of a general pattern that obscures important issues, primarily by conflating his antinuclear ideology with "the nuclear theme." In effect, while Boyer's history is startling and insightful, he leaves his reader with the erroneous impression that the only films that truly engage nuclear issues are antinuclear films and that these are few and far between.

Specifically, Boyer claims that "[a]fter 1963, the nuclear theme largely disappeared from TV and the movies. . . ." And, "After years of neglect, the movies and television rediscovered nuclear war in the early 1980s." This is clearly not correct. Let us take a look at the facts of bomb films. The overall average since 1950 is 17.89 bomb films per year. The number of bomb films in the period that Boyer describes as "the years of the Big Sleep" declined by less than 6 percent, or 1 film per year. In fact, in none of Boyer's periods, or cycles, does the average number increase or decrease by more than 30 percent from the overall average. I have tried using several different scholars' timelines as axes along which to divide bomb films into historical periods. These time lines include: major developments or events in nuclear technology, the arms race, and the cold war; major technological, economic, political, legal, and social developments of the cinema; and, more simply, decades. No matter how I divide atomic bomb cinema into historical periods, no one period varies from the overall average by more than 30 percent. Thirty percent is statistically significant, but it does not suggest "cycles" of public apathy, psychic numbing, or "years of neglect."

I have also "crunched" the numbers of bomb films into a computer, using the "Smoothing Spline Fit" technique with a "goodness of fit" of roughly 0.84 (that is, a fairly accurate generalization of the distribution of bomb films). At the risk of overgeneralizing Boyer's interpretation, he sees a pattern of peaks and valleys that describe only the tip of the iceberg, so to speak. To me, these peaks and valleys suggest that hidden beneath the surface is the main body of bomb films. Another way to put that is, to me the statistics suggest a significant basal rate of bomb film production with some variation, not wild fluctuations. I also see a generally increasing or stable production of bomb films. By "normalizing" the numbers of bomb films to the numbers of all films, and comparing them, I also found, statistically speaking, that during slumps in the film industry bomb films often outperformed all films. Professor Emeritus Takao Shōhōji, an internationally respected statistician and my colleague at Hiroshima University, disagrees with me. When he looks at my statistics, he sees periods of stable increase and periods of stable decrease. Indeed, this is true. And, without a very elaborate statistical model that compares several different factors, we can say little else with certainty. But such a model would, ultimately, require us to "weigh" our factors, or give greater relative importance to one event over another. Both the Soviet's first detonation of a nuclear weapon and the legally enforced breakup of the vertically integrated film studios, for example, took place around 1949; to which should we give greater weight? Boyer's claims about television are, in addition, impossible to verify. To calculate the appearance of the bomb in television is a practical impossibility, and Boyer's survey is not even random. In the absence of a very sophisticated statistical model, however, I think we can still say with reasonable confidence that there is little correlation between the distribution of bomb films and Boyer's history; that is, atomic bomb cinema has never "largely disappeared" from the filmgoers diet or conscious concerns. Furthermore, although there are significant qualitative differences, earlier themes and motifs continue in bomb films of the 1980s and beyond.

In this chapter we will examine both the differences and continuities in themes by examining a small but representative selection of films from the so-called Reagan era. First we will look at the *Mad Max* trilogy, an Australian production strongly received in America. Next, we will look at *Testament,* and the single most popular TV movie—and a much criticized film—*The Day After*. We will conclude with an examination of *The Terminator.*

Whenever my work becomes a topic of conversation, one of the first questions I am inevitably asked is "What do you think of *Mad Max*?" It is difficult to convince colleagues and friends that, technically, the trilogy is only peripherally important to atomic bomb cinema. Thus, the trilogy is important because it is generally believed that these films are post-apocalyptic bomb films. It has been approximately twenty-two years since the first film was released, twenty years since the second, and sixteen years since the third, and still the films remain part of people's consciousness, and the phrase "road warrior" has become a permanent feature of colloquial language. However, except for the charismatic Mad Max, played by Mel Gibson, each of the films is so different that knowledge of the other two is not necessary to appreciate any one alone. In fact, between the films there are significant changes in characters and context. Nevertheless, because of their cult status and frequent TV broadcasts, the narratives of all three films are quite well known.

In 1979 Australian director/writer George Miller and producer/writer Byron Kennedy released their low-budget film *Mad Max*. The film did extremely well in Australia, making more money than *Star Wars* (George Lucas, 1977). It did not do nearly so well in the United States.[10] *Mad Max* takes place in the near future when social order, institutions, and infrastructures have nearly collapsed. There is no bomb.

Two years later, Miller and colleagues resurrected Max. In Australia the film was released as *Mad Max II*, but in the United States the film was renamed *The Road Warrior* (1981). The film came and went very quickly. Within a few weeks, however, the film returned to second-run theaters (often as a double feature with *Mad Max*), where it played to a mixture of bikers, punks, and art and film students.

The second film begins as a flashback, then quickly becomes a conventional narrative. The narrator explains that in the time when the world was powered by the "black fuel," for unknown reasons "two mighty warrior tribes" started a war "that engulfed them all." Though the world survived the war intact (unlike in *On the Beach*, 1959), social institutions slowly collapsed and the world slipped into chaos, and yet it does promise redemption for the righteous few.

The first in the film series, *Mad Max* is clearly not a bomb film. The opening sequence in *Mad Max II* is very enigmatic, and very little attention is given to nuclear concerns. After repeatedly viewing a videotape of the opening sequence in slow motion, I have found at most two images that might possibly be construed as nuclear mushroom clouds, but these are far from certain. Each of these images is on screen for at most a second. Furthermore, there are none of the usual indexes: blinding lights, mutants, lingering radiation, forbidden zones, and so forth. The essential point of the sequence is that communications have broken down and we have no idea what has happened in the world outside Australia. The narrator describes a third world war, but not how it was fought. He describes life after the war. Like the fall of the Roman Empire, Australian civilization does not end with a nuclear bang but with a long, drawn-out whimper. As communication and commerce breaks down, the fossil fuel based infrastructures of the modern world grinds to a halt, and civilization collapses through entropy and attrition. The conclusions of both films leave Max spiritually bankrupt and abandoned in a world without redemption. In the end he is morally little different from the punk villains he defeats.

Sadly, before the production of the third *Max* film began, Byron Kennedy died in a helicopter crash, a victim of the technology he celebrated and satirized.[11] At the start of *Mad Max beyond Thunderdome* (George Miller and George Ogilvie, 1985), Max is a desert nomad. His wagon and camels are stolen, and Max traces them to Bartertown, where his goods are being sold. In Bartertown, the trilogy's first explicit references to radiation are made. But so too are other allusions made to popular culture, TV, film, art, and even Japanese ghost stories. (A sign at the entrance reads "Helping to Build a Better tomorrow"—an obvious parody of early post–World War II advertising and propaganda.) Two competing forces rule Bartertown: Aunty Entity (Tina Turner), and a midget named the Master (Angelo Rossitto). A kind of balance of power exists between the two forces. Aunty establishes Bartertown and is its ruler, but Master controls the town's crucial supply of methane gas and maintains his power through his energy "embargoes"—a familiar word to audiences in 1985. (The gas is produced from the fermentation of pig dung.) Like King Arthur and so many other legendary leaders who bring order out of chaos only to become frustrated by the laws that they have established (in part, to legitimize their rule), Aunty's own laws prevent her from killing Master and taking control of this new technocivilization. So, she offers Max new supplies in exchange for killing Master's giant protector, Blaster. The fight takes place in Thunderdome, Bartertown's last court of appeal. Max is about to kill the giant when he discovers that Blaster is the proverbial witless giant who is more of a child than a man, and so he refuses to kill him. For not living up to his agreement, Aunty has Max bound on the back of a mule and driven into the desert to die. Max is rescued by a young woman, Savannah Nix (Helen Buday), who drags him back to an oasis where she lives in a community of children and teenagers.

The children believe Max is the long awaited Captain Walker who will take them back to their homes in the cities, back to "Tomorrowmorrow land." When Max tells the children he is not Captain Walker and there are no more cities to return to, he sets off a series of events that lead him back to Bartertown. Max, some of the children, and Master escape Bartertown in the train engine used to generate the town's electricity. Having quite literally reached the end of their tracks, everyone but Max climbs into a small plane. Max sacrifices himself so everyone else can escape. At the end of the film Master and the children are living in the cities, rebuilding, and waiting for Max to return. The spiritual rebirth prophesied for the righteous that is in the second film comes true in the third film, for the final scene dissolves from children to the city, and then to Max, who is walking toward the glowing light just off the horizon. Unlike the first two films, the ending is more ambiguous, but it also holds out a greater possibility of a happy ending for the hero. The *Mad Max* saga, thus, seemed to have exhausted itself—at least, that is, until the year 2000 when George Miller announced the production of a fourth *Mad Max* film.

Many scholars seem intent on reading into the trilogy nuclear themes that simply do not exist. Weart claims that the trilogy is the peak of post-nuclear war survival films. But then in a footnote he qualifies his claim by admitting that the last film was "[T]he first explicitly post-nuclear Mad Max film."[12] Peter Fitting's more interesting and provocative article makes a similar argument. Fitting writes that in the first film, "the larger nuclear war/post apocalypse background which interests me here was hardly mentioned." Nevertheless, Fitting insists on redacting (that is, editing together disparate stories into one seemingly united story) the trilogy under his "World War III" rubric along with American films such as *The Terminator*, where the context is explicitly postnuclear, post-apocalyptic, though, again, not necessarily postwar.[13] Mick Broderick explicitly acknowledges that only the third film is a bomb film, but then he too goes on to redact the trilogy into a single, coherent apocalyptic narrative; an idea he develops, as part of his greater exploration of bomb films, over the course of several articles. Broderick, like most critics, embraces both Lifton and Boyer, but also sees many bomb films as examples of the postmodern. His approach, therefore, is through the discourse of contemporary critical theory. From time to time, however, Broderick falls victim to his own critical apparatus, and reifies Hiroshima as the beginning of the Rapture in the Christian apocalypse. Broderick writes, for example, "It seems undeniable that the atomic bombs dropped on Hiroshima and Nagasaki created a psychological, political and social rupture in the text of history, the narrative of the human project."[14] More importantly, Broderick argues repeatedly that the narratives of these films try to contain this rupture. That is to say, rather than seeing these films as an attempt to engage the bomb, Broderick cleverly uses the discourse of critical theory to argue what most other scholars have argued for over half a century: these films foster or express a denial, that is, Lifton's nuclearism and psychic numbing. Broderick's analyses of the *Mad Max* trilogy and other bomb films are insightful, provocative, sometimes even brilliant, and belong at the top of any serious scholar's reading list. But, as I have argued throughout, seeing history as a series of ruptures is, in fact, a very traditional way of constructing a history; this standard approach to criticizing bomb films as evidence of a false consciousness is, moreover, an intellectual dead end.

Like most redactors of apocalyptic texts, these scholars obscure important thematic, historical, and cultural events as they attempt to squeeze dissimilar films into a single, one-dimensional category: a nuclear third world war. Two non-nuclear historical developments, however, seem particularly relevant to our discussion of the *Mad Max* trilogy: the oil crises of the 1970s and the development of punk culture.

In 1973 the Organization of Petroleum Exporting Countries (OPEC) cartel orchestrated its first embargo and dramatic price increase. Most anyone old enough to have a driver's license by the mid-1970s remembers long lines at gas stations, and many countries began crash programs in energy efficiency. In the United States, small, fuel-efficient Japanese cars began to sell for a premium. In 1976, President Jimmy Carter launched what was for Americans an ambitious alternative energy program, including state-of-the-art solar panels for the White House. Occasional gas shortages continued to plague the world throughout the decade. The last severe fuel shortage was in the summer of 1979. (At the time of this writing, fall 2000, another fuel shortage is developing, but it does not seem to be as severe as past shortages, and its cause is very much in debate.) By this time, however, Americans had developed coping strategies. Rationing was one; businessmen who could not afford to wait on long lines began hiring students to jockey their cars. Later administrations, moreover, did as much as they could to alleviate fears over future shortages and keep a stable supply of petroleum flowing into Americans' gas-guzzlers. The Persian Gulf War will likely remain a fresh, cynical example of American energy policy in the minds of some critics, but we should not forget that the Reagan administration gutted Carter's alternative energy programs and even disassembled the solar energy system in the White House; the Bush administration then scrapped the system and sold it to a local college at a substantial loss to taxpayers.[15] Be that as it may, the increasing popularity of the *Mad Max* trilogy attests to the fact that until at least the mid-1980s the oil-consuming countries remained fearful of further oil embargoes, and this helped contribute to the general sense that America was in decline. Though the energy crises and "grinding inflation" of the 1970s affected the poor more than anyone else, social critics of every variety claim that the 1970s was to be an era in which everyone's life, liberty, and pursuit of happiness, suffered.[16] Many Americans began to fear what the punks already insisted on: the world was already too degenerate to be saved. The *Mad Max* trilogy, particularly the second film, is visually dominated by punk-like imagery.

In an intriguing and insightful analysis, British scholar Dick Hebdige asserts that when the punk subculture came to London, "Apocalypse was in the air and the rhetoric of punk was drenched in apocalypse." Hebdige may indeed be right, but punk culture—as time has proven—was too nihilistic to be a true apocalyptic or millennial movement.[17] Not being able to offer a serious criticism or alternative to contemporary society, nor even a sustainable aesthetic, the movement died. Sadly, punk never became anything more than an expression of rage and despair. To the dominant, middle-class culture, punk represented self-immolation; the rejection of punks' one-time hippie parents' values and lifestyles; and self-destructiveness. This image of nihilistic punk is spectacularly exploited in the *Mad Max* series, especially the most important second film *The Road Warrior*.

The *Mad Max* trilogy, however, is not a punk vision of the world. Max is no punk: he does not look for spectacular self-destruction. Rather, he is a jaded middle-class hero, hardened by the world but still, in the end, a supporter of redemption. Nor is the trilogy driven by fear of the bomb. Rather, these films responded to the cultural environment of the time, to the threatening visions of a world without cheap energy, and to the collapse of trusted social institutions.

In *The Road Warrior* (1981), not only does Max struggle against predatory gangs, but also against a world turned inside out, and stereotypes and audience's expectations are inverted. Wez (Vernon Wells), Max's nemesis, is the most feared, most sadistic, and most macho of the hoard. He is also gay. Wez has his young, pretty, lover chained to the back of his motorcycle. When the Feral Kid (Emil Minty) kills the lover, with a stainless-steel boomerang, Wez becomes hysterical. In a scene that is both profoundly disturbing and touching, Humungus (Kjell Nilsson) comforts and restrains Wez and promises revenge. Also, when Max first drives the tractor-cab through the hoard and into the besieged compound, he tears loose a tent. For a brief moment we see inside the tent where a heterosexual couple are making love. The woman is on top; while this is not, in itself, aberrant, in the context of the film it is yet another inversion. Thus, in not so subtle ways, the audience's expectations that motorcycle gangs are fiercely heterosexual and patriarchal are inverted. It is Max's job to destroy the degenerate hoard and ensure the community's survival.

By 1985, when *Mad Max beyond Thunderdome* was released, the social environment changed once again. Having lost the vitality and energy of its initial impetus, this third film is consciously self-referential and intentionally ironic in subverting the clichés it helped to establish; its references to cold–war era slogans and fears of radioactive fallout, as well as Japanese ghost stories, add to its campy style. Considering the normal two-year production time for most films, the energy crisis was still an active issue when the film was made. However, nuclear issues seem to have become a more immediate concern; and yet, even in this film nuclear issues are lesser, background concerns compared to the clearly foregrounded problem of energy embargoes and who controls the supply of fuel. Fitting correctly observes that both *Mad Max beyond Thunderdome* and *The Terminator* posit a postnuclear, postholocaust environment in which women (Savannah in the former and Sarah in the latter) are central to the building of a society that transcends previous social relations.[18] This revolution in gender roles, Fitting suggests, is one reason the films have been attacked by the critics. Fitting's analysis is cogent and convincing, but the film is not nearly as revolutionary as he would imagine. While the future society described in *Mad Max beyond Thunderdome* does indeed transcend all previously known social structures, this third film is more like *The Time Machine* (1960) than first the two *Mad Max* films. At the conclusion of the film the children and Master bring about the rebirth of the past era in a new and better form— an essential theme in the apocalyptic genre.

The Biblical underpinnings to the trilogy are most apparent in *Mad Max beyond Thunderdome*. Anyone who has sat through a Jewish Passover seder should recognize Savannah's "telling the tell." This "telling the tale" is a recounting of the community's past and a foretelling of the future, that is, predicting when they will return to their home in the city.

Every year at Passover Jews proclaim, "Next year in Jerusalem." Similarly, Savannah and her friends regularly proclaim their longing to go home. The seder stresses that children learn to conceptualize themselves as part of the Exodus. Likewise, at the end of *Mad Max beyond Thunderdome*, Savannah asserts for the second time that her story is "the tell of us all" and that the newborn should learn their story. There are also similarities between Moses and Max. Moses's mother abandons him in a reed basket, which she floats downriver where Pharaoh's daughter finds him. In the same fashion, Max is abandoned in the desert by Aunty, found by the woman tribal leader, and then floated down a river in a rubber raft. Both Moses and Max wander the desert before becoming the reluctant leaders of a people that wish to return to their homeland. But before they can return home, tests and preparations must be made. Finally, Moses and Max lead their peoples through the desert to the Promised Land, but neither crosses into the land of milk and honey.

From the very beginning of the film, *Mad Max beyond Thunderdome* evokes the sense of an age having finally passed and a new one dawning, but there is still one final, apocalyptic crisis to overcome. The essentials of the apocalyptic genre are, in other words, present in this narrative. For example, when Savannah "tells the tell," she reveals to Max a drawing the children made of their Captain Walker flying them back to the city. The portrait of Captain Walker bears, of course, a remarkable resemblance to Max. More importantly, Savannah interprets this revelation for Max; and, indeed, Max fulfills the prophecy. The film thus exhorts us to survive and self-actualize during oppressive times by using an otherworldly journey, revelations, revelations interpreted, final judgments, *Tikkun Olam*, and the promise of a world reborn.

The presence of a child motif, as I suggested in my discussion of *Them!* in chapter 4, is a common element in atomic bomb cinema, and it suggests both a psychic problem in the central character and the possibility of resolving that problem. Throughout the *Mad Max* series, the child motif is present, yet in the first two films Max seems to mover further and further away from a resolution of his problems. In the third film, the child, or children, are more central to the plot and the structure of the film. The biblical Abraham is commanded to sacrifice his son, but at the last moment his hand is stopped as another voice countermands the sacrifice; Max too stays his hand and spares the child. Moreover, he becomes Moses to the community of children, saving them and Master/Blaster. All this is to say that Max could not have killed the child, Blaster, without foreclosing his own chance for psychic rebirth or salvation, and slipping beyond the pal of his already ambiguous status as antihero.

There is a second, ironic sense in which *Mad Max beyond Thunderdome* evokes the passing of an age. It does, at least for those of us who were old enough (or perhaps that should be "young enough"?) to have flocked to the theaters to see the first and second *Mad Max* cult films before they became acceptable viewing to TV censors and our parents. One friend summed up the third film's failings rather succinctly: "Not enough gratuitous sex and violence." To see the irredeemably repressed savage and one-dimensionally cynical edge of the youthful Max being slowly ground into the gentleness and compassion for others that comes with middle-aged complexity makes one nostalgic. It marks not only the fact that the actors and filmmakers have survived the crises of their youth and passed into another age, but our own as well. Like all villains, for example, Darth Vader (James Earl Jones) in George Lucas' *Star Wars* series, and all antiheros, Max is interesting to us precisely because he has lost his humanity. (I would say that Satan is a perfect example of our fascination with fallen characters, except that, at the literal level, Satan is a fallen angel, and has no humanity to lose.) Villains and antiheros are foils or beacons by which we measure our own humanity. Once they recover their humanity, we lose interest in the character. The issues and conflicts that first enlivened Max's world, more importantly, no longer seem so immediate. George Miller is a masterful filmmaker and storyteller, and most likely the fourth *Mad Max* film will be a hit. Still, it will be an amazing feat to redeem, so to speak, Max from his salvation.

The *Mad Max* trilogy is important to atomic bomb cinema because it highlights how the apocalyptic imagination structures our memories of the past. From analyzing the trilogy and other films of the late 1970s and early 1980s, and the debate about these films, I draw four conclusions. First, concern over nuclear weapons and related technology did not disappear in the 1970s. There was no era of the Big Sleep. As Peter Clecak notes, "Old problems persisted, and new ones took shape: apocalypse, the nuclear arms buildup suggested, had been wrenched from divine control and made possible by human arrangement."[19] Second, though nuclear issues persisted in the 1970s, few remember the strained U.S.-Soviet relations after Afghanistan, SALT II, Three Mile Island, or the neutron bomb. The most talked about events that took place in the 1970s are Vietnam, Watergate, American hostages in Iran, OPEC, and stagflation. None of these events easily lend themselves to the forms of apocalyptic imagination that dominate American consciousness. Third, by the mid-1980s, the frightening events of the 1970s had begun to sub-side, or we had become accustomed to them. In conjunction with the continuing and/or exacerbated fears of nuclear war, this historical moment created the impression that we had left an era of the Big Sleep. Because nuclear issues readily lend themselves to the apocalyptic imagi-nation, the apparent resurgence of activism seems all the more dramatic.

Lastly, the apocalyptic imagination constrains scholars and critics as much as or more than it constrains filmmakers. Social critics are inher-ently susceptible to the apocalyptic imagination because, as Clecak states,

> the genre of social criticism itself enforces a bias toward negative views of the present—any present. And endings, especially of millennia or cen-turies, but even endings of such reified and arbitrary entities as decades, evoke a certain blend of anxiety, fatigue, and expectation.[20]

Boyer condemns the 1970s for not producing enough good bomb films, that is to say, pedantically antinuclear films. If a film does not frighten the public with images of nuclear hell, then it is ignoring the issues. For Boyer there is very little middle ground in public opinion. One is either against nuclear weapons or unconscious. Weart takes a slightly different view of the situation. He believes that because the public is so ignorant it is obsessed with the fear of nuclear annihilation; therefore, all relevant popular imagery is a psychological projection or displaced symbol of this fear. Weart, consequently, considers every postapocalyptic or postcata-clysmic narrative to be inherently about the bomb. And Fitting's concerns are so narrowly defined, so constrained by the apocalyptic imag-ination that he cannot recognize sociohistorical motifs or cultural themes that do not correspond to his version of World War III. For him, the apocalypse is the product of a third world war, which is in turn a nuclear war. These assumptions, however, are not necessary and or sufficient. Each of these scholars trims the facts to fit his theory. As redactors, they are continuing the long tradition of editing apocalyptic and Biblical nar-ratives to fit immediate historical contingencies.

Likewise, during the early 1980s, Americans became convinced that something was wrong, and so turned to Ronald Reagan, who promised to trim the facts of America in order to make it fit his vision of America. But by 1982 many factors contributed to a general sense of insecurity, and these in turn heightened fears of nuclear annihilation.[21] Middle-class, educated liberals, in particular, felt threatened on several fronts. The "sacred cows" of the welfare state—social programs begun during Roosevelt's administration and greatly expanded upon during the "movement years"—were being cut. At the same time, those people whom the welfare state was supposed to protect increasingly attacked liberals for meddling (e.g., the resentful speeches of Jesse Jackson). Economically, the middle class was coming under increased pressures; two-income/career families were no longer a luxury but a necessity. The middle-class home itself seemed to be under increasing attack from a host of social problems spilling over from their usual urban domain into the suburbs. No one was prepared for AIDS, certainly, but there seemed a surprise attack from all directions. Even if such immediate concerns could be overcome, Reagan's military buildup and provocative foreign policies made the future look bleaker then the present.

President Reagan oversaw the biggest and steepest increase in military spending since the beginning of the Second World War. Because the actual military budget is a secret kept shrouded in mystery by the high priests of national security, there are no reliable figures on just how much is spent on nuclear weapons and research. Estimates prior to 1980 range from 10 to 15 percent of the military's budget. After 1980 estimates increased to 20 to 25 percent.[22] To liberals and radicals, the president's policies seemed clearly insane; while increased spending on military defense may indeed have made many feel more secure, Reagan's saber rattling ironically made many feel more at risk. During a radio speech broadcast nationally on August 11, 1984, President Reagan told the nation that he had signed legislation outlawing the "Evil Empire," and that the bombers were on their way to the Soviet Union. The White House later claimed the president was not aware that he was on the air at the time he made the "joke." For many, such provocations appeared to be a ploy designed (perhaps by General Jack D. Ripper) to put the commander-in-chief's military to the test.

The administration's domestic policies were no less dramatic. While Nancy Reagan collected a quarter of a million dollars in tax-deductible donations for the White House's new chinaware, in the summer of 1981, Ronald Reagan dismissed ten thousand air traffic controllers and then refused to negotiate, thus busting the union. Clecak describes the political atmosphere this way:

> By mid-autumn of 1981, in the president's moment of triumph over Congress, it appeared that Reaganomics was being botched by ideological

surgeons unable to distinguish between scalpels and bludgeons. Economic recovery was postponed by the onset of the most painful recession since the Great Depression.

In addition, he notes,

Much of the Reagan economic program, then, did not mesh well with the president's expressed moral aims of restoring America's global leadership, returning government to the people, correcting injustices of the welfare state, and providing positive incentives to its victims. In the early months of 1982, even many of the faithful were given to bouts of disbelief.

In the December 1981 issue of *The Atlantic*, budget director David Stockman contributed to this disbelief by confessing that supply-side economics was in fact trickle-down economics. In other words, the administration favored more tax credits for the rich, and cut backs in social services that affected the middle class and especially the poor.[23] The poor are not a well-represented group in cinema.

In 1982 the television movie (TVM) *World War III* (David Greene) was released, but received little critical attention. The narrative is almost unique, for the film ends moments before the world is annihilated with nuclear weapons. (Some might be reminded, by this ending, of Thomas Pynchon's 1973 novel *Gravity's Rainbow*.) Concluding as it does, the narrative comes as close as any to violating the apocalyptic tradition of holding out the possibility of rebirth following Armageddon. That *World War III* was released at all suggests Americans were beginning to see nuclear war in a new way. But, again, this is only one film, and not at all exemplary.

As we have seen in other films, atomic bomb cinema is a venue for exploring a range of issues that extends far beyond nuclear war. In 1983 there were four made-for-television bomb films—three are relevant to our discussion here. (There was also one miniseries.) One film in particular uses nuclear war as an opportunity to unabashedly lament some of the issues that concerned educated, middle-class, liberals. Lynne Littman's 1983 TVM *Testament*, adapted by John Sacret Young from a novel by Carol Amen, was originally produced for the Public Broadcasting System (PBS) *American Playhouse* series, but was successful enough to be rereleased in theaters and even received an Oscar nomination.[24] Ostensibly, *Testament* is about suburban housewife Carol Wetherly (Jane Alexander) and her attempts to keep her family and town together after a surprise nuclear war. However, this is just a thinly disguised pretext for other issues.

As I will demonstrate, *Testament* has much in common with Stanley Kramer's weepie *On the Beach* (1959).

There are four major themes in *Testament*, which include the horrors of nuclear war; the need to wake up and protect the children's future; men's indifferent and abusive treatment of women; and women's suffering. These four themes are balanced by a fifth theme: the innate goodness of the American "nuclear" family.

Hiroshi (Gerry Murillo), a learning disabled Japanese boy, is an obvious and crass icon for Hiroshima and Nagasaki, and the horrors of nuclear war. To establish the need to "wake up" and protect the children a more elaborate allegory is used. The town's name is Hamelin, and Carol is directing the school play, the "Pied Piper of Hamelin." In addition to refusing to help take care of the house and raise the children, Tom (William Devane) derides Carol's involvement with the school play as its director. Littman does not trust her audience; so to drive the point home she actually stages the school play in the film. The conclusion of the play is particularly poignant, although in the context of the film, it is overkill. The King of Hamelin realizes that because of his greed, he has lost his own son and the town's children. Thus, because the town patriarchs did not "wake up" Hamelin, the town dies.

The suffering of women is depicted many times. Cathy (Rebecca De Mornay) is so "proud because she had so much milk" for her infant, but the child dies anyway. Against all odds, Carol struggles to keep her family alive and their spirits up. *Testament* is probably an advancement of sorts of *On the Beach*, for unlike Kramer's characters who accept the "painless way out," sheepishly taking the government-issued suicide tablets, Carol heroically struggles to survive.[25] This act of heroism, Carol's commitment to life and children, is her one redeeming quality. However, Carol never even attempts to answer her own question: "Who did this?" The only meaning in Carol's life is waiting for her husband and raising her children as she always has: without Tom's help. Thus, Carol fulfills her destiny as a paragon of the cult of true womanhood: She suffers. In contrast to other women in bomb films, Carol Wetherly is so powerless that she cannot even promise her children a better life in the future.

Despite all their suffering, the family and community remain a liberal haven from a heartless world. Carol even takes in two orphaned children. Brad (Ross Harris) spends all his time with the fatherly Mr. Abhart (Leon Ames), and Mary Liz (Roxana Zal) continues her piano lessons. When Brad's bicycle is stolen, he respectfully takes his father's, and Carol comments on how he has become a man in a time when being a man is meaningless. Individuals may dissipate and die, but the dignity of the family remains. Each time a person dies, the film cuts to a Super 8-quality film depicting some family event. *Testament* concludes with yet another home movie; this time it is Tom's birthday. The screen goes black, and then the following appears in the crawl:

> This film is dedicated to my family.
>
> —Lynne Littman.

Since *Testament* does not fit any previously recognized genre, I am proposing one justification for this film: "postnuclear feminist weepie." We do not need to add *dystopic* because weepies, at least as some feminist film scholars interpret them, always rob the central character of a nurturing environment. Unlike the weepies that Mary Ann Doane describes in her book on the woman's film of the 1940s, however, *Testament* raises the subtextual issues to the level of text through a pretense at realism.[26] The reality this film celebrates is the heroine's powerlessness, her status as a victim who can only wait for a miracle—an allegory, so to speak, of the suburban feminine bourgeoisie. Carol has no hope of affecting her destiny; or, even less hope than the heroines in the weepies that Stanley Cavell analyzes.[27] And because she can only ask "why" but never answer the question, the film celebrates the meaninglessness of her life outside of the roles of wife and mother. *Testament* presents itself as a feminist film, and many received it as such. If suffering and sacrifice makes one a feminist, then I guess most of us are feminists. Certainly, anyone who sat through the screaming demagoguery of *Testament* has suffered plenty.

Testament appeals only to those who are already convinced of the film's basic ideology of powerlessness: because men ignore women, women (and children) suffer. It appeals to the victims of our society, not survivors, for, rather than critiquing power relationships, the film merely wallows in self-pity. Carol never forms a deeper, more sophisticated understanding of her social or political life—not even her life as a woman. The message of *Testament* is clear: Avoid politics, reflective thinking, and criticism; salvation is found by sticking close to the family hearth. It appeals to the crass sentiments of a segment of the American population that felt alienated by the political environment. To my mind at least, *Testament* is only remotely about nuclear war. The real threat is the decaying standard of living and political powerlessness that young, educated liberals perceived in the early 1980s. *Testament* appeals to the gun-shy liberals who abandoned the movement after several WASP students were killed at Kent State University, and then became either yuppies who maintained their liberal personae or radical wannabes who sought sanctuary in the university. Unlike earlier antiwar films, say, William A. Wellman's *Wings* (1927), G. W. Pabst's *Kameradschaft/Comradeship* (Germany, 1931), or Stanley Kubrick's *Dr. Strangelove* (Britain, 1964), I fail to see how Littman's *Testament* can convince anyone, even temporarily, to buy its ideological program—except, of course, those who are already convinced.

Also released in 1983 was Nicholas Meyer's *The Day After* (ABC), the highest-rated TVM in twenty-five years of television movies: capturing a rating of 46 and share of 62, roughly 9 points higher than the next highest-rated TVM.[28] Like *Testament*, *The Day After* received tremendous critical praise. Particularly noteworthy is William J. Palmer who, sounding a bit too much like Linus Pauling, claims *The Day After* single-handedly changed the course of history because it "so catalyzed public opinion that it influenced the Reagan government to pursue more serious nuclear arms control negotiations with Russia."[29] On closer inspection, sex and family are, again, the dominant themes for this TVM.

The Day After begins with a Looking Glass plane taking off from the Strategic Air Command (SAC) post near Kansas City, Missouri. From the plane's perspective we are shown the heartland of America. The camera moves to the ground where we are introduced to several families living in and around Kansas City. The people seem as squeaky clean as the environment. No urban decay here, no racial strife, not even a hint of the economic crisis that was starting to depopulate the farm belt. Moreover, all the farms are family owned. Corporate agribusiness does not intrude on this idyllic, bucolic scene. The only intrusion is the military. Periodically, radio and television news reports inform us of a growing crisis in East Germany. People's lives are disrupted by these events, which are openly compared to the Cuban Missile Crisis of 1962. Thus, the military disrupts the physical and psychological environment.

The Day After takes approximately the first hour to set the context and introduce all the characters. It is like watching two hours of *Mayberry, R.F.D.* with no plot and even less character development: sheer torture.[30] Finally, the nuclear war begins and a few minutes later the war is over. The rest of the film is devoted to chronicling the characters' struggle for survival in a wasteland.

At the nucleus of *The Day After* is the family. There are two farm families, the Dahlbergs and the Hendrys. There is also Dr. Oakes's family, and missile-silo technician William "Billy" McCoy's family. A few important individuals are featured as well. There is Bruce (Jeff East) who is engaged to the Dahlbergs' daughter; Steve Klein, a pre-med student at the university; Nurse Bauer (JoBeth Williams); Allison, a pregnant woman (Amy Madigan); and most importantly, Dr. Sam Hachiya (Calvin Jung)—an intelligent and sensitive homage to Dr. Michihiko Hachiya, director of the Hiroshima Communications Hospital, and a very important diarist of the nuclear aftermath.[31] Although the film tries to represent the plural American society in a good light, the cultural pyramid is, nevertheless, obvious. America is squeaky clean and mostly white. Ironically, Dr. Oakes is played by Jason Robards, who also starred in *A Boy and His Dog*. In both films Robards lives in an idealized Kansas town.

Sex is this film's major motif. There seems to be one exception, and it is, not surprisingly, the one black family. What concerns Billy McCoy's (William Allen Young) family most is his getting out of the military. Let us examine the role of sex in the other three families.

The night before the war begins Denise Dahlberg (Lori Lethin) and Bruce are late for their wedding rehearsal—presumably because they are making love. That night Denise's younger sister steals her diaphragm. After retrieving the diaphragm, Denise spends the entire night making love with Bruce who, Denise says, cannot wait two more days. The next morning she and her father argue over her staying out all night. That same night, Dr. and Ellen Oakes (Georgann Johnson) also make love. After making love they reassure each other that there will be no nuclear war, and reminisce about the night President Kennedy warned the American people that nuclear war with the former Soviet Union was a very real possibility. That was the night their daughter was conceived.

The following day, news reports reveal details of increased military conflict. First conventional weapons are used, then tactical nuclear weapons, and, inevitably, strategic nuclear war. Just before the nuclear war begins, Mr. Hendry (unnamed actor) returns home for lunch. Mrs. Hendry (Antonie Becker) calls the children to the table, but they are engrossed in another ominous TV news report and ignore their mother's call. So, the parents sneak off to their bedroom for an afternoon of love-making. After making love, the wife sits contentedly, preening herself before the mirror. Suddenly there is a loud roar; she and the whole house shake. We see the Minute Man Rocket moving out of the ground—Eros and Thanatos are combined in the phallic projection from deep within, underground libidinal desire. Mrs. Hendry looks outside in time to see the missile "pop" out of the silo, and then take off into space.[32] The family quickly loads their belongings into their truck to flee. But it is too late; they are among the first to be consumed by a thermonuclear fireball.

Bruce, Denise's fiancé, is on his way home when the war begins, and he is exposed to the blast. We never see him again. Dr. Russ Oakes is also exposed, but just like Carol Wetherly in *Testament*, he drives a Volvo so he survives for a few weeks. Oakes' family, however, are all at home in Kansas City, which is leveled by Soviet ICBMs.

Before the Dahlbergs can climb into their cellar, the flash blinds Danny, their son. Jim Dahlberg (John Cullum) forces his family into the cellar for several weeks. The first evening in the cellar, the Dahlbergs give refuge to Steve Klein (Steven Guttenberg), who is on his way home. Denise's mental state slowly decays. She fantasizes that Steve is her fiancé Bruce, and begins to make love to him until her father shines a flashlight on them. (the superego strikes again!) Denise screams hysterically that she wished she had not used her diaphragm when she made love the night before the war. At least, she says, she would have had a baby. Denise runs outside. Steve brings her back, but not before both have been covered in radioactive dust.

Weeks later at a church meeting where the priest barely contains his own hysteria, Denise begins to bleed from the vagina. Steve takes her and Danny to the university hospital, leaving the three healthy Dahlbergs to care for the farm. After trying to save Danny's eyes, Dr. Hachiya releases Danny without any hope. Denise is very sick, and she and Steve have begun to lose their hair. Even though Steve claims they will recover and return home in a few days, their survival seems undercut by images of the dead and dying victims of radiation. Jim Dahlberg also dies. Jim confronts some squatters who have slaughtered one of his animals, we think. With his shotgun in hand, he tells the squatters to leave. One man shoots Jim in the back with a shotgun, and then nonchalantly slices a piece of meat off the spit.

Meanwhile, back at the university hospital, after several weeks of intense work, Dr. Oakes finally develops radiation sickness. Oakes decides that before dying he wants to again see his own home. In the rubble of his home he finds the watch he had given his wife the night before the war. Like Jim Dahlberg, Oakes finds some squatters on his land and demands that they leave. But, instead of retaliating, they offer him food. Dr. Oakes falls to his knees and cries. An aged and sick man goes to him and they embrace. This is where the narrative ends.

The issue of sex is very ambiguous in this film, for no one type of person is punished (i.e., killed by the bomb) for having sex. On the one hand, those who engage in sex for pleasure die in dramatic ways, and on the other hand the pregnant woman survives and has a healthy baby. Thus, it would seem that at the heart of this film is a frighteningly confused and puritanical attitude toward sex.

The antiwar theme is clear. We could discuss the relative merits of Kennedy's nuclear strategy versus Reagan's, but this is besides the point. Clearly, because Jim Dahlberg carried a gun he was killed. Because Russ Oakes did not carry a gun, he found sympathy and compassion. At the risk of perverting Peter Clecak's intended use of the phrase, Oakes has found "a community of like-minded others."

Also present is the theme of hope. Just before the war begins a pregnant woman enters the hospital where Dr. Oakes works. The woman is already overdue to deliver. We learn that her husband did not survive the war, and that it will be another two weeks before she gives birth. Dr. Oakes tells her that not only is she holding back the baby but she is also holding back hope. The woman dismisses Oakes's sentimentality, and says, "We knew the score for forty years. . . . Nobody cared." But just as Oakes finds the watch in his ruined home, the woman gives birth. Thus, not only is Dr. Oakes the pillar of the hospital, he is also the symbolically important oak tree of life to many.[33]

As in many films, hope no longer includes God. In both *The Day After* and *Testament*, priests try to maintain a facade but it is clear that they have lost their faith. Whether this means that God can offer no hope or that liberals have lost faith in God is not clear. Early in the film Oakes's daughter, Marilyn (Kyle Aietter), takes her father to a museum where she explains Chinese landscape paintings to him. In Chinese paintings, she says, recessional perspective is not used because the painter wants us to feel that we are part of the landscape. (Kim Newman, in *Apocalypse Movies*, suggests that in this scene *The Day After* announces its strategy: to make "[o]rdinary" viewers feel a part of its landscape.)[34] Dr. Oakes asks if the Chinese painters are not suggesting God's perspective. The daughter's response is ambiguous, suggesting her father's view of the world is parochial and only partly right. It is unclear if the film is suggesting that we have lost contact with God. It is also unclear whether

God is to be conceived of as a personal redemptive God or a modern, secular vision of nature as god.

In keeping with the general motif of the film, Oakes's daughter also tells him that she is moving to Boston where she will study art. Oakes asks if she is following her boyfriend who is a pre-med student in Boston. She admits that she is following her boyfriend, but they will not be living together. "At least not at first." So, once again sex becomes the key motif.

All that *The Day After* leaves us with is family. After escaping into their cellar, Jim Dahlberg tells Denise that "What matters is we are alive and together." However, because Denise abandons the family, first for pre-marital sex, and then later by running into the contaminated atmosphere, the family unit begins to fall apart. It seems that the individual is required to stay within the patriarchal family unit until married, when sex is then acceptable and performed only for procreation. Thus, in contrast to L. Q. Jones's *A Boy and His Dog* (1975), *The Day After* seeks to protect a pristine vision of America, a vision it establishes at the beginning of the film. Frankly, I prefer John Carpenter's vision of urban decay, corrupt government, a continuing nuclear arms race, and berserk terrorists in *Escape From New York* (1981).

Because *The Day After* is a TVM, it is very difficult to analyze. A full analysis of a made-for-TV-movie requires access to the original broadcast tape. Commercials are important. Sponsors usually spend more per minute on commercials than producers spend on programs. What comes between scenes is often as telling as the scenes themselves. *The Day After*, moreover, was surrounded by an unprecedented amount of publicity and media activity. Everyone became involved, including the White House. There were guidebooks distributed to a half-million people, and teach-ins were organized across the country. And, other versions of *The Day After* were shown in theaters or on television in forty different countries, including Japan and Poland.[35] Perhaps most importantly, following the broadcast there was even a panel discussion by "authorities." All this is important to understanding *The Day After*, but unavailable through commercial distribution.

Susan Boyd-Bowman, in a brilliant and much overlooked article, "'The Day After': Representations of the Nuclear Holocaust," does much to disentangle the complexities of this film, and its liberal ideology. But this is peripheral to our current discussion.[36] Suffice it to say that if we put aside the formal and ideological issues that distinguish television from cinema, *The Day After* is similar to other postnuclear melodramas, for example, *On the Beach* and *Testament*. These films reduce complex issues to simplistic platitudes: Somebody did something wrong, and now we all suffer. And, in *The Day After*, there is even less character development than the other nuclear melodramas. Events do not bring about new political, psychological, or other awarenesses. What we are left with is the rather mundane, very inconsequential lives of one-dimensional characters. For me, in *The Day After* the heartland is celebrated for its sentimentality, not for its important contribution to a meaningful life.

Because there are no supernatural beings, otherworldly journeys, prophesies of history beyond the immediate events, or revelations of any kind, *The Day After*, like *Testament*, depicts solely the catastrophic events of the apocalypse, the illness and suffering and death. *The Day After* describes only the manifest text of apocalypse, life in a postnuclear dystopic future, without delving into the anagogic subtext so important to the apocalyptic genre as a means to shock middle-class America into righteousness. The true message of the film seems to be that the bomb will bring sin to light and punish backsliders. Whether that is a good thing remains to be seen. However, the depiction of a nuclear war in *The Day After* may have shocked some viewers and motivated others into antinuclear activism, in which case, Sontag's imagination of disaster has done its job. More likely, in this case, people were manipulated by the film's sentimentality and conflation of sex with guilt over nuclear war.

The third 1983 TVM that we need to consider is Edward Zwick's *Special Bulletin*. Unlike *Testament* and *The Day After*, *Special Bulletin* is not a soap opera, but a gripping drama that confronts complex political realities. In *Special Bulletin* an odd collection of activists have built a nuclear weapon and are holding the port city of Charleston, South Carolina, hostage. They threaten to use the weapon unless all the nuclear detonators in the Unites State's arsenal are turned over to them to be destroyed. A special team storms the boat on which the bomb is kept, and attempts to dismantle the bomb. They fail and Charleston is destroyed. *Special Bulletin* respects the ambiguity and complexity of nuclear issues, even if the characters are somewhat clichéd. The activists include men and women, concerned scientists and homemakers, white liberals and a black radical. The film explores each person's motivations, the government's responses, and the media's coverage of the events. The film provocatively leaves the issues unanswered. The actions of the terrorists, or activists, if you prefer, are neither condemned nor condoned. Nor are anyone else's actions. The spectators are left to make their own decisions. Let us now end our discussion of television here, and return to our discussion of atomic bomb cinema.

Atomic bomb cinema is, as I have said before, a complex body of films that cannot be reduced to any single ideology. Even in the strongly anti-nuclear atmosphere of the mid-1980s, there are popular and profitable bomb films that exhort a decidedly pronuclear ideology. More precisely, since 1964, people have become increasingly worried about the bomb, yet optimism and faith still remain high. This atmosphere of cautious enthusiasm can be seen in several films. John Milius's very popular 1984 film *Red Dawn*, for example, is a defense of the Reagan administration's subscription to the Nuclear Utilization Theory (NUT), which maintains that a controlled, escalating, nuclear war can be successfully fought. In *Red Dawn*, however, it is the Soviets who successfully implement the strategy. The film also describes the domino theory, in which the Soviet block isolates and then invades the United States, fighting a very limited nuclear war. In this film many of the central characters are traumatized by the loss of family, home, and material comfort. Only a few survive. Nevertheless, the film remains true to the Leatherstocking myth, which Slotkin explains is essential to understanding American mythology (see chapter 4). The invasion, which drives the heroes and heroines westward, helps them out of the urban environment and into a communion with nature where they rediscover the true American spirit. Through the hunt, blood rituals and all, these men and women are reborn into true Americans. The bomb in *Red Dawn* is, in other words, a device that, ultimately, spawns the regeneration of Americans.

The films of writer/director James Cameron and (his former partner and his wife) producer/writer Gale Anne Hurd are among the most interesting bomb films of this or any period. They exhibit the elements of what C. W. Mills called a "sociological imagination," a combination of "the personal troubles of milieu" within the context of "the public issues of social structure."[37] In the fall of 1984 Cameron and Hurd released the first of four bomb films, the sleeper hit, *The Terminator*, followed by *Aliens* (1986), *The Abyss* (1989), and *Terminator 2: Judgment Day (1991)*. Since then Cameron has made one other bomb film, without Hurd's contribution as either writer or producer, *True Lies* (1994). The bomb features as an important motif in each of these films, and along with George Pal's *The Time Machine* (1960) and Stanley Kubrick's *Dr. Strangelove* (1964), *The Terminator* is one of the most important bomb films in atomic bomb cinema. While not the most popular film, *The*

Terminator is the most imitated film of the past two decades. And the popularity of *The Terminator* has remained so high that, seven years after its initial release, the sequel, *Terminator 2: Judgment Day*, reportedly earned back 97 percent of its record 94 million dollar price tag—before being released![38]

In this chapter we will look at the first three Cameron films and analyze *The Terminator* in depth, reserving the other films for the next chapter. When we look at the first three bomb films directed by Cameron it is abundantly clear that there is one dominant theme: women's crises, which, as we have seen in earlier films, is a theme common in the story lines of atomic bomb cinema. In each of the three films, events overwhelm the heroine. Much like some heroes in westerns, for example, in *Shane* (George Stevens, 1953), the heroines at first resist becoming involved but find themselves inextricably embroiled in the events. All three of the women, Sarah, Ripley, and Lindsey, make the axis around which the narrative develops. In *The Terminator*, society designs its own destruction, and Sarah must survive to rebuild the future. In *Aliens*, corporate greed and the desire for personal success threaten human existence, and Ripley must uncover the plot and destroy the threat. In *The Abyss*, cold war paranoia and (submarine-) pressure-induced psychosis threaten the lives of those working on a submerged oil rig; there is a threat of nuclear war against a benign, alien life form. If the aliens are to survive, Lindsey and her estranged husband Bud must disarm the nuclear device and make contact with them.

Unlike the heroes in westerns, the issues that the three heroines face are particular to women in our society, as are some of their solutions. In *The Terminator* Sarah's challenge is to become a mature, powerful, adult woman in a world where women are often powerless victims. In *Aliens*, Ripley's challenge is motherhood. (*Aliens* was the first of now several sequels to Ridley Scott's 1979 film *Alien*, which itself appears to be a remake of Edward L. Cahn's 1958 film *It! The Terror from Beyond Space*.) And, in *The Abyss*, Lindsey faces the most frightening challenge for affluent women in the late twentieth century: having a successful career and a meaningful relationship that transcends mere sex or marriage. (Cameron and Hurd's personal relationship—collaboration, marriage, and divorce—has become part of the aura that surrounds their films, sometimes misdirecting analysis.)

Of the three films, only *The Terminator* is placed within the context of a nuclear apocalypse. The film takes place in and around Los Angeles,

California, the center of the military industrial complex's high-tech research and development. Because of the time travel theme, the film's chronology can be confusing. Kyle Reese, one of two time travelers, explains that in

> [a] nuclear war a few years from now, all this, gone. Just gone. Survivors here, there. No one knew who started it. It was the machines, Sarah. defense network computers. New, powerful, hooked into everything, trusted to run it all. They say it got smart, a new order of intelligence. Then it saw all the people as a threat, not just the ones on the other side. Decided our fate in a microsecond: extermination!

The machines attempt to kill the human rebel leader, John Connor, by sending a terminator back in time to kill his mother, Sarah Jane Connor (Linda Hamilton). The Terminator is a cyborg, or robot, with human skin, and the product of automated factories. (Arnold Schwarzenegger, who reportedly turned down the role of Reese, plays the Terminator). John Connor sends one man, Kyle Reese (Michael Biehn), back in time to protect Sarah. The two time travelers and Sarah meet in a club, shoot up the place, then move on to the first of many chases. After the first car chase, the police take Sarah and Reese into custody. The Terminator attacks the police station and slaughters everyone. Kyle and Sarah escape the battle and hide in a culvert. The next morning they make their way to a hotel. The Terminator eventually locates the hotel and chases Sarah and Kyle into a high-tech factory. Inside the factory, Kyle is killed attempting to stop the cyborg. The explosion that kills Kyle also bisects the Terminator and cripples Sarah. She, however, leads the cyborg on a chase through the machines, eventually trapping and destroying the Terminator. At the end of the film Sarah, pregnant with her son John, drives to Mexico to wait for the crisis to come. As she drives, Sarah records her thoughts and feelings for her soon-to-be-born son. It is clear that Sarah has gained much from the experience. She has learned about the future and guerrilla warfare, and love, sex and motherhood. About Kyle she says that in only a few days "we loved a lifetime."

There is a history of bomb films that warn against an overreliance on machines, or rather, the human potential to become machines, such as in *The Invisible Boy* (Herman Hoffman, 1957) or *Colossus: The Forbin Project* (Joseph Sargent, 1970). And while *The Terminator* is not antitechnology propaganda, from the moment it begins, machines take on a traitorous importance. The film opens by fading into an eerie night scene of ruins. Strange helicopters fly overhead, giant stainless-steel military tanks that gleam blue in the night roll over bleached skeletons, all in search of the enemy. A lone rebel runs across the ruins and is fired upon by the machines. Mounds of skulls, pulverized under the awesome weight of a tank's tracks, evoke images of Nazi death camps—a theme that recurs later in the film. The words "Los Angeles 2029 A.D." appear atop the screen in the chiseled design of a 1980s computer typeface.[39] This explanation then follows:

> **The machines rose from the ashes of the nuclear fire. Their war to exterminate mankind had raged for decades, but the final battle would not be fought in the future.**
> **It would be fought here, in our present.**
>
> **Tonight. . .**

The scene dissolves into the title and opening credits, and then dissolves again into a night scene of another machine, a garbage truck. Over the scene, "Los Angeles 1984" and "1:52 A.M." appear. Suddenly the truck stalls. Lighting arcs illuminate the truck, much in the same way that electricity arcs across two vertical rods (sometimes referred to as a Jacob's ladder) in the 1931 film *Frankenstein* (James Whale). The camera tracks and eventually it steadies on the Terminator, standing naked to the world, yet invulnerable. Later, a naked Reese appears out of thin air and falls to the ground in a fetal position, gasping for breath like a newborn. This is just the first of many birth images.

Heavy equipment, tractors, trucks, cars, motorcycles, and motor scooters, even toy tractors, portable stereos, and home appliances all take on an ominous visage in this film. (Even the cadence of the Terminator's menacing theme music reminds us of a heavy train moving slowly down its tracks.) However, the innocuous convenience items that we often take for granted are what appear literally to ensnare Sarah. In one scene she and her roommate Ginger (Bess Motta) are apparently caught in a web of appliance cords. The Terminator then breaks in and murders Ginger's boyfriend. Ginger hears nothing because she is wearing a Walkman-type portable stereo. The Terminator shoots Ginger and also steps on her

Walkman, evoking the image of tank treads crushing human skulls, and also symbolically signaling that the music has gone out of her life. Phones seem to be especially dangerous, and Sarah's Achilles heel. In pursuit of Sarah J. Connor, the Terminator methodically kills every Sarah Connor he finds in the phone book, alphabetically. Phones, whether they are out of order, busy, or in some other way malfunctioning, betray Sarah. For example, the Terminator intercepts Sarah's phone call to Ginger, which leads him to her address book, and to Sarah's mother whom he kills. Then, in a phone conversation with Sarah, he imitates the mother's voice in order to learn from Sarah her hiding place. There is a cheeky irony to this contrived series of events. The recorded message on the two girls' message machine is in Ginger's voice, and she asks the caller to leave a message because "Machines need love too."

Televisions are also important icons in that they signify our dangerous addiction to technological conveniences. In what James Cameron calls a "future-flashback," beneath the surface of the ruins, we see children huddled around a television, only to discover that it is actually just a hollow shell in which a fire burns (yet another discomforting, albeit subversive, allusion to the mythical, Platonic cave).[40] Sarah learns about the deaths of the other Sarah Connors from news reports on TV. After the first report one friend jokingly says, "You're dead, honey." Albeit the symbol of dangerous addiction, it is the television that warns Sarah of her pursuer. The technology, therefore, has both positive and negative aspects. Likewise, guns can be used to kill or to protect. A salesman in a gun shop tells the Terminator that "any one of these is ideal for home defense." When the Terminator picks up and loads a shotgun, the clerk says, "You can't do that." The Terminator simply replies, "Wrong," and shoots the man. But then the scene cuts to Reese, who is sawing off the butt of a shotgun he stole from a police car. Reese uses this gun to protect Sarah.

Of all the characters, Reese is the most dehumanized and objectified by machines. He is trapped in burning cars, shackled with handcuffs, interrogated with video cameras (graphically imprisoning him within a machine within yet another machine: the cinematic apparatus), and killed by machines. Reese has even been tattooed with a universal price code for easy identification by a laser scan. Reese tells Sarah how "the disposal units ran night and day" and that "some of us were kept alive to work loading bodies" in the "camps for orderly disposal." Again, the Nazis' efficient factory death camps and the objectification of the human being are evoked. At one point a smarmy criminal psychologist replays the videotape of his interviews with Reese. When Dr. Silberman (Earl Boen) turns the video player off, Reese pops out of existence. Thus, Reese's death is foreshadowed as he remains trapped by technology and historical circumstances, unable to reach out to Sarah.

It is significant that as the film progresses, both Reese's and the Terminator's powers wane, and Sarah's increase. Sarah begins to take increasing control over events, and as she does, events turn in her favor. This power is symbolized through her use of technology. At first she is trapped, entangled, and dominated by technology, but as her strength increases she begins to use technology and technology begins to serve her. Understanding Sarah's development is crucial to understanding *The Terminator*.

The name Sarah means *princess*.[41] Our Sarah from the film embodies both the worst and the best character traits evoked by this appellation. At the start of the film Sarah is anything but the mature woman, warrior, or leader she is destined to become. Rather, she is more like Sleeping Beauty waiting for a man to awaken her inner life. In her emotional life she is still very much an adolescent. At work she is incompetent and frustrated, and complains that she cannot even balance her checking account. Sarah has yet to transcend her status as daughter or develop a sexual identity. When Sarah and Ginger play their messages from the answering machine, we discover it is Sarah's mother who has called. Later, against her better judgment, Sarah caves into pressure from her mother and reveals her hideout. The point here is not that the mother is wicked or evil, but that Sarah has not stopped playing the role of the dutiful, submissive daughter. Part and parcel to continuing her role as the daughter is her struggle with her sexual identity. When Sarah discovers her date has stood her up, she displaces her need to give and receive affection onto Pugsley, her pet iguana. When Sarah kisses the lizard, Ginger, who seems far more sexually active, exclaims, "That's disgusting." Thus, in the context of the film, it is no wonder that Sarah is stood up by her date.

While it is clear that the film operates within the prevalent norms of heterosexual society, it would be wrong to accuse it of promoting rigid gender roles or punishing Sarah for being single, as does, for example, *On the Beach* (1959). Peter Fitting agrees that *The Terminator* demonstrated a first step toward feminist filmmaking that addresses gender inequality. In his qualified praise he says that although Sarah is the "'new' woman of the '80s . . . she will be saved by a man from the future."[42] But is she really saved by Kyle Reese? At the mundane level, yes. One could argue that even though Sarah destroys the Terminator, she could not have done so without Reese's intervention; but this argument does not work at the anagogic or psychological levels of analysis. The point here is not that Sarah is the type of helpless heroine that we often see in film and television, a woman waiting to be saved or transformed by a man's love; it is obvious that Sarah rises as a full-blown heroine, and that her vulnerability, or need for love, is no different from the mature male hero's need. And, regardless of anyone's final conclusion, the film remains important because it explores Sarah's crisis of identity in a way that is most relevant to contemporary society.

Sarah works in the sterile environment of a franchise restaurant where the food is a generic industrial product and the employees are undifferentiated. Sarah, to push a metaphoric comparison with her antagonist, is a *robot* (the Czech word for *worker*). Her work environment is far from nurturing: we never see her eat there, and even though she is first made aware of the crisis at the restaurant, the TV news report elicits no action or cognitive response. The anesthetizing quality of Sarah's postindustrial, part-time "organization man's" life is reinforced by the fact that the second time she is made of aware of the crisis it is again in a restaurant. The second restaurant, however, is entirely different from the first. It is a dark place, a bar with mostly men, a hangout for lounge lizards. Ironically, this seedy restaurant's aura of libidinal desires, in the broad sense, provides not only sustenance (that is, she eats), but also the heightened emotional energy that allows her to recognize her crisis. This time when she sees the TV news report she not only responds, she takes action. Thus, she wakes up, so to speak, before Kyle Reese enters her life.

Sarah's crisis is one of empowerment, including those aspects of power normally reserved for men in our society. The reader will recall that a crisis is a razor's edge between destruction and rebirth to a higher psychic state. The dual nature of the crisis manifests itself in the Terminator and Kyle Reese.

On the one hand, the Terminator represents the individual's potential for unthinking, unrestrained destructiveness. The Terminator is one of George Romero's living dead, a manifestation of our society's, indeed any society's, ability to burn a village in order to save its people. James Cameron suggests that audiences "see him almost from the beginning as this implacable, sexless, emotionless machine—in the form of a man, which is scary, because he's a perfect male figure."[43] Perfect, that is, according to our society's abstract definitions of maleness: a *robot*. Bereft of the emotional life normally reserved for women, he is systematic and ruthless, yet unimaginative. He is nothing more than, to paraphrase Reese, a hyperalloy combat chassis with human skin. Indeed, he epitomizes the absolute soldier—the goal of the basic training we see so clearly and brutally depicted in, for example, Stanley Kubrick's Vietnam War film *Full Metal Jacket* (1987). Tellingly, early in the film the Terminator acquires an olive-green military jacket, one most commonly associated with, at that time, the Vietnam veteran. In an early scene, the Terminator confronts a group of punks and demands their clothes. The punks refuse and threaten him with switchblades. The Terminator grabs one punk by the throat, drives his hand through the thoracic cavity and rips the punk's heart out, leaving a pool of blood at the Terminator's feet and holding the pumping heart in his hand. (Here's a notable observation: Is it not strange that we always refer to the Terminator as *he* or *him*, and not more properly as *it*?) This seemingly gratuitous act foreshadows the Terminator's function: to kill Sarah. In a later scene, Reese warns the police,

> You still don't get it do you. He'll find her. That's what he does. That's all he does. You can't stop him. He'll wait for you, grab her throat and pull her fucking heart out!

While on the surface of the text the Terminator's function is to kill Sarah, at the subtext level he symbolically represents that element—psychic or social—that stops our hearts, just as it stopped the tragic hero's heart in *The Amazing Colossal Man*, and prevents us from developing, overcoming our crises, and reaching our fullest potential as human beings.

Reese, on the other hand, is a strong warrior, tempered by compassion, creativity, and love. And yet, when asked to describe the women of his time, all he can say is that they are good fighters. While this is no mean compliment, it lacks the response of one living in a "kinder, gentler nation." (In one future-flashback, we observe the pained expression that comes across Reese's face when his partner, a woman, is blown to pieces by one of the gleaming cyborg tanks.) Reese is the wounded warrior who commonly appears in atomic bomb cinema and Hollywood in general, a war veteran who is still capable of love but too scared to act on his feelings for Sarah. So it is Sarah who initiates their romance, and when they make love she is, for a time, on top, a suggestion of feminine empowerment.

More importantly, their intertwined fingers relax at the same time. That is to say, their suggested simultaneous orgasm evokes their emotional proximity and equality.

Kyle's name means *firth* or *channel*.[44] Although this connection may have been unintended, and it certainly would not come across obviously to the viewer, it is, nevertheless, through Kyle that Sarah can access the strength and powers that are normally reserved for men. More importantly, it is through Kyle that Sarah finds her own strengths. Their lovemaking may perhaps symbolize Sarah's integration of Kyle's psychic functions. Dialectally speaking, one might then conclude that Kyle gives Sarah something she did not always possess, and, therefore, it must not really be hers. This is in part true, but only at the mundane level of gender politics. While Sarah matures beyond Kyle and survives the crisis by developing classical resourcefulness, Kyle succumbs to the crisis and dies. Therefore, their love serves as a catalyst to the nascent powers residing within Sarah, not Kyle.

After Sarah and Kyle make love, the Terminator bursts through their hotel door and instinctively fires into their soiled bed. The Terminator is again being systematic. Since anagogic transformations occur in the bed via sexual communion, it is therefore the locus of greatest threat to the Terminator. One can argue that he is just being logical. He arrives too late, however, and his powers begin to wane while Sarah's and Kyle's powers strengthen. For the first time, the two act on the offensive. When the Terminator rushes back through the door Kyle rams his pickup truck into the unsuspecting cyborg.

The two flee the hotel; the Terminator gives chase and shoots Kyle. Sarah, who is driving, rams her truck into the Terminator's motorcycle, causing both truck and cycle to crash. The Terminator, limping on his left leg (a sure sign of wounded masculinity), commandeers a gasoline tanker and attempts to crush Sarah and Kyle just as the tanks crush the mounds of skulls in the future-flashbacks. Sarah drags the unconscious Kyle out from the overturned truck and revives him. Kyle places one of his pipe bombs, filled with homemade plastic explosives, into the tanker. The glorious explosion makes perfect use of the Soviet-style film editing known as *montage* by rapidly and disjointedly cutting to different shots of the same scene to heighten the sense of movement and energy.

The Terminator crawls out of the tractor cab and is consumed by the fire, or so we think. Typical of most psychological processes, bringing repressed energies to the surface only plays a small part in achieving the resolution. What is repressed (the potential for becoming a terminator) must also be owned, or integrated. Otherwise, what is not owned will be falsely projected onto external forces. Thus, the true Terminator, a metallic skeleton clearly built to look like Schwarzenegger, arises out of the ashes and takes up his pursuit. The Terminator's hyperalloy combat chassis gleams with the same tint of blue that we saw on the tanks in the opening scene, and moves with the elegance of a Ray Harryhausen creation.[45]

Sarah and Kyle drag each other to safety. As they run toward a building, Sarah picks up a large tubular piece of debris to break open the door. This action is important, for Sarah has developed masculine powers (not to mention taken control of the phallus-like object). Sarah has held such objects before, but this is the first time she initiates the action. The limping Terminator breaks through the barricade and into the automated factory where Sarah and Kyle are hiding. Kyle turns on all the equipment to distract the Terminator's sensitive tracking equipment. So, as Sarah becomes stronger, and Kyle and the Terminator become weaker, the technology around her begins to work in her favor.

Kyle again collapses and Sarah again drags him to his feet. In a voice worthy of a military drill instructor, Sarah demands, "Move it Reese. On your feet soldier. On your feet!" Eventually the Terminator catches up with them inside the factory. Kyle sacrifices himself for Sarah by attacking the Terminator. Again we must take careful note of the symbolic nature of imagery in this scene and the scenes that follow. After the Terminator unwittingly knocks Reese down, Reese places a phallic-looking pipe bomb into the Terminator's pelvis, in effect castrating the Terminator with his own sexual energy.

The explosion kills Reese and injures Sarah. From her left thigh (the same side as the Terminator's injury) Sarah removes a large metal shard that was once part of the Terminator's chassis. The shard penetrating Sarah's body symbolizes her incorporation of the Terminator's powers or psychic function. The pain that accompanies this union is not to be confused with sexual violence. Rather, it is the pain that accompanies every crisis, particularly crises in which we learn about our own potential for violence, that Sarah experiences. For example, the miraculous births of Aphrodite and Venus symbolize this type of emotional pain, as does the less well-known birth of Dionysus (Bacchus), in which the male diety Zeus cuts a gash in his own thigh so that he could serve as a surrogate mother for the fetus of his child. One can assert that these myths describe the pain that comes with all creative or anagogic growth. Sarah's pain is the pain of her own potential for survival and creative self-actualization; that is, rebirth. And this is borne out in what follows.

The Terminator is not dead, merely cut in half. In the final chase, both Sarah and the Terminator crawl. This time, however, Sarah leads the Terminator purposefully through the machines. She manages to stay ahead of the Terminator as she passes through a giant press. Again, whether intentional or not, the press works as a birth channel. Because she passes through the press, Sarah is, symbolically, reborn. Now she can destroy the Terminator. Sarah's method of destroying the Terminator is very different from Kyle's; she does not depend on weapons such as homemade, phallic-looking pipe bombs. Instead, she relies on her available resources. Once out of the birth channel, Sarah closes the steel gate behind her. Trapped in the press, the power womb so to speak, the Terminator reaches through the gate for Sarah's throat. As he does, Sarah exclaims, "You're terminated, fucker!" and activates the press that crushes him.

Thus, the power of the consuming mother, and the *vagina dentata*, often lampooned in Western society, is turned to Sarah's advantage. This uniquely female ability to destroy and reorganize life—a key theme in Japanese bomb films—is only part of Sarah's empowerment. She extends well beyond the limits of the men in her life, for she has not only learned to destroy (in order to preserve life) but also to love, create, and cherish life.

The question of empowerment arises in a social context, and *The Terminator* has much to offer about this context. This film takes the cynicism of others like *Dr. Strangelove* or *A Boy and His Dog* in a new direction. In *Dr. Strangelove* human error and a series of improbable coincidences override an otherwise foolproof technology. *A Boy and His Dog* mocks the leadership of the liberal establishment, totalitarian Marxists, and Libertarian reactionaries alike, and celebrates the postapocalyptic dystopia as an opportunity for the rebirth of manliness. While *The Terminator* continues in this tradition of cynicism about contemporary society, it remains hopeful that through individual redemption humanity and civility may survive.

In *The Terminator*, Cameron and Hurd strip away the nonchalant characters, the humor, and playful quality of *A Boy and His Dog* and leave us with one of the most frightening visions of the future ever created on screen. The future is not merely a brutal struggle for scarce resources, but a struggle against what Cameron coined an "implacable, sexless, emotionless" foe of our own creation. In fact, it is the very promise of abundance and safety through technology that promotes scarcity and fear. It is not merely that the technological systems cannot protect us from danger, they *are* the danger. It is the "Skynet" computers, Cameron's fictional twenty-first-century upgrade to the Strategic Air Command and the North American Air Defense Command designed to deter nuclear war, that initiate nuclear war against all of humanity and not just the other side. At the same time, the guiding hand of the welfare state is too ill-equipped to solve urban decay or direct its restless youth into more fruitful paths. Moreover, beneficent social institutions no longer function adequately, leaving us vulnerable. When after being put "on hold" many times Sarah finally gets police protection, even thirty well-armed and valiant policemen and policewomen cannot protect her from the Terminator.

While *The Terminator* depicts the inevitable destruction of our society and a dystopic future filled with pain, fear, and depravation, it remains, oddly enough, hopeful. The locus of hope, however, no longer lies in the social institutions, as we saw in earlier films, but in the individual who exists in a social system that is slowly decaying into the anarchy-ridden world of *The Road Warrior*. What Peter Clecak calls social justice and a community of like-minded others are, in films like *The Time Machine* (1960), necessary and sufficient for self-fulfillment. However, just the opposite is true in *The Terminator*. Justice and community are predicated on the individual's ability to self-actualize. *The Terminator* does not eschew politics; rather, it suggests that the available political systems, for better or worse, have little to offer the psychological needs of the individual. In other words, contemporary political debate does not resolve the paradox of the one or the many at the human level. Thus, in true apocalyptic and biblical fashion, only after Sarah has been empowered and the earth has been purged can her son bring forth justice and community out of anarchy and discord.

The Terminator is an apocalyptic bomb film. Many elements of the apocalyptic genre have wonderful twists that show the plasticity and vitality of the genre. And like most apocalyptic narratives, *The Terminator* draws on a large variety of sources. Benjamin Urrutia points out several influences, starting with chapters 12:2–6 in The Revelation of John (The Apocalypse). Urrutia also argues that Reese, whom Sarah, and everyone else, at first considers a murderous madman, can be traced through J. R. R. Tolkien's Aragorn, and Byron's messianic hero, to Isaiah 53:3–4.[46] While Reese's character is certainly informed by biblical and literary precedents, these precedents may or may not be sources that directly influenced Cameron and Hurd's unique vision of the future; nevertheless, the creators were certainly employing elements of the many narrative traditions that spring from the apocalyptic genre.

Within the structures of this genre, Reese serves several functions. For instance, he is the traveler who goes to an otherworld and he is also the sage to whom history is unfolded. Cameron and Hurd, however, add a unique twist. Kyle Reese travels to a past world, not the future. In addition, Kyle is also the supernatural being who interprets another's revelation. Sarah is unexpectedly caught up in events, she is told about the future and even dreams about the future, but none of it makes sense. After dreaming about the postapocalyptic future while sleeping in the culvert, Sarah tells Kyle, "I was dreaming about dogs." He explains, "We use them to spot Terminators." Sarah replies with a shiver, "Your world is pretty terrifying.

Biblical characters frequently referred to in early apocalyptic literature also inform Sarah's character. Like Moses, Daniel, and other significant biblical figures, it is difficult for us to explain why Sarah is chosen, just as it is also difficult for the chosen ones to explain. Or, in the secular language, why chance should happen to pick Sarah. While hiding in the culvert, Sarah asks, "Are you sure you've got the right person?" Kyle replies, "I'm sure." Sarah continues:

> Come on, do I look like the mother of the future? I mean, am I tough, organized? I can't even balance my checkbook. Look Reese, I didn't ask for this honor and I don't want it, any of it.

With great sympathy and compassion for Sarah's obvious state of confusion and fear, Kyle tells her that he has a message from her son.

> Thank you, Sarah, for your courage through the dark years. I can't help you with what you must soon face except to say that the future is not set. You must be stronger than you can imagine you can be. You must survive or I will never exist.

Thus, we have a revelation and its interpretation, a prophecy of trials and tribulations, and the promise of better times. This prophecy makes us question just what role Sarah plays in this cosmological drama.

When *The Terminator* was released, it quickly moved to center stage in the scholarly debate over Hollywood's ideology, and the debate became unusually wild and vociferous. A brief review of this debate will advance our understanding of *The Terminator* and atomic bomb cinema as well as their place in American society. J. P. Telotte, on the one hand, concludes that *The Terminator* and two other films resist "what promises to become a 'dominant ideology': the desire to see the mind as machine."[47] Hugh Ruppersburg, on the other hand, considers *The Terminator* to be one of several recent messianic science fiction films that "are, finally, reactionary in their rejection of science and their advocacy of the supernatural."[48]

In addition to these more general debates, *The Terminator* divided the ranks of feminist film scholars. The three most prominent voices in this debate are Constance Penley, Lillian Necakov, and Margaret Goscilo, all of whom base their analyses on a liberal interpretation of Freudian psychoanalytic theory and a cavalier understanding of the Bible. Foremost is Constance Penley's oft-cited and anthologized article, "Time Travel, Primal Scene and the Critical Dystopia," in which she argues that *The Terminator* recreates Freud's notion of the primal scene. That is to say, the film fulfills our desire to see ourselves conceived or born. Penley concludes that in the final analysis *The Terminator* is no different from the mainstream.[49] Lillian Necakov comes to a more progressivist conclusion. She asserts that not only does the film, ultimately, subvert mainstream Hollywood ideology, but also it "overthrows the 'correct' Oedipal resolution."[50] Such arguments are clear misreadings of the film's narrative, for it is Kyle who travels back in time to be Sarah's lover, not her son John. Taking this debate one step further, Margaret Goscilo argues that *The Terminator* is ideologically reactionary, for "Sarah's pregnancy encompasses her heroism . . . however strong [she] may become," though Goscilo never explains why pregnancy prevents a woman from being strong or heroic. (Having witnessed my wife give birth to our two children, and as she is now their primary caregiver, I can only say that motherhood can be an empowering, heroic journey as worthy as any other.) Moreover, Goscilo, who also bases her argument on psychoanalytic theory, goes as far as to insist, in a bizarre bit of frustrated wishful thinking, that "[u]ltimately, Sarah Connor does not kill Arnold Schwarzenegger."[51] Of course, the fictional character Sarah Connor does not kill the actor Arnold Schwarzenegger—she kills the Terminator.

Necakov and Goscilo, as well as others, also argue that Sarah is, as Necakov puts it, "a new Virgin Mary." Several reasons are offered. First, Necakov writes, she is one of the few women not persecuted for "having a child outside of wedlock." Second, the conversation in the culvert "can be viewed as the Annunciation, with Reese as the angel Gabriel, telling Sarah/Mary that she is going to have a son." Lastly, Reese, Sarah, and John form a sort of Holy Trinity. Necakov sees this as a kind of Mariology that supports the film's progressivist ideology, while Goscilo argues that "such a religious underpinning can only prove unfavorable to the film's image of women."[52] Whatever else we may say about these scholars' interpretations of the film, their equation of Sarah with Mary, which is largely accepted in scholarly and popular critical literature, is weak for several reasons.

In *The Terminator* at least three births must be taken into account—that is, if we do not include Sarah's psychological rebirth among them. There is one evil birth (the Terminator) and two good births (Kyle Reese, who asserts that traveling through time "is like being born," and John Connor). All three births have obvious eschatological connotations,[53] but none are necessarily of "the Messiah." There is, after all, a love scene, which would indicate no evidence of an Immaculate Conception. All too frequently film scholars have interpreted *The Terminator* with only a very limited understanding of biblical, let alone apocalyptic, tradition. These scholars erroneously conclude that Sarah must represent the Virgin Mary and that John Connor must represent the Messiah.[54]

On the one hand, Necakov's argument that Sarah symbolizes the new, improved, feminist Mary seems feasible. On the other hand, this argument also constrains our understanding of the original Immaculate Conception. For instance, Sarah is not named after the New Testament's mother of the Messiah, but the Old Testament's wife of Abraham and mother of Isaac, with whom God made his covenant (Genesis 17:19–21).[55] In the Old Testament, Sarah is the defender of her genealogy, "a mother of Nations" (17:16). Also, because God gives her a child at a very late age, Sarah complains to God, "everyone that heareth will laugh on account of me" (21:6). Similarly, Sarah in *The Terminator* is a mother of nations; she is laughed at for believing Reese's story of time travel, which others consider "lunatic." In the sequel, *Terminator 2: Judgment Day* (1991), she is not only laughed at but imprisoned for what is deemed her insane belief in her extraordinary conception. Furthermore, Isaac is not the Jewish "one like the son of God" nor the Christian "Savior." And, because apocalyptic visions draw on many different traditions and sources for imagery and ideas, we should expect the central character of *The Terminator* to be especially multivalent and polysemic.

I maintain that although the name John Connor can easily be interpreted as a messianic allusion to Jesus Christ, it is a mistake to consider Sarah only as the new Mary, and John only as the Messiah. Her name, after all, implies that she is not strictly a medium through which God acts; she is not the weak woman who depends on Joseph—or a distinctly male God for that matter—for protection. According to Flora Haines Loughead, the name John, Sarah's son, means "the Lord graciously giveth: Jehovah is gracious."[56] John is both Sarah's and Kyle's gift to humanity. However, it is Sarah alone who raises John to be a leader. Moreover, in Biblical and apocalyptic texts there is also a figure referred to as "the wonderful counselor" who should not be confused with "the Messiah."[57] Thus, Sarah Conner is actually the new Sarah of an older Genesis that does not owe its allegiance to the patriarchal past.

Cameron and Hurd add a novel twist to the apocalyptic dimension of atomic bomb cinema by making Sarah—perhaps unwittingly—a combination of three biblical persons: Mary and Sarah, as we have already seen, but also Eve. The equality of Sarah and Reese, which the film goes to great lengths to demonstrate and on which Necakov so emphatically insists, relies on Genesis 1:27 rather than Genesis 2:21–24. Genesis describes two different versions of the origin of Adam and Eve. In the second version, chapter 2 of the book of Genesis, woman is made from man. Because it seemingly justifies women's second-class status, chapter 2 has become one of the pillars of Western patriarchal dogma. However, in Genesis 1:27, we read that "God created man in His own image, in the image of God He created him; male and female created He them." God not only makes Adam and Eve in His own image, He also blesses them both equally (1:28).

The Terminator draws on the oracle and testament narrative traditions, which are related to the apocalyptic genre. From oracles the film derives its use of: propaganda, determinism, the prophesying of events after the fact, and women prophets. Collins writes that

[t]he suggestion of determinism in the oracle form, enhanced by the frequent use of *ex eventu* prophecy, lent an air of inevitability to the sibyl's message. In all, then, this was a medium well suited for Jewish propaganda in the Hellenistic world.

One of the more important bodies of oracles is the Sibylline Oracles. The Sibyllines were women, powerful figures who influenced the politics of their day.[58]

In *The Terminator*, the prologue directly addresses the spectator, propagandizing us to see ourselves as participants, as soldiers in the rebellion against the machines. In other words, like an inverted retelling of the Exodus at the Passover seder, those attending are encouraged to say *we will be* oppressed and not *you were* oppressed. At the same time, the narrative suggests that the course of some events, but not all, are already determined: we learn that Reese is the father, that John is born, and that Reese returns to destroy the Terminator and to be a father to John. Also, the narrative clearly prophesies events after they have already occurred *ex eventu*. At one point a confused and bewildered Sarah decries the film's paradox by insisting to Reese, "You're talking about things I haven't done yet in the past tense. It's driving me crazy." Lastly, at the end of the film, Sarah, like the Sibyllines, records her own prophecies of events that will dramatically alter the course of global history; she has foreknowledge, and she is using it to guide the world.

The paradox of free will or determinism, so apparent throughout the apocalyptic genre, is also strongly felt in *The Terminator*. We are told that in the future there will be an Armageddon, an era of trials and tribulations, the destruction of the wicked and the salvation of the righteous. All this is determined. And yet individuals are subject to their volitions. When Sarah asks Kyle if he comes from the future, he says "One possible future from your point of view, I don't know tech stuff." Thus, *The Terminator* heightens the dramatic tension by guaranteeing the future, but also allows the individual to choose between damnation and redemption, annihilation and rebirth.

The film scholars I have cited, as well as others, fail to acknowledge the ambiguity, ambivalence, and paradox common to our lives as well as their representation in film. Not only does *The Terminator* use these aspects of human experience to build dramatic tension, but it also evokes recognition of the ineffability and evanescence of human experience at both the conscious and unconscious levels. It seems that James Cameron is very much aware of the paradoxical natures of the human psyche. In an interview he explains,

> There is a little bit of the terminator in everybody. In our private fantasy world we'd all like to be able to walk in and shoot somebody we don't like, or to kick a door in instead of unlocking it; to be immune, and just to have our own way every minute. The terminator is the ultimate rude person. He operates completely outside all the built-in social constraints. It's a dark, cathartic fantasy. That's why people don't cringe in terror from the

terminator but go with him. But then when we go back to Reese and Sarah, you get the other side of it, what it would feel like to be on the receiving end.[59]

Cameron articulates the point so clearly. One can only wonder why some scholars resist acknowledging the ambiguous nature of human experience that allows for multiple readings of a text or film. For some, this resistance comes from ideological stridency, be it an antinuclear or profeminist agenda. For others, it demonstrates an inherent weakness in strident adherence to a single intellectual tradition. The critical theory movement, in particular, has the unfortunate tendency to inculcate devotees with the false impression—an arrogance, really—that as long as one has read theory one can easily disregard the object of inquiry—for example, the text (in this case the Bible) or the film narrative—in favor of one's own critical apparatus when forming a critical opinion. We will too soon encounter this problem again in the scholarly literature on Japanese films, in chapter 8.

Within the context of the apocalyptic dimension of atomic bomb cinema, *The Terminator* is an important film because it transcends Fowler's third phase of generic development. *The Terminator* illustrates a syncretic development of all three phases, for the optimism of the first and second phases exists simultaneously with the cynicism of the third. Likewise, the film both incorporates aspects of the dominant ideology, and subverts aspects of the dominant ideology. On the one hand, *The Terminator* symbolizes a typical apocalypse in that it promises that after Armageddon, after a period of trials and tribulations, a cosmological revolution back to a pristine state will provide salvation. On the other hand, the film clearly shows that accepted social institutions no longer fulfill their functions, and thus the viewers can no longer afford to be passive spectators to their lives.

To conclude this chapter, let us briefly look at another darling of the antinuclear Left, the satirical and cynical *Miracle Mile* (Steve DeJarnatt, 1989). As war begins and the film ends, the lovers (Anthony Edwards and Mare Winningham) are trapped in Los Angeles's La Brea Tar Pits. The hero reassuringly predicts that "a direct hit" by a thermonuclear weapon will "metamorphosize" (*sic*) them "into a diamond"; they will be found by future generations and displayed "in a museum." *Miracle Mile* disturbs, in part because it ironically embraces not Tikkun Olam, but the promise of the Christian apocalypse: continuance and perfection after the end. My point here, however, is simply that most films, even those of the cyclical 1980s, *Miracle Mile* included, cannot envision an end to story-telling; that is, in accord with the apocalyptic imagination, bomb films exhort survivance and self-actualization. Let us now return to the questions posed at the beginning of the chapter.

At the start of this chapter we explored the seemingly contradictory cultural developments in the United States during the early- and mid-1980s. I am struck by the paradox of this era. During this time a number of Americans rallied to the Reagan administration's policies, particularly increased military spending. During this time, popular pro-nuclear, pro-Reagan films did exist. For instance, John Milius's *Red Dawn* was released the same year as *The Terminator* (1984) and it packed theaters. And, many of the same viewers saw both films more than once. At the same time that Americans flocked to the Reagan platform, more Americans watched the antinuclear *The Day After* than any other TV movie before, and probably since. Moreover, the image of the future in popular bomb films and TV movies became increasingly dystopic. As James Cameron says,

> It's depressing when you watch the interviews with high school kids the day after *The Day After* and see that they've come to accept the inevitability of nuclear war. In *The Terminator* the fact of nuclear war is thrown away, with the complete understanding that people will buy it. It's just part of the fabric of the story. On the other hand, it tried to say that you take responsibility for your own life, and for the life of society. *The Terminator* looks like death, and if you want to read into it, it's a death image. Linda Hamilton's character faces that image of death or fate and survives.[60]

After films became increasingly dystopic and ideologically arcane some critics began to rediscover apocalyptic images. But because those critics misinterpret these images through their own political agendas, they have erroneously equated nuclear war or nuclear annihilation with World War III and the apocalypse. Peter Fitting, for example, stretches the definition of war beyond a useful point when he insists that the nuclear holocaust in *The Terminator* is World War III; it is, in fact, really a computer malfunction.[61] This rather bizarre situation suggests to me that while Americans embraced Reagan's vision of a revitalized America, they remained skeptical—fearful, even—of the outcome. Americans were generally anxious about the heating up of the Cold War, but did not back away from the Reagan program. And, at the same time, many people in other nations embraced and imitated the Reagan program as a way to enhance their own nation-states, with equal numbers of people fearful of the program. Perhaps the apocalyptic promise of salvation outweighed the possibility of apocalyptic dystopia.

At the same time that Americans trekked with Reagan backward to find an idyllic America, Americans also pushed forward toward a more just society. During the 1980s women moved increasingly closer to the axis of economic, political, and sociocultural power, and, very importantly, closer to the axis of the nuclear dilemma. Everywhere, outspoken women started to dominate antinuclear campaigns. Women, and the feminine element, moreover, have always been vitally important characters in atomic bomb cinema. In the 1980s, however, women take on increasing importance, moving to the center of bomb film narratives and resolving the crises often in unexpected ways; this is at least noteworthy if not remarkable for a patriarchal society. It would seem, therefore, that while the apocalyptic imagination remains fundamentally the same, there are significant changes in the way Americans imagine the bomb.

As I will make clear in the chapters that follow, American films seem to be increasingly moving toward the Japanese model: the bomb and all it represents is clearly the product of an overly powerful patriarchy while only women can resolve the crisis and restore harmony and balance to the social and natural world. Like Japanese films, American films are also increasingly concerned with environmental issues, not simply nuclear annihilation. In the most important of all Japanese bomb films, Inoshirō Honda's 1954 film *Gojira* (a.k.a., *Godzilla, King of the Monsters*, 1956), the central character is a woman, Emiko Yamane (Momoko Kochi).[62] While men discuss what to do about the monster Gojira, only Emiko has the moral strength to decide if and how Gojira is to be killed. Ultimately, she is responsible for Gojira's destruction and what I refer to as the restoration of balance and harmony in the natural and social world. Sarah in *The Terminator*, like her predecessor Emiko, also faces an implacable foe that threatens to destroy all of humanity, and only she can destroy that foe. Sarah is acting out the tradition of Tikkun Olam, which is similar to the tradition of restoring harmony and balance in its commitment to repairing a fractured world. In addition, both *Gojira* and *The Terminator* have a male character who is so emotionally scarred by battle that he cannot survive the crisis (Dr. Serizawa and Reese both have physical injuries that are clearly stigmata or somatic symbols of emotional injuries). Both men pass their knowledge on to women, for only Emiko and Sarah can use the knowledge to save humanity. And like Emiko, only through empowerment can Sarah contribute to the restoration of balance and the world be saved. In both films, hope that a just society will arise out of the rubble of a world racked by inequity surfaces.

Finally, I would stress again that bomb films of the 1980s are important because they are challenging to analyze, and because they indicate profound changes in public consciousness about the bomb. They also serve as entertainment. Despite the general dismissal of bomb films in the scholarly literature, these are insightful cultural texts—insightful because they employ what C. Wright Mills calls the "sociological imagination"— they explore "the personal troubles of milieu" within the context of "the public issues of social structure." Not only does atomic bomb cinema continue to evolve along the lines of Fowler's phases of generic development, but at the same time it continues to adapt to the changing sociocultural environment. In so doing, it further spreads the hopeful message that rebirth and self-actualization, or salvation, are possible—all of which is consistent with and essential to the apocalyptic imagination and narrative tradition.

7

1990 to 2001
The post–cold war years

The atomic bomb is shit. . . . This is a weapon which has no military significance. It will make a big bang—a very big bang—but it is not a weapon which is useful in war.

—J. Robert Oppenheimer to Leo Szilard, May 31, 1945,[1]

The atom bomb is a paper tiger which the U.S. reactionaries use to scare people. It looks terrible, but in fact it isn't. Of course, the atom bomb is a weapon of mass slaughter, but the outcome of a war is decided by the people, not by one or two new types of weapon.

—Mao Tse-Tung, August 1946, *Selected Works of Mao Tse-Tung.*[2]

The end of the cold war is variously placed between 1989 and 1991.[3] Even before this we can find indications of change in the shape of atomic bomb cinema and foreshadowings of changes off the silver screen. In *Iron Eagle II* (Sidney J. Furie, 1988, Canada-Israel), for instance, American and Soviet pilots join forces to destroy a nuclear arsenal in the Middle East. But there have been few essential changes in how the bomb is imagined. The bomb, as depicted in Hong Kong filmmaker John Woo's stunning *Broken Arrow* (1996), is still described as "the power of God," the hubris that leads actor John Travolta's character, Air Force Major Vic Deakins (a telling name considering his charismatic character) to his downfall. And, in one scene, the bomb is graphically rendered as Deakins's self-destructive phallic projection, just as it was rendered Air Force Major T. J. Kong's (Slim Pickens) self-destructive phallic projection in *Dr. Strangelove* (Stanley Kubrick, 1964). The resolution of crisis, the cessation of suffering, the American quest, otherworldly journeys, and the gaining of mystical knowledge remain key elements in contemporary bomb films. Living as we are in the early post–cold war era, it is too early to draw any grand conclusions about our own time. The available quantitative data on this period is far from complete, and the period's qualitative shape is still very much in flux. But it is still possible to analyze the data and observe the trends, from which we can draw some firm, albeit tentative, conclusions about atomic bomb cinema and the new "millennium."[4]

Of great importance are the dramatic changes that have affected the motion picture industry itself in recent years, in particular, the proliferation of multiplex cinemas, cable television movies (CTVMs), "multimedia" computers, DVDs, the production of alternate versions of the same film for different overseas markets, the sale of films to foreign markets only, the burgeoning of direct-to-video releases of motion pictures, and, perhaps, most importantly, the fact that even successful films now make their profit not in the theater but from sales and rentals to cable TV, TV, and individual consumers. In addition, the tracking of the film industry in the various film references and databases has become increasingly sophisticated and complete, thus possibly skewing comparisons of, say, the 1990s with the 1950s. All this influences our understanding of atomic bomb cinema. Statistically, the 1990s can be described as a period of stable decline in the production of bomb films; nevertheless, the actual numbers of bomb films remain high. The number of bomb films released from 1990 to 1999 reached 187 films (this number includes only a few TV movies, CTVMs, and direct-to-video releases), or an average of 18.7 films per year. This is about 1 percent higher than the average for all postwar years. While the modal year for all decades remains 1966, with 41 films released, in 1990 (the modal year of the 1990s) 31 films were released—versus 1992, when only 11 films were released. Some of these films were, of course, in production before the end of the cold war. Still, 187 films is a conservative estimate, and these numbers are very much in keeping with the statistical trends we have observed thus far, if not higher; thus, while the much-anticipated "Peace Dividend" went bankrupt, the production of bomb films remained high. In the year 2000 at least 13 bomb films could be seen in theaters.

FIGURE 1

The Beginning or the End (1947). Matt (Tom Drake, center) takes an other-worldly journey into the Manhattan Project, where secrets are revealed and interpreted—all common elements in apolcalyptic narratives. From the promotional brochure *Facts about the Making of M-G-M's Remarkable Motion Picture "The Beginning or the End."* Copyright © 1947 by Turner Entertainment Co. A Time Warner Company. All rights reserved.

FIGURE 2

The Incredible Shrinking Man (1957). On an otherworldly journey, Scott (Grant Williams) encounters a giant spider, a potent symbol for the centers of both the universe and his own psyche. Copyright © 1957 by Universal Studios, Inc. Courtesy of MCA Publishing Rights, a Division of Universal Studios, Inc. All rights reserved.

FIGURE 7

Gojira tai mosura/Godzilla vs. the Thing. Two larvae (left and right) encase Gojira (center) in a chrysalis, symbolizing the ascent of the feminine and the restoration of balance and harmony in Japanese society. Copyright © 1964 by Toho Co., Ltd.

<figure>

FIGURE 8

Hachigatsu no rapusodī/Rhapsody in August (1991). Kane's (Sachiko Murase) calmness suggests that after years of torment, balance and harmony have been restored, and she can die at peace. Courtesy of Kinnevik Media Properties, Ltd.
</figure>

That the production of bomb films remains high is itself very suggestive. The end of the cold war and the greatly reduced threat of global nuclear annihilation have not translated into the end of a cycle of concern over the bomb. To put this another way, the theory, advocated by Boyer, Evans, and others, that the production of bomb films expresses a cyclical alternating of nuclear paranoia and numbness in mass consciousness, at best describes only the peaks in the production of bomb films. The generally constant, high rate of bomb film production, and its continuing popularity, however, suggests that there still exists a basal level of concern about the bomb, and that bomb films address this concern. Furthermore, the continuing relevance of such films indicates that atomic bomb cinema adapts and responds to changes in the world. Thus, if the persistent popularity of atomic bomb cinema reflects human consciousness, then, regardless of any other changes, the apocalyptic imagination remains a persistent and prevalent presence even after the end of the cold war.

Atomic bomb cinema has entered a new period of reorganization, one similar to Fowler's second phase in which the generic type is consciously used and shaped to fit a new sociopolitical context. This new period of reorganization, however, is already quite sophisticated for, as we will see, it integrates the ironic and subversive elements of Fowler's third phase of generic development. This includes not merely subversive or clever allusions to other texts, but the reorganization of earlier bomb films. In this context, it is not a stretch to see, for example, in *Independence Day* (Roland Emmerich, 1996) a mythological reworking of *The War of the Worlds* (1953), or in *Waterworld* (Kevin Reynolds, 1995) a similar reworking of *The Time Machine* (1960).

Out of this new period of reorganization three important characteristics have emerged. First, bomb films of the 1990s struggle to define or redefine the cold war and the post–cold war eras. This struggle revolves, of course, around a variety of themes or concerns. Some films explore, for example, what the end of the cold war means in martial terms, while others try to reform public perceptions of social problems that have been left unattended as a result of the cold war. Still more films resurrect the notion of the "peaceful atom," an important theme in the early years just after World War II, as a viable use of the technology in the post–cold war era.[5] The strongest of these themes concerns the environment, which we will study in regard to exactly how the bomb will impact our future existence. Second, none of these themes are necessarily exclusive; they are often blended in unexpected ways. That is to say, a fusion of various sociological and mythological themes give rise to mosaic-like complexity in film narratives of the 1990s. This contextual complexity would have possibly baffled and disappointed earlier audiences, and is taken for granted in the post–cold war era in part, I believe, because it mirrors the complexity and ambiguity of the times in which we live. The third defining characteristic is, of course, the importance that continues to be placed on the apocalyptic imagination as the major structuring element in atomic bomb cinema.

In this chapter I will begin with the first and end with the third characteristics, but discuss the second characteristic throughout. In order to explicate each, I will briefly examine several films, and analyze in depth a few key recent bomb films: *The Adventures of Baron Munchausen* (1989), *Total Recall* (1990), *Terminator 2: Judgment Day* (1991), *Waterworld* (1995), and *Godzilla* (1998). Let us begin with those bomb films that evoke the first important characteristic: the struggle to make sense of the past and current eras.

As we struggle to define what the end of the cold war means in the 1990s, films also engaged in the struggle will offer very simple ideas about geopolitical relations; from these ideas we will begin to work our way toward the more complex, even twisted, vision of *Total Recall*. In Andrew Davis's 1989 film *The Package*, certain reactionary groups within the American and Soviet military–industrial complexes use their covert forces in an attempt to prevent the end of the cold war. They plan to assassinate Premier Gorbechov before he and President Bush can sign an arms control treaty in Chicago—the site of the first nuclear reactor. Fortunately, an average Joe American career military officer (Gene Hackman), aided by an average Jane American career military officer and former wife (Joanna Cassidy) and an average Joe Chicago police officer buddy (Reni Santoni), foil the assassination attempt. If you have not seen *The Package*, imagine a slightly cynical 1990s thriller directed by Frank Capra. In this "Mr. Smith Goes to the Cold War," superpower conflict is defined as the product of individual greed, misguided loyalties, and the subversion of real political process, not ideology or geopolitical realities; and the outcome of the cold war rests on the integrity of a few characters. In 1990, filmmaker John Frankenheimer entered the post–cold war fray with *The Fourth War*. Frankenheimer is the king of American cold war film directors. Perhaps his most psychologically complex film is *The Manchurian Candidate* (1962). (Frank Sinatra, who starred in the film, was a friend of President Kennedy. After the assassination, Sinatra was so disturbed by similarities in the film that he had it withdrawn from circulation until 1987.) While *The Manchurian Candidate*, imbued with Mills's sociological imagination, focuses on individual characters struggling to survive as they are used first as foot soldiers and then as pawns in an unimaginable machination, *The Fourth War* is a more tawdry affair. The 1990 film is about two soldiers, one American (Roy Scheider) and one Soviet (Jurgen Prochnow), who have been fighting the cold war for so long that they cannot stop. The two central characters are not struggling to survive the conflict, they *are* the conflict. The personal struggle between these two cold warriors is synecdochical for the larger conflict; thus, the cold war is, again, redefined as the product of character rather than ideology, and in this case psychopathology. Fortunately, the film reassures us, cooler heads do prevail in the military.

While American films have been, from the start, generally enthusiastic about the end of the cold war, British films remain somewhat incredulous about the New World Order. British spy films, especially, have always had a cynical edge. John Mackenzie's 1987 film *The Fourth Protocol* has the heads of Britain's MI5 and Russia's KGB (their equivalents of the CIA) openly colluding to further their own careers, even at the risk of nuclear terrorism and provoking another world war. As in *The Package*, however, it is, again, the man on the ground, the insubordinate, peace-loving spy living next door (Michael Caine) who prevents disaster. But unlike in *The Package*, the central character does not preserve the system; he threatens the system, and thus puts himself and his family in perpetual jeopardy as a result of his ultimate powerlessness to effect real change.

The many bomb films derived from the literary works of British spymaster John LeCarré are even more cynical. Fred Schepisi's 1990 film *The Russia House* is an American adaptation of LeCarré's first post–cold war novel. *The Russia House* is about how the American and Soviet military–industrial complexes, and not just a few renegades, have mobilized to ensure their continued existence. In other words, the cold war has not really ended at all; the post–cold war era is defined as a sham. As always, the more intelligent and slightly more reasonable British agents are caught between the shrewd Soviets and the bungling Americans. Ironically, in *The Russia House*, Sean Connery stars as an apolitical, alcoholic book dealer who is co-opted by MI5 but eventually gives up on politics and betrays his own country for love. More like *The Manchurian Candidate* than, say, *The Fourth War*, *The Russia House* looks at character in a geopolitical context. The only way to survive, however, is to do as the lovers in Matthew Arnold's poem "Dover Beach" do: turn their backs on a beguiling world, "which seems to lie before us like a land of dreams," where no one is who they seem to be. Similarly, the hero in *The Fourth Protocol* or Clayton Forester in *The War of the Worlds* do likewise. What is ironic is that not only did Sean Connery make the British superspy James Bond a household name, he also starred in an anti-Soviet bomb film that was released a few months earlier: John McTiernan's *The Hunt for Red October* (1990).

In *The Hunt for Red October*, a film that portrays the cold war as a time when men (and only men) could prove themselves, Connery plays a Soviet submarine captain who defects to the United States. Few American films are as nostalgic for the cold war as *The Hunt for Red October*, and most American films seem naively optimistic compared to British spy films. While *The Hunt for Red October* wistfully longs for the macho clarity of the cold war, *The Russia House* gleefully rubs our noses in the rueful fact that the cold war, which is populated by mostly impotent and pathetic men, has yet to come to an end.

In the fallout of the post–cold war era the spread of weapons of mass destruction, which is itself the cause of tremendous changes in cold war–era political relationships, has become a topic of serious concern—one that has helped to redefine the post–cold war era and redirect atomic bomb cinema. In fact, there seems to be a minor industry devoted to just churning out cheap films about stolen nuclear materials and weapons. The plot lines of these films are usually quite similar: the stolen materials are recovered by sometimes bungling and sometimes successful elite forces who are, inevitably, hampered by corrupt people in high places. There are also very expensive productions that exploit this same theme, such as the DreamWorks SKG production company's much anticipated first theatrical release *The Peacemaker* (Mimi Leder, 1997). Greedy Russian military officers, accustomed to a cushy lifestyle that the newly democratized Russian government can no longer afford, supplement their income by selling valuable military weaponry on the black market. This time, the black marketers kill trainloads of their own soldiers in a far-reaching conspiracy to sell nuclear weapons to terrorists somewhere within the once introspective now war-ravaged Balkan region of the former Soviet Union. The plot device in this film is a well-worn cliché, a sensitive artist (Marcel Lures) is so bereaved by the loss of his family that he seeks to revenge himself on an indifferent world, particularly those governments who helped fuel the conflict by selling arms to the various sides. The terrorist's target is the United Nations. Fortunately, two attractive warriors in the fight against nuclear proliferation (played by George Clooney and Nicole Kidman) charge to the rescues and stop the mad terrorist-artist. But, of course, the hero and heroine show great sensitivity to the artist's anguish, and insist on entering into a therapeutic dialogue about his emotional state. When the talking cure fails they kill him, disarm the nuclear device, have a shower and a swim, and then go out for a beer. In short, the film, though promising to be a psychologically complex thriller, redefines cold warriors in terms of the therapeutic culture: more in touch with their emotions and the emotions of others, but no less lethal or convinced of their mission.

At first, the James Bond film *Tomorrow Never Dies* (Roger Spottiswoode, 1997) also seems to be about the spread of nuclear weapons but is really about redefining yet another cold war–era theme: the threat of television. A Rupert Murdock–like media mogul (played by Jonathan Pryce) is a charismatic villain who orchestrates a nuclear war between China and Great Britain. His whole purpose is to get exclusive broadcast rights to the lucrative yet underdeveloped China market. Of course, Bond (Pierce Brosnan), in collaboration with his sexy female Chinese counterpart (Michelle Yeoh), prevent the war and have lots of sex along the way. Unlike some of the other Bond films, such as *Goldfinger* (Guy Hamilton, 1964), in *Tomorrow Never Dies* the bomb, while a linchpin to the plot, seems rather stale and uninteresting. Far more interesting is how the film demonstrates the entertainment industry's ability to profit or regenerate by publicly cannibalizing itself.

Let us move on to another important theme found in films characterized by the struggle to define the cold war and post–cold war eras. In some American bomb films, the end of the cold war ushers in a time to redress those social issues that were put on the back burner while fighting the Soviet threat (a common theme heard also in public and scholarly debates). In Tony Scott's 1995 film *Crimson Tide*, the bomb is again a MacGuffin to discuss racial issues. The film takes place on a U.S. submarine that is cut off from the chain of command just as they are receiving orders on how to respond to nationalist rebels in the former Soviet Union. The rebels are a threat to world stability, one that could lead to nuclear war. The ship's highly regarded captain (Gene Hackman) orders a nuclear strike but his new executive officer (Denzel Washington) refuses to carry out the order, claiming the captain is not following proper procedures. This leads to a power struggle and mutiny. As the conflict between the white captain and the black executive officer reaches its climax, racial issues come to the fore. In a very tense standoff that has the divided crew waiting for reconfirmation of their orders, the captain coolly taunts the executive officer with a fallacious story about using cruelty and torture to train show horses. The story reveals, in a not so subtle way, the underlying racial tensions of the situation. Finally, however, the executive officer is not only vindicated but also proven correct in his judgment. In the denouement the captain retires from the service and offers an apology to his former executive officer. The black officer's gentlemanly acceptance of his tormentor's apology suggests that the cold war–strained race relations, and black Americans, need to accept a kind of amnesty for racism. But of course, themes regarding races relations have been dealt with in many bomb films over the years, including early films like *Five* (1951) or *The World, the Flesh, and the Devil* (1959). Then there is James B. Harris's 1965 film *The Bedford Incident*, which also uses a ship as a metaphor for society and the bomb as a MacGuffin to explore black-white race relations.

Finally two recent if unlikely films, both romantic comedies, explore the bomb's relationship to unresolved social issues. *Blast from the Past* (Hugh Wilson, 1999) is about a young man born, raised, and educated in a 1950s bomb shelter. He emerges from the shelter into a world very different from the one his parents knew to become the perfect foil for critiquing both the 1950s and the 1990s. In *Pleasantville* (Garry Ross and John Lindley, 1998), a TV repairman (Don Knotts of *Andy of Mayberry*, and *Mayberry R.F.D.* TV fame) sends twin teenagers from the 1990s into a 1950s-like black-and-white TV situation comedy, *Pleasantville*, to become the two central characters. There they cause change and are changed by the experience, again foils for the critique of both the cold war era and the late 1990s. Both the narrative and the visual style of this film have much in common with *The Wizard of Oz* (Victor Fleming, 1939). The one reference to the bomb is a TV remote control unit (that sends the two into the TV program) milled with a fifties hi-tech look. On its surface is the then all-too-familiar symbol for radiation. This one symbol, momentarily seen, speaks loudly about how the bomb is perceived in the 1990s as the overshadowing context for understanding the 1950s; *Pleasantville*, however, does not address the bomb directly, is more about what we have become in the 1990s, and thus is somewhat tangential to atomic bomb cinema.

Another 1990s theme is actually familiar to older films. While optimism about what Paul Boyer refers to as the use of "peaceful atoms" declined after the early 1950s, it never completely disappeared from atomic bomb cinema. In the post–cold war era, moreover, peaceful atoms seem to have renewed currency. In particular, films like *Deep Impact* (Mimi Leder, 1998), *Armageddon* (Michael Bay, 1998), or even *Flubber* (Les Mayfield, 1997) demonstrate that nuclear energy, including nuclear weapons, has legitimate peaceful uses. Of course, in current films, the peaceful use of nuclear weapons is depicted as far more limited, and much less dramatic, than what was prophesied in, for example, *The Beginning or the End* (1947). In *Deep Impact* and *Armageddon*, nuclear weapons are successfully used to destroy a meteor that threatens life on earth. The use of nuclear weapons to stop meteors, and other extraterrestrial threats to Earth, is hardly new. In fact, Sean Connery starred in one such film called *Meteor* (Ronald Neame, 1979). This particular film, and other similar films, however, is less concerned with the peaceful use of nuclear weapons then with overcoming cold war–era politics. The optimism of films like *Deep Impact* and *Armageddon*, nevertheless, stands in direct contrast to films such as *China Syndrome* (James Bridges, 1979), and films of the 1980s that viewed any use of nuclear energy with great distrust; thus, it appears that with the decline of cold war tensions the dream of not merely disposing of nuclear weapons but putting them, and other nuclear technologies, to more productive uses has again captured people's imaginations—as will be made evident by several of the films discussed in this chapter. The peaceful use of nuclear technologies has, again, very limited applications due to their long-term destructive effects. And this brings us to the final, and perhaps most important, theme in the struggle to define or redefine cold war and post–cold war eras: the impact of the bomb on the environment and how that impact will change the way we lead our lives in the future.

The modern environmental movement began before the end of the cold war and its roots run well into antiquity, as do the roots of our degradation of the environment. Michael Ortiz Hill, in *Dreaming the End of the World: Apocalypse as a Rite of Passage*, traces these roots and finds intimate connections among the bomb, humanity's fear of death and the natural world, destruction of the natural environment, and the apocalyptic imagination; and, in the post–cold war era this connection has come to the fore in people's dreams.[6] Hill also exhorts the reader to a revolutionary return to ancient ways of imagining humanity's place in the natural world; that is, only a neopagan relationship to the natural environment can save us from self-destruction. If we observe atomic bomb cinema closely, however, we can see that the connection between nuclear and environmental issues has always been present in bomb films, even if at the time we did not recognize it as such; and, we can also find foreshadowings of Hill's argument for a revolutionary return to a neopagan worldview. Since the 1950s, moreover, there have been very few unreservedly pronuclear films, and most films on the political right of the nuclear issue portray the bomb as a necessary evil. Nevertheless, I think Hill is correct in that humanity's relationship to the natural environment, not war, is the new context in which the bomb must be made meaningful and thus exists at the foreground of our apocalyptic imaginings in the post–cold war era. We can see this in atomic bomb cinema.

An exhortation to protect the natural environment, and condemn those who would pollute it, has always been an element of atomic bomb cinema. Consider *Gojira* (Inoshirō Honda, 1954), *Them!* (1954), *The Time Machine* (George Pal, 1960), *Silent Running* (Douglas Trumbull, 1971), *China Syndrome* (James Bridges, 1979)—which Paul Boyer credits for revitalizing the antinuclear movement—and *Silkwood* (Mike Nichols, 1983). These are just a few examples of popular mainstream bomb films from the 1950s to the 1980s that clearly express strongly conservationist—though not necessarily liberal—concerns for the environment.

Perhaps the most outspoken yet least heard proenvironmental voice in atomic bomb cinema is the Troma film production company. Since at least the mid-1980s Troma has been producing a unique brand of cheap but commercially successful exploitation films that attract mostly younger audiences and little critical attention. Some of these films include Troma's *Toxic Avenger* series (1985, 1989, 1989) and their *Class of Nuke 'Em High* series (1986, 1991, 1995). Though often morally conservative, even reactionary, these films have an intentionally tasteless, subversive, and cynical comic edge to them, particularly in their antinuclear, antiestablishment, and proenvironmental stridency. To some extent Troma's films pay tribute to the genre and production style developed most fully by the Japanese, particularly Inoshirō Honda and Eiji Tsuburaya. As we will see in the next chapter, Honda's Godzilla and Mothra films are among the earliest films to make a connection among industrialization, the bomb, and the destruction of the natural environment. By the 1990s, however, the degradation of the natural environment seems to have become an inescapable issue in atomic bomb cinema, and part of the mosaic of sociological and mythological themes that characterize films of the post–cold war era.

At the other end of film-culture spectrum from the Troma films are the three *Teenage Mutant Ninja Turtles* films (1990, 1991, 1993). The first, directed by Steve Barron, is the fourth highest-grossing film of 1990, and an apologia for Reaganomics.[7] White, middle-class parents who are too busy with their careers, and poor people of color who are too busy just trying to stay alive need not worry about their kids. Radioactive waste, illegally dumped "ooze," helps children through the crisis of adolescence. Actually, it transforms their animal companions into superheroes. The children simply return to their parents and the status quo without any deeper emotional understanding of themselves or deeper political understanding of the world. Thus, the children merely come to accept their parents' authority. In Erikson's identity-formation psychology, children can move from reactive formation to role fixation. Problems are merely compensated for, not resolved—a keystone to Reagan politics.

In the political context of the 1990s, any depiction of the bomb in a film must be counterbalanced by some sort of textual disclaimer. Roland Emmerich's 1996 summer spectacular *Independence Day* clearly articulates, albeit briefly, an exhortation against the use of nuclear weapons—that is, within the earth's atmosphere. When the president (Bill Pullman) orders a nuclear strike against the alien invaders, other characters, one outspoken "scientist" (Jeff Goldbloom) in particular, challenge the decision and warn against the disastrous environmental consequences that would result, even if the weapon should prove effective. Predictably, the bomb is not effective, and the president regrets his hasty decision, which has rendered a large part of the United States uninhabitable. Later, however, the very same scientist helps to defeat the enemy aliens by destroying their mother ship with a nuclear weapon, which proves effective, but, this time, the target lies outside the earth's atmosphere. Other bomb films, needless to say, are not merely careful about taking a politically correct stance toward the use of nuclear weapons, but have more fully developed critiques of environmental issues.

Early in the post–cold war era, one bomb film made a clear, proenvironmental statement that was both cynical and hopeful. David Zuker's *The Naked Gun 2½: The Smell of Fear* (1991) seems like an ostensibly and unlikely choice, but nonetheless it is an ingenious production in atomic bomb cinema. As did Kubrick's *Dr. Strangelove*, *The Naked Gun 2½* uses comedy as a tool for social criticism, and ironic subversion of atomic bomb cinema. Some critics, however, claiming that the comic tradition is apolitical, attacked the film. Such a narrow-minded vision of the comic tradition not only throws any standard film history text out the window, but also excludes Charlie Chaplin, the Marx Brothers, Frank Capra, Woody Allen, Mel Brooks, and even Stanley Kubrick. Be this as it may, indeed there is a method to Zuker's comic madness. What at first may seem like an uncontrolled mix of screwball gags is, actually, a sophisticated mosaic of themes and styles established by other filmmakers. The film's title is both an obvious homage to Fellini's 1963 masterpiece *8 ½*, and, of course, a spoof on the hit 1991 bomb film *Terminator 2: Judgment Day* (James Cameron). Zuker's film openly spoofs dozens of other films, such as *Mr. Smith Goes to Washington* (Frank Capra, 1939), and *Goldfinger* (Guy Hamilton, 1964); in particular, the wheelchair-bound scientist and the president sitting on the toilet poke fun at Kubrick's *Dr. Strangelove* (1964). Like all good burlesque, there is a critical undercurrent to the parody. *The Naked Gun 2 ½* spoofs these films in order to set up a cogent and unabashed attack on America's political leadership.

In *The Naked Gun 2 ½* the Democrats are inept, and President Bush's administration is led by a bunch of corrupt fat cats who are willing to destroy the environment in order to line their own pockets. The film views America's politics quite cynically. *The Naked Gun 2 ½* remains, nevertheless, humorously optimistic about the individual's ability to change the system—even a bungling individual. In the film's climax, at the last possible moment, the hero, Detective Frank Drebin (Leslie Nielsen) succeeds in disarming a nuclear weapon only by tripping over and accidentally unplugging its electric power cord from the outlet in the wall. The message is clear: Just unplug the devices. Because of its dumb humor, *Naked Gun 2 ½* is one of the few films with an environmental and political message that does not bury its wit in maudlin sentimentality.

The more recent *Godzilla* (Roland Emmerich, 1998) is another fascinating American film that foregrounds environmental issues. Midway through the film, one of the main characters, Philippe Roche (Jean Reno), a French undercover agent, very apologetically acknowledges that France's nuclear weapons tests are responsible for an unprecedented environmental disaster. Yet ultimately, the film lays the blame at America's doorstep. Although born of a nuclear weapons test in French Polynesia, Godzilla heads for New York City. The film never explains this fact. Most animals, most notably salmon, return to the place of their birth to nest and hatch offspring. People in some cultures (e.g., many Japanese women) do this as well. Thus, on the surface, it would seem that Godzilla would make his nest in the Bikini Atoll (or other similar place) in the South Pacific. This animal, however, is born of a nuclear disaster. Godzilla returns not simply to America, the place where the bomb originated, but to Manhattan—as in "The Manhattan Project."[8] Ironically, Manhattan, or, more accurately, Ellis Island, is the celebrated entry point for many immigrants, including several scientists who helped to develop the bomb. The web of responsibility for the bomb is very hard to disentangle.

Despite this pretense at environmental consciousness-raising, the bomb is a Hitchcock-like MacGuffin that masks a mosaic of subtextual issues missed by most reviewers and critics. Symptomatically, the July 6, 1998 cover of the Asia edition of *Time* consists of a collage, of a black-and-white picture of the original Gojira but with the head of the American Godzilla in color, taped onto the body. The headline reads: "GODZILLA! What Have They Done to Asia's Favorite Monster?" (Typical of *Time*, Japan is synonymous for Asia.) And yet, the film, and the merchandising, seems to have been reasonably popular in Japan. The Meiji foods products company, for example, marketed a *Godzilla* "Choco Snack," and the film remains very popular in the video rental markets.[9] Most of the attacks on *Godzilla* accuse it of not living up to the spirit of the original. The question is, Which original? Inoshirō Honda's 1954 film *Gojira*, or the significantly altered film that Americans first saw in 1956: *Godzilla: King of the Monsters* (directed and re-edited by Terry Morse)? Depending on which version of the original we compare *Godzilla* to, we develop very different interpretations. But let us start at the beginning, with the 1998 film.

The opening sequence is a montage of images of French Polynesia, a lot of iguana lizards, and the testing of a thermonuclear weapon. A short time later a giant creature attacks a Japanese fishing vessel, and the only survivor easily identifies the monster as "Gojira." According to Dr. Nick Tatopoulos (Matthew Broderick), however, Godzilla is not an ancient dinosaur, but a mutant from an entirely new species created by exposure to nuclear weapons tests. For most audiences, apparently, this contradiction is not important.

As the film progresses, the military becomes overly eager to destroy the creature, while Nick insists that there is a nest that must be found and destroyed first. At about this time, Nick's old flame Audrey Timmonds (Maria Pittilo) works her way back into Nick's life. Audrey reluctantly, and later remorsefully, exploits Nick's trust, getting him fired in the process, in order to make a name for herself as a reporter. Thus, the plot begins to focus on the seemingly contemporary problem of conflicts among career, meaningful relationships, and personal values. After Nick is fired, he is kidnapped by Roche. In order to earn Nick's trust and help, Roche finally reveals his true identity and his true intentions, and acknowledges France's guilt. Roche, in other words, learns to move beyond his deceptions and develop an honest relationship with the other characters. Eventually, the central characters, led by Roche, make their way into a subterranean nest deep in the bowels of Madison Square Garden, and attempt to destroy over two hundred eggs. But, the baby creatures have already begun to hatch, and Roche's original plan fails. The heroes alert the air force, and they drop incendiary bombs on the Garden, burning the hatched creatures and remaining eggs. A bereaved Godzilla is then lured onto a bridge where it is shot and killed by several air force planes. Nick then approaches the creature. Godzilla and Nick look at each other with sad expressions, and Nick watches as Godzilla dies. Nick and Audrey embrace and turn toward the crowds of cheering spectators. The last thing we see, though, is a creature hatching from an egg that survived the holocaust that consumed its siblings.

Visually, the film is constructed from scenes taken wholesale from other successful creature films. For example, the egg chamber is taken from Ridley Scott's bomb film *Alien* (1979) while the scene where Nick escapes the creatures by taking an elevator is adapted from one of James Cameron's bomb films, *Aliens* (1986); and the death of Godzilla is clearly taken from *King Kong* (Merian C. Cooper and Ernest B. Schoedsack, 1934). Other scenes are, similarly, inspired by films like *Dragonslayer* (Matthew Robbins, 1981). There are also various similarities among the characters in the 1998 *Godzilla* and the 1954 and 1956 Godzilla films. The three main characters, for example, include a reporter, a scientist, a military man, and a love interest; but, as in *The Thing from Another World* (Christian Nyby, 1951), these are hardly unusual characters in science fiction–creature bomb films.

There is an important similarity between the 1998 and 1956 Godzilla films that often eludes the critical commentary: the apology. In the 1956 film the central character, Steve Martin (Raymond Burr), an American reporter, provides both narration and narrative continuity for American audiences. Martin's commentary expresses a clear sense of guilt and responsibility for the destruction of Japan by the bomb vis-à-vis Godzilla. In the 1998 *Godzilla*, the two most important characters also express guilt and responsibility—Roche, for the bomb, and Audrey, for putting her career ahead of her relationship with Nick.

These two films have little else in common. Kim Newman astutely points out that these two films share a plot similar to the 1953 film *The Beast from 20,000 Fathoms*.[10] I would argue, however, that *Godzilla* has more in common with Gordon Douglas's classic 1954 bomb film *Them!* (see chapter 4.) All the pieces are there: the bomb has engendered a mutant species of creatures that threatens human existence (in 1998 it is lizards, in 1954 it is ants); there are underground nests containing eggs that must be burned; and there is also a love interest complicated by the seemingly contemporary issues of gender roles, career, and professional identity. The only significant change from *Them!* is that the gender roles are reversed. In the 1954 film, the female central character, Patricia, is the scientist, while in the 1998 film the scientist is Nick. Otherwise, the narrative structures are almost identical. In *Them!* the central male character, FBI agent Robert, must enter the underground nests as an instrument in the destruction of the creatures. Nick, likewise, must do the same. In both cases, this is a symbolic journey in which the male characters destroy their own psychic demons. In Robert's case, the demons are his patronizing, chauvinistic ideas about women and career; in the 1998 film, the creatures represent Nick's resentment of Audrey's career ambitions and, more importantly, his *monstrously* wounded psyche, which prevents him from accepting Audrey's genuine love. While *Them!* was filmed during the not entirely repressive cold war era, Robert learns to respect Patricia as a professional, which seems necessary for them to have a successful romantic relationship; in *Godzilla*, Audrey quits her job. Thus, Audrey serves as the central character, for she faces the toughest choices while Nick merely responds to circumstances.

Depending on how one looks at it, the resolution of the newer *Godzilla* can be, on the one hand, a reactionary response—or backlash—to women who put career and independence before family. Or, on the other hand, while *Them!* expresses the optimism of a period of ever increasing expectations and seemingly unlimited opportunity for all, the new *Godzilla* expresses the general state of diminishing expectations that has gripped the country, if not the globe, for the past several decades. Then again, the resolution can be seen as both reactionary and hopeless.

Disappointment in the newer *Godzilla* film is due, I think, to both the filmgoer's expectations and to the filmmakers' apparent misunderstanding of those expectations. To understand these expectations we need to note here briefly a few significant differences between the United States and Japanese creature film genres. In Western films the animated or mechanical creature usually represents the psychic projection (i.e., a symbolic expression) of the hero's internal monster; conversely, in Japanese films, inside the all too obvious rubber suit that represents a monster is a flesh and blood person. Also, Gojira, like most Japanese monsters, is an independent character with its own volition. Most importantly, Gojira is an expression of deeper mythical themes that go beyond the individual character's crisis and speak to the community's relationship to the natural world. (I will discuss these themes in detail in the next chapter.) The 1998 version of *Godzilla* does not fulfill the basic mythic satisfactions that audiences learned to expect from the earlier *Gojira* films. It is, therefore, not surprising that audiences and especially critics were disappointed; that is, the audiences' appetites go beyond simple name recognition or Susan Sontag's claim that they desire to witness disaster.[11]

What diminishes *Godzilla* in the end is the filmmakers' hubris. Emmerich and company seem to have thought that by simply making Gojira more high-tech, with no consideration to character, they could have a successful film. I, nevertheless, found the film a fun way to spend an afternoon. If one puts aside any expectations or looks at it as a remake of *Them!* then *Godzilla* can be an entertaining and interesting film to watch. In any case, disappointment in *Godzilla* demonstrates that there are deeper, ancient, mythic dimensions to atomic bomb cinema, particularly in the successful films that critics and scholars should take into greater consideration.

In this chapter, we have thus far examined a number of themes that characterize bomb films of the post–cold war era. These themes include: defining the meaning of the cold war, addressing social issues that were ignored during the cold war, peaceful uses for nuclear technologies, and the destruction of the environment. We have also observed that some bomb films are characterized at the subtextual level by a mosaic of sociological and mythological themes. Let us now turn our attention to another, more dominant, characteristic of post–cold war era films: the apocalyptic imagination.

One of the most important films of the immediate post–cold war era is James Cameron's 1991 film *Terminator 2: Judgment Day*. Like its 1984 predecessor, *The Terminator*, the 1991 sequel has produced images that have remained in people's imaginations years later. Released just twenty-seven days before the signing of the Strategic Arms Reduction Treaty

(START), distribution and merchandising guarantees ensured that the film was a financial success even before it opened, and was perhaps the only real blockbuster hit of 1991.[12] Its stunning visuals, particularly the "morphing" of the antagonist, were quickly imitated by other filmmakers and TV programs; the film won four Academy Awards and earned two other nominations. James Cameron again proves himself to be a master of action filmmaking, special effects, and, to a lesser extent, storytelling. This, Cameron and Hurd's final collaboration (she as coexecutive producer only), shows a greater concern for the cyborg's development than for the heroine's development. This thematic change from their other films is, perhaps, as rumored because Hurd had far less input in the film's development, and at the same time, her personal relationship with Cameron was ending. *T2*, as the second *Terminator* film has come to be known, is consequently very different from *The Terminator*. The judgment in "Judgment Day" is, nevertheless, Sarah's realization that she can control her destiny, and so determines to change the future for herself, her son, and for all of humanity. Moreover, if we observe closely, we notice that important themes run through both films, ones that highlight changing cultural attitudes toward the bomb.

In *T2* certain roles are reversed. It is 1994 and only Sarah (Linda Hamilton) knows the future, and, like Cassandra in Greek myth, no one, not even her own son, believes her; and, like her biblical ancestress, Sarah has good reason to fear that she is being laughed at by others. Sarah is incarcerated in a high-security prison for the dangerously insane. There Sarah is not merely the butt of jokes, but also a guinea pig for interns, and sexually abused by her guards. She is not psychotic. However, after spending ten years trying to prepare her son, John (Edward Furlong), for his frightening future, Sarah does, understandably, find herself sitting on the edge of insanity.

In *T2* two more terminators are sent back in time to decide the future. A new type of terminator that is made of liquid metal, known as the T-1000 (Robert Patrick), is programmed to kill John Connor, not Sarah. The future's adult John Connor, however, captures and reprograms an old model Terminator (Arnold Schwarzenegger) and sends himself a protector—a necessary change because Schwarzenegger, the former pot-smoking Mr. Olympia of *Pumping Iron* (George Butler, 1977) fame, was, by the 1990s, living clean enough to be appointed President Bush's physical fitness role model for children, as well as a wealthy contributor to the Republican Party. Suddenly, ten-year-old John

Connor discovers that two insane men are pursuing him in the way his mother was pursued back in 1984. After the Terminator rescues John from the T-1000, John realizes he possesses the ultimate boy's toy. He also realizes that his mother is not insane, so he orders the Terminator to rescue his mother without killing anyone; and so John begins his other-worldly journey.

Sarah has the Terminator recount the future, *ex eventu* history. Then, later, after the future is revealed to her in a dream—the most horrifying depiction of the nuclear holocaust that I have seen—Sarah decides she can change the course of history by "terminating" Miles Dyson (Joe Morton, who, ironically, in the same year *The Terminator* was released, starred as an alien in John Sayles's *The Brother from Another Planet*, 1984). A brilliant scientist and mild-mannered family man, Dyson is using parts from the first Terminator that Sarah destroyed in 1984 to invent the computer system called Skynet. After shooting Dyson in front of his wife (S. Epatha Merkerson) and child, Sarah cannot bring herself to kill him. John and the Terminator follow Sarah to the Dysons' home in order to stop Sarah because, as John repeatedly explains to the Terminator, "You just can't go around killing people"; in other words, killing is not the solution, it is the problem. Together, they convince Dyson to give up his research. Eventually, Sarah, John, Dyson, and the Terminator join forces to change history. They destroy all of Dyson's work and the computer laboratory where he works. The police fatally wound Dyson, so he sacrifices himself to ensure the destruction of the laboratory. The T-1000 pursues the trio. Only after a grueling battle do they destroy the T-1000, in a steel plant where it is melted down. Then, the Terminator tells Sarah to lower him into the molten steel that destroyed the T-1000; otherwise, someone else may use his parts to build Skynet. So, having changed history and averted a nuclear war, a tearful mother and son lower the Terminator to his doom. All that is left of the Terminator is a mangled forearm and hand that was caught in the teeth of a giant gear—purposeful or not, an homage to Charlie Chaplin's *Modern Times* (1936) taken to its most savage extreme.

T2, however, concentrates more on young John Connor and the old Terminator than it does on Sarah. In fact, we see more growth and char-acter development in John, or even the Terminator, than in Sarah. And, ultimately, it is the Terminator that defeats the T-1000, not Sarah. This would not be so bothersome except that in *T2* Sarah does not confront her situation as she confronted it in *The Terminator*. In *The Terminator*

Sarah found herself a victim of a world suddenly gone mad, but rose above the situation to became a survivor and a leader. In *T2*, however, Sarah does use both brains and brawn in a heroic but futile attempt to escape the mental institution, only to be rescued at the last moment by her son and the Terminator. Granted, Sarah never confronts her status as lunatic or her place in history; but she does eventually change history. Thus, whatever else we may say about *T2*, it still places the individual's struggle for physical survival and psychological rebirth within the context of contemporary social mores; and it does this through visual symbol, allusion, and metaphor.

In the final analysis *Terminator 2: Judgment Day* is an important and interesting bomb film for a few very specific reasons. The film suggests that by the 1990s not only can the individual survive the bomb and, thus, become more complex and introspective, but also that the individual can assert herself and change social reality. Also, the narrative shows that violence as a means to an end is neither necessary nor sufficient (though certainly glorified in the visuals of this science-fiction action film). Furthermore, nuclear war is no longer inevitable. Most importantly, the promise of rebirth through apocalyptic destruction is rejected as an acceptable alternative, which is a significant change from highly successful films of prior periods in atomic bomb cinema; while, at the same time, most of the elements of the apocalyptic imagination are present, including an otherworldly journey, revelations, and final judgments. *T2* is, therefore, clearly structured by the apocalyptic imagination, or the third characteristic of the post–cold war era. *T2* also struggles to redefine the cold war—that is, the first characteristic of the post–cold war era. And, *T2* offers a mosaic of subtextual sociological and mythological themes, or the second characteristic of the post–cold war era.

The most interesting and most important bomb film that explores the existential conditions of the cold and post–cold war eras is *Total Recall*, which is based on Philip K. Dick's Nebular Award–winning short story, "We Can Remember It for You Wholesale."[13] This is also the Dutch director Paul Verhoeven's second major Hollywood film, and it was released in June 1990, less than a year after the end of the Czech Velvet Revolution against a Soviet-controlled oppressive government. *Total Recall* is the quintessential apocalyptic narrative. It has an oppressive tyrant, colonies, wars, rebellions, prophets and visionaries, Sibylline oracles, mystics, mysterious temples, supernatural beings, revelations, revelations interpreted, otherworldly journeys, the unfolding of prophesied events, and mystical transformations. The film, in its depiction of the hero's "organization-man" lifestyle (early in the film), also has interesting similarities to the central character in *The Incredible Shrinking Man* (1957). The central character's vertical movement, both metaphoric and literal, between the elite and the proletariat, his eventual rebellion against his father figure, and other elements also remind us of that very important prototype to atomic bomb cinema, Fritz Lang's 1927 film, *Metropolis*. (see chapters 1 and 4). And Verhoeven adds some new science fiction twists to atomic bomb cinema.

The hero, played by Arnold Schwarzenegger, is the superspy Hauser brainwashed to think he is Quaid, a "lowly construction worker." The brainwashing is part of a plan to help Hauser infiltrate the rebellion's leadership. Bored with his life, Quaid has recurring dreams of an adventurous life on Mars. Seduced by a television advertisement, and without fully understanding why, Quaid eventually decides to implant the memory of a Mars adventure in his mind. But something unexpected happens. The implantation seems to go awry and other spies want to kill him because they unwittingly think he is a traitor, which, in the end, he becomes. Quaid has no idea what is happening until he receives a message from himself, recorded before the brainwashing, that partially explains events. Hauser tells Quaid to travel to a Mars mining colony. There he meets a psychic who reads his mind and tells him what he must do to save the oppressed people. Eventually Quaid destroys the tyrant, frees the oppressed, and brings about a cosmological revolution, or so we think, for it may all be a paranoid delusion. Ultimately, the film gives no hint as to where, if at all, Quaid's implanted memory ends and his actual adventure begins. As Quaid admits to the tyrant, after he has explained the film's plot to the hero, "That's the best mind-fuck yet."

The plot device of *Total Recall* makes it the first truly important bomb film that tries to define the issues of the post–cold war era. The tyrant (Ronny Cox) has monopolistic control over the supply of artificial air on the Mars mining colony (a unique underworld, perhaps a hyperbolic rendering of the American inner city). The tyrant uses it to control everyone, especially the mutants. He himself created the mutants by installing inadequate protection from solar radiation. Now the mutants want their freedom. Coincidentally (if coincidence exists in the apocalyptic genre), miners discover an ancient nuclear reactor designed to melt the planet's frozen core and release enough oxygen to create an atmosphere for the dead planet. The tyrant, however, keeps the reactor a secret. He claims it will cause a nuclear chain reaction that will destroy the entire planet. Since no one can explain why the aliens left the reactor unused, it appears that the tyrant truly believes the reactor is dangerous; in fact, at the end of the film he loses his own life in a desperate attempt to prevent Quaid from starting the reactor. Nevertheless, the telepathic, mutant leader of the rebellion, George/Kuato (Marshall Bell), has read Quaid's mind and convinced him to start the reactor (see figure 5). Quaid accomplishes his mission and the reactor creates fresh air and freedom for a suffocating and oppressed people. Air could be interpreted as a metaphor for the asphyxiation of freedom behind the iron curtain, or perhaps America during the cold war. In any case, *Total Recall* asks the most important question of the post–cold war era: Can a totalitarian leader remain in power if he gives up monopoly control over scarce resources? On the one hand, *Total Recall* seems to say he cannot, but never explains why not. And, on the other hand, *Total Recall* seems to say revolution and freedom may exist only in our fantasies.

Total Recall, like other bomb films, attempts to define the post–cold war era, but it does not offer a pat or reassuring definition. It gives instead an ambiguous and disturbing definition that reflects the ambiguity of our times. *Total Recall* also pieces together a complex mosaic of social and mythological themes—most importantly, that of the apocalyptic imagination. Again, the film contains many of the most important elements of the apocalyptic genre. The hero, Quaid, experiences disturbing dreams, visions, and even bizarre messages from himself—that is, several different revelations guide him on an otherworldly journey and to the rebel leader, George. Like Quaid, George has an alternate personality—the supernatural being Kuato who interprets Quaid's last revelation. This final revelation and interpretation are important precisely because both take place on-screen and are so literally supernatural, as well as because the scene is a mosaic of visual and narrative symbols. Kuato, for instance, is physically joined to the exterior of where George's womb would be if he had one, and resembles a newborn baby—who, it is often said, looks old and wrinkled. To be precise, Kuato is not only the supernatural being of apocalyptic narratives but also a particularly potent expression of "the child motif" (introduced in chapter 4) that appears frequently in bomb films. The "child's" attributes include, Jung tells us, divine or supernatural births and powers, and hermaphroditism; the child is "both beginning and end, an initial and a terminal creature," and "paves the way for a future change."[14] In keeping with the apocalyptic narrative tradition, after Quaid understands his place in future events he exhorts others to action, takes action himself, and frees those who are suffering. Implied in the film's narrative is the exhortation to social justice, a community of like-minded others, personal fulfillment, and, to some extent, a concern for the environment. But again, this may be tongue-in-cheek criticism of American-style consumer capitalism, for the narrative leaves open the possibility that the hero's adventures may be just an implanted fantasy that he purchased to assuage his feelings of hopelessness at work and at home. Atomic bomb cinema is not without irony.

Kevin Reynolds's well-known 1995 film *Waterworld* is perhaps the one apocalyptic bomb film that most obviously depicts environmental concerns. In earlier bomb films that address the destruction of the environment, with the possible exception of *Silent Running* (Douglas Trumbull, 1971), the environment still exists largely untouched. Even in a film like *On the Beach* (1959), where the dialogue describes the end of all life on earth, what we see is an environment that is depopulated but reassuringly intact. *Waterworld* dramatically departs from any prior film. It portrays a world so utterly changed that it seems environmentless, and the environment that remains is virtually a limitless body of water. The very point of the film focuses on a fictive exploration of how life would exist and endure in an environment so completely ruined by humanity's carelessness that annihilation is all but a foregone conclusion. *Waterworld*, however, cleverly gives almost no background to the story; it assumes that filmgoers are now so familiar with the postnuclear survival subgenre that we can easily fill in the details for ourselves. All we are told is that the story takes place centuries in the future and that "the ancients"—that is, we ourselves—have done something terrible that has created a new deluge. Only later does the film awkwardly make the nuclear connection clear. Less obvious is the mosaic of social and mythological themes that make this film such an important and intriguing example of atomic bomb cinema.

Waterworld opens with the hero, the Mariner (Kevin Costner), drinking his own urine, an important clue to the character's existential condition and humanity's relationship to the environment. He then travels to a manmade "Atoll" to trade. The Atoll elders ask him to impregnate a young woman in order to replenish the gene pool, but he refuses, saying that the people of the Atoll will die with or without his seed. This leads to a fight and the discovery that the Mariner is a mutant. (He has webbed feet, and functional gills behind his ears, which allow him to swim to the submerged cities on the bottom of the ocean where he scavenges for parts for his unique boat and for things to trade). The Atollers capture and piously condemn him to be "recycled" as landfill. Just as he is being lowered to his death, the Atoll is attacked by "Smokers," so named because they chain-smoke cigarettes and because their dilapidated boats, jet skies, and airplanes billow out noxious petroleum exhaust (they also drink excessively, eat processed-meat products, are violent, and live degenerately—all in all, a politically incorrect and surly group in dire need of final retribution). The Smokers are looking for a mysterious Caucasian girl, Enola (Tina Majorino), who draws pictures of things no one has ever seen, and whom most of the people on the Atoll distrustfully regard as strange. The Smokers want her because on her back is tattooed an indecipherable map that supposedly leads to "Dryland." An Atoll woman, Helen (Jeanne Tripplehorn), frees the Mariner in exchange for his taking her and Enola, whom she has adopted, to Dryland. At first, following their escape, the Mariner resents and despises his passengers, but through a series of adventures the two women soften his heart and win his friendship and love. Eventually, however, Enola is captured by the Smokers and taken to their ship, the Exxon *Valdez*. The Mariner rescues Enola, destroys the Smokers, and defeats their leader "the Deacon of the Dez" (Dennis Hopper). Helen and some of the survivors of the Atoll in turn rescue the Mariner and Enola in a hot-air balloon. Inspired by the similarity between Enola's drawings and photographs in *National Geographic* magazines, the Mariner is finally able to provide the missing clue to reading the map. The map is upside down—or rather, the world is now upside down, with the cities beneath the water; and, more importantly, the Earth's poles have been reversed (undoubtedly caused by the use of nuclear weapons). Together they make the final journey to Dryland to establish a colony for those worthy of salvation and thus save humanity (one presumes that if humanity is to survive more than a generation, they will also be joined by other survivors). A single seagull alights on their ship; this image nicely evokes the symbol of the dove carrying an olive branch, in the story of Noah and his Ark (Genesis 8:11), announcing that land is near, the deluge is receding, and God's covenant with Noah promises that there will be no more apocalypses (Genesis 9:11).[15] Once on land, Enola proclaims, "I'm home." All, needless to say, feel as though they are indeed home; except, of course, the Mariner. He must return to sea, leaving behind his lover, Helen, and his friend, Enola.

Much of what has been written about this film is on tangential issues, for example, the extreme expense it took to produce the movie (as much as $180 million), its various production problems, and its disappointing box-office and critical performance. Critics, moreover, attribute much of the film's problems to *Waterworld*'s liberal borrowings from another well-known film, *The Road Warrior* (1981). Indeed, *Waterworld*, like its scavenger hero, also borrows from a large number of other films. For example, the importance of literacy and ancient texts; the final destruction of a degenerate, predatory people; and the rebirth of society following a nuclear war are central themes in the seminal bomb film *The Time Machine* (1960); the problem of inbreeding and the need for a sperm donor from outside a hermetic community was the plot device in *A Boy and His Dog* (1975); and, the outsider hero who defends a community against a predatory or tyrannical leader has been the theme in any number of westerns and Japanese samurai films. At the level of narrative structure, however, *Waterworld* is, in fact, a mixture of *The Wizard of Oz* (Victor Fleming, 1939), the story of Moses, and, to a lesser extent, *The Searchers* (John Ford, 1956)—all points we will return to shortly.

In one of the few insightful analyses of *Waterworld*, and the apocalyptic imagination in film, Arthur Taussig asks:

> Is it possible that the usual symbolism of land and ocean have reversed (as have the magnetic poles) in this inverted world? After all, the unconscious meaning of our symbols must, ultimately, be based on some sort of translation of physical reality. If that physical reality changes, why should not the symbolic meanings attached to it? In our world, the ocean, containing the vast unknowns with both terrors and treasures, often symbolizes the unconscious, while the land, explored and known, represents consciousness. In many aspects, *Waterworld* is an admirable speculation on the symbolic consequences of a reversal of these symbols.[16]

Taussig then goes on to make clear the less obvious, symbolic commentary on contemporary life and our relationship to the natural world. He does this through an analysis of the characters, in particular the central character's existential condition:

> Today, drinking one's own urine is, if not an act of desperation, an act of self-hate. And self-hate, together with anger and anxiety, inundate *Waterworld*'s Mariner in the same way that the seas have overwhelmed the land.

Taussig's analyses stress, as suggested by the citations above, the various symbols or allusions, often ironic, in the film. Most obviously, The Exxon

Valdez is, of course, a reference to a real oil tanker, and its real drunk captain, Joseph Hazellwood, referred to in the film as "Saint Joe," who caused one of the worst oil spills in history. Names of characters and their relationships to ancient texts, especially when inverted or reversed, are particularly important. Helen, Taussig points out, like her namesake, initiates the film's plot by effectively being the face that launches the Mariner's ship (Helen frees the Mariner in exchange for her and Enola's safe passage out of the Atoll and to Dryland); and, if you don't get the connection to the Trojan Wars, there is also a character named Priam, the king of Troy. Also, Taussig points out, when the Mariner cuts Helen's hair "the inverted symbolism of *Waterworld*" becomes evident. "Unlike the Biblical Samson, rather than losing her strength after he cuts her hair, she begins taking action and increasing in power." I would argue, however, that the film is a bit more ambiguous, with a hint of misogyny. Up until the Mariner cuts both Helen's and Enola's hair, he is rather passive to events, while Helen is active and strong. But Helen is as much out of her element on a ship as the Mariner is on the motionless Atoll, and every action she takes leads them into further difficulties. Only after the Mariner cuts the women's hair does he become active, taking the initiative, while they become passive, even silent. And yet, for Helen and Enola it is also a time of learning about the sea, their protector, and themselves; that is, they endure a period of crisis that eventually prepares them for their future. The Mariner himself is scavenged from other texts. He is, Taussig writes, a failed Ancient Mariner, and a failed Flying Dutchman (who is allowed to go ashore once every seven years—a sabbatical, so to speak—to find a woman who can redeem him).[17]

Taussig, however, misses another important clue to the Mariner's character and function within the narrative. The Mariner urinates into a can, purifies then drinks his urine, and afterward he spits some into a potted fruit tree. This last action foreshadows his relationship to other humans and to Dryland. More importantly, it inverts what Taussig calls an act of hatred; it is also an act of (or at least the desire for) self-redemptive transcendence. To nurture another living thing with one's own body, from one's own mouth, demonstrates an ultimate commitment to the world; that is, a commitment to repairing and restoring a fractured world to Tikkun Olam.

The most important name in *Waterworld* is, obviously, Enola. Her name can refer to only the Enola Gay, the plane that delivered the nuclear weapon that destroyed Hiroshima.[18] This too is another inversion of the symbolic world. Taussig writes, "Enola's name in *Waterworld* is doubly strange since her parents seem to be Japanese—the last people on Earth to celebrate their own nuclear holocaust through their daughter's name."[19] Be that as it may, with Enola the connections among the bomb, the apocalypse, and the more general socioenvironmental problems that concern Hill, becomes apparent. Taussig writes that

> [t]he atom bomb, then, is a stepping stone in the process of the apocalypse; a process, which when completed will have cleansed the world and brought about a new, better, order. *Waterworld* clearly shows us aspects of both, a world in transition. The sinking of the Exxon Valdez (the Smoker's home base) celebrates the complete disappearance of the old ways—the end of consumer capitalism and Manifest Destiny. The cover of a well-preserved *National Geographic* sports the title, "Paradise Lost." Of course, the arrival of the travelers on Dryland is simultaneous with the destruction of the Deacon and his ways. The previous residents of Dryland were doomed because the world was not yet cleansed of the old ways, a process in which Enola and the Mariner are instrumental.[20]

Enola and the Mariner are indeed instrumental to the development of the apocalyptic imagination in this film. In this regard, however, Taussig's analysis does not go far enough. The apocalypse is not simply a cleansing of the world or the establishment of a heaven on earth, but a revolution or return to some prior, pristine state—in the context of *Waterworld*, for example, the tropical paradise, or Dryland, on the cover of the *National Geographic* that inspires the Mariner's solution to the mystery of Enola's tattoo. The apocalypse is a rebirth of and a return to that prior world. And, in the gnosticism of the apocalyptic imagination, the bomb is a necessary evil precondition that brings about the world's rebirth.

As we have seen many times before, essential to the apocalyptic narrative tradition is the use of both ancient and contemporary sources or texts in order to make the apocalyptic imagination speak more effectively to a specific audience. The story of Noah and his Ark, as I have already suggested, is obviously important. Three less obvious but equally important sources for understanding the narrative structure of *Waterworld* are John Ford's 1956 film *The Searchers*, the Old Testament story of Moses, and *The Wizard of Oz*. The central character in each is driven by the need to recover something, return to and reclaim their ancestral homes. There are, however, no simplistic correlations among Ethan Edwards, Dorothy Gale, and Moses to Enola and the Mariner.

Ethan Edwards (John Wayne), in *The Searchers,* is a tragic character, for he ensures his own irrelevance in the future through his maniacal quest for a white girl taken captive by a renegade "Indian"; Edwards's quest to civilize the wild frontier gives meaning to his own life. The slightly less maniacal Mariner also returns a girl, held captive by a primitive horde, to her home, helps settle the frontier, and, like Edwards, is too much a part of that wild frontier to remain in the civilization that he helps secure for others. Frederick Jackson Turner's thesis about "The Closing of the Western Frontier," no matter how discredited and how politically incorrect, obviously remains a vital myth in the American psyche; or, at least, a potent template for the construction of marketable American heroes.[21]

Like Moses, Enola's parents try to save her by sending her on a journey across the waters, where a benevolent woman adopts her; and, it is Enola's job to lead her people back to the promised land. Both Enola and Moses are associated with the creative act of drawing or inscribing things that inspire fear or awe in others. And, like Dorothy, and Moses, Enola is sent on a fantastic otherworldly adventure, but all she really wants to do is go home, which is the promised land. Also like Dorothy, Enola at first misses her chance to go home in a hot air balloon. Later, however, she and the Mariner are rescued and taken aboard the balloon, which is piloted by a rather incompetent wizard (some of whose lines come directly from the film *The Wizard of Oz*), who takes them to Dryland. This connection between Enola and Dorothy makes even more sense when we take into consideration Dorothy's and Enola's names. The name "Dorothy" literally means "gift of God," and because Frank L. Baum appended his central character with the surname Gale, today Dorothy also carries the connotation of a strong wind or emotional outburst.[22] Since 1945 the name Enola has connoted and evoked similar meanings and images.

Both the Mariner and Moses are rescued from the water by a woman. In fact, Moses' name means "saved, drawn out of the water."[23] Also, like Moses, whose tongue was burnt when he was young, the angry Mariner has conspicuously little dialog; and each spends a lot of time alone in a wilderness before being recruited to reluctantly lead the righteous few to the promised land. But once the Mariner arrives at the promised land he finds he cannot stay, just as Moses was not permitted to cross over into the land of milk and honey. And, like Dorothy in *The Wizard of Oz*, the

Mariner is filled with anger and anxiety about the world in which he lives. An unexpected encounter with a traveling wizard, who later rides in a hot-air balloon, sends Dorothy to Oz, where she frees the people from the tyranny of an evil witch and learns that "there's no place like home." A similarly unexpected encounter with an almost identical wizard sends the Mariner on a journey in which he frees the people from the tyranny of the evil Deacon and his Smoker horde, and he too learns that there is no place like home. The Mariner's heroic journey teaches him that his home is Waterworld.

As an apocalyptic text, *Waterworld* has all the essential elements: the unfolding of history, an otherworldly journey, final conflicts, judgments, an exhortation to righteousness, revelations and the interpretation of revelations, mystical knowledge gained, and the promise of rebirth beyond our oppressive conditions. In the film we also find that the hero's resolution of his personal crisis, his anger and self-hate (at, perhaps, being a mutant) coincides with the resolution of the plot and the rebirth following the apocalypse. The bomb is, of course, the mechanism that brings about the desired apocalypse, but the bomb has become part of a broader concern with environmental issues or Tikkun Olam. And, finally, we also find an exhortation to what Peter Clecak calls the American quest for the ideal self: the pursuit of social justice, a community of like-minded others, and personal fulfillment.

While *Waterworld* did not do particularly well at the box office, or with the critics, it did have a respectably long run in theaters as a summer action-adventure film (and with video rentals and sales, it was surely profitable). Although this is not unusual, it is difficult to explain. It is, perhaps, one more aspect of the ambiguous and multivalent nature of the post–cold war era. Irrespective of the reasons for the film's success or failures, *Waterworld* is a fascinating example of the apocalyptic tradition's power as a genre through which to communicate ideas, and an example of the apocalyptic imagination's ability to adapt to and critically respond to changing sociocultural conditions. Of course, it is by no means the last such film. *The Postman* (1997), directed by and again starring Kevin Costner, is apparently another apocalyptic postnuclear survival bomb film, with a proenvironmental edge. *The Postman* ran in theaters only briefly, critics dismissed it, and yet everyone was talking about the film. Perhaps this is a testament to the power of the apocalyptic imagination.

Let us now turn our attention to the last film to be discussed in this chapter, former Monty Python member Terry Gilliam's contribution to atomic bomb cinema. Released in 1989, on the very cusp of the post–cold war period, Gilliam's *The Adventures of Baron Munchausen* reconstitutes atomic bomb cinema in such a way that it foreshadows almost all the elements characteristic of other post–cold war bomb films, and in unexpected but nevertheless ingenious ways. This film is based on the life of the German soldier and nobleman Karl Friedrick Hieronymous von Munchausen (1720 to 1797), whose exploits inspired many legends and a collection of stories by Rudolf Erich Raspe. There are approximately fifteen film adaptations of these stories, including a 1911 version by French pioneer filmmaker Georges Méliès and a Nazi version directed by Joseph Von Baky in 1943. Gilliam's is the first production to be distributed widely in the United States.[24] Gilliam's film may not seem like one that belongs in the atomic bomb cinema category, but it, in fact, does. This is what makes *The Adventures of Baron Munchausen* so unusually difficult to describe, let alone analyze. Thus, let us begin our analysis of this film by retracing our steps just a little bit.

Throughout this book I have argued that the bomb has given new energies to the apocalyptic imagination, and that it is through this imagination that we give the bomb meaning. At the same time, I have also argued that some well-known bomb films are, at best, a marginal part of atomic bomb cinema. These films are marginal because they mention the bomb only in order to establish a character (in, for example, *Suddenly* [Lewis Allen, 1964]); to establish the postwar context (in, for example, *The Best Years of Our Lives* [William Wyler, 1946]); to add scientific believability (in, for example, the film series and TV programs that began iwth *Honey, I Shrunk the Kids* [Joe Johnston, 1989]); or as a MacGuffin used to explore characters' deeper existential dilemmas (in, for example, *The Lady from Shanghai* [Orson Welles, 1948]), but never really to explore the bomb or its possible meanings. As in these earlier films, the bomb appears in *The Adventures of Baron Munchausen* in only one brief scene. Gilliam's approach to the bomb, however, is so radical that it demands some re-evaluation of atomic bomb cinema itself. *The Adventures of Baron Munchausen* shows us that in the 1990s a film does not have to "be about the bomb" to be about the bomb. Where once the bomb evoked the apocalyptic imagination as a way of understanding contemporary events, in the post–cold war era the bomb still does this, but, now, the apocalyptic imagination is also understood through the bomb. The bomb, now, both completes and is emblematic of the apocalyptic imagination. And, rather than residing in the subtext, the mosaic of themes and images rise to the surface of the narrative and become the engine that drives this bomb film—a MacGuffin in reverse. *The Adventures of Baron Munchausen* is, therefore, to my mind at least, the single most important, and most interesting, apocalyptic bomb film of the early post–cold war era.

The Adventures of Baron Munchausen is a comedy, and, just as in *The Naked Gun 2½*, there is method to Gilliam's madness. The one scene in which the bomb appears, although funny, is so subtle, so straightforward in comparison to the seeming chaos of the rest of the film, that most spectators do not remember either the bomb or the scene. And yet, it is the most important scene in the film. In this scene, the central characters have encountered the Roman god Vulcan (Oliver Reed) on the top of Mount Etna. Vulcan graciously invites his guests to tour his home and his munitions factory. Vulcan, as depicted here, is an arms merchant who is "willing to supply arms and equipment to anyone that's prepared to pay the price." In defense of his rather sordid vocation, he rhetorically asks, "It's not my fault if they're crazy enough to slaughter each other, is it?" Vulcan then shows his guests a weapon, calling it his "RX, ah, Intercontinental Radar Sneaky Multi-Warheaded Nuclear Missile," that simply kills "all" the enemy. When an astonished guest reproachfully asks "Well, where's the fun in that?" Vulcan replies that "Oh, we cater to all sorts here. You'd be surprised."

Although Vulcan's suggestive choice of words to describe his weapon and clients is a kind of verbal finger-pointing that alludes to something like the psychopathology of some characters in *Dr. Strangelove* (1964), in this film the bomb explains nothing, establishes no context, character, or plot. The bomb itself, that visual mass that is the literal background to the characters' discussion, is emblematic of an entire context in which Gilliam's story telling takes place; i.e., a world in which the bomb and the apocalyptic imagination have become so mind-bogglingly intertwined that it is now perhaps impossible to tell where one ends and the other begins.

In Gilliam's film we find both a heroine clearly in the midst of a psychological crisis, and many of the apocalyptic genre's most important elements. These elements include a prolonged war, people oppressed by a foreign invader as well as a cruel tyrant, an otherworldly journey, supernatural beings, the retelling of past historical events as though they were taking place in the present or future (*ex eventu*), revelations and interpretations, mystical knowledge imparted, exhortations, judgments, retributions, and, most importantly, individual and communal rebirth or Tikkun Olam. More importantly, these elements are used to subvert the Christian and scientific worldviews while bolstering a neo-Pagan revivalism. Thus, *The Adventures of Baron Munchausen* foreshadows even Hill's exhortation to return to rituals that evoke a neopagan worldview.

Furthermore, the apocalyptic elements in *The Adventures of Baron Munchausen* are presented in less than obvious ways. There is the story of the Baron that is told by the film, the story of the Baron that is told by a fictional theater company, and the story of the Baron that is then retold by the mysterious Baron himself. At the start of the film, this telling and retelling of the same story, a weaving of a mosaic-like wide-screen mural from multiple perspectives, both within and without the fictional space of the film, leads to a disjointed, out-of-sync quality to the narrative. The chaotic pattern to the film, however, comes into sync as the central character resolves her own inner, personal crisis.

The film takes place during the late-eighteenth century, the radical zenith of the Age of Reason. The title suggests that this film is about the Baron's (John Neville) adventures. And Sally, just like Enola in *Waterworld*, can be interpreted as Jung's "child motif," a symbol that announces crisis and apocalypse but promises future possibilities and hope. At a compatible but different level of the narrative, however, the film is also about a girl on the verge of adolescence, Sally Salt (Sarah Polley), and her efforts to save her city from two opposing forces: the city's insane leader and a sultan who has laid siege to the city. At an even deeper subtextual level, the film is about what psychologist Joseph L. White, writing in the same year of *The Adventures of Baron Munchausen*'s release, calls a "troubled" adolescent's crisis—that is, a fictional narrative about a contemporary young heroine's crisis and journey to self-discovery and empowerment.[25] The Baron is a mere guide on this journey. Moreover, it is Sally who leads the Baron and his men into final victory over the Sultan and the city's leader.

At the start of the film, when Sally confronts her father, she asks him why the poster for his theater company says "The Henry Salt and Son Players" when, after all, he has a daughter and not a son. The father claims it is a tradition. So, on the surface level of the narrative, Sally's gender, her lack of masculinity is of course important to her character. However it also contributes, by the way of a genealogy that is out of sync, to the narrative disorder of the film. This issue, of Sally's gender, is seemingly pushed aside by the Sultan's threat to the city. Yet, in psycho-symbolic terms, the battle is another aspect of Sally's crisis that is brought on due to her inability, by virtue of her gender, to carry forward the patriarchy. Finally, at a deeper level, the war, waged between the city's leader and the Sultan demolishing the city, is emblematic of the battle currently affecting Western culture. The battle is between the dominant mode of thought, logic, and reason and the long-repressed emotion, fantasy, and intuition. While the city's leader is a greater direct threat to Sally and the Baron, what is repressed (represented by the Sultan) threatens to become irrational and destroy the benefits of Western progressive thought. Therefore, Sally must also resolve, or *balance* (a key theme in Japanese films), this dualism in Western culture if she is to succeed in saving her city, the theater company, and herself.

As the sultan (Peter Jeffrey) lays siege to Sally's city from without, the Right Honorable Horatio Jackson (Jonathan Pryce), the city's leader, lays siege from within. Jackson believes only reason and scientific principles can make people happy and peaceful. At one point a soldier (Sting, the musician, in a cameo appearance) is brought before him. Jackson recounts the humble soldier's extraordinary bravery, which goes far beyond the call of duty, then says,

> Have him executed at once. This sort of behavior is demoralizing for the ordinary soldiers and citizens who are trying to lead normal, simple, unexceptional lives. Aren't things difficult enough as it is without these emotional people rocking the boat?

At this point the Baron arrives at the theater and interrupts the Salt Players' performance of "The Adventures of Baron Munchausen." The rabble audience becomes entranced by the real Baron's telling of his own adventures. The Baron's performance, however, is interrupted by a mortar shell that explodes near the theater. Sally discovers the Baron unconscious, with Death, the Grim Reaper, about to take the Baron's soul; and Sally saves the Baron from certain demise. The Baron then engages Death once more before setting about rescuing the city.

In order to save the city and himself from the Sultan's wrath, the Baron sets off on more adventures, with Sally as a stowaway on his makeshift hot-air balloon. Sally increasingly becomes the center of both the adventures and the story. By having the "real" Sally participate in the Baron's adventures the film magically deceives its viewers into forgetting that they are watching a story within a story. This device, moreover, allows the film to transport Sally to the far more challenging "unreal" world, beyond set notions of patriarchal and fatherly values, where her character can come to fruition.

Throughout Sally's adventures, Jackson's logic is repeatedly lampooned. Early in their journeys, Sally observes that the Baron has gotten younger. The Baron responds that of course, one is rejuvenated by adventure. (Later, when the journey comes to a standstill, the Baron ages again.) When Sally and the Baron journey to the moon she discovers that The King and Queen of the Moon have detachable heads. The monarchs' heads spend their time in intellectual pursuits while their bodies are involved in bodily pursuits. The King is really quite mad, and it quickly becomes clear that the cause of this madness is the separation of his mind and body. It is also clear that this entire episode can be taken as an indictment of the Cartesian logical thinking that the king epitomizes. At the end of this episode the king becomes insanely jealous over the Queen's infatuation with the Baron, as does Sally to a lesser degree, and he tries to kill the Baron, Sally, and one of the Baron's missing helpers, Berthold (former Monty Python member Eric Idle). But all three escape.

The three heroes then climb onto the very tip of the moon, drop a rope and begin to climb down. (Another allusion to Méliès's 1902 *A Trip to the Moon*.) When they reach the end of their rope, literally, the Baron tells the last person to cut loose the upper end of the rope and drop it down so they can continue their descent. This works just fine until someone asks what is holding them up, at which point they fall. The point is not that questions are bad, but that an imaginative, even fanciful, understanding of the world, rather than strict logic or reasoning, not only allows the narrative to develop but serves as our salvation. Fortunately, the heroes' free-fall into Mount Etna, where the warm air rising from the volcano, fantastically enough, cushions their landing. What follows is the crucial scene in Vulcan's munitions factory, where we see the prototypical bomb. After seeing the bomb, Vulcan invites his guests for "a little fodder." During their refreshments the Baron discovers another of his lost helpers, and Venus (Uma Thurman), Vulcan's wife, appears à la Botticelli's *The Birth of Venus*.[26] There is an instant and obvious attraction between Venus and the Baron. Venus entices the Baron, both for the thrill and, we later learn, to egg on Vulcan's passionate jealousy. The Baron, no innocent himself, offers her a rose in honor of her beauty, as he did the Queen of the Moon, and then they begin to dance. (The Baron has an endless supply of roses for women, all of whom he finds equally beautiful.) Falling prey to the siren's song, as in the case of countless other adventures before this one, only delays the heroine's journey, her rescue of the city, and the cessation of a war that benefits only Vulcan's munitions business. Again, it is Sally's impatience to save her city, or perhaps her jealousy, that provokes Vulcan to throw them out of what the Baron describes as paradise.

Having been tossed down from Mount Etna, Sally, the Baron, and his two helpers fantastically end up floating in the ocean on the opposite side of the world. A giant fish then swallows them. Inside the fish, the Baron discovers his last two helpers. The two already trapped in the belly of the fish tell the new arrivals that there is no escape, that the only reasonable thing to do is submit to their fate, make themselves as comfortable as best they can, and wait for the inevitable. As though in a stupor, the Baron and his helpers sit down to play cards, and the Baron again looks old. The dealer, Sally recognizes, is Death. But, Sally again foils Death's attempts to take the Baron's life. This provokes the Baron's anger—a strong emotion. Suddenly, the Baron's lost white steed, a symbol of the Baron's own strengths, kicks its way out of a wooden structure. The Baron, now complete with his four helpers and his mount, has awakened from his stupor and decides it is time to escape. In enacting their escape, the Baron actually reenacts the first scene that Salt and company were performing in the theater when the film, and the multiple layers of storytelling, first begin.

Sally, the Baron, and the Baron's four helpers return to the city and raze the siege. When things do not go quite as planned, the Baron's helpers give up again, so the Baron decides to save the city by offering his head to the Sultan, which, as the Baron insisted all along, is what the Sultan was really after. Sally, however, rallies the helpers to rescue the Baron from the Sultan's chopping block and save the day. During the celebration, Jackson, the Baron's archenemy, shoots him. Death appears disguised as a doctor and takes the Baron's soul, and the entire city goes into mourning. Suddenly the film returns us to the present, to the theater where everyone has been captivated by the Baron's storytelling, and we realize it was all just a story (within a story); or so it would seem. The Baron then defies Jackson by leading his audience outside the city and shows that indeed the Sultan, and therefore Jackson with him, have been defeated. Sally turns to the Baron and demands, "It wasn't just a story, was it?" The Baron grins and throws Sally a rose. As the Baron rides away on his white horse, Henry Salt hands his daughter a new theater bill that reads "Henry Salt and Daughter Players."

To me, *The Adventures of Baron Munchausen* is about, no less, lampooning the entire tradition of rational thinking in the West. On the one hand, from Jackson's perspective the world of scientific and reasonable men is under siege by the emotional, instinctive, visceral, and primitive forces within man that must be repressed. But the pagan world of emotions is attacking the city because that is where it is being strangled by the turgid mentalities, or what Gerald Vizenor calls in his novels the "terminal creeds," of men without imagination. The bomb, particularly in its symbolic representation in *The Adventures of Baron Munchausen*, embodies the drama of this all too real dilemma.[27]

Perhaps earlier than anyone else, Gerhard Adler, in his 1946 lecture "Psychology and the Atom Bomb," fully grasped the symbolic significance of the bomb, which Gilliam, in *The Adventures of Baron Munchausen*, brings to life. Adler writes, somewhat personally,

> I can't help feeling that there is a deep symbolic meaning in the story of the atom bomb. It is the shattering force that has come out of our human autarchy, it is the *enantiodromeia* to man as the creator, it is the divine symbol of fate hidden in the human sin of reliance on rationality and reasonability. It is a tremendous and terrifying question-mark to man.[28]

What Adler had to say about that question mark, that is, about that which the bomb had quickly come to symbolize, is as true now as it was in 1946, and very important to understanding the continuing narrative of inner chaos provoked by the Baron through his fantastical threats to civilization:

> Every repressed content, however, sooner or later becomes active, but then, as it is repressed, active in a primitive and unpleasant, perhaps even a most destructive way. Just as, if I refuse to acknowledge the power of love and the need for relationship, I find myself one day in the most unpleasant entanglements which are most incompatible with my life (a situation of which the well-known film "The Blue Angel" gave an excellent example).[29]

In *The Adventures of Baron Munchausen*, it is up to Sally to rescue the city by reviving imagination and finding a balance between it and disciplined logical thought.

This balance is reached through the heroine's journey of self-discovery. In each episode of Sally's and the Baron's adventure, they confront a twisted logic that threatens to destroy them—to which Sally and the Baron respond accordingly. This twisted logic reaches its apex in the scene of Vulcan's nuclear missile factory, after which a giant fish, à la Jonah, swallows the heroes. However, unlike the fish in the Judaic Biblical story, this fish does not signify a place for introspection and resignation to one's fate as determined by a Jewish God. Nor is it symbolic of Lifton's psychic numbing. Rather, within the context of Enlightened Christendom, the giant fish, which dwells deep beneath the sea—a common symbol of the unconscious—might be seen as representing Adler's "fate hidden in the human sin of reliance on rationality and reasonability." The fish, thus, is a place of repressed emotion, conformity, dogma, and indifference to political realities. But, like the metaphor of the Emperor's new clothes, the fish does not deceive children as easily as adults (i.e., those aspects of the psyche that children and adults represent). Instead of giving into the fish, Sally resists, and inspires others to resist as well. Thus, it is Sally's lack of reasonability, her jealous anger, her emotions that rock the boat, both literally and figuratively, that saves the Baron and company.

The Baron, despite his advanced age, has tremendous sexual vitality, and with each adventure he grows younger and more virile—just as Odysseus was regenerated by his journey. The only thing the Baron fears, however, is doctors. This is an inversion of the usual trust in scientists—who typically disbelieve in the regenerative powers of mystical experience—that one usually finds in the West. Doctors in the West (and elsewhere) are, or at least are supposed to be, men of science who see the human being as divisible into different functional systems, a mechanism governed by laws. In the doctor's scientific worldview, people simply do not grow younger, more virile. Thus, when Death finally takes the Baron, he comes in the guise of a doctor. In each episode or adventure, the Baron is saved by his sexual vitality. The women of the town give him their knickers so he can make a hot air balloon and escape. As the balloon swells erect, one of the male characters humorously lampoons "the Age of Reason," in which they are supposed to be living, by proclaiming that it is the "dawning of the age of beautiful intimate things."

On the moon, it is the Queen's love of the Baron that saves them from the mad King's prison. Too much bliss, of course, can be dangerous. When the Baron flirts too much with Vulcan's wife, Venus, it is Sally's jealousy and impatience that saves the Baron from the siren's song, and gets everyone thrown out of the all-too-distracting comforts of Mount Etna. And again, it is Sally's passionate anger that helps them escape the giant fish. In each case it is sexual vitality, or Sally's nascent sexual power and desire to save her city, that saves them. Throughout the film, the Baron gives roses to all the women he meets except Sally. Only at the end of the film does the Baron give Sally a rose, perhaps suggesting that Sally is no longer a child, but on the verge of becoming a powerful woman. Sally, in other words, has, through her otherworldly journey, overcome her crisis (her identity as a woman vis-à-vis her conflict with her father and the assault on her city) and gained mystical wisdom about the nature of the universe and her place within it.

In *The Adventures of Baron Munchausen*, Gilliam brilliantly weaves a mosaic from the apocalyptic imagination; issues surrounding the bomb and modern society; C. Wright Mills's notion of the "sociological imagination"; and (Mills's student) Peter Clecak's notion of an American quest for social justice, a community of like-minded others, and self-fulfillment.[29] And yet, in the scholarly and critical literature it is often suggested that with *The Adventures of Baron Munchausen* Gilliam backs away from his earlier radical, dystopic views (e.g., *Brazil*, 1985), and lauds fantasy as the last hope of the nonconformist. Such an argument suggests that each person's ideology is rigid, unchanging, rather than responding to social and personal changes. It also suggests that intellectuals, whether artists or scholars, work on the same static problem throughout their entire lives (assumed facts that cultural critic Clecak has thoroughly debunked).[30] Throughout all his films, however, Gilliam not only explores the ambiguous division between the social and the personal—that is, between the one and the many—but he is also an intelligent enough filmmaker to have more than one idea.

In *Brazil* Gilliam demonstrates that fantasy is not a substitute for political action; however, in *The Adventures of Baron Munchausen*, Gilliam shows an imagination that can be used as an effective weapon against totalitarian mind control, and if used critically it leads to effective political action. This argument has been made elsewhere, by other people in different contexts. For example, it has been widely argued that such features of African-American culture, the rhetoric of the black church, and even the stereotypical lazy slave or "Negro worker" can be seen as imaginative and humorous strategies for coping with an oppressive environment; such strategies have been instrumental to struggling African-American communities trying to overcome an unjust sociopolitical system.[31] Gerald Vizenor also makes this same point in his Native-American trickster novels and his scholarly writing. And, of course, in the apocalyptic narrative tradition an active imagination is an essential element in surviving oppressive conditions. In 1989, Gilliam's Baron leads the people of Sally's city in a revolt against Jackson's logical but unfeeling approach to governing human affairs. That same year a poet, Vaclav Havel, led the people of Praha (Prague), Czechoslovakia, in their revolution against an equally logical and unfeeling government.

Are films such as *Total Recall*, *Terminator 2: Judgment Day*, *Waterworld*, and especially *The Adventures of Baron Munchausen* expressions of Lifton's psychic numbing, Boyer's paranoia, or a retreat to fantasy and wishful thinking? Not at all. As the Marxist critics Herbert Marcuse and Eric Fromm have pointed out, fantasy plays a significant part in social criticism.[32] More importantly, as we have seen in every apocalyptic bomb film, fantasy functions as one way for human beings to process information; furthermore, it acts as a psychic defense against a hostile and oppressive world. If atomic bomb cinema is at all an indication of human consciousness, then, regardless of anything else, we know that even after the end of the cold war the apocalyptic imagination remains a dominant theme, and it will probably continue as such into the next millennium.

8 1945 to 2001
Japan's atomic bomb cinema

In symbolism, some areas are universal while others are influenced
by cultural differences. One who fails to keep this in mind is apt to
err seriously. . . .

—Hayao Kawai, *The Japanese Psyche*[1]

The horrendous medical and social problems caused by the nuclear weapons dropped on Hiroshima and Nagasaki have made Japanese films about the bomb urgently important to Western critics and scholars, particularly Americans (who have great influence over scholarly opinion about Japan throughout much of the rest of the world).[2] Curiously, however, Japanese bomb films, whether marketed as entertainment or art, take quite a critical beating in the United States. They are frequently denounced as irresponsible and inadequate, and both the films and the culture are grossly misinterpreted. These films are, nevertheless, popular with both Japanese and American audiences. Films marketed as antinuclear consciousness raising, usually independently produced with funds from various public and private largesse, fare better with critics and scholars, but are less popular with audiences. Unfortunately, it is not possible, in the space of one chapter, to give this large and very complex body of films, Japan's atomic bomb cinema, the full attention it deserves. It is, nevertheless, possible to identify the most important elements—particularly what I call "the restoration of balance and harmony through playfulness." So, to further our understanding of atomic bomb cinema, especially the Japanese and American film responses to the bomb, we need to take a close, albeit brief, look at some key Japanese bomb films. But first we must prepare ourselves by criticizing the scholarly reception of Japanese bomb films in the United States and other countries.

Most scholars in this field, again, have a clear antinuclear agenda and write as though the world began on August 6, 1945. In the introduction to his superb anthology, *Hibakusha Cinema*, the Australian scholar Mick Broderick does an excellent job of contextualizing the development of scholarship on Japanese bomb films.[3] (The term *hibakusha*, usually rendered as "A-bomb survivors," is most accurately translated as "explosion-affected persons.")[4] Even in Broderick's writing we see the characterization of issues that is typical of the scholarly literature. Broderick, for example, writes about how during the Allies' Occupation of Japan, "a concerted effort was mounted to censor and officially deny the hazards of radiation and any long-term manifestation," while, at the same time

> US [*sic*] scientists . . . refused to treat *hibakusha* but nevertheless studied them by the tens of thousands. This seemingly blasé attitude is reflected by the American 'star' presence of Nick Adams playing a 'sympathetic' US [*sic*] researcher in [Inoshirō Honda's] *Frankenstein Conquers the World* (*Furankenshutain tai baragon*, 1965), a co-production between Toho studios and American International Pictures [*sic*]. After being thanked by a young female *hibakusha*, Adams confides to a Japanese colleague that the girl will be dead within a month, yet clearly the paternalistic staff will not inform her of this. Shortly after, inside his radiation laboratory, Adams reflects: 'Yeah, the story of Hiroshima is tragic, but it's given us the opportunity to study the [cellular] tissues of the human body. It's ironic but science progresses in this way.[5]

Broderick's analysis is insightful and provocative. However, the film itself is not so clear-cut because, after all, we are really talking about two separate films. One film is *Frankenstein Conquers the World*, where the Japanese actors' lines are dubbed in English, and the other film is *Furankenshutain tai chiteikaijū (baragon)*, where the American actors' lines are dubbed in Japanese.[6]

Broderick's point is that what is suppressed must be expressed, and in this case the *official* censorship and denial are expressed by the American character. Thus, it is important to note that Adam's next line is, "We've

got to work tragedy into happiness in the future." And, a Japanese colleague (Tadao Takashima) voices agreement with Adams's view of
scientific development. But, ironically, it is Takashima's character who is
willing to sacrifice a pathetic (foreign) boy, Frankenstein, in order to
advance science and protect the community, while Adams and another
scientist (Kumi Mizuno—who provides the love interest), try to stop
Takashima and save the boy. More importantly, in the Japanese-language
release Adams's lines are tellingly different. Broderick's crucial middle
sentence, "It's ironic, but science progresses in this way," is not spoken.
In other words, the blasé attitude toward the hibakusha that Broderick
identifies in the English-language release is anything but blasé in the
Japanese-language release. This probably has more to do with the problems inherent in dubbing a film (e.g., coordinating the sound track with
actors' mouths but still managing to maintain a coherent dialog), and less
to do with ideology. We will probably never know whether that crucial
middle line was added to the English-language release, or cut from the
Japanese-language release. Thus, the predictably antinuclear nature of the
conclusions that Broderick builds from his analysis of this film, and others, are misleading or at least clearly open to debate.

Broderick's characterization of events assumes and implies that this
blasé attitude is the product of official censorship and denial of the bomb;
that is, what Lifton calls "nuclearism" and global "psychic numbing."
But such blasé attitudes characterize the entire history of medicine.
Clearly, the nonchalance of Nazi doctors in their grotesque medical
experiments on Jews and other "degenerate" peoples, or the infamous
"Wartime Human Experimentation Program" conducted by Japan's
monstrous Unit 731, cannot be traced back to nuclearism.[7] Nor can
America's darkest moment in medical history, the Tuskeegee Syphilis
Study (1932 to 1973), be the product of nuclearism.[8] Rather, the bomb
is doubtlessly the product of a more fundamental numbing to the human
condition. In any case, it is a mistake to assume that everything Western
audiences find politically incorrect in *Frankenstein Conquers the World*,
some thirty-five years after its initial release, is a reflection of the American
character.

Broderick, nevertheless, implicates the American influence when he
writes that "clearly the paternalistic staff will not inform" the dying
woman that her death is imminent. While this criticism is reasonable on
some levels, it ignores both parts of the narrative and important cultural
traditions that precede the bomb. Not only does the fictional hospital's

staff include both Americans and Japanese, but in the Japanese health care system a paternalistic attitude is expected of any attending physician. Even today, very few doctors will give patients anything more than a general explanation of their illnesses, and almost none would inform a patient that they have a terminal illness. Although attitudes are slowly changing, in surveys many Japanese claim they do not want to be informed, do not think a loved one should be directly informed, or at least feel uncertain about the need for a patient to know the status of their own condition.

The official censorship and denial is, moreover, as much Japanese as American, as several articles in *Hibakusha Cinema* make clear. Indeed, considerable evidence indicates that successive Japanese governments have continued to suppress knowledge of the bomb, and are in a state of denial over the hibakusha. But, again, this probably has less to do with the bomb than Japanese culture itself. Enduring, or *gaman*, for decades even, is how the Japanese, at the individual and corporate levels, deal with most crises, not simply with the bomb.[9] Thus, who is censoring or denying what, and why, in *Frankenstein Conquers the World*, is very unclear. My point is not to diminish the far-reaching significance of censorship and denial, nor to dismiss Broderick's perceptive criticisms. Rather, my point is to contextualize these films into a more precise cultural, historical, and international context then even Broderick has given them.

Modern Japan was not born out of the ashes of the two atomic bombs dropped by the Americans. For more than one hundred years Japan has been a key economic, industrial, and military player on the world scene. The cinema is, furthermore, an international medium and the filmmaking traditions of different societies and cultures influence one another. Since the development of the cinema, Japan has been a major consumer of films produced throughout the world, particularly Europe and North America. We may, therefore, find similar visual, narrative, or symbolic elements in Japan's bomb films. The meanings of these elements might be universal, or these elements might carry culturally specific meanings, or both. This additional layer of complexity in cross-cultural film analysis is often missed in the scholarly literature on Japanese films, particularly bomb films. As Japan's most influential clinical psychologist, Professor Hayao Kawai, puts it, "We Japanese have been strongly influenced by Western mythologies"; and yet, "[i]n symbolism, some areas are universal while others are influenced by cultural differences. One who fails to keep this in mind is apt to err seriously."[10] Such errors, we will see, lead some dangerously close to reconstructing a new "Orientalism."[11]

The Japanese people's relationship to nature is a linchpin to my analyses of Japan's atomic bomb cinema. In order to understand nature's role in Japanese responses to the bomb, in the cinema at least, we must be sensitive to how their expressive forms of culture evoke the natural world. Poetry is Japan's preeminent expressive form. In the "Kana Preface" to the *Kokin Wakashū* (ca 905), one of the most important collections of poetry, we read that

> Japanese poetry has the human heart as seed and myriads of words as leaves. It comes into being when men use the seen and the heard to give voice to feelings aroused by the innumerable events in their lives. The song of the warbler among the blossoms, the voice of the frog dwelling in the water—these teach us every living creature sings. It is song that moves heaven and earth without effort, stirs emotions in the invisible spirits and gods, brings harmony to the relations between men and women, and calms the hearts of fierce warriors.[12]

The contemporary poet and scholar Gerald Vizenor, in his analysis of Japan's haiku poetry, metaphorically suggests a similarity between haiku, oral storytelling, and film. "Haiku is a word cinema," Vizenor writes, "a visual experience, earth toned, closer to the visual memories of the oral tradition than to written grammatical philosophies bound in print." (Indeed, oral traditions remain a vital undercurrent in Japanese expressive forms of culture.) The key element in these visual memories, says Vizenor, is the natural world, for the earth "must speak through the lives she bears, the memories she endures in human dreamscapes," and, elsewhere, he writes that "elements from the environment . . . connect the reader to the earth and shared experiences in nature." Vizenor also persuasively asserts that "the real master of haiku" is not the skilled poet but "the imaginative reader who finds a dreamscape in natural harmonies beneath the words."[13] The earth, in other words, does not speak merely through the poet, but through the reader's reception of the poem; that is, the earth speaks through that mystical moment when reader, poem, poet—everything, in fact—are experienced as the transcendent oneness that haiku refers to so eloquently. The same is even truer for the film spectator, who must be sensitive to harmonies not only beneath the word, but also the narrative structure and the image. All this is to say that, just as in the apocalyptic narrative tradition as manifested in Western films about the bomb, Japan's atomic bomb cinema is more poetic than pedantic in its ability to evoke and exhort. And what these films evoke is a passion, both serious and playful, for living in accord with the natural world—in all its beauty and terror. Poetic dreamscapes, intended to evoke a reawakening to the natural world, however, have all too frequently been turned into a cult, or used to justify an ideology.

Living in accord with nature is a virtue described in many ancient texts, both domestic and imported; the most important is the Buddhist scripture the *Kegonkyō*.[14] It is also a virtue still exalted in both contemporary popular and scholarly literature. Indeed, the first thing any student of Japan is told, by both Japanese and non-Japanese alike, is that the Japanese have a special relationship to nature, and this is the explanation *sine qua non* for everything Japanese. While there are many English-language popularizers of Japanese culture, Daisetz T. Suzuki's essay "Love of Nature" is seminal in this regard.[15] That the Japanese live in harmony with nature rather than dominate it as in Western civilization is now, despite any evidence to the contrary, an insidious self-fulfilling prophecy in the scholarly literature on Japan. In *Japanese Identity*, Isamu Kurita, writes that "The 'essence' of Japanese identity is most plainly manifested in the attitude toward nature and the four seasons." And, "[f]or over two thousand years" this attitude toward nature has been Japan's "unbroken thread of civilization." Thus, Kurita concludes, the notoriously small living spaces in Japan's denatured, monolithic apartment complexes are not "rabbit hutches" at all, because the Japanese "do not conceive of their homes as independent parcels of space cut off from nature." Kurita takes this logic a step further, arguing that this supposedly unique attitude toward nature is the cause of all cross-cultural misunderstandings between Japan and the rest of the world. Even "[t]he trade imbalance . . . is tied to [this] basic culture gap."[16] While there is a grain of truth in what Kurita writes, it is surprising how many people, Japanese and non-Japanese alike, still accept this argument as the only possible explanation.

This "traditional" connection to nature, moreover, is exemplary of the many elements of Japanese culture that are usually assumed to be ancient, but often are not. Stephen Vlastos, in the opening essay to his 1998 anthology *Mirror of Modernity: Invented Traditions of Modern Japan*, writes, "Especially since 1945 and the eclipse of the ideology of the emperor-centered family-state, Japanese have come to know themselves, and to be known by others, through their cultural traditions." (Vlastos, however, may have been premature in announcing this "eclipse"; in a controversial May 15, 2000 speech, Prime Minister Mori declared, "Japan is a country of God with the Emperor as its Center.")[17] And yet,

Vlastos continues, "Readers will be surprised to discover the recent origins of 'age-old' Japanese traditions. Examined historically, familiar emblems of Japanese culture, including treasured icons, turn out to be modern."[18] Almost paradoxically, the Japanese are infatuated with the new, disdain anything outdated, and are not sentimental about revising, amending, or discarding "tradition." And yet, they talk endlessly about how their maintenance of ancient "traditions" distinguishes them from other cultures. Additionally, much that is seen as exemplifying this "traditional" love of nature is the product of a hermetic, elite, urban leisure class; so we must be careful in talking about a singular "Japanese culture." My interest here, however, is not in reinforcing or debunking any particular construction of the Japanese identity. My interest is in analyzing how such expressed reasoning structures Japanese responses to the bomb as expressed in bomb films. Nature is, again, the key element in this response, and there are others.

The closest equivalent to the apocalyptic imagination in Japan is the *masse* tradition. Unlike the apocalypse, masse describes the complete end of the world, and the beginning of an entirely new world.[19] Very few bomb films come even close to describing the complete end; David Greene's 1982 TV movie, *World War III*, is, again, one such film (see chapter 6). The closest example of a complete narrative closure, however, may be observed in Muneyoshi Matsubayahsi's 1961 film *Sekai dai sensō* (*The Last War*). It is an unambiguous, linear narrative that ends with a nuclear war that reduces peace-loving Japan to a molten rock, and annihilates the world. Only the small crew of an oceangoing vessel survives. In Japanese philosophy, linguistics, and theology, the individual's identity is derived from the cultural context; thus, for all intents and purposes, the crew is already dead. Knowing this, the crew decides to return to what once was their home to die. The ending of *Sekai dai sensō* is very disturbing because it forecloses the possibility of anyone surviving. (And yet, as in *On the Beach*, the presence of a camera that records and tells a story after the end implies that some survived.) Since complete narrative closure is an anathema to Western consciousness and the apocalyptic imagination, let us concentrate, instead, on the American release of *Sekai dai sensō*, or, *The Last War*. The American release was greatly re-edited, beginning with the nuclear war, the ship's crew deciding to return to Japan, then the first mate's voice-over narration and a dissolve that leads into a flashback that constitutes the bulk of the narrative. The re-edited version, to put it another way, creates a narrator who describes to the audience a *crisis* that he has survived (global nuclear annihilation). That is to say, at the level of narrative structure, *The Last War*, as opposed to *Sekai dai sensō*, reassures the spectator that humanity can survive nuclear war. The narrator is, after all, alive to tell his story. And, similar to *On the Beach*, the film engenders, in the audience, that sense that we too have survived to hear the story.

The re-editing of *Sekai dai sensō* into *The Last War* suggests, most obviously, that the apocalyptic narrative tradition is so entrenched in Western consciousness that it can, or must, reorganize even the most distant cultural traditions to fit its norms. The relative scarcity of Japanese films like *Sekai dai sensō*, however, also suggests that though the apocalyptic imagination is nearly universal, it is more prominent in some cultures than others. Masse is an obscure tradition in Japan, and more important themes deserve our attention.

As in American atomic bomb cinema, Japanese films frequently use the bomb as a MacGuffin to explore other issues. Perhaps the clearest example of this may be viewed in Katsuhiro Otomo's 1988 animated feature *Akira*, which has attained worldwide cult status among *anime* (animation) or "Japanimation" fans. Freda Freiberg notes, "*Akira* was made . . . by and for a generation of Japanese who have no personal memory of Hiroshima and Nagasaki."[20] And, indeed, for that generation the bomb allows for an exploration of adolescent crises and fantasies about empowerment, rebirth, and regeneration within the contemporary Japanese sociocultural context. This context includes a large number of disaffected and disillusioned youth who feel bound by traditions that no longer seem relevant, and by social institutions that seem oppressive, even corrosive.[21] *Akira* is more about the crises inherent in contemporary Japanese youth culture than what the bomb means; nevertheless, the film does hint at the core issues in Japanese bomb films. We will return to these core issues shortly.

As in the United States, a great deal of variety in the treatment of bomb-related issues exists, including Japan's equivalent to nuclear bathos (see *On the Beach*, in chapter 3). Tokihisa Morikawa's film *Natsushōjo* (*Summer Girl*) is an independently produced film that has yet to be released in theaters, but has had many limited public screenings. It was first shown in Hiroshima in 1995, the year that marks the fiftieth anniversary of Hiroshima's destruction. Significantly, Gyō Hayasaka, a well-known TV and film screenwriter, wrote the screenplay for *Natsushōjo*. Hayasaka's works include the extraordinarily popular 1986

TV serial *The Diary of Yumechiyo* (*Yumechiyo-nikki*), which then became a theater play, and later the serial was re-edited for a film. Maya Morioka Todeschini refers to this earlier film as an "'A-bomb soap opera' or 'A-bomb tear jerker.'"[22] For our purposes, an analysis of the more obscure *Natsushōjo* will bring us closer to understanding Japan's atomic bomb cinema.

Natsushōjo is ostensibly about a family of three that lives on an island near Hiroshima. Both the father (Kanpei Hazama) and the mother (Kaori Momoi) were children when the bomb was dropped, and are therefore hibakusha. The mother seems to support the family by operating a shuttle boat between the island and the mainland. At the very beginning of the film the mother is transporting both a bride and the bride's mother to a wedding, and returning a man with a funeral urn of ashes. The symbolism of the film is clear. The mother can easily traverse the primal sea of limitless, life-giving potential, and is herself in transition between death (the funeral urn) and rebirth (the bride; women wear a white kimono three times in their lives, for birth, marriage, and death, and men, only twice, for birth and death). The father is consumed by the experience, particularly his guilt over a female classmate that he could not save, and drowns his guilt in the bottom of a bottle and in self-pity. He, more importantly, is physically and psychically unable to move at the beginning of the film. When he finally does move it is to drive his delivery van the wrong way down a one-way street. Though a hackneyed use of a symbolic cliché, it is clearly an ominous foreshadowing for the fate of the father.

The couple has one middle-school-aged son, Mamoru (Takeshi Fujioka), whose name means "to protect." In his first scene, he climbs a fence and traverses a playground; thus, like his mother, and unlike his motionless father, he is in a state of transition as he crosses boundaries. He is also a troubled boy, and so his teacher takes a special interest in him. On the evening of August 6, the family sits on the banks of Hiroshima's Ōta River, where, as part of the annual memorial, candle lanterns are sent floating downstream in a symbolic gesture meant to ease the suffering souls of the dead hibakusha and return them to heaven. (In Buddhist tradition, rising heat and smoke help carry the dead souls to, or back to, heaven.) Disregarding the father's insistence that it is best to forget and never talk about the past, the mother explains that they are hibakusha; and, that, though Mamoru is well, his older sister died *in utero*. The mother believes the fetus died because both parents are hibakusha. One day the son finds a roof tile (*kawara*) on the shore (again, near the water) that was partly melted by the A-bomb. An old woman explains that the *kawara* are the souls of those killed by the atomic bomb. Soon thereafter, the mother, father, and son begin seeing apparitions of a young girl (Asako Yazaki) who begins to dominate their lives. The mother comes to believe that the girl is her aborted child. The father believes it is the ghost of the girl he could not save, and he dies chasing after the son and apparition. Eventually we learn that there are other spirits of dead hibakusha living on this island and elsewhere.

The conclusion to the film comes abruptly, and its resolution is unusual for a Japanese narrative, even bizarre. The mother takes the boy and girl out on her boat to swim in the ocean (again, deep waters). The girl leaves a trail of blood in the water. She has begun to menstruate. At this point, the mother reconciles herself with the girl, and accepts her as her real, flesh and blood daughter. The film's abrupt ending and vague resolution, even by Japanese standards, leaves the viewer surmising that the three live happily ever after, *sans* father. How are we to explain this abrupt ending and fascination with the dead?

Hayao Kawai argues that abrupt or open-ended conclusions in which nothing happens (or nothing seems to happen), transgressions of taboos—imposed by women, rather then men—without punishment, and the loss of potential happiness without unhappiness are common features of Japanese narrative structure. In Western narratives, Kawai argues, it is most often the man who imposes the prohibition, and the woman is punished yet ultimately rewarded with profound happiness.[23] Thus, at first glance *Natsushōjo* seems at best an odd mixture of Japanese and Western narrative structures. And yet, because the narrative of *Natsushōjo* so clearly violates some sacred prohibitions in Japanese culture, we must begin to think of the possibility of a new genre. And, we must continue to look within Japanese tradition for something that explains this film's abrupt resolution and strong attachment to the dead and coincides with Japanese narrative structures.

Masaki Kobayashi's brilliant 1964 film *Kwaidan* is composed of four different ghost stories, all based on a very popular 1904 collection by Lifcadio Hearn, also known as Yakumo Koizumi (1850 to 1904).[24] (The number four, or, *shi*, is important because it is a homonym for death.) In one story, "Black Hair," a samurai (Rentarō Mikuni) abandons his faithful wife (Michiyo Aratama) only to remorsefully return to her years later. The surprisingly still youthful and faithful ex-wife welcomes him home, and makes their bed. When he wakes up, he discovers he has been sleeping with the skeletal remains of his ex-wife, and by doing so he too has been turned into a ghost or hideous demon.

Contact with the souls of the dead is normal and healthy in the Japanese imagination; it is a transcendent experience that helps the living endure what is, in Buddhist philosophy, a world of suffering. A common narrative structure in Nō, Bunraku, and Kabuki theater, film, and literature, is for a spirit seeking cathartic release to inhabit the body of the living, tell her or his story, and then return to the spirit world. Through the telling of the story, the spirits of legend suffer and the audience finds cathartic release. Symbols of the living and the dead, however, must never be mixed. In funeral ceremonies, the bones of the cremated deceased are passed from person to person with chopsticks; therefore, food is never passed in this way, and pairs of chopsticks must never touch during a meal. Breaking this taboo has a strong visceral effect on people, even today. The dead, moreover, must return to their own world. During the *Obon* festival, celebrated throughout Japan each August, spirits of the dead visit the living for a short period. The festival climaxes with ecstatic rituals, including dancing and building bonfires, that help the spirits return to their world. Thus, more than abandoning his wife, the samurai's crime involves the breaking of Japan's very strict taboos against mixing the symbols of life and death. To make a family with the dead, as in *Natsushōjo*, is to invite disaster. Elements within *Natsushōjo*, therefore, suggest a narrative trajectory too horrifying to realize.

The filmmakers had, in a sense, painted themselves into a corner that could only be escaped by an abrupt ending of the film; for, if the narrative continued the mother and her son would surely have been turned into the living dead, like the samurai in "Black Hair," the spirits that inhabit the *kawara* tiles in *Natsushōjo*, or the tormented souls that still haunt Hiroshima and Nagasaki. After the screening of *Natsushōjo* concluded, one tearful hibakusha cornered my wife and me in the lobby, and would not let us go until she had told us her own wretched story. I have heard other hibakusha tell their stories, but this was different.

To find a film with high production values, and well-known actors and actresses, that is so clearly marketed to exploit the emotions and life experiences of such a small, singular group is, at first sight, unusual. In a sense, all films try to exploit certain raw emotions in the audience. But *Natsushōjo* demands a re-evaluation of what we mean by an "exploitation film," and suggests the consideration of a new genre, what I would call "hibakusha exploitation films." *Natsushōjo*, more importantly, casts many

better-known Japanese bomb films, from Kaneto Shindō's classic
Genbaku no ko (*Children of the Bomb*, or *Hiroshima no ko*, or *Children of
Hiroshima*, 1952) to Shōhei Imamura's *Kuroi ame* (*Black Rain*, 1989),
in a new light. The ubiquitous woman teacher enters her students' lives,
learns about their suffering, and tries to fix them. (This is a common role
for teachers in Japanese films, including Yoshimitsu Morita's 1984 satiric
Kazoku gēmu, or *Family Game*.) A song must be written and sung to
appease the tormented souls of the dead. In *Natsushōjo*, Mamoru's
teacher is struggling to finish her masterpiece in time for the children to
perform it at the August 6 memorial. The ghostly young girl helps her
complete the song. In *Natsushōjo*, moreover, the two most-desired
women, the young girl and a female lover in a subplot, are supernatural
beings who are made more attractive, more desirable because of their sufferings. Maya Morioka Todeschini writes that "the stigma attached to
radioactive 'contamination'" has made hibakusha, particularly women,
pariahs in Japanese society, genetic pollutants that must avoided.[25]
Todeschini argues, however, that films about women hibakusha, including *Kuroi ame*, aestheticize and fetishize women's suffering.[26] Suffering
and enduring suffering selflessly only enhances women's beauty. They
transcend their suffering only through suffering and dying beautifully,
and become supra- or supernatural beings. These are familiar elements in
Japanese culture and films, particularly those that exploit hibakusha
issues.

Having said all this, I am somewhat abashed by my own criticism. On
April 12, 2000, five years after seeing *Natsushōjo* and well after having
written this critique, I had the opportunity to talk with the producer, and
exchange our ideas about his film. On the one hand, Mr. Noriaki
Uchinotani explained that he saw the mushroom cloud from a safe distance, and is motivated to make antinuclear films. He privately financed
his film (the various hibakusha and antinuclear groups refused to give him
financial support for the project). Mr. Uchinotani and the writer,
Hayasaka, specifically wanted to address the problem of discrimination
against hibakusha, especially women. But, they wanted to avoid the "realism" and "dripping flesh" horrors of "most A-bomb films." Much like
Kurosawa, Mr. Uchinotani insisted that his film is a fantasy, and that if
one understands both "the pain of the A-bomb" and "human love," then
one can understand the film's message. Children usually get the message,
he claims, but adults often complain that his film is "not really about the
A-bomb." Understandably, Mr. Uchinotani had a hard time articulating

that message. However, he insisted that the final scene is not to be understood literally but metaphorically; the mother, as opposed to the father, shows that it is possible to overcome one's victimhood and find peace in this life. On the other hand, however, he also pointed out that Hayasaka's screenplay is partly based on the folktale or ghost story, *zashikiwarashi*, which is about the tutelary spirit of a child, either female or very feminine in character, that haunts people's houses. More importantly, all of Hayasaka's writings are based on his personal experiences—*Natsushōjo* in particular. In brief, Hayasaka had an adopted sister, and although the two had a falling out, they reconciled and were even engaged. As fate would have it, the sister/fiancée disappeared in the destruction of Hiroshima, but Hayasaka was far away. He (and his mother who later suffered from radiation illness) went to Hiroshima but could not find her, and he still bears that wound—the true subject of his writing.

With Hayasaka's story in mind, the image of the child becomes increasingly significant to our understanding of Hayasaka, the film, and, without digressing too far, the image of children in other Japanese films. In *Natsushōjo* we see a clear example of Jung's "child motif." The child, as a symbol, appears in conjunction with a crisis and indicates unforeseen possibilities and the "anticipation of future developments"; in Japanese terms, balance and harmony are restored. As we will see, in many of the Japanese bomb films that we will be discussing this child motif is vitally important.[27]

Natsushōjo is a fascinating and important film. Mr. Uchinotani's interpretation of the film's conclusion is valid and bears due consideration, and his sincerity and simplicity of vision are humbling. Nevertheless, although I do not want to use biography to justify my own interpretation, what he revealed about the screenwriter supports, I believe, my contention that *Natsushōjo* is a hibakusha exploitation film, and that it mongers its message. To my mind the film is a profound exhortation of what Gerald Vizenor calls "survivance" (see chapter 1), but it is burdened by an even greater expression of guilt and victimhood. Like most hibakusha exploitation films, *Natsushōjo* does not resolve any of the conflicts or issues in a way that allows the characters to move beyond their crises or sufferings; rather, they just simply exploit the audience's vulnerabilities by wallowing in wishful thinking, such as that the dead will return to life. Intellectuals respond well to such films.

Rather than reading the lack of a resolution in such films as itself an indication of the culture's ongoing struggle to find meaning in the bomb, scholars have raised it to the level of an aesthetic or even a cultural imperative, something both ontologically essential and unique to being Japanese. Particularly noteworthy, in this regard, is Donald Richie's influential 1962 article "'Mono no Aware'/Hiroshima in Film," which is considered by many to still be the standard and best text on the subject.[28] Not only does Richie single out Shindō's *Genbaku no ko* (*Children of the Bomb*) for praise as "a very good reflection of a genuine Japanese attitude," he insists on a single "authentic Japanese attitude." This "true attitude," moreover, engenders "the unique Japanese inability to cry over spilt milk." Richie equates this attitude with Buddhist philosophy, epitomized by the phrase *mono no aware*, and translates this as a "lament[ing] . . . feeling for the transience of all earthly things." Kawai translates it as "softly despairing sorrow."[29] But these are inadequate translations. The term *aware* does indeed evoke the concept of *shogyō mujō*, or the impermanence of all things, but it also suggests a profound sympathy that is more difficult to define. It is an appreciation of the bittersweet beauty of an existence in which everything is born and dies in time but the essential nature of things does not change. The art historian Tsuji Nobuo, in his revolutionary 1986 book *Playfulness in Japanese Art*, writes that *aware* "expresses deeply emotional feelings about the mutability of things and the evanescence of man's existence, as well as the beauty of nature and the arts."[30] Tsuji's introduction of "the arts" to a discussion of *aware* is a bit ambiguous. *Aware* also suggests Buddhism's sense of resignation to a separation between *here* and whatever lies *beyond* that cannot be closed through Cartesian ratiocination. This separation can, however, be momentarily transcended by activities such as *zazen* ("sitting zen") meditation or the arts, including theater and—by extension—the cinema; and thus, the tremendous importance of art in Japanese culture and any discussion of *aware*. In the seminal Nō play *Obasute* (*The Deserted Crone*), which takes place during the fall moon-viewing season, we read the line: "Ten thousand miles of sky." This figure, ten thousand, traditionally suggests completeness or wholeness, even the infinite or eternity. We also read:

> But here the moon through its rift of clouds,
> Now full and bright, now dimly seen,
> Reveals the inconsistency of this world
> Where all is perpetual change.[31]

The moon is a recurring symbol in Japanese expressive forms, especially in Nō Theater, and we will return to it shortly. What is important for us here is that the notions of completeness or wholeness and impermanence coexist in natural harmony with one another; these antitheses are equally evoked by viewing the moon in the sky, and expressed by the term *aware*. In other ways, Richie's description of *aware* is substantially incomplete and misleading because it rests on a fundamentally flawed understanding of *aware* that pervades the scholarly and popular literature on Japan.

In Japanese philosophy and culture, especially its aesthetics, *balance* is a fundamental principle. Balance, however, is something fluid, dynamic, and transient; it is neither a Sisyphean effort nor a static state of achievement, but a perpetual process of forces counterbalancing each other. Tsuji, a thoughtful and provocative scholar, points out that the phrase *mono no aware* came into use during the Fujiwara period of art (Late Heian, 894 to 1185). The Fujiwara nobility, however, sought not only things that evoked a sense of *aware*, writes Tsuji, but

> also sought things lighthearted and gay that would enliven and unbind their hearts. This is not unrelated to their bountiful curiosity in regards to the reality of life. When coming across something that was unusual they would utter the word *okashi* (funny or amusing). This feeling of *okashi* was also directed towards art.[32]

And, Tsuji makes clear the importance of a balance between *aware* and *okashi* (or *wokashi*):

> in the tradition of expressionism in Japanese art, the two extremes of seriousness and playfulness do not necessarily contradict each other. Even in works of the utmost seriousness the spirit of playfulness creeps in, preventing the work from being too stiff-looking, and giving it a warm-hearted feeling.[33]

Tsuji clearly demonstrates, moreover, that a "childlike playfulness extends to all . . . manifestations [of Japanese art] including the art of the court." This "whimsical" side to even the very serious samurai, says Tsuji, is "beyond the comprehension of today's Japanese."[34]

In his conclusion, Tsuji writes that "following the Meiji period [1868 to 1912], the Japanese placed much emphasis on seriousness and sobriety as virtues." Tsuji speculates, and I think correctly, that "Surprised by the vastness and profundity" of Western civilization, "today's Japanese . . . feel a sense of shame that within the traditions of their own country there is much that is frivolous or lowbrow in a spiritual dimension." (Indeed, in my own interactions with Japanese people, I have seen that this sense of shame is quite real.) Thus, since the Meiji era the Japanese have been dominated by "An excessive seriousness . . . and the spirit of playfulness which had continued within the tradition of Japanese art could not find an outlet." Be that as it may, Tsuji himself goes against the current of contemporary mainstream Japan by celebrating the playful; and, he considers it "one major source of strength and life in Japanese art." This source of strength and life, moreover, has not died:

> Yet the hearts of the Japanese which seek after the excitement of the fabulous in art most likely endure. The popularity of comic books and strips in Japan today suggests this. . . . As seen before, for more than a thousand years the Japanese have loved comic art and have been successful in frequently joining a comic expressionism to the highest art forms.[35]

To this I would add two points. First, the modern era redaction of Japanese aesthetic tradition is also the product of other forces, including the Edo or Tokugawa era (1615 to 1868) social reforms and the ongoing program of building a nation-state identity initiated in the Meiji era (1868 to 1912).[36] Second, Tsuji seems a bit too close to his ancient subject to have a clear perspective on contemporary Japanese culture. One can still find venues where the playful spirit does find expression, but nowhere so forcefully as in works on that most serious of subjects: the bomb.

Mono no aware, to summarize, is only half of a very complex aesthetic, one that must be balanced by playfulness, which shapes the Japanese response to the bomb. This "spirit of playfulness which exists as an essential component of Japanese art to the same extent as seriousness, or perhaps even more so," is precisely what is missing from Richie's (but not only Richie's) excessively serious and historically inaccurate argument.[37] Thus, Richie's argument reifies Buddhist philosophy into the culture itself, while at the same time reducing a highly complex society into a single, authentic "Japanese" response to the world. Anything that does not fit this patterned response is simply not "Japanese." This response, moreover, it is argued, is uniquely Japanese. Surely Isaiah 40:8—"The grass withereth, the flower fadeth; But the word of our God shall stand for ever"—evokes the same sense of evanescence.[38] However, neither culture can be reduced to the sayings of the Buddha or Isaiah. Richie's argument is not only fallacious; it at once dehumanizes the Japanese by reifying an element of Japanese culture, and is too easily adopted by noteworthy apologists for us to forego our suspicions.

The Japanese are inherently no more nor no less able to cry over spilt milk or be aware of the evanescence of life than any other group of people that has ever populated the earth. The single most popular narrative in Japanese literature, theater, TV, and cinema must be *Chūshingura*.[39] This is the true story of "The Loyal Forty-Seven Ronin," besmirched samurai who avenge their dead lord, then assure themselves a place in history by committing ritual suicide (*seppuku*) en masse. *Chūshingura* is the very celebration of crying over spilt milk, which is perhaps still the highest virtue in modern Japan. Although Richie's analyses of individual films and the history behind them are invaluable, his broader argument demonstrates here the pitfalls of putting exuberance before precision—especially in cross-cultural film analysis. The Japanese as a unique people is part of the official mantra for outsider critics not befitting the precision of Richie's observations in so many other areas. With all this in mind, let us now carefully examine several key Japanese bomb films.

An unlikely but pertinent film to the study of Japan's filmic response to the bomb is Hayao Miyazaki's 1984 animated feature *Kaze no tani no Naushika* (*Naushika of the Valley of the Wind*). Miyazaki's works are extraordinarily popular, both inside and outside of Japan; yet, curiously, *Naushika* (as it is known) has received very little attention outside Japan and is still not commercially available in the United States's lucrative Japanimation video market.[40] Typical of Japanese storytelling technique is that much is not explained. The story is often intricate and confusing, but the narrative itself is fairly straightforward. The subtext of the film, moreover, is of crucial importance to our line of thought.

The story takes place one thousand years after industrial society has collapsed under the burden of a polluted ecosystem and constant wars waged with thermonuclear monsters that had set fire to the world. In the aftermath, a *fukai*, or poisonous sea of rotten vegetation, threatens to engulf the world and destroy all of humanity. Only a few communities survive, and slowly they too are being desolated by the fukai. One of the surviving communities is the Valley of the Wind, an idealized techno-agrarian society that lives in harmony with nature. Yet, even in this idyllic valley, the villagers must be vigilant and burn any fukai spores that begin to grow in their forests. Central to the valley people's ethos of harmonious living with nature is their reverence for the four elements, particularly the wind, followed distantly by water, earth, and fire. Significantly, Naushika's grandmother tells us that they "are protected by the blessed wind that blows from the sea." The old woman also then points to an old painting depicting a very Christlike savior in a blue robe, who is prophesized to "guide us to the blue land" and "forge once again the lost bond with the land." (Blue, *aoi* in Japanese, can also mean green or verdant.) While the characters and locale seem to be Slavic, as Japanese people will insist, this film is really an elaborate metaphor for Japan.

Despite her tender age and gender, Princess Naushika is already a beloved village leader, she has a "mysterious power," many abilities, and is known as one who expertly "weaves the wind." (Naushika's mode of transportation is a one-person flying wing of sorts.) No mention is made of Naushika's mother, and her father lies dying of exposure to the fukai. In other ways, Naushika is a typical anime character: playful, pure of heart, childlike, even childish in demeanor, naive in her flirtations with older men, and clearly virginal; yet her exaggerated "Western" features— for example, her hyperbolic round eyes (a common feature of most anime characters), hourglass body shape that never quite looks good in kimono, and revealing short skirt—give her not merely a strong sexuality, especially compared to the other female characters, but also make her highly erotic and exotic.

Naushika's peace-loving valley is invaded and becomes the hapless pawn in a battle between city-states vying for world domination. Naushika's father is killed, and she goes into a rage, killing several soldiers before she is restrained. The invaders' plan is to hatch a dormant thermonuclear monster, then use it to destroy the fukai and unify the world under their domination—the dream of many past and present Japanese leaders.

At the climax of the film, all of which is clearly foreshadowed in the first scenes, the winds have stopped blowing and a herd of enormous, unstoppable "Ohmu insects" are heading toward the valley. A monster is unleashed on the creatures, but it suffers a meltdown and self-destructs. Naushika, who happens to be wearing a blue gown, puts herself directly in their path. She succeeds in calming the Ohmu but in the process is killed. The Ohmu, however, have the power to heal. They lift her up with their tentacles into the sky, and in a sort of reverse pietà, or perhaps, more accurately, a resurrection, they revive her. The children describe what they see to the old woman who then proclaims that the savior has come at last, and Naushika appears on screen as a vision of the savior. The film then ends with scenes of a world reborn: the fukai is no longer poisonous, the valley is more verdant than ever before, Naushika and Prince Asbel still play together, and the winds have returned.

Miyazaki's characterization of young women begs for critical analysis.[41] Suffice it to say that, particularly in a culture where talking openly about problems is abhorrent, one of the functions of these erotic and exotic depictions of fantastic foreign peoples and environments is a mechanism for the displacement and projection of anxieties about Japan. The ostensive Western setting and features of the characters allow filmmakers to create and audiences to receive intense subtextual undercurrents of criticism of very sensitive, contemporary sociocultural problems in Japan.

Visually, the film reminds us of the Japanese love for the strange and fantastic, playful depictions of hellish environments in which insect-like creatures torment the deceased, enormous or minute insects, and bizarre or exaggerated creatures.[42] The key to the film's narrative, however, is found in the title: the wind. In the thirteenth century Japan refused to accept the Kublai Khan's suzerainty and pay tribute. Angered, the Mongols twice attempted to invade and subdue Japan, first in 1274, and then in 1281. A total of 5,300 ships and 180,000 men where sent to the shores of Japan in the two assaults. During both assaults, typhoon winds destroyed much of the fleets, forcing the survivors to retreat. From this arose the belief that not only is Japan a unique place established by the gods, but that it is protected by a *kamikaze*, literally a "god wind" or "divine wind"; or, in the words of Naushika's grandmother, Japan is "protected by the blessed wind that blows from the sea." Then, in World War II, as it became apparent that the Japanese military could not stop the Allied fleet, divine forces were invoked by referring to the approximately two thousand pilots trained for suicide missions as "kamikaze."[43] Clearly, the legend of kamikaze, as it is played out in both later historical events and narratives like *Naushika*, entails not just the belief that a divine force protects Japan, but that sacred Japan is forever at risk of being invaded and polluted by foreign forces.

Not just in *Kaze no tani no Naushika* but also in numerous other films—for example, Matsubayashi's *Sekai dai sensō* (*The Last War*)—Japan, even industrial Japan, is described as an idyllic land. The Japanese are depicted as knowing the importance of living harmoniously with others and with nature. They are a "peaceful" or "peace-loving" people, with a long "humanist" tradition (claims one hears repeated ad nauseam in Japan). Unfortunately, Japan is doomed to be drawn into world events not of its making. Japan, however, prevails upon the world and foreign governments to renounce militarism and embrace the Japanese style of peaceful coexistence with others and nature. Only rarely, as in Matsubayashi's film, does the world actually destroy itself. Usually, as in *Naushika*, Japan is successful in restoring order to a world that has lost itself in anger. After killing several invading soldiers, Naushika remarks that she is afraid of herself because she killed in anger. Explaining violence as having "lost oneself in anger," just as a wounded child lashes out in anger or confusion, is a significant element in this and other narratives, a recurring theme in Taoist and Buddhist literature, and a frequent explanation in Japanese culture for all inappropriate behavior, particularly World War II.

At most levels of discourse, Japan has simply refused to acknowledge its history or participation in world events. Japan's own long history of brutal military aggression into other parts of Asia, cruel feudalism, and oppressive state control, are, in other words, often expunged from fictional narratives, state-censored textbooks, and dinner-party conversation with colleagues. In its place is substituted a vague notion of "unfortunate events" and Japan as the perpetual victim of intercultural "misunderstandings." Other cultures may make themselves appear more exotic, but also less foreign to the increasingly global economy; Japan's dominant vision of itself is as utterly and uniquely *other* to this world. Masao Miyoshi and H. D. Harootunian call this state-sponsored dogma "an ideology of cultural exceptionalism . . . (*Nihonjin-ron*)."[44] Hewing close to this ideology, many narratives, like *Naushika*, give us a whitewash of Japan's past, present, and apocryphal future.

Central to *Naushika*'s filmic rendering of that apocryphal past, present, and future is a modern invention: the "traditional" way of life, and the even more modern cult of *furusato,* or "native place." Furusato is, currently, promoted intensely by both capital investment and state propaganda, the object of popular and scholarly consumption, and a recurring theme for Miyazaki and his collaborator Isao Takahata.[45] Furusato is the legacy of Kunio Yanagita's school of *minzokugaku,* or native ethnography. Harootunian writes that Yanagita's brand of native ethnology "ultimately authorized a discipline called Japanology, which made folk, community, and culture (a synonym for race) interchangeable subjects of knowledge representing a completed history and an immutable essence." And, notes Harootunian, we can "detect [this discourse's] ghostly presence in all those shrill discussions of what differentiate 'we Japanese' from the outside world."[46] The cult of furusato renders Japan's exceptionalism absolute. It elides any internal contradictions due to conflicts between core and periphery, new and old social relations, or lord and peasant. Andrew E. Barshay suggests that the emperor and his subjects, like the folk who inhabit the Valley of the Wind, are also thought to be in a symbiotic, mutually beneficial "traditional" relationship that is immune to such foreign concepts as exploitation, alienation, or equal rights.[47] And although the emperor is the cornerstone to these harmonious relations, "'Furusato Japan,'" as Jennifer Robertson puts it, "thus imbues the state with a warm, fuzzy, familial, and ultimately maternal aura."[48]

The feminine or women's connection to nature is a powerful theme in Japanese culture. The politics of so intimately linking women with nature and the ideological construction of the feminine in Japanese society aside, these connections are very powerful. Women are empowered by their bond with nature, and those women who break that bond pay a heavy penalty; for example, the princess-general of the invading army paid that price when an insect severed her limbs. As we will see shortly, these are themes that recur throughout Japan's atomic bomb cinema, but are most obvious in *Kaze no tani no Naushika*. The theme that ties the narrative of the film together, however, is the fear of pollution.

I have already discussed the prohibition, which predates the bomb, against mixing the symbols of life and death; that the bomb is perceived as a pollutant; and that those exposed to the bomb are contaminated or are now pollutants. As the work of the famous anthropologist Mary Douglas suggests, *taboo* regarding *pollution* has existed in all cultures for eons.[49] John T. Dorsey and Naomi Matsuoka, in their analysis of Masuji Ibuse's 1967 novel *Kuroi ame* (*Black Rain*) and Imamura's 1989 film adaptation, note a "distortion of nature," but they neither define nor develop this concept.[50] In pedantic treatments of hibakusha, like *Black Rain*, the bomb is the obvious pollutant and cause of the distortion. But, in less pretentious, more pioneering films—in the sense of exploring the bomb's meaning—the bomb is symptomatic, even the product, of a far greater distortion in the relationships between people, and with nature. It is this distortion that must be analyzed if we are to understand fully Japan's atomic bomb cinema.

Certainly in Japan survival and self-actualization are important themes, as are the resolution of personal and collective crises. But, in contrast to Western films, in Japanese films there is less emphasis on the protagonist gaining self-knowledge or mystical wisdom. Rather, the emphasis is the vague but nonetheless important concept of what I call the "restoration of balance and harmony" (at the individual and collective levels) with oneself, others, and nature. This is the dominant theme that structures virtually all of Japan's atomic bomb cinema, and it is most clearly expressed in Japan's popular monster films.

The most prolific Japanese director of bomb films is Inoshirō Honda, who directed the 1954 *Gojira* (later rereleased as *Godzilla* in 1956). Honda directed more than fifty films, some acclaimed dramas, and frequently advised other directors, including his lifelong friend Akira Kurosawa. Kurosawa's film research group even authored a small monograph on Honda.[51] Over the years Honda has even gained a limited cult following; nevertheless, in both popular and scholarly circles, little is known about Honda, and he is very misunderstood. In fact, the first edition of Ephraim Katz's otherwise indispensable *Film Encyclopedia*, for example, has an entry for the special effects director Eiji Tsuburaya, but no entry for Honda.[52] (Curiously, although the producer Tomoyuki Tanaka is better known than Honda, there is still no entry for him.) Also, as late as either the 1997 or the 1998 edition of *Leonard Maltin's Movie and Video Guide*, preference was finally given to the 1954 *Gojira* release rather than the American re-edited 1956 *Godzilla*.[53] This rehabilitation of the 1954 release probably has more to do with the release of Roland Emmerich's *Godzilla* in 1998 and the short-lived nostalgia for the more *authentic* 1954 original, concomitant with baby boomers' growing nostalgia for everything from their childhood, than any real appreciation for Honda. Where Honda is discussed, he is usually dismissed as a hack director of cheap monster films. He is, nevertheless, the true pioneer of Japanese atomic bomb cinema.

Honda's best-known film is the *kaijū eiga*, or "mysterious creature film," *Gojira*, also known to us as *Godzilla* (1954)—released just two years after the end of the Allied Occupation (cf. the American release; see chapter 4). Ironically, outside of Japan this is probably the best-known Japanese film. This film establishes kaijū eiga's most important themes. Some themes focus on the domestic or personal, such as tradition, family, harmony with nature, and the centrality of women in Japanese society. Other themes focus on a broader social context, including the dangers of modernity, technology, or capitalism, and the role of the military. The most important theme, however, is the restoration of balance and harmony. The fear and wonderment of children are also an important subtextual theme, which is expressed more directly in later films' texts.

In the film, nuclear weapons tests in the Pacific awaken Gojira, or Godzilla, and make him radioactive. Gojira acts on his suffering by trying to destroy Tokyo, Japan's center of modernity (see figure 6). The military proves no more able to stop Gojira than it was the Allied forces.

Gojira rages, like a wounded child, against Tokyo, the modern city that has forgotten Japanese tradition: the first to see Gojira are young people dancing to Western music on a pleasure boat in Tokyo Bay. Like Gojira, one scientist in the film, Serizawa (Akihito Hirata), also rages against society. According to Mr. Honda, in my interview with him in 1990, Serizawa's missing eye is—at least to 1950s Japanese audiences—an emblem, or stigma, of his wartime experience and suffering. Serizawa discovers an oxygen destroyer. He shows it to his fiancée, Emiko (Momoko Kōchi) the daughter of his mentor, but swears her to secrecy because he fears his discovery could be used as a military weapon. Eventually, Emiko reveals the secret to the man she truly loves, Ogata (Akira Takarada), a naval officer. Ogata and Emiko confront Serizawa, and the two men fight. Emiko stops the fight and insists that Serizawa use his oxygen destroyer to stop Gojira, thus, also putting herself into conflict with her father—played by the internationally renowned actor Takashi Shimura—who wants to save Gojira. Serizawa agrees, but, along with Gojira he destroys himself and the formula to the oxygen destroyer and, presumably, sacrifices himself so that Emiko and Ogata can wed. Several ways to interpret this film present themselves.

One way to look at the film is as though it were a typical or derivative cold war–era monster movie made by hacks with a talent for imitation. Indeed, popular writers, including Bill Warren and Stuart Galbraith IV, and scholars such as Joseph L. Andersen and Donald Richie, and S. S. Prawer, all claim that *Gojira* is an imitation of one or several American films.[54] In the very first sentence of a prize-winning essay, "Godzilla and the Japanese Nightmare: When *Them!* is U.S.," film scholar Chon Noriega reaffirms the commonly held conceit that *Gojira* "appeared to be merely an imitation of the 1953 American film *Beast from 20,000 Fathoms*."[55] Kim Newman writes that "*Gojira* was an unauthorized semi-remake."[56] Honda, however, claimed that though there was much talk about it, no one working on *Gojira* had seen the 1953 film; in fact, *The Beast from 20,000 Fathoms* (Eugen Laurie) was released in Japan in 1954, the same year as *Gojira*. All substantial and anecdotal evidence suggests Laurie's film did not directly influence the production of *Gojira*; thus, indicating synchronic cultural responses to global events, not mimicry.[57] To say that these filmmakers are hacks, therefore, makes about as much sense as calling Shakespeare a hack because he was influenced by Italian popular literature; and it has racial overtones. To look for Western influences only in film, moreover, is a conceit. We ought to start with the French writer Jules Verne (1828 to 1905), whose works were already being translated, and very influential, even before Honda and his colleagues were born.[58] Be that as it may, monsters in American films are usually the mere projection of the central character's crisis, usually a psychosexual crisis. (Thus, when the hero or heroine fights and slays the monster, he or she is resolving or integrating some undesirable aspect of his or her own psyche.) That would make Serizawa the central character, as the perceptive Ken Hollings argues;[59] but Serizawa destroys himself, and he neither develops nor learns from his experiences, which is an essential element to Western narratives. Perhaps, then, Gojira is a projection of Emiko, who, because she is the only one who can make a decision, is clearly the central character. But, Gojira takes no interest, neither hostile nor romantic, in Emiko whatsoever; the two do not fight as heroes or heroines and their projections normally do. Clearly, Gojira's crisis and Emiko's crisis are very different.

How the Japanese themselves receive the film is, furthermore, vitally important. In comparing Japanese and Western tales, Kawai contends that

> they have a different impact: the Western one has a form of completeness which impresses the reader whereas the Japanese seems to be incomplete. But if one considers the feelings apt to be induced in its audience, the story is complete. It cannot be discussed as a whole without appreciating the feeling of *awaré* [*sic*] (softly despairing sorrow) which a Japanese would feel for [the central character] who disappears.

To this Kawai adds that we must also consider "the beauty of rancor (*urami*) which backs up that of sorrow (*awaré*)," which is expressed by the central character. "If *awaré* occurs at the sudden cessation of a process and is directed at something disappearing, then *urami* looks toward the continuation of a process and is born out of the spirit of resistance to the necessity of disappearing."[60] Indeed, some American bomb films, such as *Them!* end with what might be called a sense of regret, maybe even sorrow, about the past, and a clearly articulated foreboding for the future; but, they also end with the lead male and female characters having resolved their personal crises, thus evoking Kawai's sense of "completeness." Also, neither the characters nor the audience feel any particular sympathy for the ants. *Gojira*, however, seems to cease suddenly without an obvious happy-ever-after ending or clear resolution of the story. The decision to destroy Gojira is made reluctantly and sorrowfully by the characters; audiences also express a great deal of sorrow for the character, and Gojira himself expresses a considerable amount of rancorous resentment toward the world and resists his disappearance by returning again and again in numerous sequels—points I will discuss in detail shortly.

While relevant, analyzing *Gojira* as a typical cold war–era film depends too much on Western conventions. Indeed, compared to typical Hollywood films of the same era, Gojira's personality is more fully developed and independent of the dramatic devices or characters explored in Hollywood films. (His character continues to develop throughout the Gojira series.) As some of my students wrote in a class assignment, "A monster cannot speak, so he must express his nobility with his acts."[61] Japanese monsters are indeed independent, noble characters, so we must look elsewhere for an interpretative strategy.

The relevant scholarly literature on *Gojira* is dominated by the psychopathology argument. First, Richie condemns *Gojira* for "[i]ts very refusal to make a responsible statement" or "moral commitment"; Susan Sontag then proclaims that such films are the "emblem of ["most peoples'"] . . . *inadequate response*," and finally, Lifton determined these films to be more evidence for psychic numbing or denial of the bombing of Hiroshima, Nagasaki, and the nuclear arms race.[62] In support of his bipolar "cycles" theory, Boyer cites Honda's *Bijo to ekitai ningen* (*The H-Man*, 1958) as one of many films that "had obvious psychological roots in the fear of genetic damage from radiation."[63] Even C. J. Jung and colleagues, in *Man and His Symbols*, note in a caption to a still from *Gojira* that "Perhaps the monsters of modern 'horror' films are distorted versions of archetypes that will no longer be repressed."[64] Even if we accept Jung's notions about transpersonal archetypes, why should we assume that in our day and age they are any more pathologically "distorted" than at any other time in history? Psychopathology arguments, in other words, are too ideologically shrill to offer any useful critical insights.

The most common way to look at *Gojira* is as a condemnation of America's use of nuclear weapons against Japan. But that is much too simple of an explanation, for if we look closely this film explores, from a Japanese perspective, the depths of the human condition in the early postwar environment. The most productive way to look at this film is the restoration of balance and harmony. *Gojira* suggests that men have become too powerful because they make war; consequently, society is no longer in harmony with the natural order of things. Thus, the world is dangerously unbalanced. Something must counterbalance the male element in this film.

Emiko Yamane, the central character, is caught among three men: her father, who wants to save Gojira; Ogata, who wants to use Serizawa's formula to destroy Gojira; Serizawa, who wants to keep his formula a secret, and between Serizawa (her fiancé) and Ogata (the man she loves). The men, Ogata and Serizawa in particular, end up paralyzed by fighting among themselves, thus creating a vacuum, or *ma* in Japanese aesthetics, that draws in Emiko. Ma is frequently seen as the blank spaces in a painting or flower arrangement, but is more easily likened to the empty intervals between musical notes or dialog in premodern Japanese theater. These intervals are as important as the notes or words themselves, for they are pregnant with meaning, energy, and unforeseen potential; that is, the notes or words and the intervals are the *here* and the *beyond* in Zen philosophy (discussed above). In *Gojira*, this ma is noticeable in both the narrative and, more importantly, the visual symbology of the filmic imagery—that is, the graphic movement of the camera and the characters. To fill this void, Emiko must assert herself, in her own subtle yet nonetheless forceful way, thereby resolving her crisis and restoring harmony and balance; she literally steps between the two men. Her subtle gentleness toward Ogata is also a considerate and gentle indication to Serizawa of her changed affections. Emiko has, in effect, made the crucial decisions that allow the narrative to resolve itself in a way that brings about the restoration of balance and harmony both within human society and with nature. But, as noted before, balance is not a static phenomenon; Emiko's decision has unforeseen consequences. The disappearance of both Serizawa and Gojira at the end of the film is quite affecting because, in part, it evokes Kawai's sense of mono no aware; and, more importantly, because their absence creates a ma—one so powerful that it draws Gojira back into our lives again and again.

It is worth noting here that Emiko and her father have taken on as their ward a boy orphaned by Gojira's destruction; and yet, the all-important Japanese mother figure appears to be absent from the Yamane family. Thus, this film is very much about Emiko, how she struggles to fill several different voids, including the void in her own personal life, and fulfill her own potential. As Joy Wilemse, one of my foreign students at Hiroshima University, observes, Emiko is at first what Kawai refers to in fairy tales as a "woman of endurance" but she becomes a "woman of will."[65] Only when she has resolved what direction she will take and reveals her love for Ogata is harmony and balance restored. In Honda's later films he dispenses with the kitschy love triangle as the dramatic device, and finds subtler ways to develop more thoroughly this pattern of restoring balance and harmony at both the level of the narrative and at the more important symbolic, subtextual level.

Let us take a look at two later films by Honda, *Mosura* (1961, or, *Mothra*, Lee Kresel, 1962) and *Mosura tai Gojira* (*Godzilla vs. the Thing*, or *Godzilla vs. Mothra*, 1964). In the first film, an international expedition team, financed by wealthy Caucasian entrepreneur Clark Nelson (Jerry Itoh), investigates reports about a mysterious pacific island that had been used for nuclear weapons tests. In the inner part of the island the investigating team finds a thriving indigenous pretechnological society and a pair of toy-sized twins (played by the popular singing duo the Peanuts, identical twins Emi and Yumi Itō). Nelson and his Japanese henchmen kidnap the twins, killing some of the natives along the way, and take the twins back to Tokyo where he forces them to perform. (Remember, King Kong has a similar fate). The character that, like Emiko, truly drives the plot forward is woman news photographer Michi Hanamura (Kyōko Kagawa). She leads a group of Japanese, who were part of the expedition, on a futile campaign to rescue the miniature women. (In 1963 the current emperor became engaged to and soon married Michiko Shōda, who has been very popular with the people; while a common name to begin with, Michiko and its variants became even more popular.) Meanwhile, a giant larva, the island's protector, with which the miniature women have a telepathic connection, or psychic bond, destroys much of Tokyo in an attempt to recover the women. Nelson and his henchmen take the tiny women and flee to a Western country. The larva, having metamorphosed into a giant moth, follows them, causing global panic. The police shoot Nelson, while Michi and her male colleagues recover the kidnapped twins and return them to Mothra. This action brings about the restoration of balance and harmony.

In the second film, *Mosura tai Gojira*, both scheming entrepreneurs and Godzilla threaten one of Mothra's eggs. A woman news photographer (Yuriko Hoshi), the two tiny women from Mothra Island (the Itoh twins), and Mothra herself lead the effort to rescue the egg. Eventually, two *yōchū*, or larvae, hatch from the egg and encase Godzilla in a *mayu*, or chrysalis. Godzilla then falls back into the ocean whence he came (as he does in most films; see figure 7). Again, symbolically, it is once more the women who stabilize competing forces.

Though I have been critical of the Japanese tendency to see themselves as the victims of outside misunderstandings, foreign scholars of Japanese films really do at times err by imposing Western interpretations on Japanese symbols. (Sometimes, especially when it serves the purposes of Japanese apologists, Western interpretations, even misinterpretations, are used and eventually believed by the Japanese themselves.)[66] Foreign scholars err most exemplarily in their analyses of Japanese bomb films, particularly kaijū eiga. For instance, Chon Noriega, in his analysis of Honda's *Mosura* and *Mosura tai Gojira*, jettisons the narrative's explanation of certain pre-Christian artifacts found on Mosura Island, thereby missing the cultural and narrative context of important symbols. He can do this because, in his reading, these symbols work "at a deeper psychological level to explicate Japan's Westernization." This leads Noriega to conclude bizarrely that these films express Japan's latent Christianity.[67]

Noriega's conclusion begs the question: Can you have latent Christianity without Jews or Christians, or even the concept of sin?[68] In the dominant Christian narrative, the person most responsible for humanity's original fall from grace is female, and the person most relied upon for humanity's ultimate redemption, the one destined to establish cosmological balance and harmony, is male. In contrast, all the early *Gojira* films portray the men, and the male Gojira, as the cause of the problems (with the men receiving far less sympathy than the monster).[69] While the criminal mastermind in *Mosura* is indeed a foreigner (played by a Japanese actor), in both the 1961 and 1964 Mosura films the villains are, more importantly, men whose greed causes massive destruction in Japan. And, it is the women and female moths who struggle and sacrifice themselves to resolve the films' crises in favor of a more earthly balance and harmony in the here and now. Let us also not forget that Japan's imperial family was established by a goddess, Amaterasu Ōmikami, and that the goddess Izanami gave birth to the land of Japan (in addition, Benzaiten, one of the seven Buddhist deities of good fortune, is the Goddess of music and water—both of which are exceedingly important in Gojira films); thus, as Kawai suggests, feminine figures play a central role in Japan's myths about itself, and thereby confer tremendous powers on the feminine and women. Noriega is an astute scholar, and his contribution to the scholarly literature on kaijū eiga deserves the utmost attention. His critical apparatus (one with broad appeal to thinkers on the left), however, leads him to misinterpretations of cultural meanings. Sociologists Wade Nobles and Lawford Goddard call such misinterpretations as Noriega's "transubstantive error"; that is to say, in what appears to be part of the normal trial-and-error process of explaining another culture, Noriega has interpreted the substance of the other culture through the filter of his own.[70] This cautions us against a strident commitment to a single approach, critical theory in particular, and behooves us to look for a better explanation than the one Noriega offers, one more attentive to the paradoxical, simultaneous, universal, and culturally specific polysemous nature of filmic imagery.

In the second *Mothra* film, the two yōchū restore harmony and balance, symbolically, through encasing Gojira in a chrysalis, which has the power of transforming something crude into a higher order of being, and then Gojira falls back into the ocean. Water, as we have seen repeatedly in both Western and Japanese films, has the power to cleanse and restore. The sea is an especially significant type of water. C. G. Jung draws connections between the sea, the mother, and the child motif.[71] Deep water and the chrysalis (à la *The Silence of the Lambs* [Jonathan Demme, 1991]), however, are probably universal symbols of psychic transformation, and ubiquitous in Japanese culture. For instance, the well-known poet Tatsuji Miyoshi reminds us that part of the Chinese character, or *kanji*, for ocean, is the character for mother. Although Miyoshi's interpretation is not etymologically correct, his poem nevertheless highlights the deep connection in Japanese people's minds between mother, or the feminine, and the sea.[72] And, in ancient Japanese legal and mythological texts, the silkworm and women are intimately linked. *Mushimezuruhimegimi*, an anonymous tale found in the twelfth-century (late Heian) collection *Tsutsumi Chūnagon monogatari*, has been given various English titles, most recently *The Girl Who Loved Caterpillars*.[73] The *Kojiki* (*Record of Ancient Things*) establishes a relationship between matriarchy and silkworms, as do many folktales.[74] The thirty-third emperor gave silk culture constitutional recognition and skillfully turned silk into a cottage industry that relied on peasant women's labor. More importantly, just as the *tennō* (or emperor) is the symbolic head of the rice culture—for he plants and harvests the first shoots—the *kōgō* (or empress) is the head of the silk culture. Even in this age, the empress feeds the first mulberry leaves to the worms and harvests the first cocoons or chrysalides.[75] A chrysalis—Kimi Honda, the filmmaker's widow, pointed out to me—is, moreover, very much like a *shikyū*, or womb.[76] In these films, men have become too strong, that is, their weapons or political powers are too strong, and society is out of balance with nature; so nature, which is highly anthropomorphized in Japanese tradition, retaliates (usually against modernity). Thus, the feminine element must assert itself and transform the masculine element in order to restore balance and harmony. In this light, even the otherwise incomprehensible conclusion of Honda's *Frankenstein Conquers the World*, in which a teenage Frankenstein, the direct byproduct of WWII, is inexplicably dragged into the sea by a "devil fish," begins to make sense.

In *Gojira*, the power of the feminine to restore harmony with nature and a balanced society is located in the central character, Emiko. In the two later films, however, Mothra is the surrogate and symbolic expression of the power that is reserved for the feminine. But more than merely exercising a balancing, harmonizing influence, the feminine element in Japanese culture actually brings about a transformation in the masculine element. Thus, Gojira is encased in a womb-like mayu, then falls back into the sea. There he is transformed into Japan's protector, the role he fulfills in later films, including some directed by Honda.

One of the more common and important motifs that draw together these traditional storytelling elements is that of the angry, unwanted child (e.g., Gojira) who returns to Japan to claim the honor he is denied. This theme is exemplified by another Japanese myth. In "The Hidden Gods in Japanese Mythology," Hayao Kawai writes about "a strange god named Hiruko (Leech Child), who was the only one not retained by the Japanese pantheon."[77]

Hiruko occasionally returns to Japan to annoy the people, thereby reminding them of his existence. Kawai concludes that the Japanese people are changing, and they are learning to accept Hiruko, or, rather, the psychic element that Hiruko represents. To my mind, at least, Hiruko represents the kid of "individualistic" personality that is broadly considered disruptive in Japanese society. When I look at the tremendous transformations that Gojira has undergone throughout many films, sometimes destroyer and sometimes protector, I cannot help but think that these films are just the latest expression, or at least the clearest modern example, of the Japanese struggle to find a way to incorporate Hiruko into their lives.

Japan's kaijū eiga and science fiction films, including some of Honda's, have other thematic and ideological agendas as well, some not so benign. In Honda's *Chikyū bōeigun* (*The Mysterians*, 1957), for example, aliens who destroyed their own planet in a nuclear war build a base in Japan.

They claim, at first, to want only a small parcel of land to resettle. A young scientist (Akihiko Hirata), who fears that humanity will similarly destroy itself, is at first sympathetic to the aliens' cause. His mentor (Takashi Shimura), however, pleads with the world to join forces and defeat the invaders before they get a foothold on the earth. Eventually, the Mysterians' true intentions to conquer the earth and use human women for breeding purposes become clear. Several women are kidnapped, but, much to their good fortune, not impregnated before the heroes rescue them. Shortly after the women are rescued, the aliens are defeated. Coming some five years after the end of the Occupation, *Chikyū bōeigun* seems to encapsulate many of the ideological forces in Japanese society that we have seen in other films, including *Kaze no tani no Naushika*. Japan's nationalist pride and isolationist tendencies, a sense of vulnerability to the outside world, resentment of foreign occupation, and fear of the polluting of the Japanese race through miscegenation are, on the one hand, rather obvious ideological imperatives in this film. Somewhat less obvious, on the other hand, are Japan's need for world recognition but without actual interrelation, its new national identity as a peaceful nation that is fostering order and cooperation among the nations of the world, and the pressures to "internationalize." The film may also be seen as working through Japan's own disastrous history of colonialism. These may seem to be irreconcilable contradictions in Japanese society, but they describe the complex modern Japanese national identity: in the world but not of it. (Conversely, foreigners may be in Japan, even celebrated, but never really of it.) In this film, moreover, the transformative power of the feminine is not so strongly developed. Nevertheless, restoration of balance and harmony structures *Chikyū bōeigun* as much as any other film. Once the women are safely back in the hands of Japanese men, the threat subsides and balance and harmony are restored.

At this juncture in our discussion of Japanese bomb films an analysis of two recent Godzilla films not directed by Honda will help begin to bring our discussion of kaijū eiga to a close. The 1992 film *Gojira tai Mosura* (Takao Ōkawara), a remake of the 1964 film, is a dramatic departure from previous films: The narrative is more complex, with a large cast, various subplots, and considerably more character development. It begins with an asteroid crashing to earth, causing earthquakes, volcanoes, and typhoons, which not only uncover one of Mosura's eggs, but also unleash two monsters, Battra and Gojira. Takuya Fujitō (Tetsuya Bessho), is imprisoned for plundering important cultural objects from an ancient tomb in Thailand. Japanese officials, including Fujitō's ex-wife, Masako Tezuka (Satomi Kobayashi), offer him freedom if he helps recover the egg. Takeshi Tomokane (Makoto Ōtake), a Japanese industrialist, sponsors the search in hopes of reaping huge profits.

Fujitō, Tezuka, and one of Tomokane's "salarymen" (white-collar employees), Kenji Andō (Takehiro Murata), discover a pair of tiny twins. The twins call themselves the Cosmos (Keiko Imamura and Sayaka Ōsawa). Together they attempt to bring the egg back to Japan by boat, but in mid-ocean the yōchū, or larva, hatches. Andō, therefore, kidnaps the Cosmos twins and delivers them to Tomokane. Trapped in the heart of Tokyo, the tiny twins call for the yōchū's help. The larva destroys much of Tokyo in its attempt to find them. Meanwhile, Fujitō abandons his family at the airport.

Tezuka, her daughter Midori (Shiori Yonezawa), and Miki Saigusa (Emi Odaka)—a woman with psychic powers—lead a rescue attempt. Ando, however, returns the Cosmos twins to Fujitō, who hands them over to the three women. Midori releases the twins, and they calm the yōchū. The yōchū then changes into Mosura, and Battra also transforms from a yōchū into a batlike creature. Mosura and Battra begin to battle, but Mosura succeeds in gaining *wakariai* (an understanding) with Battra. Together, these two kaijū (mysterious creatures) defeat Gojira. Battra and Gojira are, as always, swallowed by the sea, and Mosura flies off into outer space, leaving behind a united Fujitō family.

Many of the same concerns found in previous films also enliven *Gojira tai Mosura*. The threat of modernity is still present; there is the villainous industrialist whose greed truly sets events into motion. Nature and women are still very important; that is, they retain their psychological importance. Women continue to lead the rescue efforts, and have direct psychic contact with the forces of nature. And, in *Gojira tai Mosura* we can still see the heartbeat of ancient Japan. The mysterious feminine element continues to transform the Hiruko character into a responsible, adult male. At the same time, we can also see the changing social status of women since 1954. Long ago goddess Amaterasu Ō mikami forced the other gods to respect her. Today, Japanese women are becoming increasingly vocal in their demands for respect, equal rights, and safety. The women in *Gojira tai Mosura* are no longer just daughters, they are professionals. But, in a striking repudiation of Emiko's character in the 1954 film, who struggles and becomes a powerful figure, the 1992 film seems to say that women and weak men need to be guided by a strong male figure. Men not only supervise but also physically dominate women; thus, we might say that the film equates women and weak men.

Japan in the 1990s faced different problems than in 1954. Gone are the films in which an elderly father, an adult daughter, and a teenage brother try to survive in the modern world and maintain traditional values. In *Gojira*, Emiko struggles between two rival men, and also between her father and the man she loves. In today's films, the nuclear family struggles against urban decadence, economic dislocation, and divorce. In *Gojira tai Mosura*, moreover, Fujitō struggles between his lifestyle and the needs of his family, between his own desires and the needs of Japan. We might, therefore, conclude that the pressure on Japanese men to change and become more responsible—particularly toward women and family—is becoming a more obvious issue in the culture; thus, men replace women as the central element in Gojira films. And yet, the same structuring mythic and symbolic elements remain important.

As in virtually all Gojira films, the Hiruko character is necessary but out of control. He must be transformed by contact with the feminine aspect. Likewise, Fujitō is out of control. He is not trusted by other Japanese and is estranged from both wife and child. Fujitō even runs away when he sees his daughter. This sort of person is an anathema in Japanese culture and yet helpful in times of crisis. Only after Fujitō recovers the Cosmos twins can he be reunited with his wife and daughter. And only then can Gojira be defeated and returned to the sea, thereby leaving the Fujitō family whole and Japan safe. Thus, as in past films, the feminine aspect continues to exert a balancing, harmonizing effect on the psyche of males and on society as a whole. In a word, Fujitō is the Hiruko character.

The twenty-third and most recent Gojira film, *Gojira 2000: mireniamu* (*Godzilla 2000: Millennium*, Takao Ōkawara), was released in late December 1999. In it, Yūji Shinoda (Takehiro Murata), a former university professor, and his adolescent daughter Io (Mayu Suzuki) who is named after one of Jupiter's moons, operate the Godzilla Prediction Network (or GPN). As in the original 1954 *Gojira*, the family consists of a scientist and his daughter, with no mother. The adult Emiko in the earlier film fills the void of the missing mother but more importantly seeks to establish her own family, and the aged patriarch seems rather asexual. Typical of contemporary dramas (and not just in Japan) about single parents, in *Gojira 2000* there is considerable role confusion. Both

Io, the adolescent, and science journalist Yuki Ichinose (Naomi Nishida) compete to fill the void of the missing wife/mother for young and sexually attractive Shinoda—perhaps the Greek myth of a jealous love triangle among Zeus, Hera, and Io was always about the Oedipal tensions between daughters and their parents. In *Gojira 2000: mireniamu* this tension becomes comical, and is never clearly resolved.

Godzilla has a passion for destroying nuclear facilities (including Tōkaimura, where there is a real nuclear reprocessing plant that had a very serious accident just before the film was released). At the same time, government scientists try to raise, out of deep waters off Japan's coast, a six-thousand-year-old meteorite with "unknown chemical properties." As it turns out, the rock is a dormant alien life form. Godzilla and the alien engage in battle in Shinjuku, a hub of Tokyo, and the alien tries to morph itself by absorbing Godzilla's regenerative powers and strength. As the battle proceeds, Ichinose gains access to a supercomputer and manages to open one of the alien's computer files that was mysteriously downloaded onto her laptop. A lot of words appear in seemingly random order. A fragmented but understandable message, however, finally takes form. In *Gojira 2000: mireniamu*, the "millennium" is the alien's plan to deracinate terrestrial life from the earth and repopulate it with its own extraterrestrial life form. Godzilla, however, emerges from the battle victorious, but proceeds to destroy a large part of ultra-postmodern Tokyo. Despite the fact, or perhaps because of the fact, that Gojira then lays waste to a large part of Tokyo, the political center of Japan, most characters seem rather satisfied with the outcome. This film brings us full circle to the motifs that started our discussion of Japanese bomb films: Japan's relationship to nature and the outside world.

The Japanese may indeed "love" nature in the way D. T. Suzuki and others argue; however, what Japanese bomb films express is nothing like, for example, Thoreau's or Muir's love of nature. Nor is it anything like Freeman Lowell's (Bruce Dern) love of nature in Douglas Trumbull's 1971 bomb film *Silent Running*. According to Toho Studio's "Godzilla Official [web] Site" (*sic*), Shinoda tells us that by "studying Godzilla, we may be able to unravel the secrets of all life forms on this earth."[78] Shinoda and his GPN, however, do not hope to stop Godzilla. Rather, they hope to find a way to live in balance and harmony with him, just as one must learn to live with an often hostile natural environment: violent earthquakes, volcanoes, and typhoons. Nature is something that must be contended with, compensated and prepared for, just as traditional

Japanese architecture is said to compensate for the extreme humidity. Needless to say, one could never hope to control or fully compensate for nature; after all, to cite Toho's official Godzilla website, "As Shinoda says, Godzilla is full of surprises." In other words, if the Japanese love nature, then it is a love based first on fear and reverence.

Like baseball, Christmas, St. Valentine's Day, "chapel weddings," Noriega's "Christian" symbols, the bomb, and, in a sense, perhaps all of modernity, the "millennium," too, has been absorbed and morphed into something very Japanese; or, at least, a very Japanese perception of its relationship to the rest of the world. The millennium is yet another example of a doomed foreign force threatening to invade and pollute sacred Japan. And what saves Japan is, again, nature's violent gale—in this case Gojira's "atomic fire breath," his main weapon against the alien life form. As terrible as typhoons or Gojira can be, they also protect Japan. Thus, one must learn to *gaman*, or as the emperor Shōwa put it in 1945: "endure the unendurable," until the aliens have left. Alien life forms, Gojira, and even worse domestic monsters such as the AUM Shinrikyō cult or a decade-long recession that has increased the numbers of single-parent families through divorce and suicide by "downsized" men, are all now taken for granted. Conspicuously absent from *Gojira 2000: mireni-amu* are the panicky crowds.

In order to close this discussion of Japanese kaijū eiga, one last question remains to be answered: Why does everyone think that kaijū and science fiction films are so "bad"? In recent years scholars have begun seriously to criticize these films as artifacts of culture, but never as art or clever filmmaking. Noriega correctly observes, "Unfortunately, Godzilla (horror) films are not perceived historically, but aesthetically according to Hollywood technical standards."[79] Indeed, even the authors of mainstream cult-film books and articles, who produce most of the literature on these films, can only offer apologies for the seeming lack of filmmaking sophistication. The usual apologies include poor production facilities and low budgets in Japan's early post-Occupation years, and attacks on highbrow critics who do not understand that these films are "just good fun." No one, not even a Japanese writer, has been able to offer an aesthetic understanding of these films that contextualizes them within Japanese expressive traditions. And, this is precisely what I will do in the next few paragraphs; that is to say, I will argue seriously for contextualizing both the narrative and, especially, the visual presentation of kaijū eiga within the broader historical traditions of Japanese art.

As mentioned earlier, the first edition of *The Film Encyclopedia* had no entry for Honda. And, curiously, in my years of teaching in Japan, virtually none of my students could remember seeing a film by the renowned Akira Kurosawa, but everyone knew his name. In contrast, all could easily remember, in great detail, many Gojira films, though few could name Honda; they could, however, name more recent directors of Godzilla films. This sort of anonymity should not be surprising. In Japan, after all, the screenwriter is often far more celebrated than the director. Curiously, however, I have found that students in American classrooms similarly know Kurosawa's name but Honda's films. If we take into account both the Japanese collective mode of film production, and the desire to produce bomb films with a broad appeal to audiences throughout the world, all of this makes sense.

According to Mr. Honda, while the director takes nominal responsibility for a film's success or failure, most films are a collaborative effort involving everyone from the production crew and cast. (This mode of filmmaking also calls into question the very appropriateness of the usual sort of auteur analyses employed by most scholars, even in the discussion of so-called art filmmakers, and their usual dismissals of popular Japanese films.) Films, in Japan, therefore, are more often the product of a collective imaginative effort rather than individual artistic genius. To the extent that this collective process can, as the seminal scholar Siegfried Kracauer so emphatically argues, "reflect (a nation's) mentality," it must also be responsive to changing sociocultural conditions.[80] Kaijū eiga and their filmmakers have gained cult followings, yet these films remain more like myths and fairy tales than high drama. While scholars and critics acknowledge the importance of myths and fairy tales, maybe even secretly adore them, few would accord them the status of artistic genius. It makes sense, therefore, that while the authors of dramas are often celebrated, the authors of these modern folk tales, Tanaka, Honda, and Tsuburaya, have been eclipsed by their creations. And yet no one, except perhaps myself, would say kaijū eiga are examples of ingenious filmmaking; this is because, I maintain, there is a fundamental misunderstanding about Japanese aesthetics.

Though less than receptive to discussing kaijū eiga as a subject for serious scholarly inquiry, Professor Masatsugu Matsuo, the director of Hiroshima University's Institute for Peace Studies, was more than eager, almost ecstatic, to tell me about his own vivid childhood memories of seeing *Gojira* in a movie theater, and his even more vivid memories of Gojira's recurring image in his childhood dreams. His response is typical.[81] Japanese people also frequently describe Gojira as a pathetic child, and since female children in Japan are rarely allowed to behave as badly as Gojira, I assume it is male. Because this male child has been woken from his sleep, he is angry and needs to be lulled back to sleep by his mother. That is to say, Japanese adults, both male and female, take a very paternalistic, tender attitude toward Gojira, and seem to understand why they and their children identify with the creature so thoroughly. Also, adults tell me that children (usually boys) consider Gojira part of their *nakama*, or clique, and their protector. Indeed, in *Son of Godzilla* (*Kaijūtonokessen Gojiranomusuko*, Jun Fukuda, 1967), Gojira's role as protector becomes more explicit. In other words, because the sometimes childlike, sometimes paternal Gojira is not a mere projection of the central human character but an independent character, audiences can easily identify with Gojira. Additionally, the equivalent for the English colloquialism, to "stir up trouble," is *netako wo okosu*, or "wake up the sleeping child." (This phrase is often used, for example, in reference to minorities' issues, which can include the hibakusha.) Thus, if one is cynical enough to add fear and loathing to the list of parental responses to children, which is not inconceivable considering how monstrously destructive children (especially boys) can be, and how Gojira-like they can sound, then the circle of feelings surrounding Gojira is complete. There is every reason to believe that audiences outside Japan, especially Americans, respond to Gojira and kaijū eiga in similar ways. After all, we do not see American children playing with mutated ant dolls, but we do see them playing with Gojira dolls, and other related commercial "tie-ins"; and, in the adult world, Ken Hollings, for instance, writes about how he and others have "a feeling a lot like love" toward Gojira.[82] Needless to say, Gojira's image is ubiquitous, as are references and allusions to the film.[83]

From analyzing the film and the Japanese people's responses to it, we see that Gojira has both a serious, albeit sometimes destructive, side as well as a childlike, sometimes even childish, side. This last point is vitally important, for it brings us to the heart of Japanese aesthetics and atomic bomb cinema. The child or childlike, in Japanese culture, stirs very deep emotions. To illustrate this point, Nobuo Tsuji, the art historian, cites

a popular Heian ballad (*imayō*) which was included in the *Ryōjin hishō* that was compiled by the retired emperor Goshirakawa:

> For sport and play
> I think that we are born.
> For when I hear
> The voice of children at their play,
> My limbs, even my
> Stiff limbs, are stirred.

The manner in which the playful voices of children moved the hearts of adults has not changed with the passage of time; the poem, full of poignant emotions is still recited today.[84]

More importantly, the childlike is connected to both playfulness and the creative spirit in Japanese art (or, as Jung calls the child motif, a "person-ification of vital forces quite outside the limited range of our conscious mind").[85] According to Tsuji,

> In artistic terms, the expression "childlike" may not always be one of praise. Yet Su Shi [a Chinese philosopher that influenced Japanese artists] called the divine force that created the universe (*Zaohua*) a child. . . . Rephrasing this, ingenuous play like that of a child is the form adopted by Japanese artists.[86]

That is to say, the child or childlike is the foundation for playfulness in Japanese art. And, this playful spirit is, precisely, the all-important but unrecognized artistic element in Japanese kaijū films. Again, as Tsuji points out, the "spirit of playfulness" is an essential, balancing component to seriousness in Japanese art. But not just in art. My own experiences in Japan have shown me that a careful balance exists in daily life. While a casual attitude toward a serious subject is not appreciated, being overly serious or direct about a subject will simply alienate people. Akira Kurosawa, Mr. Honda's close friend, has stated not only that the bomb is "unfilmable," but also that he avoided "shockingly realistic scenes" because they would "prove to be unbearable" and "would not explain in and of themselves the horror of the drama."[87] In a subject as serious as the bomb and the destruction of Hiroshima and Nagasaki, we should, therefore, expect and appreciate a certain amount of what Tsuji calls "playfulness."

Mr. Honda, the director, acknowledged to me in my interview with him the serious nature of his films, and his opposition to nuclear weapons. When I persisted in asking him about his politics or feelings toward the bomb, however, he became angry and refused to answer my questions (though, later, when recounting his life story, he indirectly answered that question by openly describing his shock and disillusionment when, following Japan's surrender, he was repatriated from Manchuria to Hiroshima). Mr. Honda preferred talking about the playful. He talked about how fortunate he was to be a filmmaker, to be able to combine and develop his childhood fascination with both science, particularly paleontology, and the fantastic. And he told how he was fortunate enough to make films that explored a very serious subject, the bomb, but never in an overly serious way, and always in a playful way.

The man in the rubber suit has been the laughingstock of world cinema simply because people, including the Japanese, miss the point (see figure 6). The very depiction of Gojira, both serious and laughable in its exaggerated menacing visage, comes straight from Japanese aesthetic tradition. That is, from what Tsuji calls "the 'pictorial fallacy' (*esoragoto*), the theory that in order to inject an animated reality into a work of art a fabricated exaggeration is need." Additionally, Tsuji writes that "what the towns people of the Edo period sought from their artists and artisans was . . . a wizardlike ability to freely alter" and exaggerate the size of objects.[88] Are modern audiences really any different? Consider Tsuji's description of Shōhaku Soga's 1763 painting *A Dragon Emerging from the Sea*: "The awesome image of a dragon, which has been enlarged to cover the entire painting surface, is no longer merely a dragon but becomes a monster with a fearful forcefulness that almost puts today's movie monsters to shame." Indeed, fantastic, bizarre, and horrifying creatures abound in Japanese art, as do overwhelmingly humorous creatures. Here, consider *Elephant and Chinese Lion* (circa 1620), by "the plebeian artist" Sōtatsu Tawaraya. These paintings, Tsuji says, "are far more lovable and affectionate" than contemporaneous artists who served the taste of the elite. Or consider Rosetsu Nagasawa's pair of screen paintings *Bull and Elephant* (late eighteenth century), which Tsuji says "magnificently and humorously depict the juxtaposition of large and small, and black and white," and are "anthropomorphized, vividly theatrical expressions of the animals." Not only do Tsuji's descriptions of seventeenth- and eighteenth-century Japanese artists and paintings seem to describe the "plebeian" filmmaker Honda and his creation Gojira, but many of these creatures look like enormous, rubbery, Japanese kaijū film monsters in happy play or repose.[89]

Whether fearful, humorous, or both, fantastic creatures in Japanese art, as Tsuji points out again and again, are always depicted in a very *playful* spirit:

> The spirit of humor did not change even with *Rokudo-e* (Paintings of the Six Realms) which are didactic religious scrolls dealing with filth and the grotesque. For example, *Jigoku zoshi* (Hell Scroll) . . . contains in rich proportions a spirit of laughter that can be called black humor. . . . The artist took delight in rendering this wretched scene, while viewers of the scroll must also have been simultaneously delighted and terrified.[90]

This description and interpretation of the twelfth-century *Hell Scroll* applies equally well to the horrific scenes of destruction and misery in the film *Gojira*. For Tsuji, in other words, "Behind the facade of Japanese seriousness, a playful heart is hidden," and that playfulness has a very positive, childlike character.[91] We can see this serious facade and childlike, playful heart in the response of Japanese people to the character Gojira, the kaijū creature's graphic similarity to earlier works of Japanese art, and the spirit of playfulness that animates this very serious subject. *Gojira* and other kaijū films are not "bad" by any means; rather, they are the expression of a repressed, vital, playful spirit that, as Tsuji argues, seeks legitimate outlets. And, in kaijū eiga, *playfulness* is a MacGuffin through which the very serious elements of *balance* and *harmony* can be *restored*. Kaijū eiga is, I believe, the quintessential outlet for the Japanese playful spirit in our time.

The restoration of balance and harmony through playfulness is ubiquitous in Japan's atomic bomb cinema, and not limited to kaijū eiga. So, having completed our discussion of kaijū eiga, the last three films I will discuss will be dramas, all by the same director. Akira Kurosawa directed three bomb films: *Ikimono no kiroku* (*Record of a Living Being*, or *I Live in Fear*, and *I Knew What the Birds Knew*, 1955), *Yume* (*Akira Kurosawa's Dreams*, or, *Dreams*, 1990), and *Hachigatsu no rapusodī* (*Rhapsody in August*, 1991). Stephen Prince, in his superb study on Kurosawa, *The Warrior's Camera: The Cinema of Akira Kurosawa*, notes a "lighthearted vein" in Kurosawa's last films, particularly in *Hachigatsu no rapusodī*. Prince considers this a defect.[92] But, as Tsuji argues, and Kurosawa demonstrates, lightheartedness is a strength.

In the first of Akira Kurosawa's three bomb films, *Ikimono no kiroku*, we find that the bomb can cause intense suffering and illness, which ceases only with the restoration of balance and harmony. The central character,

Mr. Nakajima, whom everyone calls *Rōjin*, or old man, is portrayed, ironically enough, from a younger person's perspective, that of
thirty-five-year-old Toshirō Mifune. He is so worried about nuclear war
that he wants to move his family, and later even his factory employees, to
South America, where he thinks it will be safer. His family objects, and the
dispute ends up in Family Court. Eventually, the old man becomes ill, then
mentally imbalanced from frustration and worry about the bomb. The old
man's slow decline is symbolized by his progressive isolation from the
women in his life. First distance, then windows and screens, and finally
iron bars separate him from the women he cares about most. In the end,
the old man has a complete psychic collapse and is institutionalized.

The impossibility of the old man's desire to leave Japan is obvious, at
least to Japanese audiences, from the very beginning. Prince repeatedly
points out that Kurosawa saw himself as a "global citizen" but nevertheless insisted "he made movies for the Japanese audience."[93] Thus, as we
saw in the example of *Sekai dai sensō*, above, even if Japan is destroyed by
nuclear war there is nowhere else to go. Mayumi Tanaka, one of my students at Hiroshima University, thoughtfully observes, "To reveal
something is to find something that is hidden," and though apocalyptic
bomb films give "us the chance to reflect on what will happen . . . we cannot continue [our] thought[s] of the future" because it is unknowable.
Ms. Tanaka is not arguing that we should ignore the bomb, but because
it is impossible to know what is hidden we must not dwell on the future.
She thus concludes that from a Japanese point of view, Nakajima "ruined
himself" because he "thought about what will happen after the end of the
world too much."[94] Taken to its logical extreme, Ms. Tanaka's argument
is highly suggestive. *Ikimono no kiroku* can be read as implying that the
bomb is the outcome of Western hubris, that is, the tragic belief that we
can learn hidden secrets before they are revealed to us; or that those
obsessed with the bomb, be they pro- or antinuclear, are doomed because
they dwell in fantasy. Although these interpretations seem valid, I am not
sure they are the most fruitful, for the film does offer Nakajima a way out
of his dilemma. To understand this way out, we must examine the character of the narrator.

The narrator of the story is a dentist, Dr. Harada (Takashi Shimura),
who is one of the court's judges by virtue of the status accorded a man of
science, particularly medical science, in Japan's patriarchal society.[95] In the
last act, the dentist goes to visit the old man in his cell at the mental hospital. The dentist is defeated and confused because his science cannot

explain or ease the old man's suffering. Nor can it ease the dentist's grow-ing concerns about the bomb. In the final scene, the weary dentist descends the stairs of the mental hospital as the old man's second and favored mistress, Asako Kuribayashi (Akemi Negishi), and their baby ascend the stairs. Like most scholars, Prince argues that "this sequence embodies stasis, confinement, and hallucinations of oblivion," but to me this is a definite misreading.[96] Visually, the family's symbolic absence and the dentist's graphic descent creates a *ma* or vacuum that draws in the mis-tress and baby, just as it drew in Emiko in *Gojira*. This ending, to an otherwise very serious film visually hints at the playful, "optimistic side of the Japanese disposition."[97] This scene also makes apparent the dentist's hubris and his comeuppance, but without the punishment of death or being turned into a ghost, thus suggesting the possibility for learning and growth. And, in addition to the symbolic power of the feminine, the pres-ence of children, Emperor Goshirakawa reminds us, can ease an old man's suffering. Thus, with the descent of patriarchal, scientific consciousness, and the ascent of the transformative powers of the feminine and the child-like, the film suggests that the old man has reached the apex of his crisis, and some further development toward a higher stage of consciousness is now possible. This symbolic conclusion of the film further suggests that, with the restoration of balance and harmony, the old man will no longer suffer, will recognize that you cannot run from the bomb, and, as the medical humanist Eric J. Cassell says, will be enlarged by his experiences.[98]

Ikimono no kiroku depicts a frightening reality. The bomb need not necessarily cause an "illness"; the mere fear of the bomb can lead to the most intense suffering and crisis. At the same time, modern institutions, like family courts or medical science, which cannot ameliorate or even understand one's suffering, intensify the crisis. And herein lies the para-dox of Japan. The authority and power of "science," especially in medicine, is so institutionalized that other therapies—for example, clini-cal psychology and even "traditional" (or what we incorrectly call "alternative") Asian therapies—are largely distrusted.[99] And yet again, the autochthonous message of restoration of balance and harmony in films like *Ikimono no kiroku* or *Mosura tai Gojira* is very appealing to Japanese audiences. These films are, I believe, all the more powerful because they express the restoration of balance and harmony through symbol and in the subtext.

Yume, Kurosawa's second bomb film, is composed of several different sequences, each based on a different dream Kurosawa had and later painted. (In his youth, he studied painting.) The subjects of these sequences focus on, again, traumatic loss—for instance, the loss of connection to family when a child's protomilitarist mother turns him out of the house and forces him to beg for forgiveness or commit suicide merely because he was curious (about a group of anthropomorphized foxes marching in a wedding procession); the traumatic loss of connection to the natural world when a boy's family cuts down a sacred peach orchard (the gods, in Shintō tradition, alight on trees); or the loss of friends and comrades to the spirit world. Some of the sequences also directly address the threat of technology, nuclear technology in particular, to our connection to the natural and social worlds. These sequences have much in common with the kaijū eiga or mysterious creature film genre, both visually and thematically; that is, their balancing of the serious or horrific with the playful in the exploration of the bomb's meaning. The seminal kaijū eiga director Inoshirō Honda, in addition to being one of Kurosawa's closest friends and a frequent collaborator, was also Kurosawa's special effects director for *Yume*.[100]

Although pedantic, these bomb or technology-related sequences are not without irony and humor. In the "Mount Fuji in Red" sequence, Japan's scandalously incompetent nuclear power industry causes a catastrophic meltdown, and throngs of panicky Japanese—ubiquitous in kaijū eiga—leap to their deaths like lemmings, just as they are said to have leapt off the cliffs of Saipan when the Americans invaded. And in "the Weeping Demon" sequence, global nuclear war strips away the human facade of Japan's corrupt ministerial industrial complex (the target of Kurosawa's ire in other films) and reveals its denizens to be the demons they are. Prince says the "camera work" in this episode "is flat and uninteresting, and the images . . . are unpersuasive."[101] It is indeed flat, and for a reason. The image of the tormented demons dancing in and around polluted waters bears an uncanny visual and stylistic resemblance to the *Hell Scroll* that Tsuji describes. In the final sequence or coda, "Village of the Watermills," a hiker wanders into an anachronistic village. There, an old man, the Luddite voice of the film and presumably the director, lectures the hiker on the evils of technology and losing the old ways, then joyously, or, shall we say "childishly" and "playfully," joins a funeral procession for his unrequited love. Thus, what makes *Yume* so disturbing is that it first shocks the audience with images of how science and technology create massive destruction, then reassures the audience that somewhere there is a *furusato* (or "native place") where the wellspring of

Japaneseness continues to flow free and pure.[102] After all the nightmarish tumult and anxiety the first seven sequences evoke in the spectator, the final sequence is a palliative. For many, myself included, this works to undermine *Yume*'s success. And yet, a close analysis of the film reveals not dementia, as some claim, but a complex and coherent film. The structural underpinning that connects these disparate sequences together into a coherent exhortation is, nevertheless, the final sequence in which we see balance and harmony restored through playfulness.

In *The Motion Picture Encyclopedia*'s online database, the reviewer remarks that the film begins with "a wedding that looks more like a funeral and end[s] with a funeral that looks more like a wedding."[103] Indeed, to anyone who has attended Japanese weddings and funerals, this is an unintentionally perceptive commentary. While weddings are rather restrained, at funerals there is an outpouring of emotion. Although funerals are sad, painful events, there is an almost joyous, celebratory atmosphere. (The late Jūzō Itami's 1984 film, *Osōshiki*, or *The Funeral*, is an excellent example of this mix of sadness and joy.) Perhaps this is because, on the one hand, weddings are small, either Shintō or mock-Christian rites, and one is more likely to invite business associates than family or friends to a wedding reception. Funerals, on the other hand, are open to virtually anyone who ever knew the deceased, and it is a Buddhist rite that marks the deceased's passing from this world of suffering and delusion to a higher plane of existence. In another interesting symbolic reversal, both the first and the second sequences take place in rural environs, yet the first is virtually depopulated, while the latter is not only well populated but filled with children—in reality, today's rural villages are in sharp decline as young people migrate to the cities. *Yume*'s final scene is, moreover, filled with not only lots of children (Jung's child motif), but also childlike playfulness. The foxes' very serious wedding processional, in the first sequence, is transformed into a playful and joyous funeral march in the final sequence. Thus, in keeping with Japanese tradition, death is, or can be, the ultimate restoration of balance and harmony.

There is considerable confusion about the title of Kurosawa's third bomb film, so let us be clear: Mr. Kurosawa intended the film to be known as *Hachigatsu no rapusodī*.[104] The central character, Kane (Sachiko Murase), an old grandmother, lost her husband in the destruction of Nagasaki, which she witnessed. Through an encounter with her

American nephew (Richard Gere, reportedly a practicing Buddhist), the
son of her brother who emigrated to the United States and married a
Caucasian woman before World War II, the grandmother resolves her crisis and learns to forgive both herself and others for all the terrible things
done in the war. With the rift in her family resolved, balance and harmony are thus restored, and the old woman can successfully make the
transition to the next stage in life. This reconciliation takes place under a
full moon, which, the grandmother says, can wash the mind clean, thus
suggesting psychic completion, the cycles of life, and purification. At the
end of the film, the old woman psychically lets go of this world in prepa-
ration for death, and rushes into a storm where her umbrella literally
inverts (see figure 8). At that moment we hear a chorus of children
singing Franz Peter Schubert's *Nobara*, or *The Wild Rose*. *Nobara* is
based on a Goethe poem about a boy who tries to pluck a wild rose and
pricks himself on a thorn. The song is used throughout the film, as is the
rose. In an earlier scene, during a memorial for those who died in
Nagasaki on August 9, 1945, a grandson does, indeed, follow a trail of
ants to a wild red rose. The rose's color is noteworthy because the indigenous wild rose is white; although enigmatic, the red rose suggests, at
least, that some elements of the West have taken root in Japan. Earlier in
the film the American-born nephew overhears his younger cousins
singing *Nobara*. He is moved by their singing and says they have the voices of angels. *Nobara* is one of three "classical" European songs in every
music textbook, a song that every school child learns, and adults associate it with their childhood. The image of the solitary grandmother and
the chorus fades to black and silence, and the film ends.

This final scene alone, an eclectic montage of themes and symbols,
speaks to Kurosawa's gift—one, I argue, common to all successful
Japanese artists—for drawing from and weaving together multiple aesthetic traditions. The inverted umbrella is a particularly important and
suggestive symbol.[105] Graphically, its shape reminds us of an atomic mushroom cloud. When inverted, its funnel-like shape suggests that the psychic
energies that the cloud has been drawing from the grandmother for half a
century are now being directed back into her. Umbrellas, even inverted
umbrellas, abound in Japanese works of art. The most famous, easily recognized, and ubiquitous—one company even includes miniature
reproductions in its packages of rice seasoning (*ochazuke*)—is Hiroshige's
(1787 to 1858) *Shirasame* (or, *White Rain*), from the Shōno station area,

in his late-Edo era series *Fifty-three Stations of the Tōkaidō Road*. The image of the grandmother holding an umbrella and making her way in the storm alludes to or reminds us of this very important Japanese work of art.

The visual and sound images in the final scene, more importantly, are potent symbols for the reversals that take place between the stages of life. The umbrella's symbolic potency derives from its visual similarity to what is probably the most famous scene in all of Kabuki theater. In the conclusion to *Shunkan*, a play based on twelfth-century persons and events, the tragic central character, Shunkan, loses his composure (just as the pivotal Lord Asano, in *Chūshingura*, and Naushika, do) and foils his own chance to leave the small, uncivilized island on which he has been exiled.[106] Shunkan then, heroically, sacrifices himself so his family can return safely to the Japanese homeland. In the climatic finale, he is standing on a cliff overlooking a bay, watching his family sail for home. As he holds on to the branch of a pine tree for support, waving his final farewell, the pine branch breaks off in his hand. The pine tree is a common symbol of long life. The branch breaking off in Shunkan's hand symbolizes that Shunkan's own connection to life is broken, and he is making his way into the next world. The final scene, at least, of *Hachigatsu no rapusodī* owes much to the play *Shunkan*.

The old woman's children and grandchildren rush pell-mell after her into the torrential storm, where they stumble and trip in the mud. Only the grandmother seems stable, no longer fighting the winds that buffet her but in harmony with their rhythms as she progresses ever so slowly toward the conclusion of that final journey that we all must make alone. The inverted umbrella evokes the same powerful emotions in the audience, both Japanese and foreign, as does the broken pine branch, and the film itself exhorts the restoration of balance and harmony through the childlike or playful. As one grandchild observes, the "clock in her head is running backwards" to before the end of World War II. I would say her mind is running as far back as the time when the grandmother was a schoolchild and had, most certainly, been singing *Nobara*. Thus, the voice-over of *Nobara* may well be the grandmother's inner voice. Additionally, the voice-over of children singing *Nobara* has an effect similar to Emperor Goshirakawa's ballad about the voice of children. Rainwater, once again, is a universal symbol with the power to cleanse and restore. In the context of the film's conclusion, the image of the old woman with her inverted umbrella, the rain, and the angelic voices of children singing *Nobara* are woven together into an image that transcends sight and sound. This final, transcendent moment of the film, therefore, evokes that subtle, dynamic tension in the harmonious balance between the serious and the comic that comes with the bittersweet recognition of the evanescence of life and the redemptive potential for childlike playfulness in us all.

Critics and scholars have praised Kurosawa's use of such symbolic devices in his other films, but not in *Hachigatsu no rapusodī*. When Kurosawa used a similar symbolic reversal in *Ikiru* (1952), where the central character (Takashi Shimura) spends his last night in a playground on a swing, happily singing, and covered with snow—another form of water—the film was lauded both for its style and "humanism." (This very serious film is punctuated by scenes in which the central character tries to recover and express his childlike, playful spirit, but only in his final moments does he find an honest way to express that spirit; thus, paving the way for his transition to the next world.) Stephen Prince repeatedly praises Kurosawa for his brilliant and subtle mastery of new Western aesthetics, but, equally important, that Kurosawa "infused cinema" with the Japanese "traditional aesthetic values" found in *sumi-e* (ink-painting) and Nō theater. Donald Keen tells us that the moon is a frequent symbol in Nō plays. Indeed, in the play *Obasute*, discussed earlier, there is the line "I will gaze at the moon and cleanse my heart."[107] Earlier than even *Ikiru*, in *Sugatasanshirō* (*Sanshiro Sugata*, 1943— which Prince singles out as one of Kurosawa's seminal films), we see Kurosawa's use of such aesthetics and symbols, but in a more youthful, heavy-handed way: the hero, immersed in pond water, stares at a moonlit white *hasu*, or lotus, flower until he bluntly announces his enlightenment.[108] Because the pure white hasu flower grows out of filthy waters it is a common Buddhist symbol for the possibility of enlightenment in this world. But, in *Hachigatsu no rapusodī* Kurosawa uses the enigmatic red rose of the West to suggest not only a growing awareness in the characters but also what Prince calls Kurosawa's "experiments at cross-cultural fertilization."[109] And, with great economy, Kurosawa has Kane chastise her children for their duplicity and greed, simply explain to her grandchildren that looking at the moon can cleanse the mind, and then they sit quietly, rapt by the moon. This scene alone demonstrates Kurosawa's mastery of his art. Elegant beyond words, the scene realizes the full potential of art in Japanese culture: the power to momentarily cleanse the spectator's mind. In a later, poignant scene, Kane and Clark reconcile under that same moon. At the level of the text, *Hachigatsu no rapusodī* may not always be so subtle, and therefore not a "good" film. At the more important subtextual levels, however, it is a symbolic expression of the restoration of balance and harmony, not ham-fisted malediction.

But *Hachigatsu no rapusodī* has been criticized in the United States for the usual reasons. For example, Linda C. Ehrlich, a scholar whose thoughtful work is usually characterized by judicious temperance, begins her essay "The Extremes of Innocence: Kurosawa's Dreams and Rhapsodies" by noting that the film "was greeted with a mixture of antic-ipation, trepidation and anger." Indeed, rather than critical distance, Ehrlich can barely contain her own disappointment and anger, which is, again, exemplary of the blinding passions and moral self-righteousness that cripples the scholarly debate about the bomb. Ehrlich, on the one hand, rightly points out, "When Kurosawa allows the power of the images their own say, they do so eloquently." But, on the other hand, she argues that "*Dreams* and *Rhapsody* are opportunities missed . . . for a voice respected throughout the world to present images of the effects of war that are at once penetrating and extensive."[110] James Goodwin, in his article "Akira Kurosawa and the Atomic Bomb," similarly concludes that *Hachigatsu no rapusodī* "culminates without the undercurrents of exis-tential and tragicomic absurdity that give . . . unsettling insights into human experience in the atomic age."[111] In "Memory and Nostalgia in Kurosawa's Dream World," Prince, echoing Richie and Sontag, uses the vague phrase "insufficient visualization" to describe the nuclear-related sequences in *Yume*, and wrongfully complains that unlike other Kurosawa characters, Kane in *Hachigatsu no rapusodī* is trapped in the past, "a character fully formed and completed and faces no significant moral chal-lenges or choices."[112] Kurosawa, in particular, is held to a double standard: he must be the artistic genius of fictions that transcend the human condition, but he must also be the world's teacher.

Films about the bomb, by Japanese filmmakers especially, are again judged by an unattainable measure, defined by Richie and Sontag, of absolute *responsibility* and *adequacy*. Ehrlich, Goodwin, and Prince are so blinded by the need to judge Kurosawa's bomb films according to this measure that they completely miss the beauty and evocative powers of the film's symbolic imagery. The most important difference between *Hachigatsu no rapusodī* and *Ikiru* is that in *Ikiru* the central character is dying of stomach cancer somewhere in Tokyo, not wasting away in Hiroshima or Nagasaki. It is this geographical difference that allows most critics to maintain a clearer perspective on the film *Ikiru*. Nevertheless, what makes *Hachigatsu no rapusodi* an unusually powerful bomb film, and every much as "good" as *Ikiru*, is that it uses these symbolic reversals, and elements common to the culture and other hibakusha films, to ask the audience to confront difficult issues. *Hachigatsu no rapusodi* tells us that a meaningful and peaceful resolution of the issues is possible. Prince, who considers the film a lesser work, is right in stating that Kane and the grandchildren "represent, in symbiosis, the grounds for a cultural healing of the war's trauma."[113] The film, moreover, decentralizes Japan, and exhorts a global resolution. Finally, the structure of this resolution is, as always, the restoration of balance and harmony. And, throughout—for example, in the relationship of the children to their grandmother, the American cousin's uninhibited friendliness, the visual *esoragoto* or exaggerations in the grandmother's vision of the bomb, and the visual effect of the final scene itself—the film uses a childlike, playful spirit to achieve this restoration. Sadly, although many U.S. scholars and critics continue to look to Japanese films for a responsible and adequate response to the bomb, they remain as disappointed and contemptuous as always.

Americans have criticized *Hachigatsu no rapusodi* for another reason that deserves our attention. Prince acknowledges his passion for Kurosawa's works, and it is his strength but also his weakness. In an apologia he tries to bolster Kurosawa's status as an auteur by diminishing the importance of his last films. "Had he ceased filmmaking after *Ran* [1985], he'd have ended his career on a note of high accomplishment." (After *Ran*, Kurosawa made *Yume*; *Hachigatsu no rapusodi*; and *Mādadayo*, or *No, Not Yet*, 1993). Kurosawa ended his career on a low note because, Prince contends, he abandoned the "crucial collaborative filmmaking" process and authored his last three screenplays by himself.[114] But, on the one hand, the sociologist Howard S. Becker has repeatedly shown that the production of all art, not just film, is collaborative, and, on the other hand, I can see no particular reason to consider screenwriting essentially more collaborative than other types of writing; thus, the suggestion that the films are flawed because Kurosawa wrote them himself really tells us nothing about them.[115] Prince's claim, moreover, may be a "transubstantive error" for Prince appears to be giving primacy to what Aoki calls the Western "written dialogue drama" over the films themselves.[116] By attacking these last three films in this way, Prince appears to undermine Kurosawa's auteur status by largely dismissing his last films—and discrediting and humiliating Kurosawa himself. On the first page of the first chapter, Prince begins not with a discussion of Kurosawa's films but of his "dilemma" and attempted suicide. Prince then asserts that "to lay the burden of Kurosawa's artistic problems exclusively on the greed or crassness of the contemporary industry is to miss seeing the very painful dead end, internal to the works, in which Kurosawa the filmmaker was stranded after 1965.[117] Kurosawa's attempted suicide is no secret. But, by framing the films within such loaded and romantic ideas as artistic dilemmas and dead ends, an artist being stranded inside his own work, and attempted suicide, Kurosawa's films become metaphors or symptoms of an undiagnosed psychopathology. In the therapeutic culture of America, at least, those who suffer from a pathology are seen as pitiable victims; thus, within the logic of Prince's argument, we may safely disregard Kurosawa's failures, his last three films in particular, and celebrate Kurosawa as an unparalleled film auteur. Although Prince's analyses and criticism of Kurosawa's films are extraordinarily insightful, his portrait of Kurosawa the person is neither sufficient nor necessary for our appreciation of Kurosawa's films. But such caricatures of Kurosawa are hardly unusual.

Many critics, Japanese and non-Japanese alike, charge that Kurosawa is really too Western to be a representative Japanese filmmaker. For instance, Kathe Geist's article, "Late Kurosawa: *Kagemusha* and *Ran*" is a fine example of scholarship, yet it too ultimately falls back on a clichéd reductive argument that in contradistinction to filmmaker Yasujirō Ozu, Kurosawa's "late" films are evidence that his artistic development is "more akin to that of classical European painters"; that is, Kurosawa's pathology is his lack of authentic Japaneseness.[118] Curiously, though, no one would similarly say that Japanese Nobel Laureates in the sciences, most of whom did their Nobel-winning work in Western countries, are not representative Japanese scholars; quite the opposite in fact: they are usually held up as exemplars of their race or culture. Be that as it may, as I have shown, in *Hachigatsu no rapusodī* Kurosawa excels in his mastery of both his art and Japanese traditions. Finally, in "*Mādadayo*: No, Not Yet, for the Japanese Cinema," published just before Kurosawa's death in 1998, David Desser, an authority on Japanese films, offers a new twist to the psychopathology argument. Kurosawa's last three films were, Desser claims, commercial and artistic failures because Kurosawa was a fraud and "senile."[119]

Desser claims that Kurosawa did not give his close friend, Honda, screen credit for his work on *Yume* or *Hachigatsu no rapusodī*, but I clearly recall Honda's credit when I saw the films in the theater, and my video copies of these films credit Honda.[120] More to the point, Desser offers no medical records or evidence (e.g., a brain pathology) of Kurosawa's dementia, does not refer to any authoritative text on the subject (for instance, *DSM-IV* or the growing body of literature on age and aging in different cultures), and does not offer a definition of senility.[121] Desser argues that Kurosawa's artistic decline began in 1965, at the age of fifty-five, and suggests that senility is the cause.[122] By accepted medical standards, fifty-five would be an extremely "early onset."[123] Desser's only evidence is that Kurosawa was notoriously imperious. In a rhetorical question, Desser needlessly conflates the historical subject and central character of *Mādadayo*, retired educator or *sensei* Hyakken Uchida (Tatsuo Matsumura), and the director: "Was ever a teacher so honored, so beloved as to merit not only life-long friendship and devotion, but virtual financial and personal protection his whole life? . . . Does Kurosawa expect this kind of reverence, not simply from his own proteges [*sic*], but . . . even from all of Japan? There is a sense that this is so."[124] Desser is as ill-informed about some aspects of Japanese culture as he is about dementia. The general term for teacher, *sensei*, applies to anyone, in any walk of life, who has achieved the proper age and status. The behavior that Desser describes as demented is, moreover, not only common and accepted, but also expected. Even my rebellious colleagues, who find such behavior distasteful, openly fear that they will be unable to resist the pressures to conform and, inevitably, they too will assume the imperious manners of their own professors. In even more important ways, Kurosawa's behavior fits the norms of Japanese culture. In *Taming Oblivion* John Traphagan, a gerontological anthropologist, points out that common to the Japanese discourse on senility is "the idea that the key to a good old age is to find a reason for being, an *ikigai*"; and Prince repeatedly makes the point that Kurosawa saw his filmmaking as his "life's project."[122] Traphagan suggests that in Japan a commitment to one's life's project is considered essential not only to the individual's maintenance of body and mind in old age but also to a healthy society.[126] And if we ask ourselves which characters in Japanese culture Desser's portrait of Kurosawa most resembles, the image of the devoted artist or Buddhist monk comes easily to mind. Even if socially frowned upon, an extreme dedication to one's "life's work," as exalted in *Chūshingura*, is admirable in Japanese society. Few Japanese would seriously say Kurosawa was demented. Childish, perhaps, or childlike in his obsession with his art; that is to say, filled with Tsuji's spirit of *Zaohua*.

Peter Clecak has shown, in his study of postwar radical thinkers, *Radical Paradoxes*, that the life process changes an intellectual's perspective on the very questions that can occupy her or him for a lifetime. Younger thinkers, however, see these perspectives gained in age as betrayals of positions taken in youth, or as intellectual decline.[127] This is perhaps even truer of artists or filmmakers and their audiences. Kurosawa has always been concerned with age and aging, and as I have shown, his last films demonstrate artistic mastery and subtlety, and the perspective of someone who has reached an advanced age. Desser's ad hominem attacks are blatantly bigoted (ageist), indecorous, and grossly inaccurate. I have not made my point clear; I will forthwith. Neither Desser nor Prince claim to be qualified clinicians, and I do not think that being a film scholar qualifies one to make clinical judgments about another individual's state of mind. Because Prince and Geist work from publicly available texts, their approaches are valid, even necessary for the development of cinema scholarship; and yet I personally find their arguments about Kurosawa troubling. Desser's argument is repugnant.

As the scholarly response to *Hachigatsu no rapusodī* suggests, Americans have a curiously complex relationship with Japan. (And America tends to define the Western world's relationship to Japan.)[128] Ironically, just a few short months after the international controversy over the Smithsonian Institution's proposed exhibition of the Enola Gay, the new Nagasaki Atomic Bomb Museum opened to a similar imbroglio that, predictably, received only scant coverage in the Japanese press.[129] American critics, however, were conspicuous in their silence. I do not mean to suggest that there is no criticism of Japan. If one looks hard, there is to be found a considerable amount of informed, intellectually sound criticism of Japan. Rather, I am arguing that there is an imbalance in the critical exchange. This imbalance is due in part to differences in the victimology, legal, political, educational, and social systems of the two countries. From my geopolitical point of view, Japanese people are freer, even entitled, to criticize, to petition, to hold press conferences, to take legal action, and even to meet with the American president in order to air their grievances over a broad range of issues, while Japanese officialdom carefully insulates itself from outside criticism.

Illustrating this point, a series of August 1999 *Asahi shinbun* newspaper articles detail how one Hiroshima antinuclear group, allied with the Communist Party, successfully petitioned the National Atomic Museum, in Albuquerque, to stop selling Fat Man and Little Boy earrings.[130] Their success is significant for several reasons. Although the Japanese prime minister and other dignitaries participate in Hiroshima's annual memorial service, not until 1999 did a prime minister visit the monument for those Koreans, forcibly brought to Japan, who died in Hiroshima. This historic event received scant coverage compared to the flap over the earrings.[131] Albuquerque, moreover, has no monopoly on kitsch and bad taste, as a trip through the gift shops in Peace Park will demonstrate. (The relative silence over Japan's bribing of International Olympics Committee members, while Salt Lake City was being scourged for the same crimes, is another clear example of the more general hesitancy to criticize Japan.)[132] My own attempt at raising consciousness, about the sale of Black Face Toothpaste in the student store at Kyoto University, has left me in doubt about the efficacy of censoring other cultures' bad taste and enforcing cross-cultural political correctness.[133] Be that as it may, foreign criticism generally seems limited to economic policies, and such criticisms are usually dismissed, by both Japanese and many foreigners, as cultural misunderstandings, Japan bashing, or sour grapes. Some Western criticism, also, reads more like an apology. This is often because Japan is still seen as a "traditional" culture.

This imbalance in the critical exchange is an enormously complex subject, and beyond the scope of this study. Nevertheless, without digressing too much further from our discussion of Japanese bomb films, I would like to put forth four interrelated factors that foster an environment conducive to self-censorship and duplicity, or at least timidity and reluctance when one would otherwise be candidly outspoken. These factors pertain in particular to American scholars, but not exclusively to Americans or scholars.

First, as I have suggested throughout my discussion of Japanese films, there has been considerable internal suppression of facts and debate regarding the bomb in Japan; and, it might well be that there is less discussion now than in the past. Also, there is a great deal of self-censorship out of fear of *netako wo okosu* ("stirring up trouble") with the powerful hibakusha lobbies that vociferously attack anyone or anything that does not "reflect the hibakusha mind." (Japan's brand of political correctness, "word hunting," can be quite vile.) Kurosawa Productions, on the one hand, has been very supportive of my research and the publication of this book. Japan Railway West and Tsuburaya Productions companies, on the other hand, declined my request for permission to reproduce their images of the Jamila monster (see chapter 4), but only after learning the title of this book. In all fairness I must point out that, according to widespread popular reports, hibakusha groups attacked Tsuburaya Productions for one of its *Ultraman* episodes.[134] The company has suppressed this episode and, quite understandably, now carefully avoids any connection to the bomb. Also, Japan Railway West later apologized, saying that it is not the title of my book but their contract with Tsuburaya Productions that prevents them from giving me permission to reproduce their poster. Furthermore, some film companies in the United States have been reluctant to license images for this book. Fear of stirring up trouble by raising these issues impedes discussion at the domestic and global levels.

Second, it is not an ad hominem attack to say that the Japanese are masters of propaganda, and that immediately following the destruction of Hiroshima those in power began to, and continue to, effectively "spin" the events to their advantage. This is not the symptom of some racial pathology, or an evil plan to undermine Western civilization. Rather, it is, to a large degree, a function of the Japanese language and culture, and internal politics. Precisely for those reasons, the spin is especially difficult to penetrate and criticize.

Third, although a leading member of the Organization for Economic Cooperation and Development (OECD), Japan remains a decidedly closed country. The number of foreign students, researchers, and educators, is (even by Japan's Ministry of Education, Culture, Sports, Science and Techology's standards) very low. Foreign academics and other intellectuals who do come to Japan are both constrained and rewarded in such a way as to maintain or coerce a uniform vision of Japan that is presented to the outside world.[135] Thus, there is a one-sided exchange in knowledge and intellectual property.

Finally, a sense of permanent victimhood is the core reason why criticism of Japan is so disproportionately tempered. I believe that, in the minds of many Americans, particularly scholars, the Japanese are strategically located in a conceptual place similar to that which Gerald Vizenor argues has been occupied by Native Americans—a space where they are permanent victims—not survivors—of the ideology of tragedy and domination. (The Japanese, needless to say, have their own ideological and narrative strategies that legitimize and enhance their domination of others.) Vizenor calls this strategy "manifest manners"—that is to say, the manners of those still governed by a belief in their, or their group's, own manifest destiny.[136] These four factors contribute to an environment in which intellectually sound cultural criticism languishes. In such an environment, moreover, popular films and filmmakers become all too easy targets for cathartic criticism.

As a foreigner living in Hiroshima, I have heard from many Japanese, survivors included, that they no longer wish to be thought of as innocent victims of a tragic event. But the (local, national, and international) politics and economics of victimization prevents them from speaking out. I have personally experienced the pall that can cover any discussion of hibakusha or the bomb. Hibakusha groups, at the same time, have large pools of money to support favorable propaganda, or *hibakusha exploitation* projects, which usually become fodder for the "peace education" of schoolchildren. And when, as recently happened, schoolchildren begin to question the propaganda they have been force-fed all their lives, special interest groups, which produce these educational programs, call on the government for even more mandatory "peace education" in the schools.[137] In light of the intense international politicking to make the A-Bomb Dome (the domed building that was closest to the epicenter, or ground zero, and is now an icon of Hiroshima and nuclear destruction) a United Nations World Historical Site, and for Japan to gain a permanent seat on the U.N. Security Council, while at the same time liquidating some of the West's most treasured paintings without a trace, there is something irresponsible and inadequate about the international community's responses to Japan's official distortions of history.[138] As the Smithsonian incident shows, there is relatively more public debate about these issues in the United States than in Japan, but it too is usually derailed by the politics and economics, and the *manners*, of victimization. Japanese bomb films, like American bomb films, are clearly testaments to survivance (see chapter 1). But in the climate of victimization that prevails in Japan, the United States, and elsewhere, it is little wonder that *Hachigatsu no rapusodī* has been ignored or dismissed as "inadequate" and "irresponsible," as has atomic bomb cinema in general.

CONCLUSION

Demonic cinema

[T]he ultimate sufferer [of a "bad explanation"] is the interpreter himself.
—C. G. Jung, "The Psychology of the Child Archetype"[1]

[S]tories matter, and matter deeply, because they are the best way to save our lives.
—Frank McConnell, *Storytelling and Mythmaking*[2]

Shadows of life and death capture the imagination. The bomb is not simply a category of being. It is a very real, tangible thing. However, through atomic bomb cinema and other modes of communication, it has worked its way into the history of human consciousness as an emblem of the apocalyptic imagination. In this sense, as a product of modern physics, it has transcended even its own physical threat and found its place with the most ancient symbols and most primal forms of reconciliation with life itself. That is to say, reconciliation with death, because life itself must end. And, because the apocalyptic imagination is bound up with and energized by modern ideas about personal crisis, or the American or global quests, all under the shadow of the bomb, the physical atomic bomb itself has been reimagined into a symbol of its own shadowy archetype. In other words, the apocalyptic imagination, in turn, gives meaning to the bomb. Or, more simply, atomic bomb cinema exhorts in us the hope for survival and self-actualization even under the oppressive threat of nuclear annihilation. All this is in keeping with the apocalyptic narrative tradition that structures they way so many of us, at the dawn of a "new millennium," continue to see the world.

As I come to the conclusion of this study I am abundantly aware that I am leaving many important parts of atomic bomb cinema largely unexplored. Time permitting, I would have liked to include separate chapters on introverted scientists, alienated children, frustrated adolescents, destructive creatures, crazed mutants, interrupted marriages, and several other interesting themes of atomic bomb cinema. Be that as it may, I have briefly touched on these recurring themes in my pursuit of the dominant motif, the apocalyptic imagination.

In the course of this pursuit I have also shown that, for more than fifty years, the production and popularity of bomb films have remained consistently high. Some films have, moreover, achieved strong followings. These films are popular because they address important cultural issues in a way that is meaningful to a broad spectrum of the filmgoing public. Nevertheless, most scholars who write on the bomb and culture contend either that most people have ignored or have overreacted to nuclear issues. While this may be true about some segments of the American population, the argument is fallacious for several reasons:

a. Most scholars who make these arguments have their own pro- or antinuclear agendas and, consequently, argue tautologically.

b. Being pronuclear, or *not* antinuclear, is a valid ideological position, not to be confused with ignoring the issues.

c. Being satisfied with the status quo is a similarly valid ideological position.

d. Being undecided or ambivalent about nuclear issues is no less valid than any other ideological position.

e. Being more concerned with other issues is as valid an ideological position as any other.

Regardless of any opinion poll or critical measure of American apathy and activism, it is clear to me that most Americans, whether filmgoers or filmmakers, are deeply concerned with the threat of nuclear war and technologies.[3] They just express it in different ways than do scholars. As

Collins says, "Apocalyptic literature was not governed by the principles of Aristotelian logic but was closer to the poetic nature of myth."[4] And while any one person, myself included, may wish that Hollywood represented a broader range of cultural and political perspectives, atomic bomb cinema demonstrates that Hollywood is not blind to diversity, just a little nearsighted. The solution, however, has never been censorship or condescending criticism of so-called popular tastes. Again, the problem is not Hollywood, but how people respond to Hollywood. If Hollywood's influence over public attitudes suggests anything about our society, it is that in a media-saturated world, Americans are receiving an inadequate education, and the society as a whole has abdicated the role of guiding the young. Hollywood simply fills the void we have already created.

This void has, I believe, specific historical roots. In his history of the atomic bomb, Richard Rhodes writes that rather than achieving Bohr's dream of an *open world*, "The national security state that the United States has evolved toward since 1945 is significantly a denial of the American democratic vision: suspicious of diversity, secret, martial, exclusive, monolithic, paranoid."[5] (Is it any wonder that Robert Anton Wilson claims his *Illuminatus* novels—which are about secret societies, conspiracies, and machinations—have increased in popularity?)[6] The national security state has put enormous pressures on people from all walks of life, including the entertainment industry and academe—for example, the Hollywood Ten and Wen Ho Lee. According to *Time* magazine, between 1996 and 2000, due process has been suspended in some twenty cases of "national security."[7] There are other important historical roots to this void that are not so apparent, but in our discussion one in particular deserves mention. The increasing commodification of university education, research, and publication; the declining status of the humanities and teaching in general; the hiring crisis and glut of under and unemployed doctorates; and, especially in humanities scholarship, the cultivation of a disdain for and an inability to communicate with mainstream society have all worked to frustrate and marginalize academics, thus exacerbating the void. Within this political context—that is, the context of this void—the stories we tell ourselves serve a very important function. As tribal storytellers N. Scott Momaday and Gerald Vizenor put it, "Man tells stories in order to understand his experience, whatever it may be," and "should we lose our stories," we would lose our lives.[8] Again, the problem is not Hollywood, and the remedy is not censorship or academic posturing. Hollywood is, as Frank

McConnell deftly shows, a part of the solution.[9] Atomic bomb cinema is important because, as Collins points out, the apocalyptic genre is the language of people living under oppressive conditions.

The apocalyptic imagination asks us to confront complex sociocultural and anagogic issues; but it can, however, also give the impression that everything is simply a sign of goodness or evil at work. Consequently, what one person or group opposes can very quickly be turned into a demon. The temptation to demonize others is very hard to resist, even today, because it provides us with a convenient scapegoat and simple answers to complex problems. (It also provides a simple formula for interpreting ambiguous texts.) This temptation to demonize has real-life consequences. And, no one, not even the most studied scholar, is free from this temptation's grip. This point is so important that it requires a clear example.

In July of 1995, Bowling Green University sponsored the only conference of its kind, *The Atomic Age Opens: American Culture Confronts the Bomb*. At this conference we saw the pairing off of what are, perhaps, the two greatest surviving intellectual cold warriors: Edward Teller, the man most responsible for the hydrogen bomb, and Robert J. Lifton, the man most responsible for defining the discourse surrounding the bomb. Teller was the keynote speaker at the conference's formal banquet; the following day Lifton gave the final lecture and was honored guest at the closing reception.

Like Wagner's Wotan walking among the mortals, Professor Teller entered the room carrying a wizard's conical, hardwood staff that towered above him, and he sat at the front, where he delivered his position with Delphic certainty. Teller was speaking before a largely hostile if guardedly respectful crowd; knowing this, he was both charming and inflammatory, as were some of the carefully asked questions he later answered. If one listened to Teller's speech, the man seemed to exist in Einsteinian time: all events were not teleological, but relative. He spoke of his main enemies, the Hun (who invaded his native Hungary long ago), the "Browns" (Nazis), the "Reds" (Communists), and the "Greens" (environmentalists—and, by implication, Lifton), as if they were of a singular, timeless narrative moving toward some great apocalyptic conclusion. Teller himself seemed to be both victim and hero of his own story. He also suggested that everyone imbibe in small doses of radiation, now and again, just to reduce their chances of getting cancer. After jousting with a few of the less-subtle members of the audience, his attendants, concerned about his health, took Teller's royal presence back to his hotel. The man is not senile, as some later chimed; he just sees the connections between events from a different, perhaps "Old World," point of view. Listening to such a strongly opinionated man who has been at center stage of so many of the twentieth century's important events, a man nearing the end of his journey in this world, was a moving experience. It is ironic, though, that unlike Lifton, the social psychologist, Teller, the physicist, could name his own demons.

According to the conference's chief organizer, Professor Lifton had at first refused to participate in the conference for a variety of reasons ranging from family obligations to the low honorarium. Later, however, the organizer received a call from Lifton's secretary. She stated that, having heard that Teller would be speaking, Lifton demanded a chance to present his own case; and, would accept no less than what Teller was receiving.[10] When Lifton arrived at the university, I happened to be in the foyer talking with the conference organizers, so I stood by as the organizers greeted Lifton. Talk soon turned to Teller's speech the previous night. While the tittering and snide commentary was in poor taste but predictable, Lifton's comments were shocking. He suggested that it is probably only Teller's love of disputing, even taunting, his detractors that brought him to the conference. Then, Lifton added, that for a man of Teller's age, "it is probably the only thing that keeps him going." Lifton, in other words, was as quick to demonize Teller as Teller was to demonize the "Greens" and Lifton. More poignantly, as I looked at the aging antinuclear warrior, Lifton, I thought how easily he fit his own caricature of Teller.

In contrast to Teller, Lifton spoke before an adoring crowed that considers him a hero. Following his lecture, Lifton accepted questions, and I took the opportunity to challenge the antinuclear camp for a very simple reason. Though claiming the moral and intellectual high ground, the antinuclear camp does not hesitate to commit the same error that it accuses the pronuclear camp of committing: demonizing the opposition. When Lifton demurred, I pointed out that earlier in the day I overheard "someone say that the only thing that's kept Teller going is the fight itself." Much to my relief, only Lifton recognized his own words, and he was, quite literally, physically taken aback. After regaining his composure, he spoke eloquently, and I think sincerely, about how demonizing the opposition does not benefit the antinuclear movement. What Lifton had to say about the demonization of President

Harry S. Truman was particularly insightful. Not everyone, however, seemed to hear the message.

Later that night, during the reception, and in response to another of my questions, Lifton also criticized the psychologist Robert Coles. He called into doubt Coles's conclusions regarding children's responses to adults' questions about the bomb, because Coles has a strong pronuclear agenda; here again, similar criticisms can, of course, be made of Lifton's own work. Lifton agreed to answer a more personal, metacritical question. I pointed out that all of us at the conference, to one degree or another, and Lifton more than most, built their careers on the suffering of others; and yet, we never talk about this fact. How, I asked, did he reconcile this problem? At this question, one of his groupies literally gasped and said "Jerome, you can't ask him that!" Professor Lifton brushed aside the comment, remarking that it is a problem we must never stop struggling with, and proceeded to give his own personal insights into the problem. The next day I had a chance to talk with him privately about other things as well. While I cherish the short time I spent with Professor Lifton, my point is that he is no less human than the rest of us—only perhaps, a bit more willing to accept (with a little nudging) that the demons he perceives are of his own making.

Professor Lifton and his followers in the therapeutic community have ostensibly disavowed the existence of demons. Yet, while inappropriately extrapolating from data on communities to conclusions about worldwide populations, they have, ironically, provided us with a convenient scapegoat for our times: psychopathology, and in this case, the psychically numb. Rather than seeing people as human beings struggling to survive and make sense of complex social issues and rapid technological change, Lifton and his followers see virtually everyone else as trapped in debilitating psychological denial. Messy cultural conflicts, clashes of national character, disharmony over racial or sectarian destiny, differences in ideology or political philosophy, and issues of personal or collective responsibility are, therefore, reduced to mere expressions of how the psychically numb act out their emotional traumas. Armed with the very reassuring explanations of the therapeutic culture, we can dismiss our opponents with impunity by turning them into culturally acceptable demons. Those cast down from the heaven of absolute psychological well-being abound: everyone from scientists, who, as J. Robert Oppenheimer opined, had known sin when they built the bomb, to Leslie R. Groves, to Oppenheimer himself, and, most symptomatically, to

Truman. The psychopathology theory also provides conveniently simple answers to even more difficult problems.

Lifton and coauthor Greg Mitchell's 1995 book is boldly titled *Hiroshima in America: A Half Century of Denial.* In a 1996 follow-up essay that was circulated internationally, "The Presidents Have No Regrets," the authors write that "a divisive debate over the atomic bombings continues."[11] The very titles of their book and essay, however, evoke an emphatic denial of the vitality, validity, importance, and the very *meaning* of this debate. Lifton and Mitchell also urge an official statement of unequivocal regret for using nuclear weapons. The simplicity of their diagnoses and prescriptions are highlighted by, ironically enough, a subscriber to the psychopathology theory. Paul Boyer, in a virtually forgotten 1985 essay, "The Cloud over the Culture," makes a profound and compelling argument for an expression not of regret but a more complex sense of "sorrow."[12]

It must be pointed out that in its proper setting—that is, clinical psychology—denial is not necessarily bad, though it can be in certain stages; denial is, simply, a natural part of the process of survival and the healing that follows a trauma. Not everyone, furthermore, believes that solving a problem is essential to health. As one Japanese psychologist explained to me, "Solve the problem, kill the soul."[13] That is to say, in "Oriental medicine" health is a matter of achieving balance, and that includes learning to live with one's problems; otherwise, we waste our short lives in the delusional pursuit of perfect health. But in the Western, particularly the American, frame of mind, health is defined in dualistic terms—that is, as the absence of pathology and the achievement of perfection. Every problem must, therefore, be identified, named (e.g., original sin and denial), and exorcised. Consequently, when used outside the clinical context, particularly as a tool to manipulate social policy, psychopathology becomes such a "bad explanation" that it injures the entire community. In classrooms, for instance, psychic numbing is taught frequently and dogmatically. Some students may, of course, genuinely find such an explanation for mass behavior—that is, their own behavior—intellectually appealing. Be that as it may, in the classroom psychic numbing is the supreme example of pedagogic self-fulfilling prophecy. Under the threat of a failing grade, students have no choice but to embrace this ideology, and this can only lead to intellectual complacency, self-hate, and denial in the student and arrogance in the teacher. In other words, telling people, outside the clinical context, that they are psychically numb is no less injurious than telling them that they are stupid. And yet, in our time "denial" is such a powerful, insidious argument that it has become the explanation *sine qua non* for scholars in many disciplines. This includes respected historians like Boyer, and now Gar Alperovitz. In his 1995 book *The Decision to Use the Atomic Bomb and the Architecture of an American Myth*, Alperovitz makes an even-handed and convincing argument stating that it is a "myth" to claim that the atomic bombs were used against Japan for essentially military reasons, that it is a "myth" that atomic bombs were essential to saving millions of lives and forcing the Japanese to surrender on America's terms, and that in actuality, the real reasons have been largely expunged from history, are probably political, and have been replaced by these "myths."[14]

To support his hypotheses, Alperovitz again and again puts forth the theory that so many have come to accept as an a priori truth. "In connection with the more difficult issues," (that is, the "obvious psychological reality concerning why the Hiroshima myth has been sustained for so long,") "silence mostly reigns—and denial."[15] Once upon a time, not long ago, myths and other narratives were thought to be vehicles for expressing eternal truths. Since at least the postwar introduction of French scholar Roland Barthes's writings, however, there has evolved in America a belief, generally held by liberals, that, imbedded in the architecture of all myth or narrative is mind-twisting ideology, and behind that, inevitably, is pestilential denial. (Nevertheless, as I have argued throughout, there are some important truths to be found in these narratives!) Exposure of the ideology and the denial, furthermore, is a necessity of the highest order, for it leads to real truths, psychological well-being, and universal harmony. This is the liberal myth.

The liberal myth—that is, the journey from denial, to ideology, to myth, to exposure, to utopia itself—is, of course, a narrative. Being a narrative, it is inevitably subject to the liberal laws regarding myth, and must, therefore, be dismissed for at root masking the denial of something. Thus, in order to expose the denial underlying other myths, devotees of the liberal myth must strategically locate themselves outside the mainstream of thought and culture. They can do this by virtue of their knowledge of the architecture of myth, and because they have already publicly repented their own denial. These public displays of gut-wrenching self-examination, usually the introductory chapter, often read like a religious confession (e.g., Alperovitz and Boyer), or its modern equivalent, the "recovery" or "self-help" narrative (e.g., Newman, and especially Berger).[16] In apocalyptic narrative terms, devotee scholars construct themselves not as the ordinary human on an otherworldly journey for wisdom, but the supernatural being capable of interpreting divine revelation. In more conventional language, having survived the crisis of publicly exposing the inner "numb" or denying self, the devotee scholar is no longer part of the greater culture's efforts toward understanding and critiquing itself, but reborn as society's self-anointed psychotherapist. Consequently, Alperovitz and others are inevitably led to characterizing, perhaps unintentionally, virtually the entire American population as unrepentant victims of the denial Hiroshima once engendered in themselves. Those of us still in denial are not, in other words, a people struggling, no matter how awkwardly, to come to terms with the contradictions of our own history; we are, rather, demons of denial. But by and large, the biggest demon, and most common scapegoat, in American society, is not the denial itself. Our biggest demon is, rather, the cinema—or more correctly, "Hollywood." For, as Boyer puts it in his portrait of the demon, to cite just one example, "Hollywood contributed its bit to the larger cultural process of" the American people's denial.[17]

Cinema studies scholar Robert Sklar has shown that "[f]or much of their history . . . movies had been a site of struggle over cultural power."[18] They still are. Consider, for example, the critical response to Michael Medved's 1992 book *Hollywood vs. America*.[19] The glossy trade journal *The World and I* commissioned three prominent cultural critics—conservatives Stanley Rothman and Benjamin J. Stein, and radical Todd Gitlin—to comment on the book.[20] After much equivocation over their various disagreements with Medved on certain academic points, all three ultimately embrace Medved's demonization of Hollywood.[21] Then, on May 31, 1995, World War II and cold war hero and Senate majority leader Robert Dole launched his successful bid for the 1996 Republican Presidential nomination by attacking Hollywood. Dole was defeated by his incumbent Democratic opponent, William Jefferson Clinton, who was skillful enough to steal Dole's issues. More recently, in the 2000 campaign for the presidency, the Democratic candidate, Vice President Albert Gore Jr., warned student leaders about the "unintended" impact of "violent imagery."[22] As one *New York Times* writer put it, both Gore and the Republican candidate, Governor George W. Bush, were trying to "outdo each other in expressing outrage" at the entertainment industry.[23]

Hollywood, it would seem, has outlasted virtually all other threats to American society, including the cold war, to become America's preeminent demon.

Elsewhere, Sklar makes it abundantly clear that in the struggle over cultural power, intellectuals have never hesitated to demonize Hollywood.[24] And, as we have seen, this is particularly true of Boyer, Caldicott, Lifton, Richie, Sontag, and virtually all of the scholarly literature on atomic bomb cinema. Ironically enough, F. Scott Fitzgerald—who worked in Hollywood, of course—chided intellectuals, "who should know better," because "they never see the ventriloquist for the doll." Fitzgerald continues, "tell them pictures have a private grammar, like politics or automobile production or society, and watch the blank look come into their faces."[25] Alas, Fitzgerald's message seems to have gone largely unheeded. The culture has given the cinema a clear mandate to entertain and thereby make a profit. No similar mandate exists to inform and educate or otherwise serve the public interest. That is not to say that films do not educate. Rather, the culture has clearly mandated other media to inform and educate as well as entertain, for example, television and computers, and other social contexts, such as the classroom and the family TV or computer room, but not the cinema. Scholars, pundits, and politicians, nevertheless, persist in writing and speaking as though Hollywood's mandate to raise public consciousness is an a priori truth or a commandment written in stone, and that this mandate has been subverted.

The widely respected cultural theorist Raymond Williams has clearly shown that every institution has competing ideological elements.[26] Few scholars today would challenge Williams. And yet, as I have shown throughout this study (and elsewhere), most critics of Hollywood—from across the political and cultural spectrum—persist in describing Hollywood as a monolithic and malevolent entity, while at the same time prophesying a utopian society, beyond some apocalyptic future, that is free from the evil clutches of moving pictures.[27] This struggle over cultural power—at the dawn of a new millennium—is being waged, even in the scholarly literature, with polemics and demonization rather than reasoned argument. This is because the bomb and the apocalyptic imagination have, I believe, enflamed the long-standing and acrimonious debate over American society and the cinema. More than any other body of films, atomic bomb cinema is the paradigmatic site of struggle over cultural power for our times.

NOTES

Notes to Introduction

1. Gerhard Adler, "Psychology and the Atom Bomb." *Guild Lecture No. 43* (London: The Guild of Pastoral Psychology, August 12, 1946): 1, 21.

2. *Japanese Children's Stories*, ed. Florence Sakade, ill. Yoshio Hayashi (Rutland, VT: Charles E. Tuttle Company, 1966, first printed in 1952).

3. *Godzilla, King of the Monsters*, adapted in 1956 by Terry Morse from *Gojira* (Inoshiro Honda, 1954).

4. Robert J. Lifton and Greg Mitchell, *Hiroshima in America: Fifty Years of Denial* (New York: G. P. Putnam's Sons, 1995); Donald Richie, "'Mono No Aware'/Hiroshima in Film," in *Film: Book 2, Films of Peace and War*, ed., Robert Hughes (New York: Grove Press, Inc., 1962); 67–86. Susan Sontag, "The Imagination of Disaster," in *Against Interpretation* (New York: Farrar, Straus and Giroux, 1967), 209–25; also anthologized in *Film Theory and Criticism: Introductory Readings*, 3d ed., ed. Gerald Mast and Marshall Cohen (New York: Oxford University Press, 1985), 451–63; Paul Boyer, *By the Bomb's Early Light: American Thought and Culture at the Dawn of the Atomic Age* (New York: Pantheon Books, 1985); Gar Alperovitz, *The Decision to Use the Atomic Bomb and the Architecture of an American Myth* (New York: Alfred A. Knopf, 1995).

5. Jacques Derrida, "No Apocalypse, Not Now: (full speed ahead, seven missiles, seven missives)," trans. Catherine Porter and Philip Lewis, *Diacritics* 14, no. 2 (summer 1984): 23 [full text, pp. 20–31].

6. Frederic Jameson, "Postmodernism and Consumer Society," in Hal Foster, ed., *The Anti-Aesthetic: Essays on Postmodern Culture* (Seattle: Bay Press, 1983), 111–25. An example of the subsequent appropriation of Jameson's ideas is Freda Freidberg's insightful essay "*Akira* and the Postnuclear Sublime," in *Hibakusha Cinema: Hiroshima, Nagasaki and the Nuclear Image in Japanese Film*, ed. Mick Broderick (London: Kegan Paul International, 1996), 94, 102.

7. Jonathan Schell, *The Fate of the Earth* (New York: Avon Books, 1982).

8. Frank Kermode, *The Sense of an Ending: Studies in the Theory of Fiction* (New York: Oxford University Press, 1968), 95.

9. C. G. Jung, *Memories, Dreams, Reflections*, ed. Aniela Jaffé, trans. Richard and Clara Winston (New York: Random House, 1961), 333.

10. Many historians have discussed the wartime censorship of references to nuclear energy in the United States. Kyoko Hirano's *Mr. Smith Goes to Tokyo: Japanese Cinema Under the American Occupation*, 1945–52 (Washington, DC: Smithsonian Institution Press, 1992), is now considered the standard text on Occupation-era film censorship. However, for a broader introduction to what happened in Japan during and after the Occupation, see Mick Broderick, ed., *Hibakusha Cinema* (London: Kegan Paul International, 1996) for several relevant articles.

11. Boyer, *By the Bomb's Early Light*, xviii.

12. Robert Coles, *The Moral Life of Children* (Boston: Atlantic Monthly Press, 1986), 243–83.

13. David A. Cook, *A History of Narrative Film* (New York: W. W. Norton & Company, 1981), 10–11.

14. Robert Sklar, "*Oh! Althusser!* Historiography and the Rise of Cinema Studies," in *Resisting Images: Essays on Cinema and History*, ed. Robert Sklar and Charles Musser (Philadelphia: Temple University Press, 1990), 20–21.

15. Richie, "'Mono No Aware'/Hiroshima in Film, 78.

16. Sontag, "The Imagination of Disaster," 224.

17. Robert J. Lifton, *Death in Life: Survivors of Hiroshima* rev. (Chapel Hill: University of North Carolina Press, 1991), 461–63, 570.

18. Daniel Patrick Moynihan, *The Negro Family: The Case for National Action* (Washington, D.C.: U.S. Department of Labor, Office of Planning and Research, March, 1965). Lee Rainwater and William L. Yancey, eds., *The Moynihan Report and the Politics of Controversy* (Cambridge, MA: MIT Press, 1967), 39–124.

19. The literature on African-American culture is extensive and beyond the scope of this study. The reader is referred to Wade W. Nobles and Lawford L. Goddard, *Understanding the Black Family: A Guide for Scholarship and Research* (Oakland: The Institute for the Advanced Study of Black Family Life and Culture, 1984); Joseph L. White, *The Psychology of Blacks: An Afro-American Perspective* (Englewood Cliffs, NJ: Prentice-Hall, 1984); and, James Berger, *After the End: Representations of Post Apocalypse* (Minneapolis: University of Minnesota Press, 1999), xix, 192–97, 214–15, 248 n. 16.

20. Boyer, *By the Bomb's Early Light*, xviii, 195; epilogue, "From H-Bomb to Star Wars: the Continuing Cycles of Activism and Apathy," 352–67, especially 352, 365; *see also* 356, 361.

21. Joyce A. Evans: *Celluloid Mushroom Clouds: Hollywood and the Atomic Bomb* (Boulder, CO: Westview Press, 1998), 77; also, re: realism, *see* pp. 137–39, 144, 149, 153, 159, 165, 169. Evans also specifically cites Boyer, on pp. 14, 35, and 51; Toni A. Perrine, *Film and the Nuclear Age: Representing Cultural Anxiety* (New York: Garland, 1998), 9, 154, 232, 237.

22. Berger, *After the End*, 219.

23. Kim Newman, *Apocalypse Movies: End of the World Cinema* (New York: St. Martins Griffin, 2000), 108.

24. Christian Metz, *The Imaginary Signifier*, trans. Celia Britton et al., (Bloomington: Indiana University Press, 1982), 9.

25. Mick Broderick, *Nuclear Movies: A Critical Analysis and Filmography of International Feature Length Films Dealing with Experimentation, Aliens, Terrorism, and Other Disaster Scenarios, 1914–1989* (Jefferson, NC: McFarland & Company, 1991), xvii–xix. First published by Post-Modern Publishing, Melbourne, Australia, 1988.

26. H. Bruce Franklin, *Countdown to Midnight: Twelve Great Stories about Nuclear War* (New York: DAW Books, 1984), 28.

27. Perinne, *Film and the Nuclear Age*, 28–29, 239.

28. These other scholars and their works include, Nora Sayre, *Running Time: Films of the Cold War* (New York: Dial Press, 1982); Peter Biskind, *Seeing Is Believing: How Hollywood Taught Us to Stop Worrying and Love the Fifties* (New York: Pantheon Books, 1983); Jack G. Shaheen, ed., *Nuclear War Films* (Carbondale: Southern Illinois University Press, 1978); William J. Palmer, *The Films of the Eighties: A Social History* (Carbondale: Southern Illinois University Press, 1993); H. Bruce Franklin, *War Stars: the Superweapon and the American Imagination* (New York: Oxford University Press, 1988); Spencer R. Weart, *Nuclear Fear: a History of Images* (Cambridge, MA: Harvard University Press, 1988); and, most recently, Evans: *Celluloid Mushroom Cloud*. The obvious exception is Peter Fitting, "Count Me Out/In: Post-Apocalyptic Visions in Recent Science Fiction Film," in *CineAction* no. 11 (December 1987): 42–51. The article's one major weakness is its failure to conceptualize a few 1980s films as part of the larger apocalyptic film and narrative tradition.

29. Robert Warshow, "The Gangster as Tragic Hero," in *The Immediate Experience: Movies, Comics, Theater and Other Aspects of Popular Culture* (New York: Atheneum, 1972), 128.

30. Susan K. Langer, "Discursive Forms and Presentational Forms," in *Philosophy in a New Key: A Study in the Symbolism of Reason, Rite, and Art*, 3d ed. (Cambridge, MA: Harvard University Press, 1974), 79–102.

31. Kermode, *The Sense of an Ending*, 95.

32. Melvin J. Lasky, *Utopia and Revolution: On the Origins of a Metaphor, or Some Illustrations of the Problem of Political Temperament and Intellectual Climate and How Ideas, Ideals, and Ideologies Have Been Historically Related* (Chicago: University of Chicago Press, 1976).

33. See the description of *The Way We Were* in James Monaco, *The Movie Guide: A Comprehensive Alphabetical Listing of the Most Important Films Ever Made* (New York: Baseline II, 1992), 1040–41.

34. There is much debate over what "classical" cinema is. David Bordwell, Janet Staiger, and Kristin Thompson attempt to codify definitively the "classical" Hollywood cinema in *The Classical Hollywood Cinema: Film Style and Mode of Production to 1960* (New York: Columbia University Press, 1985). This study ultimately fails because the statistics that serve as the very foundation of their methodology are highly flawed. In order to affect scientific objectivity, the authors

use a coding technique that selects films at random. Once the authors have reduced the extant Hollywood filmography to a manageable number of films, however, they abandon their statistical methods and choose only those films that prove their hypothesis; thus, they carefully ignore and fail to explain the more numerous counterexamples.

35. Raymond Williams, *Marxism and Literature* (Oxford: Oxford University Press, 1977), 121–27.

36. Mick Broderick, "The Rupture of Rapture: Recent Film Narratives of Apocalypse," in *Southern Review* (March 1994): 70–78. My research is based on an earlier draft of this paper available online at <http://www.1earth.net/~postmodm/m/text/rupture.html>, p. 2 of 10.

37. Stanley Cavell, *Pursuits of Happiness: The Hollywood Comedy of Remarriage* (Cambridge, MA: Harvard University Press, 1981), and *Contesting Tears: The Hollywood Melodrama of the Unknown Woman* (Chicago: University of Chicago Press, 1996).

38. The geopolitical conditions following the Second World War and the Vietnam War were dramatically different. Suffice it to say that while exhaustive research has been done in Hiroshima and Nagasaki, little reliable research has been conducted in Vietnam. The research that has been conducted, however, increasingly points to an unparalleled environmental and human disaster. The literature—both scholarly research and mass-media reporting—is scant, sometimes contradictory, but chilling. See Peter C. Kahn, et al., "Dioxins and Dibenzofurans in Blood and Adipose Tissue of Agent Orange—Exposed Vietnam Veterans and Matched Controls," *The Journal of the American Medical Association* (March 18, 1988): 1661ff. See also Peter Korn, "Agent Orange in Vietnam: The Persisting Poison," in *The Nation* (April 8, 1991): 440–46; Liane Clorfene Casten, "Anatomy of a Cover-Up," *The Nation* (November 30, 1992): 658ff; James H. Dwyer and Dieter Flesch-Janys, "Editorial: Agent Orange in Vietnam," *American Journal of Public Health* (April 1995): 476ff; Arnold Schecter et al., "Agent Orange and Vietnamese: The Persistence of Elevated Dioxin Levels in Human Tissue," *American Journal of Public Health* (April 1995), 516ff; Philip M. Boffey, "Agent Orange in Vietnam, 30 Years Later," *New York Times*, (September 8, 1998): editorial, A24; and Catherine M. Cooney, "Study Alludes to Deformities from Dioxin in Vietnam," *Environmental Science and Technology* (January 1, 1999): 12A. Also, Cooney briefly reports on research conducted by a Canadian consulting firm specializing in dioxin sampling, and provides a website for the firm: <http://www.hatfieldgroup.com>. Others argue that dioxin has not been conclusively proven to be harmful, and the birth defects seen in Vietnam are probably due to malnutrition. See, <www.junkscience.com>.

39. Boyer writes, "If each upward spiral of the nuclear arms race has spawned its progeny of ever more terrible weapons, so has each cycle of antinuclear activism bequeathed to the future its legacy of cultural documents and political experience"; (see Boyer, *By the Bomb's Early Light*, 366). Also, Franklin, for instance, accepts most of Boyer's conclusions, in *War Stars*, 227 n. 3. Evans, too, is essentially making the same argument that Boyer made before her; see Evans, *Celluloid Mushroom Clouds*, 77, 166.

40. Seth Ward, "The Evasive Epoch: Jewish Perspectives on the Millennium and other Calendrical Conundrums," paper presented at the Twelfth Annual Klutznick Symposium. See <http://puffin.creighton.edu/klutznick/abstracts/htm>.

41. The yearly average numbers of films seen by teens and adults comes from a statistical survey reported in the *U.S. News & World Report*, and was cited by Cable Network News (CNN) programs in Japan on June 23, 1994.

42. Film noir is a genre that began in earnest after World War II and lasted for just a few years. Some critics say film noir began in 1941 with Orson Welles's *Citizen Kane* and ended in 1948 with Welles's *The Lady From Shanghai*. Others claim the genre ended with Welles's *Touch of Evil* (1958), which then inspired France's own version of film noir, i.e., the French New Wave cinema. Regardless of its precise beginnings or endings, in their authoritative text, Alain Silver and Elizabeth Ward identify a total of 303 noir films released over a forty-nine year period, 1927–1976. *See Film Noir: An Encyclopedic Reference to the American Style*, ed. Alain Silver and Elizabeth Ward (Woodstock, NY: Overlook Press, 1979).

43. Franklin, *War Stars*, 1991, chapters 14, "Triumphs of Nuclear Culture," and 15, "Arms Control?" particularly 180–83, and 191–94.

44. Dipesh Chakrabarty, "Afterword: Revisiting the Tradition/Modernity Binary," in *Mirror of Modernity: Invented Traditions of Modern Japan*, ed. Stephen Vlastos (Berkeley: University of California Press, 1998), 295.

45. Takao Aoki, "The Paradoxical Rebirth of Traditional Theater through the Moderization of Japan: The Case of the Noh Play," paper presented at the Asia-Pacific Traditional Arts Forum, Taipei, Taiwan, October 1, 2000.

46. Warshow, "Author's Preface," in *The Immediate Experience*, 26.

47. Donald Davidson, *Inquiries into Truth and Interpretation* (New York: Oxford University Press, 1984), 157.

48. John Locke, *An Essay Concerning Human Understanding*, ed. Peter H. Nidditch (London: Oxford University Press, 1975), 697–706.

49. Gerald Vizenor, *Bearheart: The Heirship Chronicles* (Minneapolis: University of Minnesota Press, 1990), passim.

50. Stanley Cavell, *Pursuits of Happiness*, 37.

51. *The Chicago Manual of Style*, 13th ed. (Chicago: University of Chicago Press, 1982), 271–72.

Notes to Chapter 1

1. Siegfried Kracauer, *From Caligari to Hitler: A Psychological History of German Film* (Princeton: Princeton University Press, 1947), 8.

2. Paul Boyer, *When Time Shall Be No More: Prophecy Belief in Modern American Culture* (Cambridge, MA: Harvard University Press, 1992).

3. Frank Kermode, *The Sense of an Ending: Studies in the Theory of Fiction* (New York: Oxford University Press, 1968), 94.

4. It is commonly believed that Dr. Caldicott established PSR. Paul Boyer, however, claims that Bernard Lown founded PSR in the 1950s. See Paul Boyer, *By the*

Bomb's Early Light: American Thought and Culture at the Dawn of the Atomic Age (New York:Patheon Books, 1985), 353. Eric Semler writes that Lown founded PSR in 1961 but it "became dormant in the 1960s and was revived in the 1970s by Dr. Helen Caldicott." See Eric Semler et al., *The Language of Nuclear War: An Intelligent Citizen's Dictionary* (New York: Harper & Row, 1987), 220.

5. Dr. Helen Caldicott, "Forward," in Mick Broderick, *Nuclear Movies: A Critical Analysis and Filmography of International Feature Length Films with Experimentation, Aliens, Terrorism, Holocaust and Other Disaster Scenarios, 1914–1989* (Jefferson, NC: McFarland & Company, 1991), xiv–xv.

6. George P. Elliott, "Think Films: A New Hollywood Creation," *Esquire* (March 1960): 118. See also Pauline Kael, *Kiss Kiss Bang Bang* (Little, Brown, and Company, 1968), 207, and in *Nuclear War Films*, ed., Jack G. Shaheen (Carbondale: Southern Illinois University Press, 1978), 31.

7. Boyer, *By the Bomb's Early Light*, 367.

8. Christopher Lasch, *The Minimal Self: Psychic Survival in Troubled Times* (New York: W. W. Norton, 1984), 17, 19.

9. Robert J. Lifton, *Death in Life: Survivors of Hiroshima*, rev. ed. (Chapel Hill: University of North Carolina Press, 1991).

10. Michael Ortiz Hill, *Dreaming the End of the World: Apocalypse As a Rite of Passage*. (Dallas: Spring Publications, 1994).

11. Jonathan Schell, *The Fate of the Earth* (New York: Avon Books, 1982), 65, 231.

12. Michael Tolkin, "The Entertainment of Apocalypse the Apocalypse of Entertainment," keynote address, Third Annual Conference of the Center for Millennial Studies, Boston University December 6, 1998. See, <www.mille.org/confprodec98/tolkin>, p. 1.

13. Derrida, "No Apocalypse, Not Now: (full speed ahead, seven missiles, seven missives)," trans. Catherine Porter and Philip Lewis, *Diacritics* 14, no. 2 (summer 1984): 23.

14. Erik H. Erikson, *Identity: Youth and Crisis* (London: Faber and Faber, 1968), 16; see also 40–41, 261–62.

15. John J. Collins, *The Apocalyptic Imagination: An Introduction to the Jewish Matrix of Christianity* (New York: Crossroad, 1989).

16. I am indebted to Professor Seth Ward of Denver University for responding to drafts of several chapters; his many e-mail messages, with extensive notes, over the course of a year (October 1999 to September 2000); for his insights into Jewish, thought and culture, *Tikkun Olam*, the Golem, Maimonides, Hasidic and Jewish mystic narratives; and for his friendship.

17. Hal Foster, "Postmodernism: A Preface," in Foster, *The Anti-Aesthetic: Essays on Postmodern Culture* (Seattle: Bay Press, 1983), xi.

18. Kim Newman, "Author's Note," *Apocalypse Movies: End of the World Cinema* (New York: Saint Martin's Griffin, 2000), copyright page.

19. Stephen Prince, *The Warrior's Camera: The Cinema of Akira Kurosawa*, rev. and exp. ed. (Princeton: Princeton University Press, 1999) 24, 160, 243, 314.

20. Susan Sontag, "The Imagination of Disaster," in *Against Interpretation* (New York: Farrar, Straus and Giroux, 1967), 209–25. See also Robert Torry, "Apocalypse

Then: Benefits of the Bomb in Fifties Science Fiction Films," *Cinema Journal* 31 (fall 1991): 7–21. Although different narrative traditions share common elements, Torry, I think, wrongly labels as apocalyptic *The Day the Earth Stood Still* (Robert Wise, 1951), which is closer to a biblical testament narrative, and *When Worlds Collide* (Rudolph Maté, 1951), which is closer to a deluge narrative.

21. Lasch, *The Minimal Self*, 17, 19, 83.

22. Collins, *The Apocalyptic Imagination*, 3.

23. David Miller, "Chiliasm: Apocalyptic with a Thousand Faces," in *Facing Apocalypse*, ed. Valerie Andrews, Robert Bosnak, and Karen Walter Goodwin (Dallas: Spring Publications, 1987), 5.

24. Richard Freund, "The Apocalypse According to the Rabbis: Divergent Rabbinic Views on the End of Days," paper presented at the Twelfth Annual Klutznick Symposium. See <http://puffin.creighton.edu/klutznick/abstracts/htm>.

25. Collins, *The Apocalyptic Imagination*, 1–32.

26. Toni A. Perrine, *Film and the Nuclear Age: Representing Cultural Anxiety* (New York: Garland, 1998), 204. *See also*, Paul Coates, "Chris Marker and the Cinema as Time Machine," *Science Fiction Studies* 14 (1987): 307–15.

27. Collins, *The Apocalyptic Imagination*, first citation, 9;. elements of apocalypses, 3–8, 22; Alistair Fowler, "The Life and Death of Literary Forms," *New Literary History* 2 (1971): 199–216.

28. Northrop Frye, *Anatomy of Criticism: Four Essays* (Princeton: Princeton University Press, 1957).

29. Anthony Paul Kerby, *Narrative and the Self* (Bloomington: Indiana University Press, 1991), 3, 4.

30. Collins, *The Apocalyptic Imagination*, 205, 11, 14, 214.

31. David P. Barash, "Nuclear Psychology," in *The Arms Race and Nuclear War* (Belmont, California: Wadsworth, 1987), 319–35.

32. Melvin J. Lasky, *Utopia and Revolution: On the Origins of a Metaphor, or Some Illustrations of the Problem of Political Temperament and Intellectual Climate and How Ideas, Ideals, and Ideologies Have Been Historically Related* (Chicago: The University of Chicago Press, 1976).

33. Harris Lenowitz, "Time Place, the Millennium and the Messiah," paper presented at the Twelfth Annual Klutznick Symposium. See <http://puffin.creighton.edu/klutznick/abstracts/htm>.

34. Freund, "The Apocalypse According to the Rabbis."

35. I am indebted to the learned Rabbi Mel Silverman for his careful reading of my work, suggestions, and insightful criticisms; private conversations with Rabbi Mel Silverman, including those shared in April and May 1993, July 1995, in Costa Mesa, California; and, personal correspondence dated September 15, 1998.

36. *The Holy Scriptures: According to the Masoretic Text* (Philadelphia: The Jewish Publication Society of America, 1955), 12.

37. Steve Lipman, *Laughter in Hell: The Use of Humor during the Holocaust* (Northvale, NJ: Jason Aronson, 1993), 134–35, 153. Rabbi Weiner's quotation comes from Ulrike Migdal, *Und die Musik spielt dazu: Chansons and Satiren aus dem KZ Theriesinstadt* (Munich: Piper, 1986), 24, cited in Lipman, 153.

38. *A Passover Haggadah: As Commented Upon by Elie Wiesel* (New York: Touchstone, 1993), 35.

39. Daniel Boyarin, *Intertextuality and the Reading of Midrash* (Bloomington: Indiana University Press, 1994), xi.

40. Regarding the term "survivance," see Gerald R. Vizenor, *Manifest Manners: Postindian Warriors of Survivance* (Hanover, NH: Wesleyan University Press, 1994), passim. Vizenor more clearly defines his use of "survivance" in *Fugitive Poses: Native Indian Scenes of Absence and Presence* (Lincoln, NE: University of Nebraska Press, 1998), 15.

41. Sontag, "The Imagination of Disaster," 213.

42. For example, see Peter Biskind, *Seeing is Believing: How Hollywood Taught Us to Stop Worrying and Love the Fifties* (New York: Pantheon Books, 1983); Boyer, *By the Bomb's Early Light*; Broderick, *Nuclear Movies*; H. Bruce Franklin, *War Stars: The Superweapon and the American Imagination* (New York: Oxford University Press, 1988). See also Jeff Nuttal, *Bomb Culture* (New York: Delacorte Press, 1968); Nora Sayre, *Running Time: Films of the Cold War* (New York: Dial Press, 1978); Jonathan Schell, *The Fate of the Earth*; Shaheen, ed., *Nuclear War Films*; Spencer R. Weart, *Nuclear Fear: A History of Images* (Cambridge: Harvard University Press, 1988); and Freda Freidberg, "*Akira* and the Postnuclear Sublime," in *Hibakusha Cinema: Hiroshima, Nagasaki and the Nuclear Image in Japanese Film*, ed. Mick Broderick (London: Kegan Paul International, 1996), 91–102.

43. "Apocalypse Then," 7–8, 12–13, 14.

44. Sontag, "The Imagination of Disaster," 225.

45. See, for example, Boyer, *When Time Shall Be No More*; Norman Cohn, *The Pursuit of the Millennium: Revolutionary Millenarians and Mystical Anarchists of the Middle Ages*, rev. and exp. ed. (New York: Oxford University Press, 1970); Andrew M. Greeley, "Varieties of Apocalypse in Science Fiction," in *Journal of American Culture* 2, no. 2 (summer 1979): 279–87; Frank Kermode, *The Sense of an Ending*; and, Margarita Stocker, *Apocalyptic Marvell: The Second Coming in Seventeenth-Century Poetry* (Sussex, England: Harvester Press, 1986), xii.

46. Interview with Professor Moshe Lazar, spring 1990, University of Southern California.

47. David A. Cook, *A History of Narrative Film* (New York: W. W. Norton & Company, 1981), 15.

48. Bill Warren, *Keep Watching the Skies*, vol. 1 (Jefferson, NC: McFarland & Company, 1982): 2.

49. *A History of Narrative Film*, 13–18. Film historian Hiroshi Komatsu of Japan has said that all the films discussed in this chapter were quite accessible in Japan at the time of their release (private conversation in Tokyo, January 1987).

50. Frank Beaver, *Dictionary of Film Terms: The Aesthetic Companion to Film Analysis*, rev. ed. (New York: Twayne, 1994), 115.

51. In Cirlot's description the angel of destruction is considered "creative and beneficent," thus, destruction is an important element to salvation. *See* J. E. Cirlot, *A Dictionary of Symbols*, 2d ed., trans. Jack Sage (New York: Philosophical Library, 1971), 284.

52. There are several important historical facts about this film that bear mentioning: (1) some sources list the date of the film as 1926; I am using Katz's date; (2) according to Lang, the film was "mutilated" after he lost control of the film; (3) I am using Giorgio Moroder's 1984 reconstruction of the film, which is the most complete at this time; and (4) Lang and Harbou were married at the time they made the film. See Ephraim Katz, *The Film Encyclopedia* (New York: Perigee Books, 1982), 687.

53. Catherine Wessinger, "Understanding Contemporary Millennial Movements, Peaceful and Violent," paper presented at the Twelfth Annual Klutznick Symposium. See <http://puffin/creighton.edu/klutznick/abstracts/htm>.

54. Kracauer, *From Caligari to Hitler*, 32, 33, 163. Kracauer also devotes an entire chapter to despotic rulers, which is directly relevant to his argument about this film.

55. Cohn, *The Pursuit of the Millennium*, 16, 37–53, 281, 284.

56. S. S. Prawer, *Caligari's Children: the Film as Tale of Terror* (New York: Da Capo Press, 1980), 17.

57. Colllins, *The Apocalyptic Imagination*, 4.

58. *Ibid.*, 78. The seminal text for understanding "internal colonialism" is Robert Blauner's *Racial Oppression in America* (New York: Harper & Row, 1972). See also Michael Omi and Howard Winant, *Racial Formation in the United States: From the 1960s to the 1980s* (New York: Routledge & Kegan Paul, 1986).

59. See note 39, interview with Moshe Lazar.

60. Prawer's list includes films from Alfred Clark's *The Execution of Mary, Queen of Scots* (1895) to Edward Porter's *The Great Train Robbery* (1903), and from the Edison Company's adaptation of *Frankenstein* (1910) to Robert Weine's *The Cabinet of Dr. Caligari* (1919); Prawer, *Caligari's Children*, 8, 9.

61. Arnold L. Goldsmith, *The Golem Remembered, 1909–1980* (Detroit: Wayne State University Press, 1981), 15–16. No one agrees on the dates of the first film; however, it seems to have been made sometime between 1913 and 1915. According to Katz, the other two films are *Der Golem un de Tänzerin* in 1917, and *Der Golem: Wie er in die Welt Kam*, or *The Golem: How He Came into the World* in 1920 (*The Film Encyclopedia*, 1217). Goldsmith gives an excellent account of the later Golem-type films in *The Golem Remembered*, 143–51.

62. *Die Nibelungen* is composed of two feature length films. The dragon appears in *Siegfried*, the first part. The second part is *Kriemhilds Rache*, or *Kriemhild's Revenge*.

63. Ray Harryhausen, *Film Fantasy Scrapbook*, rev. ed. (Cranbury, NJ: A. S. Barnes and Co., 1974), 10–23.

64. Interview with Inoshirō and Kimi Honda in Tokyo on April 1, 1990.

65. Joseph L. White, *The Troubled Adolescent* (New York: Pergamon, 1989), 3.

66. I. C. Jarvie, *Movies As Social Criticism: Aspects of Their Social Psychology* (Metuchen, NJ: Scarecrow Press, 1978), 36–37.

67. James B. Twitchell, *Dreadful Pleasures: An Anatomy of Modern Horror* (New York: Oxford University Press, 1985), 219.

68. Prawer, *Caligari's Children*, 9.

69. Kracauer, *From Caligari to Hitler*, 163.

70. Perhaps the two most famous computers are the doomsday machine in Stanley Kubrick's *Dr. Strangelove* (Britain, 1964), and HAL in Kubrick's *2001: A Space*

Odyssey (Britain, 1968) and again in *2010* (Peter Hyams, 1984); the first two are bomb films. Two other computers appear in the famous bomb films *Colossus: The Forbin Project* (Joseph Sargent, 1970), and *Demon Seed* (Donald Cammell, 1977).

71. Isaac Asimov's three laws of robotics include: (1) A robot may not injure a human being, or, through inaction, allow a human being to come to harm; (2) A robot must obey the orders given it by human beings except where such orders conflict with the first law; (3) A robot must protect its own existence as long as such protection does not conflict with the first or second laws. See Prawer, *Caligari's Children*, 63.

72. Ibid., 24.

73. Boyer, *By the Bomb's Early Light*, xvi, xviii.

74. Arthur Schlesinger, "Space Program Brought Back Down to Earth After Giant Leap for Mankind," *Daily Yomiuri*, (August 29, 1994): 6.

75. Associated Press, "U.S. Museum to Change A-Bomb Display," *Daily Yomiuri* (August 31, 1994): 3.

Notes to Chapter 2

1. Murry Green, Colonel, USAF-Ret., "Silver Plate: A Case Study in Military Secrecy," *Retired Officer Magazine* (August 1990): 39.

2. C. G. Jung, *Memories, Dreams, Reflections*, ed. Aniela Jaffé, trans. Richard and Clara Winston (New York: Random House, 1961), 342, 344.

3. Richard Rhodes, *The Making of the Atomic Bomb* (New York: Simon & Schuster, 1986), 765. Weapons' yields and other data also from Rhodes, 734, 740–42.

4. Ibid., 402, 599.

5. "State Trends in Alcohol: 1979–92," in *U.S. Alcohol Epidemiologic Data Reference Manual*, vol. 5, 1st ed. (National Institutes of Health, September 1996), 10. See also Donald R. Shopland, "Tobacco Use and Its Contribution to Early Cancer Mortality with a Special Emphasis on Cigarette Smoking," *Environmental Health Perspectives* 103, supplement 8 (National Cancer Institute, November 1995), abstract.

6. "How Many Minamata Disease Victims Are There?" in *Ten Things to Know about Minamata Disease*, rev. ed. (The Minamata Environmental Creation Development Project Steering Committee, September 1997, available online at <http://www.fsinet.or.jp/%7Esoshina/10tisiki/10tiski_e.html>.

7. Rhodes, *The Making of the Atomic Bomb*, 736.

8. Thomas H. Etzold and John Lewis Gaddis, eds., *Containment: Documents on American Policy and Strategy, 1945–1990* (New York: Columbia University Press, 1978), 362.

9. Rhodes, *The Making of the Atomic Bomb*, 378, 562, 621, 757. See also Etzold and Gaddis, *Containment*, 366, 367.

10. Henry L. Stimson, in *Harper's* (1947), as cited in Godfrey Hodgson, *America in Our Time: From World War II to Nixon, What Happened and Why* (New York: Doubleday & Company, 1976), 25.

11. Rhodes, *The Making of the Atomic Bomb*, 530–31, 767.

12. Hodgson, *America in Our Time*, 40.

13. Paul Boyer, *By the Bombs Early Light: American Thought and Culture at the Dawn of the Atomic Age,* (New York: Pantheon Books, 1985), 194–95.

14. See Richard Slotkin, *Regeneration Through Violence: The Mythology of The American Frontier, 1600–1860* (Middletown, CT: Wesleyan University Press, 1973).

15. John W. Dower, *War Without Mercy: Race and Power in the Pacific War* (New York: Pantheon Press, 1986), 3–14.

16. Neil A. Lewis, "Searching Only in Profiles Can Hide a Spy's Face," *New York Times,* Weekly Review (September 17, 2000): 3. See also Andrew Goldstein with Edward Barnes, "Rights of the Accused: The Far Reach of the Law," *Time* (Asia edition, September 24, 2000): 40.

17. Early *Superman* cartoons: "Superman," "Terror on the Midway" (date unavailable); "Billion Dollar Limited," "The Mechanical Monster," 1941; "Arctic Giant" (note similarities to the later *Beast from 20,000 Fathoms* and *It Came From Beneath the Sea*); "Bulleteers," "Destruction Inc." (saboteurs in U.S. munitions factory), "Electric Earthquake," "Eleventh Hour" (Lois Lane is "interned" in Yokohama); "Japoteurs," "Jungle Drums" (Nazis); "The Magnetic Telescope," "Show Down," "Secret Agent" (Nazi Saboteurs); "Volcano" 1942; "The Mummy Strikes," "The Underground World" (note similarities to *Unknown World*), 1943.

18. Dave Aldwinckle, February 2, 2000. See <http://www.voicenet.co.jp/~davald/essays.html#ninkiseigallagher>.

19. Donald Spoto, *The Art of Alfred Hitchcock: Fifty Years of His Motion Pictures* (New York: Hopkins and Blake, 1976), 161–62.

20. Donald Spoto, *The Art of Alfred Hitchcock: Fifty Years of His Motion Pictures,* 2d ed. (New York: Anchor Books, 1992), 146.

21. See Joyce A. Evans, *Celluloid Mushroom Clouds: Hollywood and the Atomic Bomb* (Boulder, Westview Press, 198), 24; Kim Newman, *Apocalypse Movies: End of the World Cinema* (New York: Saint Martin's Griffin, 2000), 70–71; Toni A. Perrine, *Film and the Nuclear Age: Representing Cultural Anxiety* (New York: Garland, 1998), 124.

22. Spoto, *The Art of Alfred Hitchcock,* 1976 edition, 165.

23. Ibid., 1992 ed., caption to photograph of Grant and Bergman inspecting a bottle of wine, 154.

24. Ibid., xi.

25. Ibid., 1976 edition, 162–64, 167.

26. Boyer, *By the Bomb's Early Light,* 11.

27. Leonard Maltin, *Leonard Maltin's TV Movies Video Guide: 1991 Edition* (New York: Signet Books, 1990), 531.

28. Mick Broderick, *Nuclear Movies: A Critical Analysis and Filmography of International Feature Length Films Dealing with Experimentation, Aliens, Terrorism, and Other Disaster Scenarios, 1914–1989* (Jefferson, NC: McFarland & Company, 1991) 4–5.

29. Pam Cook, ed., *The Cinema Book: A Complete Guide to Understanding the Movies* (New York: Pantheon Books, 1985), 19.

30. *Film Noir: An Encyclopedic Reference to the American Style,* ed. Alain Silver and Elizabeth Ward (Woodstock, NY: Overlook Press, 1979), 77.

31. Anonymous, "Hollywood and the Atom Bomb," *Science Illustrated* vol. 1, no. 7 (October 1946): 42.

32. Jack G. Shaheen and Richard Taylor, "The Beginning or the End," in *Nuclear War Films*, ed. Jack G. Shaheen (Carbondale: Southern Illinois University Press, 1978), 8.

33. "Hollywood and the Atom Bomb," *Science Illustrated*, 43, 44. While the article has an interesting history of the film and statements by the filmmakers, it offers no critical insights.

34. Ruth Rivkin, "Movies and Theatre: The Story of the Atomic Bomb," in *United Nations World* 1, no. 3 (UN World Inc., New York, April 1947): 64.

35. Broderick, *Nuclear Movies*, 60.

36. Shaheen, ed., *Nuclear War Films*, 8–10.

37. Boyer, *By the Bomb's Early Light*, 266. While Boyer's book does not include a reference to Shaheen's work, during a personal interview with Professor Boyer, we discussed Shaheen's book (spring 1987, UCLA campus). See also Garth S. Jowett, "Hollywood, Propaganda, and the Bomb: Nuclear Images in Post World War II Films," in *Film and History* 18, no. 2 (May 1988): 32–33; Evans: *Celluloid Mushroom Clouds*, 2, 34, 43. In her book, Evans includes a question mark at the end of the film's title, but there is none on screen or in any reference book that I have seen.

38. Boyer, *By the Bomb's Early Light*, 266.

39. Robert Jay Lifton and Greg Mitchell, *Hiroshima in America: Fifty Years of Denial* (New York: G. P. Putnam and Sons, 1995), 74, 359–73. The other two films are *Above and Beyond* (Mevlin Frank, 1952) and *Fat Man and Little Boy*.

40. Ibid., 74. See also Broderick, *Nuclear Movies*, 101.

41. Lifton and Mitchell, *Hiroshima in America*, 359–72, 427, see also inside dust jacket.

42. John W. Dower, *War Without Mercy: Race and Power in the Pacific War* (New York: Pantheon Press, 1986), 3–14.

43. Sam Keen, *Faces of the Enemy, Reflections of the Hostile Imagination: The Psychology of Enmity* (San Francisco: Harper & Row, 1986), 10–14.

44. Melvin J. Lasky, *Utopia and Revolution: On the Origins of a Metaphor, or Some Illustrations of the Problem of Political Temperament and Intellectual Climate and How Ideas, Ideals, and Ideologies Have Been Historically Related*, 519.

45. J. E. Cirlot, *A Dictionary of Symbols*, 2d ed., trans. Jack Sage (New York: Philosophical Library, 1971), 353–54.

46. Hayao Kawai, *The Japanese Psyche: Major Motifs in the Fairy Tales of Japan*, trans. Hayao Kawai and Sachiko Reese (Dallas: Spring Publications, 1988), 1–26.

47. Erik H. Erikson, *Identity: Youth and Crisis* (London: Faber and Faber, 1969), 40.

48. Collins, *The Apocalyptic Imagination: An Introduction to the Jewish Matrix of Christianity* (New York: Crossroad, 1989), 87.

49. Robert J. Lifton, *Death in Life: Survivors of Hiroshima*, rev. ed. (Chapel Hill: University of North Carolina Press, 1991), 509–10; see also *The Broken Connection: on Death and the Continuity of Life* (New York: Simon & Schuster, 1979).

50. Rhodes, *The Making of the Atomic Bomb*, 614, 662, 777. See also Spencer R. Weart, *Nuclear Fear: A History of Images* (Cambridge, MA: Harvard University Press,

1988), 101–3; and John Else's 1981 documentary *The Day after Trinity*. In Manhattan Project lore, fusion devices are often referred to as "the gadgets."

51. Paul Fussell, "Thank God for the Atom Bomb," in *Thank God for the Atom Bomb and Other Essays* (New York: Summit Books, 1998), 18–35.

52. John J. Deleaney, *Dictionary of Saints* (Garden City, NY: Doubleday & Company, Inc.), 394–95.

53. Collins, *The Apocalyptic Imagination*, 22, and Lifton, *Death in Life*, 481–82.

54. Tom Carson, "Nuclear waste," *L.A. Weekly* (October 20–October 26, 1989): 39. In addition, I recall hearing Joffé speaking, in a TV documentary/trailer for the film, about the Faustian image in his film.

55. Lifton, *The Broken Connection*, 355.

56. Shaheen, ed., *Nuclear War Films*, 8. The still also appears in a rare explanatory film brochure.

57. John J. Collins, *The Apocalyptic Imagination: An Introduction to the Jewish Matrix of Christianity* (New York: Crossroad, 1989), 3.

Notes to Chapter 3

1. C. G. Jung, *Memories, Dreams, Reflections*, ed. Aniela Jaffé, trans. Richard and Clara Winston (New York: Random House, 1961), 253, 268.

2. Mick Broderick, *Nuclear Movies: A Critical Analysis and Filmography of International Feature Length Films Dealing with Experimentation, Aliens, Terrorism, Holocaust and Other Disaster Scenarios, 1914–1989* (Jefferson, NC: McFarland & Company, 1991), 78.

3. Many reasonably consider *The Last Woman on Earth* to be a bomb film. But unlike even other Corman films, the cause of the catastrophe is never explicitly stated, so I do not include it in my own filmography.

4. Tzvetan Todorov, *The Conquest of America: The Question of the Other*, trans. Richard Howard (New York: Harper Colophon Books, 1984), 153–54, 171.

5. Hollis Alpert, "All This and Heaven Too," *Saturday Review* (May 2, 1959): 31, cited by Frank W. Oglesbee in *Nuclear War Films*, ed. Jack G. Shaheen (Carbondale: Southern Illinois University Press, 1978), 29.

6. H. Bruce Franklin, *War Stars: The Superweapon and the American Imagination* (New York: Oxford University Press, 1988), 184; Spencer R. Weart, *Nuclear Fear: A History of Images* (Cambridge, MA: Harvard University Press, 1988), 222.

7. *The Portable Conservative Reader*, ed. Russell Kirk (New York: Viking Penguin, 1982), xi.

8. Melvin J. Lasky, *Utopia and Revolution: On the Origins of a Metaphor, or Some Illustrations of the Problem of Political Temperament and Intellectual Climate and How Ideas, Ideals, and Ideologies Have Been Historically Related* (Chicago: University of Chicago Press, 1976), 227–33, 310.

9. Harry Bates, "Farewell to the Master," in *Astounding Science Fiction* (October 1940), cited in Bill Warren, *Keep Watching the Skies: American Science Fiction Movies of the Fifties* (Jefferson, NC: McFarland & Company, 1997), 25–26.

10. Richard Rhodes, *The Making of the Atom Bomb* (New York: Simon & Schuster, 1986), 31, 621.

11. John J. Collins, *The Apocalyptic Imagination: An Introduction to the Jewish Matrix of Christianity* (New York: Crossroad, 1989), 112–14.

12. Thomas H. Saffer and Orville E. Kelly, *Countdown Zero* (New York: G. P. Putnam's Sons, 1982), 226–27.

13. Rhodes gives an extensive introduction to the relationship between Wells and Szilard in *The Making of the Atomic Bomb*, 14, 21, 24, 107.

14. Oppenheimer held dual posts, one at the California Institute of Technology, "Cal Tech," in Pasadena, California, and the other at the University of California, Berkeley.

15. In a 1977 survey by *TV Guide*, TV program directors were asked to choose the most popular, most-often-shown films. Out of a list of more than 20,000 titles, *The War of the Worlds* was voted the thirteenth most popular film. See Cobbett S. Steinberg, *Film Facts* (New York: Facts on File, 1980), 31.

16. This is a common editing technique used to create a transition between two different scenes. Two pieces of film are actually overlapped in the editing process, creating the image of the former scene dissolving into the latter scene.

17. For an overview of the "Just War Tradition," see "Nuclear Ethics," in David P. Barash, *The Arms Race and Nuclear War* (Belmont, CA: Wadsworth, 1987), 303–8.

18. The poem is "Hymne to God My God, in My Sicknesse" (1623 or 1631). John Donne, *The Complete Poetry of John Done*, ed. John T. Shawcross (Garden City, NY: Doubleday & Company, 1967), 344, 390–92.

19. Rhodes, *The Making of the Atomic Bomb*, 131–32, 572. See also Robert J. Lifton, *The Broken Connection: On Death and the Continuity of Life* (New York: Simon & Schuster, 1979), 370.

20. I am indebted to Professor Peter Clecak, particularly for his comments on *Dover Beach* and *The War of the Worlds*.

21. Mary Ann Doane, *The Desire to Desire: The Woman's Film of the 1940s* (Bloomington: Indiana University Press, 1987).

22. George P. Elliott, "Think Films: A New Hollywood Creation," *Esquire* (March 1960), 118; Pauline Kael, *Kiss Kiss Bang Bang* (Boston: Little, Brown and Co., 1965), 207; and Joseph Keyerleber, in Shaheen, ed., *Nuclear War Films*, 31.

23. Boyer, *By the Bomb's Early Light: American Thought and Culture at the Dawn of the Atomic Age* (New York: Pantheon Books 1985), xvii, 353.

24. Robert Warshow, "The Legacy of the '30s," in *The Immediate Experience: Movies, Comics, Theatre and Other Aspects of Popular Culture* (New York: Athenum, 1972), 33–48.

25. Peter Clecak, *Radical Paradoxes: Dilemmas of the American Left 1945–1970* (New York: Harper & Row, 1973); See also *Crooked Paths: Reflections on Socialism, Conservatism and the Welfare State* (New York: Harper & Row, 1977); and *America's Quest for the Ideal Self: Dissent and Fulfillment in the 60s and 70s* (New York: Oxford University Press, 1983), passim.

26. Boyer, *By the Bomb's Early Light*, passim.

Notes to Chapter 4

1. C. Wright Mills, *The Sociological Imagination* (New York: Oxford University Press, 1959), 8.

2. H. Bruce Franklin, *War Stars: The Superweapon and the American Imagination* (New York: Oxford University Press, 1988), 182.

3. Mills, *The Sociological Imagination*, 8–9.

4. Richard Rhodes, *The Making of the Atomic Bomb* (New York: Simon & Schuster, 1986), 652, 670.

5. Peter Clecak offers three explanations for contemporary intellectuals' disdain for religion, and especially Christian revivalism. First, "[I]ntellectuals—especially left and left-liberal intellectuals—despised the political beliefs, actions, and inactions they imputed to evangelicals and neo-Pentecostals." Second, "[I]ntellectuals oppose the born again Christians' constricted theological range—and its most obvious political and cultural implications." Third, "Highbrow social critics feel themselves culturally superior to most born again Christians, since evangelicals and neo-Pentecostals typically inhabit middle and lowbrow ranges of American Culture." See Peter Clecak, *America's Quest for the Ideal Self: Dissent and Fulfillment in the 60s and 70s* (New York: Oxford University Press, 1983), 138–39. For Clecak's fuller critique, see 135–44.

6. William H. Whyte Jr., *The Organization Man* (New York: Doubleday Anchor Books, 1957).

7. For an introduction to anthropological structuralism, *see* A. R. Radcliffe-Brown, *Structure and Function in Primitive Society* (New York: The Free Press, 1952).

8. Franklin, *War Stars*, 182. See also Nora Sayre, *Running Time: Films of the Cold War* (New York: Dial Press, 1982), 193, 204.

9. Peter Biskind, *Seeing Is Believing: How Hollywood Taught Us to Stop Worrying and Love the Fifties* (New York: Pantheon Books, 1983), 133.

10. Elaine Tyler May, *Homeward Bound: American Families in the Cold War Era* (New York: Basic Books, Inc., 1988).

11. Hayao Kawai, "The Woman Who Eats Nothing," in *The Japanese Psyche: Major Motifs in the Fairy Tales of Japan*, trans. Kawai Hayao and Sachiko Reece (Dallas: Spring Publications, 1988), 27–45.

12. Caleb Bendix, "The Child Archetype in Atomic Bomb Films," unpublished student paper, Hiroshima University, July 2000.

13. C. G. Jung, "The Psychology of the Child Archetype," in *The Archetypes and the Collective Unconscious*, 2d ed. (Princeton: Princeton University Press, 1980), 159, 164, 179.

14. I am indebted to Dr. Michael Treanor for his insightful comments on the image and symbolic meaning of the Joshua tree.

15. George Ferguson, *Signs and Symbols in Christian Art* (New York: Oxford University Press, 1961), 58. James Hall, *Dictionary of Subjects and Symbols in Art* (New York: Harper & Row, 1979), 178.

16. J. E. Cirlot, *A Dictionary of Symbols*, 2d. ed., trans. Jack Sage (New York: Philosophical Library, 1971), 346–50.

17. Fowler, cited in John C. Collins, *The Apocalyptic Imagination: An Introduction to the Jewish Matrix of Christianity* (New York: Crossroad, 1989), 3.

18. Stuart Galbraith IV, *Japanese Science Fiction, Fantasy and Horror Films: A Critical Analysis of 103 Features Released in the United States, 1950–1992* (Jefferson, NC: McFarland & Company, 1994), 7–14, 346–47. According to Galbraith, the film was shown in Los Angeles at the Toho LaBrea theater.

19. *The Motion Picture Encyclopedia*'s online review, <www.tvgen.com/movies/mopic/pictures/21/21842.htm>, May 27, 1998. According to the Library of Congress's online catalog, Hendrick Willem Van Loon's *The Story of Mankind* was first published in 1921 and won the first Newbery Medal. It has since been updated and republished by others (e.g., New York: Liveright, 1984).

20. Paul Boyer, *By the Bomb's Early Light: American Thought and Culture at the Dawn of the Atomic Age* (New York: Pantheon Books, 1985), 354.

21. Perrine is one of the few scholars to even note Scott's "exposure to pesticide." See Toni A. Perrine, *Film and the Nuclear Age: Representing Cultural Anxiety* (New York: Garland, 1998), 93.

22. Cirlot, *A Dictionary of Symbols*, 28.

23. Ibid., 304.

24. Dana M. Reemes, *Directed by Jack Arnold* (Jefferson, NC: McFarland & Company, 1988), 57–74. See also Richard Matheson, *The Shrinking Man* (Greenwich, CT: Fawcett, 1956), cited in Reemes, 57, 235.

25. Whyte, *The Organization Man*.

26. Eric J. Cassell, *The Nature of Suffering and the Goals of Medicine* (New York: Oxford University Press, 1991), 43, 57.

27. Ibid., 44.

28. Cirlot, *A Dictionary of Symbols*, 214–18. See also Ferguson, *Signs and Symbols in Christian Art*, 45.

29. Cirlot, *A Dictionary of Symbols*, 28. Also Ferguson, *Signs and Symbols in Christian Art*, 12–16.

30. Boyer, *By the Bomb's Early Light*, 354.

31. Sayre, *Running Time*, 193, 204.

32. Franklin, *War Stars*, 182.

33. According to one U.S. Army recruiting officer, the eagle holds lightening bolts and an olive branch in its talons (March 1999). A dealer in military medals, however, claimed the eagle holds one arrow for each of the original thirteen colonies of the United States (April 1999).

34. Various lectures, writings, and personal conversations. H. Arthur Taussig, Ph.D., professor of fine arts, Orange Coast College, Costa Mesa, California.

35. C. G. Jung, *Memories, Dreams, Reflections*, ed. Aniela Jaffé, trans. Richard and Clara Winston (New York: Random House, 1961), 273.

36. Eric J. Cassell, *The Nature of Suffering*, 44.

37. Clecak, *America's Quest for the Ideal Self*, 6–10.

38. Robert J. Lifton, *The Broken Connection: On Death and the Continuity of Life* (New York: Simon & Schuster, 1979), 16, 17.

39. Cirlot, *A Dictionary of Symbols*, 304.

40. Ibid., 201.

41. Ibid., 274, 364–67.

42. Ibid., 40, 165.

43. Madonna Kolbenschlarg, *Lost in the Land of Oz: The Search for Identity and Community in American Life* (San Francisco: Harper & Row, 1988), 32–33.

44. Taussig; see note 34, this chapter.

45. Gerald Vizenor, *The Heirs of Columbus* (Hanover, NH: Wesleyan University Press, 1991).

46. Richard Slotkin, *Regeneration through Violence: The Mythology of the American Frontier, 1600–1860* (Middletown, CT: Wesleyan University Press, 1973), 5.

47. John Block Friedman, *The Monstrous Races in Medieval Art and Thought* (Cambridge, MA: Harvard University Press, 1981) 2, 202–7.

48. The episode is "Kokyō wa chikyū" (or, "Earth Is My Home"), written by Mamoru Sasaki. The program suggests that the astronauts were French, and the captain's name is A. Jamila.

Notes to Chapter 5

1. William C. Bryson, *Bulletin of Atomic Scientists* (December 1982): 35, cited in Richard Rhodes, *The Making of the Atomic Bomb* (New York: Simon & Schuster, 1986), 742.

2. Paul Boyer, *By the Bomb's Early Light: American Thought and Culture at the Dawn of the Atomic Age* (New York: Pantheon Books, 1985), 355–56.

3. Ibid., 195.

4. The air force refused to assist Kubrick, so the film was made with sets and models. The accuracy of Kubrick's designs caused quite a stir in the military.

5. For a very helpful clarification of the use of metaphors in film, see Trevor Whittock's in-depth analysis, *Metaphor and Film* (New York: Cambridge University Press, 1990), especially chapter 5, pp. 49–69.

6. I am indebted to Professor H. Arthur Taussig for his insights into this film, particularly the jokes. Also Richard A. Spears, *Slang and Euphemism: a Dictionary of Oaths, Curses, Insults, Sexual Slang and Metaphor, Racial Slurs, Drug Talk, Homosexual Lingo, and Related Matters* (Middle Village, NY: Jonathan David, 1981), 251, 262.

7. Morris Weitz, "Analysis, Philosophical," in *The Encyclopedia of Philosophy*, vol. 1 (New York: Macmillan, 1967, reprint edition 1972), 98.

8. Peter Baxter, "The One Woman," in *Wide Angle*, 6, no. 1 (1984): 34–41.

9. Charles Maland, "Dr. Strangelove (1964): Nightmare Comedy and the Ideology of Liberal Consensus," *American Quarterly* 21, no. 5 (winter, 1979): 697–717.

10. Robert Warshow, *The Immediate Experience: Movies, Comics, Theatre and Other Aspects of Popular Culture* (New York: Athenum, 1972): 26.

11. George W. Linden, "'Dr. Strangelove' and Erotic Displacement," in *The Journal of Aesthetic Education* (January 1977): 67, 71–2, 80.

12. John J. Collins, *The Apocalyptic Imagination: An Introduction to the Jewish Matrix of Christianity* (New York: Crossroad, 1989), 3.

13. Godfrey Hodgson, *America in Our Time: From World War II to Nixon, What Happened and Why* (New York: Doubleday & Company, 1976), 3–16.

14. C. G. Jung, "The Psychology of the Child," in *The Archetypes and the Collective Unconscious*, 2d ed. (Princeton: Princeton University Press, 1980), 154.

15. Ibid., 67–98.

16. Boyer, *By the Bomb's Early Light*, 352–56.

17. Allan Casebier, conversation with the author, University of Southern California, Los Angeles, September 1989.

18. Boyer, *By the Bomb's Early Light*, 353, 367.

19. Stephen Hilgartner, Richard C. Bell, and Rory O'Conner, *Nukespeak: The Selling of Nuclear Technology in America* (New York: Penguin Books, 1983; first published by Sierra Club Books, 1982), xiii, xiv.

20. Regarding Henry Kissinger, see Maland, "Dr. Strangelove (1964)," 709.

21. Linden, "'Dr. Strangelove' and Erotic Displacement," 66.

22. *Time*, Asia ed., "Numbers" column (September 18, 2000): 18. After an extensive web search, I could find no further reference to this syndrome.

23. Susan Sackett, *Box Office Hits: A Year by Year, Behind the Camera Look at Hollywood's Most Successful Movies* (New York: Billboard Books, 1990), 174, 177.

24. Until *License to Kill* (John Glen, 1989), James Bond was strictly a company man restrained by the system, but in this film, Bond leaves the service to pursue a personal vendetta, destroy a South American drug dealer with nefarious connections to the Nicaraguan Contras, and preserve the status quo. Thus, despite his rogue status, deep at heart Bond remains a company man committed to preserving the status quo and the honor of the service. *License to Kill* differs subtly but importantly from past films. For instance, instead of the usual cold war themes, themes relating to the "war on drugs," "safe sex," and the "Iran-Contra scandal" appear definitively as well. Thus it is considered one of the first post–cold war films. In previous films Bond's sexual prowess is very important; but, though Bond is notoriously fickle, even his seductions of many beautiful women are justified as part of his service to queen and country. However, in *License to Kill*, Bond is strictly monogamous and develops a lasting relationship with a woman who is his equal. In more recent Bond films, such as *Tomorrow Never Dies* (1998), we find a return to cold war–era patterns.

25. Dialog Info Services, Inc., 1989, File 299: *Magill's Survey of Cinema* database (Englewood Cliffs, NJ: Salem Press, 1989).

26. S. S. Prawer, *Caligari's Children: The Film as Tale of Terror* (New York: Da Capo Press, 1980), 274, 275.

27. Robin Wood, *Hollywood from Vietnam to Reagan* (New York, Columbia University Press, 1986), 114–21.

28. Ibid., l, 23, 118.

29. Pete Townshend, "Won't Get Fooled Again," *Who's Next*, 1971.

30. John Brosnan, *Future Tense: The Cinema of Science Fiction* (New York: St. Martin Press, 1978), 229; and an interview with John Carpenter, *Morning Becomes Eclectic*, KCRW radio station, Santa Monica, California (spring 1990).

31. The very popular and influential *Star Trek* series aired on NBC from September

1966 to September 1969, and then went into syndication. See Alex McNeil, *Total Television: A Comprehensive Guide to Programming from 1948 to the Present* (New York: Penguin Books, 1980), 612.

32. Sigmund Freud, *Civilization and Its Discontents*, trans. James Strachey (New York: W. W. Norton & Company, 1961).

33. Theodore Dreiser, *Sister Carrie*, ed. Donald Pizer (New York: W. W. Norton & Company, 1970).

34. *Film Noir: An Encyclopedic Reference to the American Style*, ed. Alain Silver and Elizabeth Ward (Woodstock, NY: Overlook Press, 1979), 333–36.

35. Peter Clecak, *America's Quest for the Ideal Self: Dissent and Fulfillment in the 60s and 70s* (New York: Oxford University Press, 1983), 42–43.

Notes to Chapter 6

1. Harvey Gross, "The Problem of Style and the Poetry of the Sixties," in *The Iowa Review* 5 (winter 1974): 69, cited in Peter Clecak, *America's Quest for the Ideal Self: Dissent and Fulfillment in the 60s and 70s* (New York: Oxford University Press, 1983), 35.

2. Peter Clecak, *America's Quest for the Ideal Self: Dissent and Fulfillment in the 60s and 70s*, 43.

3. Frances FitzGerald, "The Poseurs of Missile Defense," *New York Times*, Weekly Review (June 4, 2000): 7.

4. Paul Boyer, *By the Bomb's Early Light: American Thought and Culture at the Dawn of the Atomic Age* (New York: Pantheon Books, 1985), 355–62. Weart, however, claims that the movement began in Japan; see Spencer R. Weart, *Nuclear Fear: a History of Images* (Cambridge, MA: Harvard University OPress, 1988), 375.

5. Weart, *Nuclear Fear*, 378.

6. Boyer, *By the Bomb's Early Light*, 359–60.

7. See Leonard Maltin, ed., *Leonard Maltin's TV Movies and Videoguide* (New York: Signet Books, 1991), 142.

8. *The Orange County Register* (March 21, 2000), 2.

9. Boyer, *By the Bomb's Early Light*, 354. The Japanese title for this film is *Bijo to ekitai ningen*. My translation of this title is *The Beauty and the Liquid Human*.

10. Jay Robert Nash and Stanley Ralph Ross, *The Motion Picture Guide*, vol. 5 (Chicago: Cinebooks, 1985), 1791.

11. Dough Mitchell and George Ogilvie joined the company as coproducer and codirector. See Jay Robert Nash and Stanley Ralph Ross, *The Motion Picture Guide, 1986 Annual (The Films of 1985)* (Chicago: Cinebooks, 1987), 120–21.

12. Weart, *Nuclear Fear*, 388, 516.

13. Peter Fitting, "Count Me Out/In: Post-Apocalyptic Visions in Recent Science Fiction Film," *CineAction!* no. 11 (December 1987): 42–51.

14. Mick Broderick, "Witnessing the Unthinkable," page 2 of text printed from Mr. Broderick's homepage, <http://www.1earth.net/~postmodm/pmdefault.html>.

15. This was widely reported on various National Public Radio (NPR) news programs during the summer of 1991.

16. Clecak, *America's Quest for the Ideal Self*, 39, 40.

17. Dick Hebdige, *Subculture: The Meaning of Style* (London: Methuen & Co., 1979), 27.

18. Fitting, "Count Me In/Out," 50.

19. Clecak, *America's Quest for the Ideal Self*, 37.

20. Ibid., 36

21. Ibid., 335.

22. David P. Barash, *The Arms Race and Nuclear War* (Belmont, CA: Wadsworth, 1987), 280, 281.

23. Clecak, *America's Quest for the Ideal Self*, 334–38.

24. Maltin, *Leonard Maltin's TV Movies and Video Guide*, 1157. Also, Jay Robert Nash and Stanley Ralph Ross, *The Motion Picture Guide*, vol. 8 (Chicago: Cinebooks, 1987), 3319–20.

25. Joseph Keyerleber, "On the Beach," as cited in *Nuclear War Films*, ed. Jack G. Shaheen (Carbondale, Southern Illinois University Press, 1978), 37.

26. Mary Ann Doane, *The Desire to Desire: The Woman's Film of the 1940s* (Bloomington: Indiana University Press, 1987). Susan Boyd-Bowman also calls *Testament* a weepie but never takes the comparison further; see "'The Day After': Representations of the Nuclear Holocaust," *Screen* 24, nos. 4–5, (July–October, 1984): 92.

27. Stanley Cavell, *Contesting Tears: The Hollywood Melodrama of the Unknown Woman* (Chicago: University of Chicago Press, 1996).

28. Steve Weinstein, "A Quarter-Century of Television Movies . . . ," *Los Angeles Times*, Calendar section (Sunday, April 23, 1989): 24.

29. William J. Palmer, *The Films of the Eighties: A Social History* (Carbondale: Southern Illinois University Press, 1993), 11.

30. *Mayberry, R.F.D.* (CBS, September 1968 to March 1971) has a tremendous cult following, with several websites devoted to the program. It was one of the direct spin-offs from the very popular *Andy Griffith Show* (CBS, October 1960 to September 1968).

31. Richard Rhodes, *The Making of the Atomic Bomb* (New York: Simon & Schuster, 1986), 713.

32. Some missiles are "popped" out of the silo with compressed air, and then the rockets fire. This prevents the destruction of the silo by the rockets.

33. According to Cirlot, the oak is a tree sacred to Jupiter and Cybele, and it stands for strength and long life. It also attracts more lightning than any other tree. Such symbolism exists in many cultures. And, "Like all trees, it represents a world-axis." J. E. Cirlot, *A Dictionary of Symbols*, 2d. ed., trans. Jack Sage (New York: Philosophical Library, 1971), 238.

34. Kim Newman, *Apocalypse Movies: End of the World Cinema* (New York: Saint Martin's Press, 2000), 231.

35. Boyd-Bowman, "The Day After," 71, 72, 84, 97.

36. Ibid.

37. C. Wright Mills, *The Sociological Imagination* (New York: Oxford University Press, 1959), 8.

38. Reported on National Public Radio's (NPR) *Weekend Edition* on June 29, 1991, and *Morning Edition* on July 5, 1991.

39. The film takes place one hundred years after the stock market crash in 1929 and the decades of reform that followed.

40. David Chute, interview with James Cameron, *Film Comment* 21, no. 1 (January–February 1985): 60.

41. Flora Haines Loughead, *Dictionary of Given Names*, 2d. ed., rev. (Glendale, CA: The Arthur H. Clark Co., 1981), 69.

42. Fitting,"Count Me Out/In," 50.

43. Chute, interview with James Cameron, 59.

44. Loughead, *Dictionary of Given Names*, 69.

45. The skeletal Terminator model and stop-motion animation are an elegant homage to the works of Ray Harryhousen, particularly the skeletons represented in *Jason and the Argonauts* (Don Chaffey, 1963, Britain).

46. Benjamin Urrutia, "Heroic Parallels," *Mythlore: a Journal of J. R. R. Tolkien, C. S. Lewis, Charles Williams, General Fantasy and Mythic Studies* 41, vol. 11, no. 3 (winter–spring 1985): 40, 44, 45. See the *New American Standard Bible*, Open Bible Edition (Nashville: Thomas Nelson, 1960), 674, 1218.

47. J. P. Telotte, "The Ghost in the Machine: Consciousness and the Science Fiction Film," *Western Humanities Review*, vol. 42, no. 3 (autumn 1988): 253–56.

48. Hugh Ruppersburg, "The Alien Messiah in Recent Science Fiction Films," *Journal of Popular Film and Television* 14, no. 4 (winter 1987): 160.

49. Constance Penley, "Time Travel, Primal Scene and the Critical Dystopia," in *Fantasy and the Cinema*, ed. James Donald (London: British Film Institute, 1989), 187, 210. First published in *Camera Obscura* no. 15 (1988).

50. Lillian Necakov, "*The Terminator*: Beyond Classical Hollywood Narrative," *CineAction* no. 8 (March 1987): 84, 86.

51. Margaret Goscilo, "Deconstructing *The Terminator*," *Film Criticism* 22, no. 2 (winter 1987–88): 38, 45, 50.

52. Necakov, "*The Terminator*: Beyond Classical Hollywood Narrative," 86. Also Goscilo, "Deconstructing *The Terminator*," 48.

53. John J. Collins, *The Apocalyptic Imagination: An Introduction to the Jewish Matrix of Christianity* (New York: Crossroad, 1989), 136.

54. Goscilo, *Deconstructing The Terminator*," 48.

55. *New American Standard Bible*, 14.

56. Loughead, *Dictionary of Given Names*, 66.

57. Collins, *The Apocalyptic Imagination*, 136.

58. Ibid., 93, 100.

59. Chute, interview with James Cameron, 59.

60. Ibid., 60.

61. Fitting, "Count Me Out/In," 50.

62. Jerome F. Shapiro, "The Bomb, Japanese Aesthetic Traditions, and Japan's Most Important Film: *Gojira*," *Iconics* 5 (The Japan Society of Image Arts and Sciences, 2000): 93–115.

Notes to Chapter 7

1. Spencer R. Weart and Gertrud Weiss Szilard, eds., *Leo Szilard: His Version of the Facts* (Cambridge, MA: MIT Press, 1978), 185, cited in Richard Rhodes, *The Making of the Atomic Bomb* (New York: Simon & Schuster, 1986), 642.

2. Anna Louise Strong, interview with Mao Tse-Tung (August 1946) "Talk with The American Correspondent Ana Louise Strong," in *Selected Works of Mao Tse-Tung*, vol. 4 (Peking: Foreign Language Press, 1969), 100.

3. Dates for the end of the cold war range from as early as the Czech Velvet Revolution, culminating on November 17, 1989, to later events including the breaching of the Berlin Wall or to the actual dissolution of the Soviet Union.

4. The correct date of the "millennium" is not at all clear, and it is of little importance to many societies. In Japan, for instance, the official numbering of years is based on the reign of the current emperor. For most Japanese the recent millennium was of little consequence and only a "trendy" Western event sold to consumers. Regarding the dating of the millennium, see Seth Ward, "The Evasive Epoch: Jewish Perspectives on the Millennium and Other Calendrical Conundrums," paper presented at the Twelfth Annual Klutznick Symposium. See <http://puffin.creighton.edu/klutznick/abstracts/htm>.

5. Paul Boyer, *By the Bomb's Early Light: American Thought and Culture at the Dawn of the Atomic Age* (New York: Pantheon Books, 1985), 118.

6. Michael Ortiz Hill, *Dreaming the End of the World: Apocalypse As a Rite of Passage*. (Dallas: Spring Publications, 1994).

7. Anne Thompson, "Risky Business: Year in Review, Tops and Flops of 1990," in *L.A. Weekly* (January 4–January 10, 1991): 29.

8. I am indebted to Professor H. Arthur Taussig for pointing out this connection.

9. In the Japanese market, video rentals may serve as a more accurate measure of popularity. According to the CD & Video Rental Association, as late as the week of December 28, 1998 to January 3, 1999, *Godzilla* came in sixth among the top ten rented videos. See *Living Higashi-Hiroshima* (January 7, 1999): 5.

10. Kim Newman, "Godzilla 1998," *Sight and Sound* (July 1998): 23.

11. Susan Sontag, "The Imagination of Disaster," in *Against Interpretation* (New York: Farrar, Straus and Giroux, 1967).

12. After nine years of negotiations, American president Bush and Soviet president Gorbachev signed the controversial START in Moscow on July 31, 1991.

13. The story first appeared in the April 1966 issue of *The Magazine of Fantasy and Science Fiction*, and received the prestigious Nebula Award for that year.

14. C. G. Jung, "The Psychology of the Child Archetype," in *The Archetypes and the Collective Unconscious*, 2d ed. (Princeton: Princeton University Press, 1980), 164–67, 173–78.

15. I am indebted to my student Caleb Bendix, in my class on atomic bomb cinema, for pointing out this symbolic parallel to me (July 19, 2000).

16. Arthur Taussig, "Waterworld," *Film Analyst* 43 (September 1995): 2–3.

17. Ibid., 3–5.

18. The pilot, Paul Tibbits, named the plane after his mother. "Enola" is not listed in any book on names that I have seen, and I cannot imagine anyone naming their child Enola. Moreover, naming a character Enola in a film released on the fiftieth anniversary of Hiroshima makes it hard to escape the connection.

19. Taussig, "Waterworld," 5.

20. Ibid., 5.

21. Frederick Jackson Turner, *The Significance of the Frontier in American History* (New York: Holt, Rinehart, and Winston, 1962).

22. "Dorothy is the English feminine form of Greek *Dorotheus*, 'gift of God.'" See *The Ultimate Baby Name Book*, Kent Evans, consultant and contributing writer (Lincolnwood, IL: Publications International, 1994), 361. *See also Webster's New Collegiate Dictionary* (Springfield, MA: G. & C. Merriam Co., 1980), 465.

23. In order to save her infant from an even worse fate, Moses' mother places him in a basket and floats him down the Nile where the daughter of the Pharaoh rescues him. The name the infant was given is probably Egyptian, and means, simply, "child." However, "Because the ancient Hebrews didn't understand the meaning of the Egyptian name he was given, they interpreted it as meaning 'saved, drawn out of the water.'" Evans, *The Ultimate Baby Name Book*, 203.

24. *The Motion Picture Guide, 1990 Annual (The Films of 1989)* (Evanston, IL: Cinebooks, 1990), 4.

25. Joseph L. White, *The Troubled Adolescent* (New York: Pergamon, 1989).

26. Sandro Botticelli, *The Birth of Venus* (circa 1480).

27. Gerald Vizenor, *Bearheart: The Heirship Chronicles* (Minneapolis: University of Minnesota Press, 1990), passim.

28. Gerhard Adler, "Psychology and the Atom Bomb," Guild Lecture no. 43 (London: The Guild of Pastoral Psychology, August 12, 1946, 17.

29. Adler, *Ibid.*, 16.

30. C. Wright Mills, *The Sociological Imagination* (New York: Oxford University Press, 1959), 8–9; Peter Clecak, *America's Quest for the Ideal Self: Dissent and Fulfillment in the 60s and 70s* (New York: Oxford University Press, 1983), 6–10.

31. Peter Clecak, *Radical Paradoxes: Dilemmas of the American Left: 1945–1970* (New York: Harper and Row, 1973), develops this idea in its most explicit form; he then uses it in other contexts throughout *Crooked Paths: Reflections on Socialism, Conservatism, and the Welfare State* (New York: Harper & Row, 1977), and *America's Quest for the Ideal Self* (1983).

32. See Joseph L. White, *The Psychology of Blacks: An Afro-American Perspective* (Englewood Cliffs, NJ: Prentice-Hall, 1984); and Wade W. Nobles and Lawford L. Goddard, *Understanding the Black Family: A Guide for Scholarship and Research* (Oakland, CA: Institute for the Advanced Study of Black Family Life and Culture, 1984).

33. Clecak, *Radical Paradoxes*, 197. For an overview of Fromm, see Christopher F. Monte, *Beneath the Mask: An Introduction to Theories of Personality*, 2d ed. (New York: Holt, Rinehart and Winston, 1980), 484–509.

Notes to Chapter 8

1. Hayao Kawai, *The Japanese Psyche: Major Motifs in the Fairy Tales of Japan*, trans. Hayao Kawai and Sachiko Reece (Dallas: Spring Publications, 1988), 26.

2. Masao Miyoshi and H. D. Harootunian, "Japan in the World," *Boundary* 2 (fall 1991): 4–5.

3. Mick Broderick, "Introduction," in Broderick, ed. *Hibakusha Cinema: Hiroshima, Nagasaki and the Nuclear Image in Japanese Film* (London: Kegan Paul International, 1996), 1–19.

4. James Goodwin, "Akira Kurosawa and the Atomic Age," in Broderick, ed., *Hibakusha Cinema*, 182.

5. Broderick, "Introduction," 3–4. Broderick omits the word "cellular," but such an omission is a minor point.

6. This film is frequently referred to as, more simply, *Furankenshutain tai Baragon*.

7. The activities and contributions to medical science of Nazi doctors Holzloehner, Rascher, Finke, Hirt, Brandt, and especially Josef Mengele, are well known and widely studied. Shamefully, Japan's equally criminal medical experiments are hardly known in the West. For an introduction to this very black period in Japanese history, see Hal Gold, *Unit 731: Testimony* (Tokyo: Yenbooks, 1996).

8. Accounts of the Tuskeegee Syphilis Study, even of its official title, vary. However, it seems fairly clear that in the course of the study impoverished black men were infected with syphilis but neither informed of their illness nor treated. They were, furthermore, allowed to die at a rate twice that of the control group, and potentially life-saving penicillin injections were withheld. Only about 25 percent of the men survived long enough to learn of their guinea-pig status.

9. "Stonewalling" might, at times, seem like a better translation for *gaman*; however, that term, in English, is laden with negative connotations that do not necessarily reflect Japanese values.

10. Hayao Kawai, *The Japanese Psyche*, 14, 26.

11. Edward W. Said, *Orientalism* (New York: Pantheon Books, 1978).

12. *Kokin Wakashū: The First Imperial Anthology of Japanese Poetry, With Tosa Nikki and Shinsen Waka*, trans. and annotated by Helen Craig McCullough (Stanford, CA: Stanford University Press, 1985), 3.

13. Gerald Vizenor, *Matsushima: Pine Islands Haiku* (Minneapolis, MN: Nodin Press, 1984). Quotes are found in the unnumbered "introduction" on pages 3, 7, 11.

14. I am indebted to Professor Emeritus Yasuo Sakakibara of Doshisha University, himself a Buddhist priest, for directing me toward the *Kegonkyō*. See Thomas F. Cleary, trans., *The Flower Ornament Scripture: a Translation of the Avatamsaka Sutra*, 3 vols., (New York: Random House, 1984–1987). There are many secondary texts on this sutra, including Hayao Kawai's *The Buddhist Priest Myoe: A Life of Dreams*, trans. and ed. Mark Unno (Venice, CA: Lapis Press, 1992).

15. It is, of course, foolish to accept Suzuki's thesis—or anyone else's—uncritically. Nevertheless, he does a good job of contrasting different cultures' ideas and feelings about nature. See, for instance, Suzuki's "Love of Nature," in *Zen and Japanese Culture* (Princeton: Bollingen Paperback, 1970), 329–97; see also "Lectures on Zen

Buddhism," in *Zen Buddhism and Psychoanalysis*, ed. Eric Fromm (New York: Harper, 1960), 2.

16. Isamu Kurita, *Setsugetsuka no kokoro/Japanese Identity* (Tokyo: Shōdensha, 1987), 13, 21, 22, 25 26, 33.

17. See articles in *Asahi shinbun* (May 17, 2000): 1–3, 31; (May 18): 1–4, 35; (May 25–6): 2; (May 27) 1–3, 35; and (May 30): 1.

18. Stephen Vlastos, "Tradition: Past/Present Culture and Modern Japanese History," in *Mirror of Modernity: Invented Traditions of Modern Japan*, ed. Stephen Vlastos (Berkeley: University of California Press, 1998), 1.

19. In Buddhist canons, *masse* signifies an age of moral decadence, and in ancient times it also meant a retributive event that guides humanity. Today it just means the end of the world, a morally exhausted society, and decadence; see Izuru Shinmura, ed., *Kōjien*, 3d. ed. (Tokyo: Iwanami Shoten, 1983), 2257. Rather than connoting rebirth or the battle of good and evil, masse simply denotes punishment for crimes rather than sin. Masse does not include a cosmological reorganization as we have come to know it; rather, the world ends, and then something else takes its place. According to Professor William R. LaFleur of the University of California, Los Angeles, at one time in history medieval Japanese nobility used the imminent end of the world to justify their extravagances. (Conversation with Professor LaFleur, Tokyo, April 4, 1989). Masse does not appear to grip the Japanese imagination as the apocalypse does the Western imagination. My colleague and friend at Hiroshima University, Shin-ichi Anzai, an authority on both Japanese and Western aesthetics, has encouraged me to focus on "*mappō* [the latter days of Buddhist law] instead of, or rather as well as *masse*" (e-mail correspondence, August 4, 1998). I believe, however, that the distinction between masse and mappo is noteworthy, but too arcane for our discussion here.

20. Freda Freiberg, "*Akira* and the Postnuclear Sublime," in Broderick, ed., *Hibakusha Cinema*: 92.

21. The Ministry of Education has produced a very revealing report, the title of which can roughly be translated as *Report on "The Mental Education from Toddlers On," by the Central Education Committee of the Ministry of Education* (Tokyo: Ministry of Education, Culture, Sports, Science and Technology; date of publication is somewhat vague, but either on or after June 30, 1998, and before February 1999). This Japanese language document is accessible at <http://www.monbu.go.jp>.

22. Maya Morioka Todeschini, "'Death and the Maiden': Female *Hibakusha* as Cultural Heroines, and the Politics of A-Bomb Memory," in *Hibakusha Cinema*: 225.

23. Kawai, *The Japanese Psyche*, passim.

24. Lifcadio Hearn, *Kwaidan: Strange Stories and Studies of Strange Things* (New York: Dover Publications, 1968).

25. Todeschini, "'Death and the Maiden,'" 248 n. 9, and 252 n. 54.

26. Ibid., 222–52.

27. C. G. Jung, "The Psychology of the Child Archetype," in *The Archetypes and the Collective Unconscious*, 2d ed. (Princeton: Princeton University Press, 1980), 165.

28. Donald Richie, "'Mono no Aware'/Hiroshima in Film," in *Film: Book 2, Films of Peace and War*, ed. Robert Hughes (New York: Grove Press, 1962), 67–86; anthologized in Broderick, ed., *Hibakusha Cinema*, 20–37. Broderick's introduction also contextualizes Richie's importance, 1–19. See also Victor Or's reactionary review of

Hibakusha Cinema, "An Elegiac Outlook," in *Film and History* 28, nos. 1–2, part 1 (1998): 74.

29. Richie, "'Mono no Aware,'" 70–71. Kawai, *The Japanese Psyche*, 22.

30. Nobuo Tsuji, *Playfulness in Japanese Art*, trans. Joseph Seubert (Lawrence, KS: Spencer Museum of Art, University of Kansas, 1986), 21. I am indebted to Linda C. Ehrlich for bringing this book to my attention in her article, "The Extremes of Innocence: Kurosawa's Dreams and Rhapsodies," in Broderick, ed., *Hibakusha Cinema*, 169, 176.

31. Zeami (1363–1443), "The Deserted Crone (Obasute)," in *20 Plays of the Nō Theater*, ed. Donald Keene (New York: Columbia University Press, 1970), 123, 126.

32. Tsuji, *Playfulness in Japanese Art*, 21. I am indebted to Shin-ichi Anzai, again, for helping me with the etymology and aesthetics of the words in question. In brief, there is considerable scholarly debate about the origin, meaning, and use of the word *okashi* during the Fujiwara period. The word has several different meanings. One group says that the adjective *wokashi* (now, okashi) is derived from the verb *woku* (to "beckon"), and that in the Fujiwara period wokashi meant "attractive," "inviting," or "tasteful"; *Iwanami Dictionary of Ancient Japanese*, ed. Susumu Ohno et al., (Tokyo: Iwanami-Shoten, 1975). However, other authorities argue that the adjective wokashi is derived from *woko* (fool[ishness]), and cite an early Heian-era dictionary, the *Shinsenzikan*, which defines wokashi as "laughable"; *Shōgakukan kogodaijiten*, or *Grand Dictionary of Ancient Japanese* (Tokyo: Shōgakukan, 1983). And, Tsuji finds ample evidence for this, the latter definition of the word, in the art and aesthetics of the period.

33. Tsuji, *Playfulness in Japanese Art*, 87.

34. Ibid., 14, 51.

35. Ibid., 88.

36. See Vlastos, ed., *Mirror of Modernity*; Darrell William Davis, *Picturing Japaneseness: Monumental Style, National Identity, Japanese Film* (New York: Columbia University Press, 1996); and Takao Aoki (Hiroshima University), "Cultural Division of Arts Through Modernization in Japan: The Transplantation of Western Arts (Geijutsu) and the Invention of Traditional Arts (Geidoh)," a paper presented at the First International Conference of Eastern Aesthetics in China, Hohhot, July 2000.

37. Tsuji, *Playfulness in Japanese Art*, 88.

38. *The Holy Scriptures According to the Masoretic Text* (Philadelphia: Jewish Publication Society of American, 1955), 583.

39. See Carol Gluck, "The Invention of Edo," in Vlastos, ed., *Mirror of Modernity*, 278.

40. My analysis is based on a videotape of the original, augmented later by a subtitled videotape distributed free of charge by Fans for Fans.

41. Miriam Silverberg, in the last paragraph of "The Cafe Waitress Serving Modern Japan," in Vlastos, ed., *Mirror of Modernity*, 208–25, makes some particularly trenchant connections.

42. Tsuji, *Playfulness in Japanese Art*, 26–27, 56–57, 69, 81–85.

43. *Japan: An Illustrated Encyclopedia* (Tokyo: Kōdansha, 1993), "Kamikaze," 727–28; "Kamikaze Special Attack Force," 728; "Mongol Invasions of Japan," 1000–1001.

44. Miyoshi and Harootunian, "Japan in the World," 2.

45. *Furusato* is addressed, either directly or indirectly, by almost all the contributors to *Mirror of Modernity*, but most explicitly in "Part Two: Village," 67–129. Regarding Miyazaki and Takahata, see Fumiko Y. Yamamoto, "Heisei *Tanuki-Gassen: Pon Poko*," in *Post Script* 18, no. 1 (fall 1998): 59–67.

46. H. D. Harootunian, "Figuring the Folk: History, Poetics, and Representation," in Vlastos, ed., *Mirror of Modernity*, 155, 158.

47. *See* Andrew E. Barshay, "'Doubly Crule: Marxism and the Presence of the Past in Japanese Capitalism," in Vlastos, ed., *Mirror of Modernity*, 243–61, especially 260.

48. Jennifer Robertson, "It Takes a Village Internationalization and Nostalgia in Postwar Japan," in Vlastos, ed., *Mirror of Modernity*, 115.

49. Mary Douglas, *Purity and Danger: An Analysis of Concepts of Pollution and Taboo* (London: Routledge & Kegan Paul, 1966).

50. John T. Dorsey and Naomi Matsuoka, "Narrative Strategies of Understatement in *Black Rain* as a Novel and a Film," in Broderick, ed., *Hibakusha Cinema*, 206.

51. *Honda Inoshirō Shi o Kakonde (Talking with Mr. Honda)* (Tokyo: Kurosawa Kenkyūkai, 1988).

52. Ephraim Katz, *The Film Encyclopedia* (New York: Harper & Row, 1979).

53. Leonard Maltin, *Leonard Maltin's Movie and Video Guide* (New York: Signet, 1998).

54. Joseph L. Andersen and Donald Richie, *The Japanese Film: Art and Industry*, expanded edition (Princeton: Princeton University Press, 1982), 262; originally published in 1959 by Tuttle. See also S. S. Prawer, *Calgari's Children: The Film as Tale of Terror* (New York: Da Capo Press, 1980), 14; Bill Warren, *Keep Watching the Skies!: American Science Fiction Movies of the Fifties*, vol. 1 (Jefferson, NC: McFarland & Co., 1997), 277; Stuart Galbraith IV, *Japanese Science Fiction, Fantasy and Horror Films* (Jefferson, NC: McFarland & Co., 1994), 9.

55. Chon Noriega, "Godzilla and the Japanese Nightmare: When *Them!* Is U.S.," *Cinema Journal* 27 (fall 1987): 63.

56. Kim Newman, "Godzilla 1998," *Sight and Sound* (July 1998): 23. Elsewhere, Newman calls the 1954 Gojira an "unofficial remake" of the American film; see *Apocalypse Movies: End of the World Cinema* (New York: Saint Martin's Griffin, 2000), 87.

57. *Kinema jumpō zōkan: Amerika eiga sakuhin zenshū*, no. 577/*Complete Collections of American Films, 1945–1971* (Tokyo: Kinema Jumpō Sha, 1972), 124.

58. Hitoshi Tomita and Masako Akase, *Meiji no Furansu no bungaku: Furansu gaku kara no shuppatsu (Meiji-era French literature: The beginnings of literature from France)* (Tokyo: Surugadai Shuppansha, 1987), 97, 108.

59. Ken Hollings, "Gojira, Mon Amour," *Sight and Sound* (July 1998): 22.

60. Kawai, *The Japanese Psyche*, 22.

61. Kōhei Ota, Atsushi Ōno, Yōji Orita, and Kōichi Kagawa, a report on *Gamera 3* (April 27, 1999).

62. Richie, "Mono no Aware,'" 78; Susan Sontag, "The Imagination of Disaster," in *Against Interpretation* (New York: Farrar, Straus, and Giroux, 1967), 224; Robert J. Lifton, *Death in Life: Survivors of Hiroshima* (New York: Random House, 1967), 461–63, 570.

63. Paul Boyer, *By the Bomb's Early Light: American Thought and Culture at the Dawn of the Atomic Age* (New York: Pantheon Books, 1985), 194–95.

64. *Man and His Symbols*, C. G. Jung, M.-L. von Franz, et al., eds. (New York: Anchor Books, 1964), 92–93.

65. Joy Willemse, "*Godzilla*, Or Emiko: the Woman of Will," unpublished paper, Hiroshima University, spring 2000). Kawai, *The Japanese Psyche*, chapter 9, and "The Women of Will," 171–90.

66. In an interview, Donald Keene comments on this tendency. "Looking Towards the 21st Century, Interviews with 100 People: the Thoughts of Donald Keene, Number 74," in *Yomiuri shinbun* (November 18, 1998): 12.

67. Noriega, "Godzilla and the Japanese Nightmare," 70–71, 74.

68. Statistically, no Jews reside in Japan. According to *Nippon: The Land and Its People*, Christianity in Japan reached its peak in the early seventh century, was vigorously repressed during World War II, and strictly controlled during the Occupation (Tokyo: Nippon Steel Corporation, 1983, 257). Based on 1993 data, only 1.2 percent of the population is baptized as Christian; Teruo Maruyama, ed., "*Shūkyō*" (Religion), *The Asahi Encyclopedia of Current Terms 1995* (Tokyo: Asahi Shinbun-Sha, 1995), 329, 953. Many Japanese Christians also continue to participate in Buddhist and Shintō practices. A large number of Japanese scholars argue, moreover, that Japan is a "shame" culture rather than a guilt or sin culture, and that there is no word or concept for sin, only for crime.

69. The dominant Christian narrative relies more heavily on Genesis 2:21–24, where Eve is made from Adam, rather than Genesis 1:27, where both are made equally in God's image. There are of course alternative readings to this dominant narrative, including those of Gnostic Christianity and the Mary cult, but these have historically been suppressed in the West and do not seem to play a very important role in either historical Japan or in Noriega's reading of Japan's kaijū eiga.

70. Wade W. Nobles and Lawford L. Goddard, *Understanding the Black Family: A Guide for Scholarship and Research* (Oakland, CA: Institute for the Advanced Study of Black Family Life and Culture, 1984), 19–22. There are two types of transubstantive errors: those made during the "natural cross-cultural process of 'trial and error knowing,'" and those that serve the "process or methodology of scientific colonialism." Noriega's errors are of the former type, and contribute to the development of film studies and cultural understanding.

71. C. G. Jung, "The Psychology of the Child Archetype," 177–78.

72. Tatsuji Miyoshi's poem is entitled "Kyōshū," or "Nostalgia." The characters he refers to are 海 , *umi* or ocean, and 母 , *haha* or mother. Miyoshi's poem was first published in a collection called *Sokuryōsen*, or *A sounding ship*, initial copyright 1930 (Tokyo: Dai Ichi Shobou). I am indebted to my colleague Satotoshi Kanagawa for drawing my attention to Miyoshi's poem. However, another colleague, Yoshimaru Yoda, Kyoto University scholar and poet, pointed out to me that Miyoshi's interpretation of the kanji *umi* is largely idiosyncratic. The kanji for *umi* comes from *mai*, which means "darkness."

73. *The Girl Who Loved Caterpillars*, adapted by Jean Merrill, illustrated by Lloyd Cooper (New York: Putnam & Grosset, 1997), copyright page. Also, *Tsutsumi Chūnagon monogatari* (Tokyo: Hokuseidō Press, 1963).

74. Donald L. Phillippi, trans., *Kojiki* (Tokyo: University of Tokyo Press, 1968), 87, 404–6. Fanny Hagin Mayer, trans. and ed., *The Yanagita Kunio Guide to the Japanese Folk Tale* (Bloomington: Indiana University Press, 1986), 312.

75. I am indebted to Dr. Kazuo Totani, retired advisor to the Imperial Household's silkworm farms, retired, for his insights into the history, science, and lore of the silkworm (interview conducted in Tokyo, spring 1990), and to his niece Professor Masako Notoji, of Tokyo University, for introducing us and interpreting; and to Sachiko Reese, of the Los Angeles C. G. Jung Institute, for her help.

76. Interview with Mr. and Mrs. Honda, conducted on May 1, 1990. Many thanks to my interpreters, Eriko Kamata and Sakura Asoda. Mr. Honda passed away on February 28, 1993; since then Mrs. Honda has continued to support my work, and I am indebted to her.

77. Kawai Hayao, "The Hidden Gods in Japanese Mythology," in *Eranos Yearbook* 54 (1985): 417; the article runs from 397 to 426.

78. <http://www.godzilla.co.jp/>.

79. Noriega, "Godzilla and the Japanese Nightmare," 74.

80. Siegfried Kracauer, *From Caligari to Hitler: A Psychological History of the German Film* (Princeton: Princeton University Press, 1947), 5.

81. Masatsugu Matsuo, conversation with the author, Hiroshima University, May 6, 1999.

82. Hollings, "Gojira, Mon Amour," 20.

83. *Gojira*, and other kaijū films are, without a doubt, the most well-known Japanese films outside of Japan. In California, where I grew up, *Godzilla, King of the Monsters* plays on local TV channels at least four times a year. Godzilla is now so ubiquitous in American culture, that it would be impossible to enumerate the instances in which it appears. Furthermore, people throughout the world seem passionately attached to these monsters and the films, as witnessed by the condemnation of the 1998 American imitator *Godzilla* for failing to live up to expectations. The same cannot be said of American creatures from films of this era. This sentimental, affectionate response to Japanese films and creatures can be seen in any number of places. In Bill Watterson's very popular *Calvin and Hobbes* cartoons (syndicated in countries throughout the world, including Japan), Godzilla is sometimes an inspiration to Calvin's trickster or Hiruko-like, playful misadventures. Clearly, Watterson and his audience respond to Godzilla in ways similar to the Japanese; see *The Essential Calvin and Hobbes: A Calvin and Hobbes Treasury* (Kansas City, MO: Andrews and McMeel, 1998), 65, 94, and especially 189. Watterson also refers once to Osamu Tezuka's animated character *Astro Boy*, or *Tetsuwan Atomu*, which was popular on American TV in the 1960s (217).

84. Tsuji, *Playfulness in Japanese Art*, 26.

85. Jung, "The Psychology of the Child Archetype," 170.

86. Tsuji, *Playfulness in Japanese Art*, 14.

87. "The Conversation: Kurosawa and Garcia Marquez," in *Los Angeles Times,* calendar section (June 23, 1991), 28; Thierry Jousese, "Entretien avec Akira Kurosawa," trans. Catherine Cadou, in *Cahiers du Cinéma* 445 (June 1991): 12; both articles are cited in Goodwin, "Akira Kurosawa and the Atomic Age," in Broderick, ed., *Hibakusha Cinema*, 196, 197.

88. Tsuji, *Playfulness in Japanese Art*, 30, 82.

89. Ibid., 58, 70, 80.

90. Ibid., 27.

91. Ibid., 13–14.

92. Stephen Prince, *The Warrior's Camera: The Cinema of Akira Kurosawa*, rev. expanded ed. (Princeton: Princeton University Press, 1999), 328.

93. Ibid., 356, passim.

94. Mayumi Tanaka, "Apocalypse and the Nuclear Image," unpublished paper (Hiroshima University, spring 2000).

95. Dentists are called *haisha-san*, meaning "dental medical doctor," and have about the same status as an M.D. in the United States.

96. Prince, *The Warrior's Camera*, 169.

97. Tsuji, *Playfulness in Japanese Art*, 16.

98. Eric J. Cassell, *The Nature of Suffering and the Goals of Medicine* (New York: Oxford University Press, 1991), 44. Also, Hayao Kawai, interview with the author, Kyoto, May 6, 1990.

99. Referring to therapies that predate modern medical science as "alternatives" is a clear misnomer, and a further example of who has hegemonic power in the world of medicine.

100. Jerome F. Shapiro, "The Bomb, Japanese Aesthetic Traditions, and Japan's Most Important Film: *Gojira*," *Iconics* 5 (The Japan Society of Image Arts and Sciences, 2000): 93–115.

101. Prince, *The Warrior's Camera*, 314.

102. See Vlastos, ed., *Mirror of Modernity*, passim.

103. See <http://www.tvgen.com/movies/mopic/pictures/34/34165.htm>.

104. Misunderstandings about Japanese film titles are frequent and difficult to avoid. Linda Ehrlich and James Goodwin, among others, incorrectly refer to Kurosawa's film as "*Hachigatsu no Kyōshikyoku*" (in Broderick, ed., *Hibakusha Cinema*, 160 and 178). According to Kurosawa Productions, the *rubi* (indicating a word's pronunciation) on Mr. Kurosawa's screenplay, distributed to all cast and crewmembers, clearly indicates that the word is "rapusodī" Likewise, the rubi on the official film brochure sold in Japanese theaters indicates "rapusodī." Kurosawa Productions prefers that the title be referred to as *hachigatsu no "rapusodī"* but the company does not go out of its way to correct writers who use "kyōshikyoku." Also, the rubi in the reference book *Cinema Club* indicates "rapusodī" (Tokyo: Pia, 1996, 468).

105. I am indebted to Dr. H. Arthur Taussig, Professor of Film and Photography at Orange Coast College, Costa Mesa, CA, and Shin-ichi Anzai of Hiroshima University, for sharing their insights into this film, and for suggesting some of these trains of thought.

106. According to my colleague, Aoki Takao, the story was "depicted in such works as *Genpei-seisuiki* and in the famous medieval epic *Heike monogatari*." The original author of the play *Shunkan* is unknown; however, it is clear that the Kabuki version is derived from Nō and Bunraku puppet plays, particularly Chikamatsu Monzaemon's 1719 Bunraku play *Heike Nyogono-shima*.

107. Prince, *The Warrior's Camera*, passim, 250. Keene, *20 Plays of the Nō Theater*, 123.

108. See Prince's description of this scene in *The Warrior's Camera*, 49–50.

109. Ibid., 29.

110. Linda C. Ehrlich, "The Extremes of Innocence: Kurosawa's Dreams and Rhapsodies," in Broderick, ed., *Hibakusha Cinema*, 160, 172, 173.

111. James Goodwin, "Akira Kurosawa and the Atomic Age," in Broderick, ed., *Hibakusha Cinema*, 200.

112. Stephen Prince, "Memory and Nostalgia in Kurosawa's Dream World," in *Post Script* (fall 1991): 37; and *Warrior's Cinema*, 298.

113. Prince, *Warrior's Cinema*, 319.

114. Ibid., xxii, 313–14, 339.

115. Howard S. Becker, *Art Worlds* (Berkeley: University of California Press, 1982); *Writing for Social Scientists: How to Start and Finish Your Thesis, Book, or Article* (Chicago: University of Chicago Press, 1986).

116. Regarding the "transsubstantive error," see Nobles and Goddard, *Understanding the Black Family*, n. 70. Regarding Aoki and the "western dialog drama," see the introduction.

117. Prince, *The Warrior's Camera*, 3, 9.

118. Kathe Geist, "Late Kurosawa: *Kagemusha* and *Ran*," *Post Script* (fall 1992): 30.

119. David Desser, "*Mādadayo*: No, Not Yet, for the Japanese Cinema," *Post Script* 18, no. 1 (fall 1998): 52–58.

120. Ibid., 58.

121. Ibid., passim. See also *DSM-IV: Diagnostic and Statistical Manual of Mental Disorders* (Washington, D.C.: American Psychiatric Press, 1994); John W. Traphagan, *Taming Oblivion: Aging Bodies and the Fear of Senility in Japan* (Albany: State University of New York Press, 2000).

122. Desser, "*Mādadayo*," 53.

123. "Dementia," *DSM-IV*, 133–55.

124. Desser, "*Mādadayo*," 58.

125. Traphagan, *Taming Oblivion*, passim, 133; Prince, *The Warrior's Camera*, passim, and 356.

126. Traphagan, *Taming Oblivion*, passim.

127. Peter Clecak, *Radical Paradoxes: Dilemmas of the American Left: 1945–1970* (New York: Harper & Row, 1973).

128. Miyoshi and Harootunian, "Japan in the World," 4.

129. While the English edition of the *Yomiuri shinbun* (Japan's largest paper), *The Daily Yomiuri*, covered the Smithsonian incident in great detail, I found only one reference to the Nagasaki incident: "Nagasaki A-Bomb Museum Opens after Photo Flap" (April 2, 1996): 2.

130. *Asahi shinbun* (August 6, 1999): 1; (August 7, 1999): 28; (August 8, 1999): 26.

131. *Asahi shinbun* (August 7, 1999): 28.

132. Nagano was rewarded by *Time* magazine with only one page of coverage, while

Salt Lake City received a grueling five pages. *Time,* Asia edition (February 1, 1999): 44–9.

133. "A Letter from Professor Shapiro: Concerning the Black Face Image in American Culture" (translated into Japanese), *Raifu sutēji,* Kyoto University COOP (February 1992), inside front cover-1.

134. I have not read the hibakushas' complaints, but I have seen a dubbed, English-language version of the episode. The bad monsters that thrive on human blood are indeed outer space hibakusha. But to complain about this one element of the story completely decontextualizes it from the antinuclear peace mongering that is intrinsic to this and virtually all *Ultraman* episodes. See "From Another Planet with Love," episode 12, *Ultra Seven,* 1967.

135. See Ivan P. Hall, *Cartels of the Mind: Japan's Intellectual Closed Shop* (New York: W. W. Norton & Company, 1998). Credible scholars also discuss these issues regularly on the Internet. Two good places to start are <fukuzawa@ucsd.edu> and Dave Aldwinckle's website, <http://www.voicenet.co.jp/~davald/>.

136. Gerald Vizenor, *Manifest Manners: Postindian Warriors of Survivance* (Hanover, NH: Wesleyan University Press, 1994); see also Professor Vizenor's lecture at the now-defunct Kyoto American Center (spring 1994).

137. "Shō-chū-sei no hansū shiranu: Hiroshima keiwa kyōiku ken chōsa (More than half of elementary and middle school students don't know: interim report on the Hiroshima peace education survey)," *Yomiuri shinbun* (July 12, 1996): 29. This periodic report is produced by the Hiroshima Institute for Peace Education.

138. Stephanie Strom, "Art Bought in Boom Disappears," *New York Times,* Weekly Review (August 22, 1999): 8.

Notes to Conclusion

1. C. G. Jung, "The Psychology of the Child Archetype," in *The Archetypes and the Collective Unconscious,* 2d ed. (Princeton: Princeton University Press, 1980), 160.

2. Frank McConnell, *Storytelling and Mythmaking: Images from Film and Literature* (New York: Oxford University Press, 1979), 3.

3. In a capitalist society there is no better indirect measure of interest than money. Considering the dollars that Americans spend on bomb films, there can be no other conclusion than that Americans are deeply concerned about, or at least interested in, the bomb and related issues.

4. John J. Collins, *The Apocalyptic Imagination: An Introduction to the Jewish Matrix of Christianity* (New York: Crossroad, 1989), 13.

5. Richard Rhodes, *The Making of the Atomic Bomb* (New York: Simon & Schuster, 1986), 785.

6. Robert Anton Wilson, interviewed by John Hockenberry on *Heat* (National Public Radio, June 25, 1990). See also Robert Shea and Robert Anton Wilson, *Illuminatus,* parts 1, 2, and 3 (New York: Dell, 1975) and Robert Anton Wilson, *Masks of the Illuminati* (New York: Timescape Books, 1981).

7. Andrew Goldstein with Edward Barnes, "Rights of the Accused: The Far Reach of the Law," *Time*, Asia edition (September 24, 2000): 40.

8. Gerald Vizenor, *Interior Landscapes: Autobiographical Myths and Metaphors* (Minneapolis: University of Minnesota Press, 1990), 197–98, 262.

9. McConnell, *Storytelling and Mythmaking*, 3.

10. Professor Christopher Geist, Department of Popular Culture, Bowling Green State University. I am very much aware of the fact that Professor Geist probably regrets having made these facts public. I am also very much aware of Professor Lifton's age, and that if this story is told at all it needs to be told now while there is still a chance for him to respond.

11. Robert Jay Lifton and Greg Mitchell, *Hiroshima in Japan: Fifty Years of Denial* (New York: G. P. Putnam's Sons, 1995); "The Presidents Have No Regrets," in *The Daily Yomiuri* (August 8, 1996): 10–11. The article is copyrighted and circulated by the *Los Angeles Times*.

12. Paul Boyer, "The Cloud over the Culture: How Americans Imagined the Bomb They Dropped," *New Republic* (August 12 & 19, 1985): 26–31.

13. This phrase was pointed out to me by Toshio Kawai, professor of psychology at Kyoto University, and a practicing Jungian analyst, as an important idea in the minds of many Japanese, particularly clinical psychologists (spring 1994).

14. Gar Alperovitz, *The Decision to Use the Atomic Bomb and the Architecture of an American Myth* (New York: Alfred A. Knopf, 1995).

15. Ibid., 5, 13.

16. Ibid., 3–14, especially 4 and 5. See Paul Boyer, *By the Bomb's Early Light: American Thought and Culture at the Dawn of the Atomic Age* (New York: Pantheon Books, 1985), xv–xx; Kim Newman, *Apocalypse Movies: End of the World Cinema* (New York: Saint Martin's Griffin, 2000), 17–18; James Berger, *After the End: Representations of Post-Apocalypse* (Minneapolis: University of Minnesota Press, 1999) xiv, 3–5, and passim.

17. Boyer, *By the Bomb's Early Light*, 195.

18. Robert Sklar, "*Oh! Althusser!* Historiography and the Rise of Cinema Studies," in *Resisting Images: Essays on Cinema and History*, ed. Robert Sklar and Charles Musser (Philadelphia: Temple University Press, 1990), 20–21.

19. Michael Medved, *Hollywood vs. America: Popular Culture and the War on Traditional Values* (New York: HarperCollins, 1992).

20. *The World and I* 12 (1992), 278–321.

21. See Jerome F. Shapiro, "Hariwuddo Eiga ga Kazōku Oyōbi Kodomo ni Ataeru Eikyō nitsuite Kōsatsu" ("A Study of Hollywood's Influence on Family and Children"), trans. Tomoko Yabe, in *Engeki to Eiga: Dorama no Henbō to Ensyutsu* (*Theater and Cinema: Changes and Directions in Drama*), ed. Takao Aoki (Kyoto: Kouyou Syobou, 1997), 279–87.

22. "Worldview," CNN International (aired in Japan September 17, 2000).

23. Todd S. Purdum, "Behind the Wheel and Driving the Nation's Culture," *New York Times*, Weekly Review (September 17, 2000): 1.

24. Robert Sklar, *Movie-Made America: A Cultural History of American Movies* (New York: Random House, 1975).

25. John Gregory Dunne, "Hollywood Falls for 'Art,'" *New York Times*, Weekly Review (March 23, 1997): 7.

26. Raymond Williams, *Marxism and Literature* (Oxford: Oxford University Press, 1977), 121–27.

27. Jerome F. Shapiro, "A Study of Hollywood's Influence on Family and Children," 279–87; "Atomic Bomb Cinema: Illness, Suffering, and the Apocalyptic Narrative," *Literature and Medicine* (spring 1998): 126–48.

SELECTED BIBLIOGRAPHY

Adler, Gerhard. "Psychology and the Atom Bomb," *Guild Lecture* No. 43. London: The Guild of Pastoral Psychology, August 12, 1946.

Alperovitz, Gar. *The Decision to Use the Atomic Bomb and the Architecture of An American Myth.* New York: Alfred A. Knopf, 1995.

Andersen, Joseph L., and Donald Richie, *The Japanese Film: Art and Industry,* expanded ed. Princeton: Princeton University Press, 1982. Originally published in 1959 by Tuttle.

Aoki, Takao. "Cultural Division of Arts through Modernization in Japan: The Transplantation of Western Arts (Geijutsu) and the Invention of Traditional Arts (Geidoh)." Paper presented at the First International Conference of Eastern Aesthetics in China, Hohhot, July 2000.

———. "The Paradoxical Rebirth of Traditional Theater through the Modernization of Japan: The Case of the Noh Play." Paper presented at the Asia-Pacific Traditional Arts Forum, Taipei, Taiwan, October 1, 2000.

Barash, David P. *The Arms Race and Nuclear War.* Belmont, CA: Wadsworth, 1987.

Berger, James. *After the End: Representations of Post-Apocalypse.* Minneapolis: University of Minnesota Press, 1999.

Biskind, Peter. *Seeing Is Believing: How Hollywood Taught Us to Stop Worrying and Love the Fifties.* New York: Pantheon Books, 1983.

Boyd-Bowman, Susan. "'The Day After'": Representations of the Nuclear Holocaust," *Screen* 24, nos. 4–5 (July–October, 1984): 71–97.

Boyer, Paul. *By the Bomb's Early Light: American Thought and Culture at the Dawn of the Atomic Age.* New York: Pantheon Books, 1985.

———. "The Cloud over the Culture: How Americans Imagined the Bomb They Dropped," *New Republic* (August 12 & 19, 1985): 26–31.

———. *When Time Shall Be No More: Prophecy Belief in Modern American Culture.* Cambridge, MA: Harvard University Press, 1992.

Broderick, Mick. *Nuclear Movies: A Critical Analysis and Filmography of International Feature Length Films Dealing with Experimentation, Aliens, Terrorism, Holocaust and Other Disaster Scenarios, 1914–1989.* Jefferson, NC: McFarland & Company, 1991.

————. "Witnessing the Unthinkable: a Meditation on Film and Nuclear Sublime," *Antithesis* 6, no. 1 (1992): 67–86. Revised copy available at Mick Broderick's homepage: <http://www.1earth.net/~postmodm/pmdefault.html>.

————. "Surviving Armageddon: Beyond the Imagination of Disaster," *Science Fiction Studies* (November 1993), 362–82. Revised copy.

————. "Heroic Apocalypse: Mad Max, Mythology, and the Millennium," in *Crisis Cinema: The Apocalyptic Idea in Postmodern Narrative Film*, ed. Chris Sharrett (Washington DC: Maissoneuvre Press, 1993), 250–72. (Revised copy.)

————. "The Rupture of Rapture: Recent Film Narratives of Apocalypse," *Southern Review* (March 1994): 70–78. Revised copy.

———— ed. *Hibakusha Cinema: Hiroshima, Nagasaki and the Nuclear Image in Japanese Film*. London: Kegan Paul International, 1996.

Buruma, Ian. *Behind the Mask: On the Sexual Demons, Sacred Mothers, Transvestites, Gangsters, and Other Japanese Cultural Heroes*. New York: Pantheon Books, 1984.

Cassell, Eric J. *The Nature of Suffering and the Goals of Medicine*. New York: Oxford University Press, 1991.

Cavell, Stanley. *Pursuits of Happiness: The Hollywood Comedy of Remarriage*. Cambridge, MA: Harvard University Press, 1981.

————. *Contesting Tears: The Hollywood Melodrama of the Unknown Woman*. Chicago: University of Chicago Press, 1996.

Cirlot, J. E. *A Dictionary of Symbols*, 2d. ed., trans. Jack Sage. New York: Philosophical Library, 1971.

Clecak, Peter. *Radical Paradoxes: Dilemmas of the American Left 1945–1970*. New York: Harper & Row, 1973.

————. *Crooked Paths: Reflections on Socialism, Conservatism, and the Welfare State*. New York: Harper & Row, 1977.

————. *America's Quest for the Ideal Self: Dissent and Fulfillment in the 60s and 70s*. Oxford University Press, New York, 1983.

Cohn, Norman. *The Pursuit of the Millennium: Revolutionary Millenarians and Mystical Anarchists of the Middle Ages*, rev. and expanded ed. New York: Oxford University Press, 1970.

Coles, Robert. *The Moral Life of Children*. Boston: Atlantic Monthly Press, 1986.

Collins, John J. *The Apocalyptic Imagination: An Introduction to the Jewish Matrix of Christianity*. New York: Crossroad, 1989.

Cook, David A. *A History of Narrative Film*. New York: W. W. Norton & Company, 1981.

Cook, Pam, ed. *The Cinema Book: A Complete Guide to Understanding the Movies*. New York: Pantheon Books, 1985.

Davidson, Donald. *Inquiries Into Truth and Interpretation*. New York: Oxford University Press, 1984.

Davis, Darrell William. *Picturing Japaneseness: Monumental Style, National Identity, Japanese Film*. New York: Columbia University Press, 1996.

Derrida, Jacques. "No Apocalypse, Not Now (full speed ahead, seven missiles, seven missives)," trans. Catherine Porter and Philip Lewis, *Diacritics* 14, no. 2 (summer 1984): 20–31.

Doane, Mary Ann. *The Desire to Desire: The Woman's Film of the 1940s.* Bloomington: Indiana University Press, 1987.

Dower, John W. *War without Mercy: Race and Power in the Pacific War.* New York: Pantheon Press, 1986.

DSM-IV: Diagnostic and Statistical Manual of Mental Disorders. Washington, D.C.: American Psychiatric Press, 1994.

Ehrlich, Linda C. "The Extremes of Innocence: Kurosawa's Dreams and Rhapsodies," in *Hibakusha Cinema,* ed. Mick Broderick. London: Kegan Paul International, 1996, 160–77.

Erikson, Erik H. *Identity: Youth and Crisis.* London: Faber and Faber, 1968.

Evans, Joyce A. *Celluloid Mushroom Clouds: Hollywood and the Atomic Bomb.* Boulder, CO: Westview Press, 1998.

Evans, Kent, consultant and contributing writer. *The Ultimate Baby Name Book.*

Ferguson, George. *Signs and Symbols in Christian Art.* New York: Oxford University Press, 1961.

Fitting, Peter. "Count Me Out/In: Post-Apocalyptic Visions in Recent Science Fiction Film," *CineAction* no. 11 (December 1987): 42–51.

The Flower Ornament Scripture: A Translation of the Avatamsaka Sutra. 3 vols., trans. Thomas F. Cleary. New York: Random House, 1984–1987.

Foster, Hal, ed. *The Anti-Aesthetic: Essays on Postmodern Culture.* Seattle: Bay Press, 1983.

Franklin, H. Bruce. *Countdown to Midnight: Twelve Great Stories about Nuclear War.* New York: DAW Books, 1984.

———. *War Stars: The Superweapon and the American Imagination.* New York: Oxford University Press, 1988.

Friedman, John Block. *The Monstrous Races in Medieval Art and Thought.* Cambridge, MA: Harvard University Press, 1981.

Fromm, Erich, ed., *Zen Buddhism and Psychoanalysis.* New York: Harper, 1960.

Fussell, Paul. *The Great War and Modern Memory.* New York: Oxford University Press, 1975.

———. *Thank God for the Atomic Bomb.* New York: Summit Books, 1988.

———. *Wartime: Understanding and Behavior in the Second World War.* New York: Oxford University Press, 1989.

Galbraith, Stuart IV. *Japanese Science Fiction, Fantasy, and Horror Films* (Jefferson, NC: McFarland & Company, 1994).

———. *Monsters Are Attacking Tokyo: The Incredible World of Japanese Fantasy Films* (Venice, CA: Feral House, 1998).

Goscilo, Margaret. "Deconstructing *The Terminator*," *Film Criticism* 22, no. 2 (winter 1987–88): 37–51.

Hearn, Lifcadio. *Kwaidan: Strange Stories and Studies of Strange Things.* Dover, 1968.

Hill, Michael Ortiz. *Dreaming the End of the World: Apocalypse As a Rite of Passage.* Dallas: Spring Publications, 1994.

The Holy Scriptures According to the Masoretic Text. Philadelphia: Jewish Publication Society of America, 1955.

Hollings, Ken. "Gojira, Mon Amour," *Sight and Sound* (July 1998): 20–23.

Jameson, Frederic. "Postmodernism and Consumer Society," in *The Anti-Aesthetic: Essays on Postmodern Culture*, ed. Hal Foster. Seattle: Bay Press, 1983, 111–25.

Jarvie, I. C. *Movies As Social Criticism: Aspects of Their Social Psychology*. Metuchen, NJ: Scarecrow Press, 1978.

Jowett, Garth S. "Hollywood, Propaganda, and the Bomb: Nuclear Images in Post World War II Films," *Film and History* 18, no. 2 (May 1988): 26–38.

Jung, C. G. *Memories, Dreams, Reflections*, ed. Aniela Jaffé, trans. Richard and Clara Winston. New York: Random House, 1961.

———. "The Psychology of the Child Archetype," in *The Archetypes and the Collective Unconscious*, 2d ed. Princeton: Princeton University Press, 1980,. 151–81.

Kawai, Hayao. "The Hidden Gods in Japanese Mythology," *Eranos Yearbook* 54 (1985): 397–426.

———. *The Japanese Psyche: Major Motifs in the Fairy Tales of Japan*, trans. Hayao Kawai and Sachiko Reese. Dallas: Spring Publications, 1988. First published as *Mukashibanashi to Nihonjin no Kokoro* (Tokyo: Iwanami Shoten, 1982).

Kermode, Frank. *The Sense of An Ending: Studies in the Theory of Fiction*. New York: Oxford University Press, 1968.

Kinema Jumpō Zōkan: Amerika Eiga Sakuhin Zenshū no. 577. *Complete Collections of American Films, 1945–1971*. Tokyo: Kinema Jumpo Sha, April 30, 1972.

Kirk, Russell, ed. *The Portable Conservative Reader*. New York: Viking Penguin, 1982.

Kojiki. Trans., Donald L. Phillippi. Tokyo: University of Tokyo Press, 1968.

Kokin Wakashū: The First Imperial Anthology of Japanese Poetry, with Tosa Nikki and Shinsen Waka, trans. and annotated Helen Craig McCullough. Stanford, CA: Stanford University Press, 1985.

Kracauer, Siegfried. *From Caligari to Hitler: A Psychological History of the German Film*. Princeton: Princeton University Press, 1947.

Kurita, Isamu. *Setsugetsuka no kokoro/Japanese Identity*. Tokyo: Shodensha, 1987.

Honda Inoshiro shi o kakonde (Talking with Mr. Inoshiro Honda). Tokyo: Kurosawa Kenkyukai, 1988.

Langer, Susan K. *Philosophy in a New Key: A Study in the Symbolism of Reason, Rite, and Art*, 3d ed. Cambridge, MA: Harvard University Press, 1974.

Lasch, Christopher. *The Minimal Self: Psychic Survival in Troubled Times*. New York: W. W. Norton, 1984.

Lasky, Melvin J. *Utopia and Revolution: On the Origins of a Metaphor, or Some Illustrations of the Problem of Political Temperament and Intellectual Climate and How Ideas, Ideals, and Ideologies Have Been Historically Related*. Chicago: University of Chicago Press, 1976.

Lifton, Robert J. *Death in Life: Survivors of Hiroshima*. Rev. Chapel Hill: University of North Carolina Press, 1991. First published in 1967 by Random House.

———. *The Broken Connection: On Death and the Continuity of Life*. New York: Simon & Schuster, 1979.

———. "The Presidents Have No Regrets," *The Daily Yomiuri* (August 8, 1996): 10–11.

Lifton, Robert J., and Greg Mitchell. *Hiroshima in America: Fifty Years of Denial*. New York: G. P. Putnam's Sons, 1995.

Lipman, Steve. *Laughter in Hell: The Use of Humor during the Holocaust.* Northvale, NJ: Jason Aronson, 1993.

Lippit, Akira Mizuta. "Catastrophic Light: Transparency, Invisibility, and Atomic Representation," *Public* 18 (Toronto, Ontario: Public Access, 1999): 14–23.

———. "Phenomenologies of the Surface: Radiation-Body-Image," in *Collecting Visible Evidence.* Visible Evidence vol. 6., eds. Jane M. Gaines and Michael Renov. Minneapolis: University of Minnesota Press, 1999. 65–83.

Loughead, Flora Haines. *Dictionary of Given Names.* 2d ed., rev. and corrected. Glendale, CA: Arthur H. Clark, 1981.

Malone, Peter. *Nuclear Films.* Richmond, Australia: Spectrum, 1985.

McConnell, Frank. *Storytelling and Mythmaking: Images from Film and Literature.* New York: Oxford University Press, 1979.

Metz, Christian. *The Imaginary Signifier*, trans. Celia Britton et al. Bloomington: Indiana University Press, 1982.

Mills, C. Wright. *The Sociological Imagination.* New York: Oxford University Press, 1959.

The Motion Picture Guide, 1990 Annual (The Films of 1989). 1990. Evanston, IL: Cinebooks.

Miyoshia, Masao, and H. D. Harootunian. "Japan in the World," *Boundary 2* (fall 1991): 4–5.

Nash, Jay Robert, and Stanley Ralph Ross. *The Motion Picture Guide,* vols. 5 and 8. Chicago: Cinebooks, 1985.

Nash, Jay Robert, and Stanley Ralph Ross. *The Motion Picture Guide, 1986 Annual (The Films of 1985).* Chicago: Cinebooks, 1987.

Necakov, Lillian. "*The Terminator*: Beyond Classical Hollywood Narrative," *CineAction* no. 8 (March 1987): 84–87.

Newman, Kim. "Godzilla 1998," *Sight and Sound* (July 1998): 23.

———. *Apocalypse Movies: End of the World Cinema.* New York: Saint Martin's Griffin, 2000.

Nobles, Wade W., and Lawford L. Goddard. *Understanding the Black Family: A Guide for Scholarship and Research.* Oakland, CA: Institute for the Advanced Study of Black Family Life and Culture, 1984.

Noriega, Chon. "Godzilla and the Japanese Nightmare: When *Them!* Is U.S.," *Cinema Journal* (fall 1987): 63–77.

Nuttall, Jeff. *Bomb Culture.* New York: Delacorte Press, 1968.

Palmer, William J. *The Films of the Eighties: A Social History.* Carbondale: Southern Illinois University Press, 1993.

Penley, Constance. "Time Travel, Primal Scene and the Critical Dystopia," in *Fantasy and the Cinema*, ed. James Donald. London: British Film Institute, 1989, 196–212. First published in *Camera Obscura* no. 15, 1988.

Perrine, Toni A. *Film and the Nuclear Age: Representing Cultural Anxiety.* New York: Garland, 1998.

Prawer, S. S. *Caligari's Children: The Film as Tale of Terror.* New York: Da Capo Press, 1980.

Prince, Stephen. *The Warrior's Camera: The Cinema of Akira Kurosawa*, rev. and expanded ed. Princeton: Princeton University Press, 1991.

Richie, Donald. "'Mono No Aware'/Hiroshima in Film," *Film: Book 2: Films of Peace and War*, ed. Robert Hughes. New York: Grove Press, 1962. 67–86.

Rhodes, Richard. *The Making of the Atomic Bomb*. New York: Simon & Schuster, 1986.

Sackett, Susan. *Box Office Hits: A Year by Year, Behind the Camera Look at Hollywood's Most Successful Movies*. New York: Billboard Books, 1990.

Said, Edward W. *Orientalism*. New York: Pantheon Books, 1978.

Sayre, Nora. *Running Time: Films of the Cold War*. New York: Dial Press, 1982.

Schell, Jonathan. *The Fate of the Earth*. New York: Avon Books, 1982.

Shaheen, Jack G., ed. *Nuclear War Films*. Carbondale: Southern Illinois University Press, 1978.

Silver, Alain, and Elizabeth Ward, eds. *Film Noir: An Encyclopedic Reference to the American Style*. Woodstock, NY: Overlook Press, 1979.

Sklar, Robert, *Movie-Made America: A Cultural History of American Movies*. New York: Random House, 1975.

Sklar, Robert, and Charles Musser, eds. *Resisting Images: Essays on Cinema and History*. Philadelphia: Temple University Press, 1990.

Slotkin, Richard. *Regeneration through Violence: The Mythology of The American Frontier, 1600–1860*. Middletown, CT: Wesleyan University Press, 1973.

Sontag, Susan. "The Imagination of Disaster," in *Against Interpretation*. New York: Farrar, Straus and Giroux, 1967. 209–25.

Spoto, Donald. *The Art of Alfred Hitchcock: Fifty Years of His Motion Pictures*. New York: Hopkins and Blake, 1976.

———. *The Art of Alfred Hitchcock: Fifty Years of His Motion Pictures*. 2d ed., completely revised and updated. New York: Anchor Books: 1992.

Suzuki, D. T. *Zen and Japanese Culture*. Princeton: Bollingen Paperback, 1970.

Todorov, Tzvetan. *The Conquest of America: The Question of the Other*, trans. Richard Howard. New York: Harper Colophon, 1984.

Traphagan, John W. *Taming Oblivion: Aging Bodies and the Fear of Senility in Japan*. Albany: State University of New York Press, 2000.

Tsuji, Nobuo. *Playfulness in Japanese Art*, trans. Joseph Seubert. Lawrence, KS: Spencer Museum of Art, University of Kansas, 1986.

Twitchell, James B. *Dreadful Pleasures: An Anatomy of Modern Horror*. New York: Oxford University Press, 1985.

Vizenor, Gerald. *Bearheart: The Heirship Chronicles*. Minneapolis: University of Minnesota Press, 1990. First published by Truck Press, 1978.

———. *Matsushima: Pine Islands Haiku*. Minneapolis: Nodin Press, 1984.

———. *Interior Landscapes: Autobiographical Myths and Metaphors*. Minneapolis: University of Minnesota Press, 1990.

———. *Manifest Manners: Postindian Warriors of Survivance*. Hanover, NH: Wesleyan University Press, 1994.

Vlastos, Stephen, ed. *Mirror of Modernity: Invented Traditions of Modern Japan*. Berkeley: University of California Press, 1998.

Warren, Bill. *Keep Watching the Skies! American Science Fiction Art Movies of the Fifties*. Jefferson, NC: McFarland & Company, 1997.

Warshow, Robert. *The Immediate Experience: Movies, Comics, Theatre and Other Aspects of Popular Culture.* New York: Athenum, 1972.

Weart, Spencer R. *Nuclear Fear: A History of Images.* Cambridge, MA: Harvard University Press, 1988.

White, Joseph L. *The Psychology of Blacks: An Afro-American Perspective.* Englewood Cliffs, NJ: Prentice-Hall, 1984.

———. *The Troubled Adolescent.* New York: Pergamon Press, 1989.

Whyte, William H. Jr. *The Organization Man.* New York: Doubleday Anchor Books, 1957.

Wiesel, Elie. *A Passover Haggadah.* New York: Simon & Schuster, 1993.

Williams, Raymond. *Marxism and Literature.* Oxford: Oxford University Press, 1977.

Yanagita, Kunio. *The Yanagita Kunio Guide to the Japanese Folk Tale*, trans. and ed. Fanny Hagin Mayer. Bloomington: Indiana University Press, 1986.

Yamamoto, Fumiko Y. "*Heisei Tanuki-Tassen: Pon Poko,*" *Post Script* 18, no. 1 (fall 1998): 59–67.

FILMOGRAPHY

Bomb films released in the United States

Introduction

This filmography is exclusive rather than inclusive. The films, foreign or domestic, must have been released in the United States. They must also meet the criteria described in the introduction. In brief, a mere allusion or reference to the bomb, as in *Operation Petticoat* (Blake Edwards, 1959), is not enough to warrant inclusion; the bomb must be a significant part of the film. Some scholars include *The Best Years of Our Lives* (William Wyler, 1946), *The Lady from Shanghai* (Orson Welles, 1948), and even *Raising Arizona* (Joel Coen, 1987) in their filmographies, but I do not because they do not meet my criteria. I have seen most but not all of the films included in this filmography. Film reviews are occasionally inaccurate. If a review or filmography suggests that a film I have not seen is a bomb film, then I corroborate by checking several other references to ensure that the film truly warrants inclusion. In some cases I even contact the reviewer. For foreign films, I use, whenever available, the date the film was released in the United States; for Japanese films I try also to note the original release date. Different references, however, give vastly different information for the same film. It is remarkable that three different directors have been credited for the Japanese animated film *Barefoot Gen 2*, and in the years 1983, 1995, and 1998. Different editions of the same reference also vary. Earlier editions of one reference give 1956 as the year for *Godzilla, King of the Monsters* and 1962 for *Mothra* (both by Inoshirō Honda), while later editions give 1954 and 1961. In only a few instances, however, did I have to make an educated judgment about whether or not to include a film. In order to avoid skewing the data in a way that overstates my case, moreover, I generally err on the side of caution and exclude the film if its relevance is questionable. I am therefore confident that this filmography, and also my statistical summaries and my quantitative interpretations, are very reliable. This filmography is based on years of exhaustive research. My sources include *TV Guide This Week* (TV Guide, Inc.), which I read weekly for several years; various editions of *Leonard Maltin's Movie and Video Guide* (New York: Penguin), which I read cover to cover; *The Motion Picture Guide* (New York: CineBooks, and online: *TV Guide* (<www.tvguide.com/movies/database/>); *Magill's Survey of*

Cinema (Englewood Cliffs, NJ: SalemPress, <http://library.dialog.com/bluesheets/html/bl0299.html/>); *The Internet Movie Database* <http://us.impd.com/>); *Yahoo! Movies* (<http://movies.yahoo.com/movies/>). I have also used the annual Japanese publication *Pia shinema kurabu* or *Pia Cinema Club: Japanese Film Data Base Book* (Tokyo: Pia) and a number of other books included in the bibliography, such as Mick Broderick's indispensable *Nuclear Movies* (Jefferson, NC: McFarland & Company, 1991). The data for the numbers of all films released in a given year come from Cobbett S. Steinberg's *Film Facts* (New York: Facts on File Inc., 1980, 42–43), and the "U.S. Economic Review" pages of the Motion Picture Association of America's website (<www.mpaa.org/>).

ABBREVIATIONS

*	A number derived statistically from preceding and succeeding years.
/	Usually indicates "and," but can also suggest "or," or an ambiguity.
CTVM	Cable television movie.
NA	Information is not available.
TVM	Television movie; some TVMs are compilations or derivative in some way.
TVMINI	TV miniseries.
TVP	TV play, playhouse, or program.
V	Direct to video.

AS	Austria	GR	Germany, pre-	PO	Poland
AU	Australia		1949, and after	RO	Romania
BE	Belgium		unification	RU	Russia
BR	Brazil	HK	Hong Kong	SA	South Africa
BU	Bulgaria	HU	Hungary	SP	Spain
CA	Canada	IC	Iceland	SU	Soviet Union
CH	China	IL	Ireland	SW	Sweden
CU	Cuba	IR	Iran	SZ	Switzerland
CZ	Czechoslovakia	IS	Israel	TH	Thailand
DM	Denmark	IT	Italy	UK	Ukraine
ES	Estonia	JA	Japan	US	United States[1]
EY	Egypt	LX	Luxembourg	WA	Wales
FR	France	MX	Mexico	WG	West Germany
FL	Finland	NO	Norway	YU	Yugoslavia
GB	Great Britain	NZ	New Zealand		
GE	Greece	PH	Philippines		

[1] *Note*: In most cases, films produced in the United States are not indicated as such unless coproduced in another country (e.g.: US/GB).

YEAR: NUMBER OF BOMB FILMS / ALL FILMS

1914: 1/NA
By Radium Rays (Turner)

1915: 0/NA

1916: 0/NA

1917: 1/687 (US films only)
Greatest Power, The (Carewe)

1918: 0/841(US films only)

1919: 1/646 (US films only)
Great Radium Mystery, The
(Hill, Serial)

1920: 1/796 (US films only)
Invisible Ray, The (Pollard, serial)

1921: 0/854 (US films only)

1922: 0/748 (US films only)

1923: 0/576 (US films only)

1924: 1/579 (US films only)
Broadway or Bust
(Sedgwick, serial)

1925: 1/579 (US films only)
God of Power, The (Wilson)

1926: 0/740 (US films only)

1927: 0/743

1928: 0/884

1929: 0/707

1930: 0/595

1931: 1/622
Danger Island (Taylor, serial)

1932: 0/685

1933: 0/644

1934: 1/622
Gold (Hartl, GR)

1935: 3/766
Phantom Empire, The
(Brower/Eason, originally a serial) a.k.a. *Radio Ranch*; *Men with Steel Faces*
Queen of the Jungle (Hill)
Tunnel, The (Elvey, GB)

1936: 4/735
Ace Drummond (Smith/Beebe, serial)
Ghost Patrol (Newfield)

Invisible Ray (Hillyer)
Walking Dead, The (Curtiz)

1937: 1/778
Nothing Sacred (Wellman)

1938: 0/769

1939: 1/761
Shadow Creeps, The
(Beebe/Goodkind, serial) a.k.a.
The Phantom Creeps

1940: 1/673
Dr. Cyclops (Schoedsack)

1941: 0/598

1942: 0/533

1943: 2/427
Batman (Hillyer, serial) a.k.a. *An Evening with Batman and Robin* ('65 TVM)
Madame Curie (LeRoy)

1944: 0/442

1945: 5/377
Charlie Chan and the Red Dragon (Rosen) a.k.a. *The Red Dragon*: *Charlie Chan in Mexico.*
First Yank into Tokyo (Douglas)
House on 92nd Street, The (Hathaway)
Manhunt of Mystery Island (Brissel/Canutt/Wallace, serial) a.k.a. *Captain Mephisto and the Transformation Machine* (1966)
Shadow of Terror (Landers)

1946: 9/467
Cloak and Dagger (Lang)
Crimson Ghost, The (Witney, serial) a.k.a. *Cyclotrode "X"* (1966 reissue)
Danger Woman (Collins)
Flight to Nowhere (Rowland)
Lisbon Story (Stein, GB)
Lost City of the Jungle (Taylor, serial)
Night Boat To Dublin (Huntington, GB)
Notorious (Hitchcock)
Rendezvous 24 (Tinling)

1947: 6/489

Beginning or the End, The (Taurog)
Black Widow, The (Spencer)
Brick Bradford (Bennet, Serial)
Jack Armstrong (Fox, Serial)
My Favorite Brunette (Nugent)
Operation Swallow: The Battle for Heavy Water (Vibe-Müller, NO/FR) a.k.a. *La Bataille De L'eau Lourde*

1948: 6/459

Iron Curtain, The (Wellman)
Krakatit (Vávra, CZ) remade as *The Black Sun* (1979)
Sofia (Reinhardt)
Under the Frozen Falls (Catling, GB)
Walk a Crooked Mile (Douglas)
Who Killed "Doc" Robbin? (Carr)

1949: 3/470

Beauty and the Devil (Clair, FR) a.k.a. *La Beaute Du Biable; The Devil's Beauty*
Dick Barton Strikes Back (Grayson, GB)
Project X (Montague)

1950: 10/622

Atom Man versus Superman (Bennet, serial)
Destination Moon (Pichel)
D.O.A. (Maté)
Experiment Alcatraz (Cahn)
Flying Missile, The (Levin)
Flying Saucer, The (Conrad)
Mister Drake's Duck (Guest, GB)
Rocketship X-M (Neumann)
Seven Days to Noon (Boulting, GB)
Utopia (Joannon, FR) a.k.a. *Atoll K*

1951: 10/654

Captain Video (Bennet, serial)
Day the Earth Stood Still, The (Wise)
Five (Oboler)
Flying Disk Man From Mars (Brannon, serial), a.k.a. *Missile Monsters* (1958)
House in the Square (Baker, GB)
Lost Continent (Newfield)
Ma and Pa Kettle Back on the Farm (Sedgwick)

Superman and the Mole Men (Sholem)
Thing From Another World, The (Nyby)
Unknown World (Morse)

1952: 12/463

Above and Beyond (Frank/Panama)
Atomic City, The (Hopper)
Captive Women (Gilmore) a.k.a. *1000 Years from Now; 3000 AD*
Carmen's Pure Love (Kinoshita, JA) a.k.a. *Karumen junjōsu*
Children of the Atomic Bomb, The (Shindo, JA) a.k.a. *Genbaku no ko; Children of Hiroshima*
I'll Not Forget the Song of Nagasaki (Tasaka, JA) a.k.a. *Nagasaki no uta wa wasureji*
Invasion USA (Green)
Radar Men from the Moon (Brannon, serial) a.k.a. *Ritik, the Moon Menace* (1966, TVM)
Red Planet Mars (Horner)
Thief, The (Rouse)
White Corridors (Jackson, GB)
Zombies of the Stratosphere (Brannon, serial) re-edited as *Satan's Satellites* (1958)

1953: 19/534

Atomic Blonde (Landers) a.k.a. *Run for the Hills*
Beast from 20,000 Fathoms, The (Lourie)
Bell of Nagasaki, The (Oba, JA) a.k.a. *Nagasaki no kane*
Canadian Mounties vs. Atomic Invaders (Adreon)
5000 Fingers of Doctor T, The (Rowland)
49th Man, The (Sears)
I'll Get You (Friedman, GB) a.k.a. *Escape Route*
Invaders from Mars (Menzies)
Lost Planet, The (Bennet, serial)
Magnetic Monster, The (Siodmak)
Mr. Potts Goes to Moscow (Zampi, GB) a.k.a. *Top Secret*
Number Three (Harrison, GB TVM)
Pickup on South Street (Fuller)

Robot Monster (Tucker)
Savage Mutiny (Bennet)
Silver Dust (Room, SU) a.k.a.
Sieriebristaya Pyl
Split Second (Powell)
U-238 and the Witch Doctor
(Brannon) a.k.a. Jungle Drums of
Africa
War of the Worlds, The (Haskin)

1954: 22/427

Atomic Attack (Motorola)
Atomic Kid, The (Martinson)
Beat the Devil (Huston)
Child's Play (Thomson, GB)
Colonel March: "Case of the
Misguided Missile"
Fusion Bomb, The (NA, NA)
Godzilla (Honda, JA) a.k.a. Gojira;
Godjira
Gog (Strock)
Hell and High Water (Fuller)
Killers from Space (Wilder)
Living It Up (Taurog)
Operation Manhunt (Alexander)
Paris Playboys (Beaudine)
Port of Hell (Schuster)
Stranger from Venus (Balaban) a.k.a.
Immediate Disaster
Target Earth (Rose)
Terror Ship (Sewell, GB)
Them! (Douglas)
This Island Earth (Newman)
Tobor the Great (Sholem)
20,000 Leagues Under the Sea
(Fleischer)
World for Ransom (Aldrich)

1955: 18/392

Atomic Man, The (Hughes, GB)
Bride of the Atom (Woods) a.k.a.
Bride of the Monster
Bullet For Joey, A (Allen)
Canyon Crossroads (Werker)
Carolina Cannonball (Lamont)
Case of the Red Monkey (Hughes,
GB)
Creature with the Atom Brain (Cahn)
Devil Girl from Mars (MacDonald)
Hiroshima (Sekigawa, JA 1953)

It Came from Beneath the Sea
(Gordon)
King Dinosaur (Gordon)
Kiss Me Deadly (Aldrich)
McConnel Story, The (Douglas)
Record of a Living Being (Kurosawa,
JA) a.k.a. Ikimono no kiroku; I
Knew What the Birds Knew; I
Live in Fear
Shack Out on 101 (Dein)
Strategic Air Command (Mann)
Tarantula (Arnold)
Voices, The (Vance, GB, TVM)

1956: 18/479

Calabuch (Berlanga, SP/IT)
a.k.a. The Rocket from Calabuch
Day the World Ended, The (Corman)
Dig That Uranium (Bernds)
Forbidden Area (Frankenheimer,
TVM)
Forbidden Planet (Wilcox)
Godzilla, King of the Monsters
(Honda, JA; Morse, USA; note:
Toho's date is 1955) a.k.a. Kaijū
Ō Gojira
Gamma People, The (Gilling, GB)
Jungle Boy (Cerf) a.k.a. Jungle Hell
Phantom from 10,000 Leagues
(Milner)
Plan 9 from Outer Space (Wood)
Rodan (Honda, JA) a.k.a. Sora no
daikaijū Radon
Satellite in the Sky (Dickson, GB)
Spy for Germany (Klinger, WG) a.k.a.
Spion für Deutschland;
Meisterspion Gimpel
Uranium Boom (Castle)
Warning from Space (Shima, JA)
AKA Uchūjin Tokyō ni arawaru;
The Mysterious Satellite
Werewolf, The (Sears)
World Without End (Bernds)
"X" the Unknown (Norman, GB)

1957: 23/533

Amazing Colossal Man, The
(Gordon)
Attack of the Crab Monster (Corman)
Beginning of the End (Gordon)

Bombers B-52 (Douglas)
Cyclops, The (Gordon)
From Hell It Came (Milner)
Giant Claw, The (Sears)
Incredible Shrinking Man, The
    (Arnold)
Invisible Boy, The (Hoffman)
I Was a Teenage Werewolf (Fowler)
King in New York, A (Chaplin, GB)
Kronos (Neumann)
Mad Little Island (Relph, GB) a.k.a.
    Rockets Galore!
Monster That Challenged the World,
    The (Laven)
Monsters from Green Hell (Crane)
Mysterians, The (Honda, JA) a.k.a.
    Chikyū bōeigun
Night the World Exploded, The (Sears)
Not of this Earth (Corman)
Quatermass II: Enemy from Space
    (Guest, GB)
Spies, The (Clouzot, FR) a.k.a. Les
    Espions
Story of Mankind, The (Allen)
Story of Pure Love, A (Imai, JA) a.k.a.
    Jun'ai monogatari
27th Day, The (Asher)

1958: 27/507

Astounding She-Monster, The
    (Ashcroft, NA)
Attack of the 50 Foot Woman (Juran)
Brain from Planet Arous, The (Juran)
Cosmic Monster, The (Gunn, GB)
Crawling Eye, The (Lawrence, GB)
Curse of the Faceless Man (Cahn)
Day the Sky Exploded, The (Heusch,
    IT/FR) a.k.a. Death Come from
    Outer Space; La Morte Viene
    Dallo Spazio
Earth vs. the Spider (Gordon)
Fabulous World of Jules Verne, The
    (Zeman, CZ)
Fearmakers, The (Tourneur)
Fiend without a Face (Crabtree, GB)
Frankenstein–1970 (Koch)
Giant from the Unknown (Cunha)
H-Man, The (Honda, JA) a.k.a. Bijo
    to ekitai ningen
It! The Terror from Beyond Space
    (Cahn)

Lost Missile, The (Berke)
Mark of the Phoenix (Rogers, GB)
Monster on the Campus (Arnold)
    a.k.a. Monster in the Night
Night of the Blood Beast (Kowalski)
Queen of Outer Space (Bernds)
Rally 'Round the Flag Boys
    (McCarey)
Secret Man, The (Kinnoch, GB)
Space Children, The (Arnold)
Teenage Caveman (Corman)
Terror from the Year 5,000 (Gurney)
    a.k.a. Cage of Doom
War of the Colossal Beast (Gordon)
    a.k.a. Revenge of the Colossal
    Beast; Terror Strikes
War of the Satellites (Corman)

1959: 22/439

Alligator People, The (Del Ruth)
Angry Red Planet, The (Melchior)
Atomic Agent (Decoin, FR) a.k.a.
    Nathalie, Agent Secret
Atomic Submarine, The (Bennet)
Attack of the Giant Leeches
    (Kowalski)
Caltiki, the Immortal Monster
    (Hampton, IT)
City of Fear (Lerner)
Cosmic Man, The (Greene)
First Man into Space (Day, GB)
4D Man (Yeaworth)
Giant Behemoth, The (Lourie, GB)
    a.k.a. Behemoth, The Sea Monster
Gigantis, the Fire Monster (Odo, JA
    1955) a.k.a. Gojira no gyakushu;
    Godzilla's Counterattack; The
    Return of Godzilla
Hideous Sun Demon (Clarke)
Invisible Invaders (Cahn)
Island of Lost Women (Tuttle)
Li'l Abner (Panama/Frank)
Lucky Dragon No. 5 (Shindo, JA)
    Daigo fukuryū maru
Mouse That Roared, The (Arnold,
    GB)
On the Beach (Kramer)
Rocket Attack, U.S.A. (Mahon)
30-Foot Bride of Candy Rock, The
    (Miller)
World, the Flesh, and the Devil, The

(MacDougall)

1960: 16/387

Amazing Transparent Man, The
(Ulmer)

Battle in Outer Space (Honda, JA)

Beyond the Time Barrier (Ulmer)

Final War, The (Hidaka, JA) a.k.a.
*World War III Breaks Out;
WW III: 41 Hours of Fear; Dai
sanji sekai taisen-yonju-ichi jikan
no kyofu; 41 jikan no kyofu*

First Spaceship on Venus (Maetzig,
EG/PO) a.k.a. *'60 Der
Schweigende Stern, & Milczaca
Gwiazda*

Follow That Horse (Bromly, GB)

Hiroshima, Mon Amour (Resnais,
FR/JA 1959) a.k.a. *Nijūyo jikan
no jyōji*

I Aim at the Stars (Thompson)

Neutron vs. The Death Robots (Curiel,
MX) a.k.a. *Los Autómatas de la
Muerte*

Revenge of the Dead (Wood) a.k.a.
Night of the Ghouls

S.O.S. Pacific (Green, GB)

Thousand Eyes of Dr. Mabuse, The
(Lang, WG)

Time Machine, The (Pal)

Twelve to the Moon (Bradley)

Village of the Damned (Rilla, GB)

War (Bulajic, YU), a.k.a. *Rat*

1961: 14/462

Absent-Minded Professor, The
(Stevensen)

Atlantis, the Lost Continent (Pal)

Atom Age Vampire (Majano, IT),
a.k.a. *Seddok, L' Erede di Santana*

Beast of Yucca Flats, The (Francis)

Candide (Carbonnaux, FR)

Final War, The (Hidaka, JA) a.k.a.
*Dai sanji taisen-yonju-ichi jikan
no kyofu*

Flight That Disappeared, The
(LeBorg)

Last War, The (Matsubayashi, JA),
a.k.a. *Sekai dai sensō*

Most Dangerous Man Alive, The
(Dwan)

Neutron and The Black Mask (Curiel,
MX), a.k.a. *Neutrón el
Enmascarado Negro*

Poisoned Earth, The (Wrede, GB,
TVM)

Ship That Couldn't Stop, The (Cooke,
GB, TVP)

Voyage to the Bottom of the Sea (Allen)

X-15 (Donner)

1962: 20/427

Bomb Has Been Stolen, A (Popescu-
Gopo, RO), a.k.a. *S-A Furat O
Bomba; A Bomb Was Stolen*

Creation of the Humanoids, The
(Barry)

Day Mars Invaded Earth, The
(Dexter)

Day the Earth Caught Fire, The
(Guest, GB)

Devil's Messenger, The (Strock/
Siodmark, US/SW)

Dr. No (Young, GB)

*Great Big World and Little Children,
The* (Sokolwska, PO) a.k.a.
Wielka Wielksza Najwielksza

Mothra (Honda, JA '61; Kresel,
USA), a.k.a. *Mosura*

Neutron vs. the Amazing Dr. Caront
(Curiel, MX), *Neutrón Contra El
Dr. Caronte*

Nine Days of One Year (Romm, SU)
a.k.a. *Devyat Dnei Odnogo Goda*

Neutron vs. the Maniac (Crevenuna,
MX)

Nuovo Mond, Il (Godard, IT/FR)
short in the film, *RoGoPag*, a.k.a.
*Laviamoci il cervello; Let's Have a
Brain Wash*

Panic in Year Zero (Milland)

Slime People, The (Hutton)

Sun and Shadow (Vylchanov, BU),
a.k.a. *Sinceto I Sjankata*

This Is Not a Test (Gadette)

Three Stooges in Orbit, The (Bernds)

Time of the Heathen (Kass)

Varan, the Unbelievable (Honda, JA
1958; Baerwitz, US) a.k.a.
Taigaijū Baran

Winter Light (Bergman, SW)

1963: 19/420

Atragon (Honda, JA) a.k.a. *Atragon, The Flying Super Sub; Kaitei gunkan*

Attack of the Mushroom People (Honda, JA), a.k.a. *Matango*

Brain That Wouldn't Die, The (Green)

Danger Zone (O'Ferrall, GB, TVM)

Dogora, the Space Monster (Honda, JA) a.k.a. *Uchū daikaijū dogora; Space Monster Dogora*

From Russia with Love (Young, GB)

Gathering of Eagles, A (Mann)

Haber's Photo Shop (Vorkonyi, HU), a.k.a. *Foto Haber*

King Kong vs. Godzilla (Honda, JA 1962; Montgomery, US) a.k.a. *Kingu Kongu tai Gojira*

Ladybug, Ladybug (Perry)

Lord of the Flies (Brook, GB)

Man Wants to Live (Moguy, FR) a.k.a. *Les Hommes Veulent Vivre*

Master Spy (Montgomery, GB)

No Survivors, Please (Albin, WG) a.k.a. *Der Chef Wuenscht Keine Zeugen*

Prize, The (Robson)

Shock Corridor (Fuller)

Son of Flubber (Stevenson)

Twice Told Tales (Salkow)

Voyage to the End of the Universe (Polak, CZ) a.k.a. *Ikarie XB-I; Icarus XB-I*

1964: 21/502

Atomic Rulers of the World (Ishi/Mitsuwa/ Akasaka, JA) apparently compiled from 1956 TV's *Kotetsu no kyojin;* a.k.a. *Supergiant; Super Giant 3&4.*

Children of the Damned (Leader, GB)

Crunch, The (Elliot, GB, TVM)

Demon from Devil's Lake, The (Marker)

Dr. Strangelove or: How I Learned to Stop Worrying and Love the Bomb (Kubrick, GB)

Fail Safe (Lumet)

Ghidora, The Three-Headed Monster (Honda, JA) a.k.a. *Sandaikaijū Chichūsadai no kessen; King Ghidorah*

Godzilla vs. the Thing (Honda, JA) a.k.a., *Mosura tai Gojira; Godzilla vs. Mothra* (TV title)

Goldfinger (Hamilton, GB)

Horror of Party Beach (Tenney) a.k.a. *Invasion of the Zombies*

Human Vapor, The (Honda, JA) a.k.a. *Gasu ningen dai ichigo*

Jetée, La (Marker, FR)

Kissin' Cousins (Katzman)

License to Kill (Decoin, FR)

Monocle, The (Lautner, FR) a.k.a. *Le Monacle Rit Jaune*

Monstrosity (Masceli), a.k.a. *The Atomic Brain*

Seven Days in May (Frankenheimer)

633 Squadron (Grauman, GB)

Sky Above Heaven (Ciampi, FR/IT) a.k.a. *Le Ciel sur la Tête; Sky Above; Sky Beyond Heaven; Heaven on One's Hand*

Time Travelers (Melchoir)

Zombie (Tenney) a.k.a. *Voodoo Blood Bath; I Eat Your Skin* (1970 rerelease)

1965: 18/452

Bedford Incident, The (Harris)

Carry on Spying (Thomas, GB)

Crack in the World (Marton, US)

Die, Monster, Die! (Haller)

Dr. Who and the Daleks (Flemyng, GB)

Exterminators, The (Freda, FR)

Frankenstein Conquers the World (Honda, JA) a.k.a. *Furankenstein tai chiteikaijū* (Baragon)

Heroes of Telemark, The (Mann, GB)

Nick Carter and Red Club (Savignac, FR/IT) a.k.a. *Nick Carter et le Treile; Nick Carter Reviens*

Man with the Iron Mask, The (De Martino, WG/IT) a.k.a. *Der Mann Mit Den 1,000 Masken; The Spy with Ten Faces*

Mirage (Dmytryk)

Operation Atlantis (Flemming, IT);
a.k.a. *Agent SO3; Agent 003
Operazione Atlantide*
Planet of the Vampires (Bava, IT)
Sins of the Fleshapoids (Kuchar)
Spy Who Came in From the Cold, The
(Ritt)
These Are the Damned (Losey, GB),
a.k.a. *The Damned* (made 1961;
GB release 1963; US Release
1965)
Thunderball (Young, GB)
War Game, The (Watkins GB TVM)

1966: 41/451
AD 3 Operation White Whalefish
(Lewis, IT) a.k.a. *AD 3
Operazione Squalo Bianco;
Operation White Shark*
Agent Z 55 (Montero, FR/IT/SP),
a.k.a. *Agent Z 55: missione disper-
ata; Desperate Mission*
An Affair of States (Drechsel, WG)
a.k.a. *Zwei Girls von Roten Stern*
Ape and Essence (Benedictus, GB)
Atomic War Bride (NA)
Big Duel in the North Sea (Fukuda,
JA) a.k.a. *Nankai no dai ketto;
Godzilla vs. the Sea Monster*
Cyborg 2087 (Adreon)
Defector, The (Levy)
Dimension 5 (Adreon)
Dr. Goldfoot and the Girl Bombs
(Bava, IT)
Finders Keepers (Hayers, GB)
Funeral in Berlin (Hamilton, GB)
Gamera the Invincible (Yuasa, JA)
Gamara vs. Barugon (Tanaka, JA),
a.k.a. *Gammera tai Barugon*
Godzilla vs. Monster Zero (Honda,
JA 1965) a.k.a. *Kaijū daisensō;
Invasion of Astro-Monster;
Monster Zero*
Godzilla vs. the Sea Monster (Fukuda,
JA) a.k.a. *Gojira · Ibira · Mosura
Nankai no daikettō; Ebira,
Horror of the Deep*
Goldsnake "Anonima Killers" (Baldi,
FR)

Heart of Hiroshima, The (Kurahara,
JA) a.k.a. *Ai to shi no kiroku*
How We Stole the Atomic Bomb
(Fulci, IT) a.k.a. *Come
Rubammo la Bomba*
In the Claws of the Golden Dragon
(Parolini, WG/IT) a.k.a. *In Den
Klauen Des Goldenen Drachen*
In the Year 2889 (Buchanan) a.k.a.
2889; Year 2889
Island of Terror (Fisher, GB)
Judoka Agent Secret, Le (Zimmer,
FR/IT)
Kiss the Girls and Make Them Die
(Levin)
Missile Base at Taniak (Adreon,
TVM)
Night of Violence (Mauri, IT) a.k.a.
Le Notti della Violenza
Operation Apocalypse (Malatesta,
IT/SP) a.k.a. *Missione Apocalisse;
087 Mission Apocalypse*
Operation Lady Chaplin
(De Martino, IT/US) a.k.a.
*Missione Speciale Lady Chaplin;
Operazonione Lady Chaplin*
O.S.S. 117—Terror in Tokyo
(Boisrond, FR/IT) a.k.a. *Terror
in the Sky; Atout Coeur à Tokyo
pour O.S.S. 117*
*Russians Are Coming, the Russians
Are Coming, The* (Jewison)
Santos versus the Martian Invasion
(Crevenuna, MX) a.k.a. *Santo
Contra la Invasion de los
Marcianos*
Secret Agent Fireball (Martino a.k.a.
Donan, IT) *Les Espions Meurent à
Beyrouth*
Silencers, The (Karlson)
Spy with My Face, The (Newland)
Superago versus Diabolicus (Nostro,
IT/SP) a.k.a. *Superago Contro
Diabolicus*
Terror Beneath the Sea (Sato, JA)
a.k.a. *Kaitei daisensō*
That Man in Istanbul (Isasmendi,
IT/US)
Torn Curtain (Hitchcock)

War of the Gargantuas (Honda,
JA/US production)
Where the Bullets Fly (Gilling)
Wild World of Batwoman (Warren)
a.k.a. *She Was a Hippy Vampire*

1967: 24/462

Aliens from Another Planet
(Allen/Martin, TVM) from *Time
Tunnel*, TVP
Battle beneath the Earth (Tully, GB)
Casino Royale (Huston, et al., GB)
Coplan Saves His Skin (Boisset, FR)
a.k.a. *Coplan Sauve Sa Peau*
Day the Fish Came Out, The
(Cacoyannis, GE/GB)
Diabolik (Bava, IT/FR)
*End of August at the Hotel Ozone,
The* (Schmidt, CZ) a.k.a. *Konec
Srpna V Hotelu Ozon*
*Doomsday Machine (Sholem and
Hope)* a.k.a. *Escape from Planet
Earth; Doomsday; Armageddon
1975*
Fathom (Martinson)
Gamera vs. Gaos (Yuasa, JA) *Gamera
tai Gaos*
In Like Flint (Douglas)
It (Leder, GB/US) a.k.a. *It!; The
Golem*
Journey Beneath the Desert (Ulmer,
FR/IT), a.k.a.*L'Atlantide;
Antinea, L'Amante Della Citla
Sepolta; L'Altantitude-Antinee*
King Kong Escapes (Honda, JA)
Kingu Kongu no gyakushū
Mad Monster Party? (Bass,
animation)
Peking Blonde (Gessner, FR) *The
Blonde from Peking*
Rififi in Amsterdam (Hathaway,
SP/IT)
Son of Godzilla (Fukuda, JA) a.k.a.
*Kaijūtō no kessen Gojira no
musuko*
Syndicate, The (Goode, GB)
They Came from Beyond Space
(Fancis)
To Commit a Murder (Molinaro, FR)
Unknown Man of Shandigor, The

(Roy, SZ), a.k.a. *L'Inconnu De
Shandigor*
Vulture, The (Huntington, GB/CA)
You Only Live Twice (Gilbert, GB)

1968: 13/454

Brides of Blood (De Leon, US/PH)
a.k.a. *Blood of Brides; Brides of
Death*
Destroy All Monsters 1968 (Honda,
JA) a.k.a. *Kaijū sōshingeki*
Gamera vs. Outer Space Monster Vira
(Yuasa, JA) a.k.a. *Gamera tai
Viras; Destroy All Planets*
Ice Station Zebra (Sturges, US)
Lost Sex (Shindo, JA '66)
a.k.a.*Hon'nō; Ilono*
Mister Freedom (Klein, FR)
Night of the Living Dead (Romero)
Omegans, The (Wilder, US/PH)
Panic in the City (Davis)
Planet of the Apes (Schaffner)
Salt and Pepper (Donner)
Shame (Bergman, SW)
Shoes of the Fisherman, The
(Anderson)

1969: 15/412

Beneath the Planet of the Apes (Post)
Bambi Meets Godzilla (Newland, CA,
animated short)
Bed Sitting Room, The (Lester, GB)
Christmas Tree (Young, FR/IT)
a.k.a. *L'Alberto di Natale*
Color Me Dead (Davis, AU)
Day the Hot Line Got Hot, The
(Perier, FR/SP)
Deserters and the Nomads, The
(Jakubisco, CZ) a.k.a. *Zbehove a
Tulaci*
Gamera vs. Guiron (Yuasa, JA) a.k.a.
Gamera tai Guiron
Godzilla's Revenge (Honda, JA) a.k.a.
*Gojira Minira ·Gabara ōru kaijū
daishengeki; All Monsters Attack*
Green Slime, The (Fukasaku, JA/US)
Latitude Zero (Honda, US/JA) *Ido
zero daisakusen*
Looking Glass War, The (Pierson, GB)
Mosquito Squadron (Sagal, GB)
Topaz (US, Hitchcock)

Windows of Time, The (Fejer, HU)
a.k.a. *Az Ide Ablakaj*

1970: 13/367
Aatomik (Tugunov, ES animation)
Aquarians, The (McDougall)
Beyond Reason (Mangiamele, AU)
City beneath the Sea, (Allen, TVM)
Challenge, The (Smithee, TVM)
Colossus: the Forbin Project (Sargent)
a.k.a. *The Forbin Project; The Day
the World Changed Hands*
Delta Factor U.S.A., The (Garnett)
Gamera vs. Jiger (Yuasa, JA) a.k.a.
*Gamera tai Daima tai daimajū
Jaigā; Monsters Invade Expo 70*
Horrors of the Blood Monsters
(Adamson) a.k.a. *Vampire Men of
the Lost Planet*
I Killed Einstein, Gentlemen (Lipsky,
CZ)
Kremlin Letter, The (Huston)
Love War, The (McCowan)
Man Who Left His Will On Film, The
(Oshima, JA) a.k.a. *Tōkyō sensō
sengo hiwa*

1971: 16/432
Alien Terror (Hill/Ibanez, MX)
a.k.a. *La Invasion Siniestra;
Sinister Invasion; The Incredible
Invasion*
Assault on the Wayne (Chomsky,
TVM)
Andromeda Strain, The (Wise)
Earth II (Giries, TVM)
Escape from the Planet of the Apes
(Taylor)
Gamera vs. Zigra (Yuasa, JA) a.k.a.
Gamera tai shinkai kaijū Jigra
Glen and Randa (McBride)
H-Bomb (Chalong, TH/HK), a.k.a.
Great Friday; Operation Alpha
Octa-Man (Essex)
Omega Man, The (Sagal)
$1,000,000 Duck (McEveety)
President's Plane Is Missing, The
(Duke, TVM)
Silent Running (Trumbull)
Steagle, The (Sylbert)
THX 1138 (Lucas)

Wild in the Sky (Naud/Dunne)

1972: 7/376
Blood of Ghastly Horror (Adamson),
a.k.a. *The Fiend with the Atomic
Brain; Psycho a Go Go; The Love
Maniac, The Man with the
Synthetic Brain; The Fiend with
the Electronic Brain*
Delphi Bureau, The (Wendkos, TVM)
Doomwatch (Sasdy, GB)
Godzilla on Monster Island (Fukuda,
JA) a.k.a. *Chikyō cōgeki meirei
Gojira tai Gaigan; Godzilla vs.
Gigan*
Godzilla vs. The Smog Monster
(Banno, JA 1971) a.k.a. *Gojira
tai Hedora; Godzilla vs. Hedorah*
Madame Sin (Greene, TVM)
Memories of Underdevelopment (Alea,
CU) a.k.a. *Memories De
Subdesarollo*

1973: 11/463
Barn of the Naked Dead (Rudolph)
Battle for the Planet of the Apes
(Thompson)
Genesis II (Moxey, TVM)
Ground Zero (Flocker) a.k.a. *The
Golden Gate Is Ground Zero*
Idaho Transfer (Fonda)
Innocent Bystanders (Collinson, GB)
Invasion of the Bee Girls (Sanders)
Last Days of Man on Earth, The
(Fuest, GB) a.k.a. *The Final
Programme*
Neptune Factor, The (Petrie, CA)
a.k.a. *Neptune Disaster, An
Underwater Odyssey*
O Lucky Man (Anderson, GB)
Refuge of Fear, The (Ulloa, SP) *El
Refugio del Miedo*

1974: 10/550
Blondy (Gobbi, FR/WG) a.k.a.
Germicide
Chosen Survivors (Roley)
Dark Star (Carpenter)
Dead Don't Die, The (Harrington,
TVM)
Godzilla vs. The Cosmic Monster

(Fukuda, JA) a.k.a. *Gojira tai
Mekagojira; Godzilla vs. the Bionic
Monster*
Hoax, The (Anderson)
Missiles of October, The (Page, TVM)
Planet Earth (Daniels, TVM)
Prophesies of Nostradamus (Masuda,
JA) a.k.a. *Nosutoradamusu no
daiyogen Catastrophe—1999;
Catastrophe 1999; The Last Days
of Planet Earth*
Space 1999 (Katzin, GB/IT)

1975: 8/604
Boy and His Dog, A (Jones)
Collision Course (Page, TVM)
Cranes are Flying, The (Kalatozov,
RU), a.k.a. *Letyat zhuravli*
Giant Spider Invasion, The (Rebane)
Give 'em Hell, Harry (Binder)
People Who Own the Dark
(de Ossorio, SP)
Terror of Mechagodzilla (Honda, JA)
a.k.a. *Mekagojira no gyakushū*
Ultimate Warrior, The (Clouse)

1976: 9/575
Barefoot Gen (Yamada, JA anima-
tion); a.k.a. *Hadashi no Gen*
Big Bus, The (Frawley)
*Francis Gary Powers: The True Story
of the U-2 Spy Incident* (Mann,
TVM)
Gemini Man, The (Levi, TVM) a.k.a.
Code Name: Minus One
Godzilla vs. Megalon (Fukuda, JA
'73) a.k.a. *Gojira tai Megaro*
Infra-Man (Hua-Shan, HK) a.k.a.
*Zhongguo Chaoren; The Super
Infra-Man*
Kingston: Power Play (Day, TVM)
a.k.a. *Kingston and the Newspaper
Game*
Logan's Run (Anderson)
Riding with Death (Levi/McDougal,
TVM)

1977: 23/560
Alpha Incident, The (Rebane)
Amazing Spider-Man (Swackhamer,
TVM)

Billy Jack Goes to Washington
(Laughlin)
Damnation Alley (Smight)
Day It Came to Earth, The (Braden)
Day of the Animals (Girdler) a.k.a.
Something Is Out There
Demon Seed (Cammell)
Empire of the Ants (Gordon)
End of the World (Hayes)
Golden Rendezvous (Lazarus, SA)
a.k.a. *Nuclear Terror*
Hills Have Eyes, The (Craven)
Incredible Hulk, The (Johnson,
TVM)
Kentucky Fried Movie, The (Landis)
MacArthur (Sargent)
Operation Ganymed (Erler, WG)
a.k.a. *Helden—Operation
Ganymed*
Red Alert (Hale, TVM)
Return of the Incredible Hulk (Levi,
TVM)
Space Cruiser Yamato (Nishizaki, JA,
animation) a.k.a. *Unchusenkan
Yamato*
Spiderman (Swackhamer, TVM)
Spy Who Loved Me, The (Gilbert)
Twilight's Last Gleaming (Aldrich
US/WG)
Warhead (O'Connor)
Wizards (Bakshi, animation)

1978: 22/354
Amazing Captain Nemo, The
(March)
Bermuda Depths (Kotani, TVM)
Blue Christmas (Okamoto, JA) a.k.a.
*Burū kurisumasu; Blood Type:
Blue*
Chinese Web, The (McDougal, TVM)
Cruise Missile (Martinson, IR, IT, SP,
US, WG) a.k.a. *Missile X: The
Neutron Bomb Incident; The
Teheran Incident; Missile X—
Geheimuu Ftrag
Neutraonenbombe*
Dawn of the Dead (Romero) a.k.a.
Zombie(s)
Deathsport (Suso)
Dr. Scorpion (Lang)

Piranha (Dante)
Return from Witch Mountain
(Hough)
Don't Cry (Ertaud, FR) a.k.a. Ne
Pleure Pas
Escort to Danger (NA)
Gray Lady Down (Greene)
Holocaust 2000 (De Martino,
IT/GB) The Chosen; Holocaust
2000: The Chosen
Incredible Melting Man, The (Sachs)
Matter of State (NA, TVM) a.k.a.
Photo Finish
Slithis (Traxler)
Spiderman Strikes Back (Satlof,
TVM) a.k.a. Spiderman: the
Deadly Dust; Deadly Dust
Superman: The Movie (Donner)
Swarm, The (Allen)
Top Secret (Leaf, TVM)
Uranium Conspiracy, The (Golan, IS)

1979: 17/414*

Alien (Scott)
Beyond the Poseidon Adventure
(Allen)
Black Sun, The (Vávra, CZ) a.k.a.
Cerne Slunce; Dark Sun; (cf.,
Krakatit 1948)
Bride of the Incredible Hulk
(Johnson, TVM)
Captain America (Holcomb, TVM)
China Syndrome (Bridges)
Doomsday Chronicles (NA)
Express to Terror (Curtis, TVM)
H. G. Wells' The Shape of Things to
Come (McCowan, CA)
Late Great Planet Earth, The
(Amram)
Man Called Intrepid, A (Carter,
TVMINI)
Man Who Stole the Sun (Hasegawa,
JA) a.k.a. Taiyō o nusunda otoko;
The Boy Who Stole the Sun
Meteor (Neame)
Plutonium (Erler, WG, TVM)
Ravagers, The (Compton)
Screamers (Martino, IT/US) a.k.a.
L'Isola Degli Uomini Pesce
Stalker (Tarkovsky, SU)

1980: 22/414*

Aftermath, The (Barkett)
Chain Reaction (Barry, AU) a.k.a.
Nuclear Run
Children, The (Kalmanowicz) a.k.a.
Children of Ravensback
Deadline (Nicholson, AU)
Denmark Closed Down (Tschernia,
DM) a.k.a. Danmark Er Lukket
Die Laughing (Werner)
Enola Gay: The Men, the Mission, the
Atomic Bomb (Rich, TVM)
Final Countdown, The (Taylor)
Golem, The (Szulkin, PO)
Hangar 18 (Conway) a.k.a. Invasion
Force
Island Claws (Cardenas) a.k.a. Night
of the Claw
Lathe of Heaven, The
(Loxton/Barzyk, TVM)
M Station Hawaii (Lord)
Martian Chronicles, The (Anderson,
TVM)
Nightmare City (Lenzi, SP/IT)
Once upon a Spy (Nagy, TVM)
Plutonium Incident, The (Michaels,
TVM)
Power Within, The (Moxey, TVM)
Superman II (Lester)
Stronger Than the Sun (Apted, GB,
TVM)
Virus (Fukasaku, JA/US) Fukkatsu
no hi
Wild and the Free, The (Hill, TVM)

1981: 7/414

Escape from New York (Carpenter)
Fire on the Mountain (Wrye, TVM)
For Your Eyes Only (Glen, GB)
Malevil (Chalonge, FR/WG) a.k.a.
Malevis Countdownder Neutronen
Bombe
Modern Problems (Shapiro)
People from the Forest (Jackson, GB,
TV)
Super Fuzz (Corbucci, IT/US)

1982: 14/474

Alone in the Dark (Sholder)
Atomic Cafe, The
(Rafferty/Rafferty/Loader)

Big Meat Eater (Windsor, CA)
Cafe Flesh (Dream)
Final Option, The (Sharp, GB) a.k.a.
  Who Dares Wins
In the King of Prussia (de
  Antonio/Hanlon,
  CTVM/Docudrama)
Lola (Fassbinder, WG)
Old Men at the Zoo, The (Burge, GB,
  TVMINI)
Soldier, The (Glickenhaus)
State of Things, The (Wenders, WG)
Survival Zone (Rubens, AU/US/IT)
Warlords of the 21st Century (Cokliss)
World War III, parts 1&2
  (Greene/Sagal, TVM)
Wrong Is Right (Brooks)

1983: 30/395

All the Wrong Spies (Kwan a.k.a.
  Robin, HK) a.k.a. Wo Qui Ye Lai
  Xiang
Being, The (Kong)
Blood Rush (Richmond)
Children of Nagasaki (Kinoshita, JA)
  a.k.a. Kono ko o nokoshite
Daniel (Lumet)
Day After, The (Meyer, TVM)
Due to an Act of God (Boldt, WG)
  a.k.a. Im Zeichen Des Kreuzes
Endgame (Benson [D'Amato],
  US/IT) a.k.a. Gioco finale
Kennedy (Goddard, US/GB, TVMI-
  NI)
Last Kids on Earth, The (NA)
Never Say Never Again (Kershner)
Octopussy (Glen, GB)
Raiders of Atlantis (Franklin)
Rats (Mattei AKA Dawn, FR/IT)
  a.k.a. Les Rats de Manhattan;
  Ratti: notee di terrore; Rats:
  Night Terror
Return of the Man from U.N.C.L.E.
  (Austin, TVM)
Sans Soleil (Marker, FR)
She (Nesher, IT)
Silkwood (Nichols)
Special Bulletin (Zwick, TVM)
Stryker (Santiago, PH/US)
Superman III (Lester)

Taking Tiger Mountain (Huckabee,
  WA)
Teacher, The (Ōsawa, JA) a.k.a. Sensei
Testament (Littman, TVM)
2019: After the Fall of New York
  (Dolman/Martino, US/IT)
Undercovers (Perry-Rhine)
War and Peace (Schlongdorff/Boll,
  WG) a.k.a. Krieg und Frieden
War Games (Badham)
Warriors of the Wasteland (Castellari,
  IT) a.k.a. The New Barbarians; I
  Nouvi Barbari
Yor: Hunter from the Future
  (Dawson a.k.a. Margheriti,
  IT/US)

1984: 33/410*

Atomic Station (Jonsson, IC)
Blade Master, The (Hills, IT), a.k.a.
  Ator the Invincible; Cave Dwellers
Call to Glory (Carter, TVM)
Countdown to Looking Glass (Barzyk,
  CTVM)
C.H.U.D. (Cheek)
Def-Con 4 (Donovan, CA)
Dreamscape (Ruben)
Dune (Lynch)
Future Is Woman, The (Ferreri,
  IT/WG/FR) a.k.a. Il Futuro è
  Donna
Future-Kill (Moore)
Hell Squad (Hartford)
Inside Man, The (Clegg)
Last Battle, The (Besson, FR) a.k.a.
  Le Dernier Combat
Massive Retaliation (Cohen)
Nasushika of the Valley of the Wind
  (Miyazaki, JA) a.k.a. Kaze no tani
  no Naushika; Warriors of the
  Wind
O-bi, O-ba: The End of Civilization
  (Szulkin, PO)
One Night Stand (Duigan, AU)
Prince Jack (Lovitt)
Rage (Ricci a.k.a. Richmond, IT/SP)
  a.k.a. Rabbia; A Man Called
  Rage
Red Dawn (Milius)
Repo Man (Cox)

Revenge of the Mermaid (Ikeda, JA)
a.k.a. *Ningyo densetsu*
Sakharov (Gold, HBO TVM)
Sex Mission (Machulski, PO) a.k.a.
Seksmisja
Terminator, The (Cameron)
Threads (Jackson, GB, TVM)
Time Bomb (Krasny, TVM)
2010 (Hyams)
V, Part 5 (Johnson, TVM) a.k.a. *V,
The Final Battle*
Velvet (Lang)
Warrior of the Lost World (Worth, IT)
Where the Green Ants Dream
(Herzog, WG/AU)
Z for Zachariah (Garner, GB, TVM)

1985: 34/425

Access Code (Sobel)
Back to the Future (Zemeckis)
Big Snit, The (Condie, CA, animated
short)
Blunt—The Fourth Man (Glenister,
GB, TVM), a.k.a. *Blunt*
Bombs Away (Wilson)
Bootleg (Prescott, AU)
Day of the Dead (Romero)
Defense of the Realm (Drury, GB)
Desert Warrior (Santiago)
a.k.a. *Wheels of Fire; Pyro;
Vindicator*
Edge of Darkness (Campbell, GB,
TVMINI)
Exterminators of the Year 3000
(Harrison, IT/SP)
Future Hunters (Santiago, PH) a.k.a.
Deadly Quest; Spears of Destiny
Future-Kill (Moore)
Godzilla 1985 (Hashimoto, JA '84)
a.k.a. *Gojira; Godzilla 1985: The
Legend Is Reborn; The Return of
Godzilla*
Hills Have Eyes, Part 2, The (Craven)
Hydra (Green, US/SP)
Insignificance (Roeg, GB)
Jigsaw Man, The (Young, GB)
Land of Doom (Maris)
Life Force (Hooper)
Mad Max beyond Thunderdome
(Miller/Ogilvie, AU) a.k.a. *Mad

Max III: Beyond Thunderdome*
Morons from Outer Space (Hodges,
GB)
92 Grosvenor Street (Larry, US/GB)
a.k.a. *Behind Enemy Lines*
Orion's Belt (Solum, NO) a.k.a.
Orions belte
Return of the Living Dead
(O'Bannon)
Secret Shore (Jones, WA)
Spies Like Us (Landis)
Static (Romanek)
Toxic Avenger, The (Herz/Weil)
2020 Texas Gladiators (Mancuso IT)
View to a Kill, A (Glen, GB)
Warriors of the Apocalypse (Suarez)
What Waits Below (Sharp)
Weird Science (Hughes)

1986: 31/432

Aliens (Cameron)
America 3000 (Engelbach)
Barefoot Gen 2 (Hirata, JA) a.k.a.
Hadashi no Gen (animation)
*Choke Canyon: On Dangerous
Ground* (Bail) a.k.a. *On
Dangerous Ground; Choke Canyon*
Class of Nuke 'Em High (Haines)
C.A.T. Squad (Friedkin, TVM) a.k.a.
Stalking Danger
*Dead End Kids: A Story of Nuclear
Power* (Akalaitis)
Desert Bloom (Corr)
Edge, The (Burrow, CA)
Fifth Missile, The (Peerce, TVM)
Final Executioner, The (Guerrieri, IT)
I-Man (Allen)
Letters from a Dead Man
(Lopushanski) a.k.a. *Disma
Myortvogo Cheloveka*
Manhattan Project, The (Brickman)
a.k.a. *The Manhattan Project: The
Deadly Game*
Misfits of Science (Parriott/Zanetos,
TVM)
Nuclear Conspiracy, The (Erler,
WG/AU, TVM) a.k.a. *News—
Bericht über eine Reise in eine
strahlende Zukunft*
Patriot, The (Harris)

Population: One (Daaalder)
Project "A" Ko (Nishijima, JA)
Radioactive Dreams (Pyun)
Raiders of the Living Dead (Piper)
Robot Holocaust (Kincaid)
Sacrifice, The (Tarkovsky, SW/FR)
a.k.a. *Offret*
Short Circuit (Badham)
Star Trek IV: The Voyage Home
(Nimoy)
State of Emergency, A (Bennet)
Thunder Run (Hudson)
Unmasking the Idol (Keeter)
Warlords (Ray)
When the Wind Blows (Murakami,
GB, animation)
Whoops Apocalypse (Bussman, GB)

1987: 27/494

Amazing Grace and Chuck (Newell),
a.k.a. *Silent Voice*
Big Bang, The (Picha, BE/FR) a.k.a.
Le Big Bang
Control (Montaldo, CTVM)
Creepozoids (DeCoteau)
Defense Play (Markham)
Delta Force Commando (Valenti)
Empire of the Sun (Spielberg)
Equalizer 2000 (Santiago, Video
Movie)
Fourth Protocol, The (Mackenzie, GB)
Gate, The (Takacs, CA)
Ground Zero (Pattinson/Myles, AU)
Heaven and Earth (Lommel)
Hell Comes to Frogtown (Kizer and
Jackson)
I Was a Teenage Zombie (Michalakis)
Last Emperor, The (Bertolucci,
IT/GB/CH)
Last of England, The (Jarman, GB)
Living Daylights, The (Glen, GB)
Plutonium Baby (Hirschman)
Project X (Kaplan)
RoboCop (Verhoeven)
Rock and Rule (Smith)
Slugs (Simon)
Steel Dawn (Hool)
Superman IV: The Quest for Peace
(Furie)

Survivor (Shackleton, CA/GB)
Time Guardian (Hannant, AU)
Urban Warriors (Warren)

1988: 24/466

Akira (Ōtomo, JA, animation)
Chief Zabu (Cohen, Zuker)
Crime Zone (Llosa)
Curse II: The Bite (Goodwin)
Death Ward (Fahmy, EY) *Anbar El
Mawi*
Disaster at Silo 7 (Elikann, TVM)
D.O.A. (Morton)
Frantic (Polanski)
Incredible Hulk Returns, The (Corea,
TVM)
Iron Eagle II (Furie, CA/IS)
Mutants in Paradise (Apostoulo)
Not of This Earth (Wynorski)
Pursuit of Happiness, The (Ansara,
AU)
Rock and the Alien (Rondinella)
Sisterhood (Santiago, US/PH)
Sons of Steel (Keady, AU)
Stranger on My Land (Elikann,
TVM)
Terror Squad (Maris)
Tomorrow (Kuroki, JA) a.k.a. *Ashita*
Uninvited (Clark)
Very British Coup, A (Jackson, GB
TVMINI)
War of The Worlds
(Bloomfield/Bond, TVM pilot)
World Gone Wild (Katzin)
Zombie 3 (Fulci, IT/US) a.k.a.
Zombi 3

1989: 28/472

Abyss, The (Cameron)
*Adventures of Baron Munchausen,
The* (Gilliam, GB/WG)
Back to the Future II (Zemeckis)
Black Rain (Imamura, JA) a.k.a.
Kuroi ame
Day One (Sargent, TVM)
Deadly Spygames (Sell)
Deadly Weapon (Miner)
DeepStar Six (Cunningham)
Desert Warrior (Goldman, PH)
Fat Man and Little Boy (Joffe)

Godzilla vs. Biollante (Ōmori, JA)
  Gojira tai Biorante
Handmaid's Tale, The (Schlöndorff)
Millennium (Anderson, US/CA)
Miracle Mile (de Jarnatt)
Moontrap (Dyke)
Murder By Moonlight (Lindsay-Hogg,
  GB, TVM)
My Dissident Mom (NA, TVM)
Nightbreaker (Markle, CTVM)
Package, The (Davis)
Personal Choice (Saperstein) a.k.a.
  Beyond the Star; Secret
Quartermass Conclusion, The
  (Haggard, GB,TVMINI)
Rift, The (Simón, SP) a.k.a. *La*
  Grieta Endless Descent
Robotjox (Gordon)
Toxic Avenger: Part II, The
  (Herz/Kaufman)
Toxic Avenger: Part III, The
  (Herz/Kaufman) a.k.a. *The Last*
  Temptation of Toxie
Trial of the Incredible Hulk, The
  (Bixby, TVM)
War Birds (Lommel)
Young Einstein (Serious, AU)

1990: 31/469
Akira Kurosawa's Dreams
  (Kurosawa, JA/US) a.k.a. *Yume*
Back to the Future Part III
  (Zemeckis)
Blood of Heroes, The (Peoples, AU)
  a.k.a. *The Salute of the Jugger*
Burndown (Allen)
By Dawn's Early Light (Sholder,
  CTVM)
Death of the Incredible Hulk, The
  (Bixby, TVM)
Death Merchant, The (Winburn)
Decay (Bellkov, US/UK) a.k.a.
  Raspad
E.A.R.T.H. Force (Corcoran, TVM-
  Pilot)
Flesh Gordon Meets the Cosmic
  Cheerleaders (Ziehm)
Emissary, The (Stoltz)
Fourth War, The (Frankenheimer)
Full Fathom Five (Franklin)

Future Force (Prior)
Future Zone (Prior, V) a.k.a. *Future*
  Force 2
Hardware (Stanley, GB)
Hiroshima: Out of the Ashes (Werner,
  TVM)
Hunt for Red October, The
  (McTiernan)
Killer Crocodile 2/II (De Rossi,
  US/IT)
Reflecting Skin, The (Ridley,
  GB/CA)
RoboC.H.I.C. (Hansen/Mandell)
Russia House, The (Schepisi)
Secret Weapon (Sharp, US/AU,
  CTVM)
Shadowzone (Cardone)
Spontaneous Combustion (Hooper)
Star Quest: Beyond the Rising Moon
  (Cook)
Teenage Mutant Ninja Turtles
  (Barron)
Time Troopers (Samann/Neiman,
  AU/US)
Total Recall (Verhoeven)
Unbelievable Truth, The (Hartley)
Waiting for the Light (Monger)

1991: 21/423
American Ninja 4: The Annihilation
  (Sundstrom)
Born to Ride (Barker)
Chernobyl: The Final Warning (Page,
  CTVM, US, GB, Russia)
Class of Nuke 'Em High Part 2:
  Subhumanoid Meltdown (Louzil)
Delta Force Commando 2 (Valenti,
  IT)
Delta Force 3: Young Commandos
  (Firstenberg)
Eve of Destruction (Gibbins)
Flight of Black Angel (Mostow,
  CTVM) a.k.a. *War Birds 2* (over-
  seas V, 1990)
Godzilla vs. King Ghidorah (Ōmori,
  JA) a.k.a. *Gojira tai Kingu*
  Gidora
Going Under (Travis)
Highlander 2: The Quickening
  (Mulcahy)

Meet the Applegates (Lehmann)
Naked Gun, 2¹/₂: The Smell of Fear, The (Zucker)
Never Leave Nevada (Swartz)
Rhapsody in August (Kurosawa, JA)
  a.k.a. *Hachigatsu no rapusodī*
Space Avenger (Pressman)
Teenage Mutant Ninja Turtles II: The Secret of the Ooze (Pressman)
Terminator 2: Judgment Day (Cameron)
Touch and Die (Solinas, GB+)
Tribulation 99: Alien Anomalies Under America (Baldwin)
Until the End of the World (Wenders, FR+)
Xtro 2: The Second Encounter (Davenport, CA)

1992: 11/425

Bloodfist IV: Die Trying (Ziller)
Close to Eden (Mikhalkov, SU/FR)
Critters 4 (Harvey)
Escape from . . . . Survival Zone (Jones) a.k.a. *The Runner*
Godzilla vs. Mothra (Ōkawara, JA)
  a.k.a. *Gojira tai Mosura; Godzilla vs. Mothra: The Battle for Earth*
Miracle Beach (Snider)
Neon City (Markham, CA)
Raspad (Belikov, US/SU)
Roadside Prophets (Wool)
Under Siege (Davis)
Welcome to Oblivion (Tamayo/Tent)

1993: 15/440

CIA—Code Name Alexa (Merhi)
Detonator (Jackson)
Executioners (Kei-Fung/ Siu-Tung, HK
Firehawk (Santiago)
Godzilla vs. Mechagodzilla II/2/Two (Ōkawara, JA) a.k.a. *Gojira tai Mekagojira*
Hard Hunter (Sidaris)
Honor and Glory (Hall, US/HK)
Invaders (Cook)
Matinee (Dante)
Metamorphosis: The Alien Factor (Takakjian)

Nostradamus Kid, The (Ellis, AU)
Philadelphia Experiment 2, The (Cornwell)
Return to Frogtown (Jackson) a.k.a. *Frogtown II; Hell Comes to Frogtown II*
Teenage Mutant Ninja Turtles III (Gillard)
Year of the Dog, The (Aranovich, RU/FR)

1994: 21/410

American Cyborg: Steel Warrior (Davidson)
Bloodfist VI: Ground Zero (Jackobson) a.k.a. *Assault at Ground Zero; Ground Zero*
Blue Sky (Richardson)
Breach of Conduct (Matheson)
C.I.A. II Target: Alexa (Lamas)
Crawlers, The (Laurenti, IT)
Digger (Turner, US/CA)
Fantastic Four, The (Sassone)
Frostfire (Greene, US/CA, TVM)
Godzilla vs. Spacegodzilla (Yamashita, JA) a.k.a. *Gojira tai Supēsugojira; Godzilla vs. Space Monster; Godzilla vs. Super-Godzilla*
I.Q. (Schepisi)
MacGyver: Trail to Doomsday (Correll, TVM)
New Crime City: Los Angeles 2020 (Rossovich)
Night Siege Project: Shadowchaser 2 (Eyres) a.k.a. *Project Shadow Chaser II; Armed and Deadly; Night Siege*
No Escape (Campbell)
Operation Plutonium (Ockermueller, GR, TVM)
Royce (Holcomb)
Shadow, The (Mulcahy)
Stargate (Emmerich, US/FR)
Terminal Impact (Wein)
True Lies (Cameron)

1995: 17/370

Captain Nuke and the Bomber Boys (Gale)
Carnosaur II (Morneau)

Class of Nuke 'Em High 3: The Good,
   the Bad, and the Subhuman
   (Louzil)
Crimson Tide (Scott)
Detonator I: Night Watch (Jackson,
   TVM) a.k.a. *Allistar MacLean's*
   "Night Watch" (TVM)
Digital Man (Roth)
Gamera: The Guardian of the
   Universe (Kaneko, JA) a.k.a.
   Gamera daikaijū kūchū kessen
Godzilla vs. Destororoyah (Ōkawara,
   JA) a.k.a. *Gojira tai Desutoroia;*
   Godzilla vs Destroyer
Op Center (Teague, TVM) a.k.a.
   Tom Clancy's Op Center
Project Shadow Chaser 3000 (Eyres)
Spitfire (Pyun)
Suspect Device (Jacobson, TVM)
Timemaster (Glickenhaus)
Truman (Pierson)
Under Siege 2: Dark Territory
   (Murphy)
Warhead (Roper, US/SA)
Waterworld (Reynolds)

1996: 18/420

Alien Chaser (Roper)
Beneath the Bermuda Triangle (Levy,
   CA, TVM) a.k.a. *Time Under Fire*
Big Wars, The (Takizawa/Kume, JA)
   a.k.a. *Daisenki* (93, animation)
Broken Arrow (Woo)
Chain Reaction (Davis)
Crash Dive (Stevens)
Danger Zone (Eastman)
Dogfighters, The (Zetlin)
Down Periscope (Ward)
Independence Day (Emmerich)
Infinity (Broderick)
Jackie Chan's First Strike (Tong, HK)
John Carpenter's Escape from LA
   (Carpenter)
Mars Attacks (Burton)
Mullholland Falls (Tamahori)
Mystery Science Theater 3000: The
   Movie (Mallon)
Star Trek: First Contact
   (Frakes/Leonetti)

Steel Sharks (McDonald)

1997: 21/461

Air Force One (Petersen)
Counter Measures (Ray/Raymond)
   a.k.a. *Crash Dive II*
Dead Men Can't Dance (Anderson)
Doomsday Rock (Trenchard-Smith)
   a.k.a. *Cosmic Shock*
Double Team (Hark)
Falling Fire (D'or, CA) a.k.a. *3*
   Minutes to Impact
Fifth Element, The (Besson, FR)
Flubber (Mayfield)
Hope (Hawn, TVM)
Hostile Waters (Drury/Curtis,
   FR/GR/GB/US, TVM)
Jackie Chan's First Strike (Tong)
Kiss or Kill (Bennet, AU)
Mighty Ducks: The First Face-Off
   (Murphy et al.)
Operation Delta Force 2: Mayday
   (Wein)
Peacekeeper (Forestier) a.k.a.
   Hellbent; Red Zone
Peacemaker, The (Leder)
Postman, The (Costner)
Rapid Assault (Scott, V) a.k.a. *Steel*
   Sharks 2
Starship Troopers (Verhoeven)
Sub Down (Smithee/Champion,
   LX/USA)
Tomorrow Never Dies (Spottiswoode,
   US/GB)

1998: 18/490

Armageddon (Bay)
Atomic Dog (Thenchard-Smith)
Austin Powers: International Man of
   Mystery (Roach)
Butcher Boy, The (Jordan, IL)
Crazy Six (Pyun)
Deep Impact (Leder)
Dr. Akagi (Imamura, JA) *Kanzō*
   sensei
Enemy Action (Howell/Mandylor)
Godzilla (Emmerich)
Hamilton (Zwart, SW)
Michael Kael vs. the World News
   Company (Smith, FR) a.k.a.

*Michael Kael contre la World
News Company; Michael Kael in
Katango*
Operation Delta Force 3: Clear Target
(Roper) a.k.a. *Clear Target*
Pandora Project (Terlesky/Wynorski)
Seven Islands (Wournell, CA) a.k.a.
Separate Interests
Six String Samurai (Mungia)
Vanishing Man, The (Stroud, GB,
TVMINI)
Viimeiset humalaiset (NA, FL)
World War Three (Knopp/Stone,
GR)

1999: 14/490
Airboss III: The Payback (Ingvordsen)
Atomic Train (Jackson/Lowry,
TVMINI)
Blast from the Past (Wilson)
*Citizen Toxie: The Toxic Avenger
Part 4* (Kaufman)
Clown Smiles, The (Besnard, FR)
a.k.a. *Le sourire du clown*
Deterrence (Luri)
Diplomatic Siege (Graef-Marino)
Doomwatch: Winter Angel (Battersby,
GB, TVM)
Gamera 3: Revenge of Iris (Kaneko)
a.k.a. *Gamera 3 Irisu kakusei*
Icebreaker (Giancola)
Out of Courage 2: Out for Vengeance
(Wilson)
Shapeshifter (Browning)
Top of the Food Chain (Paizs)
World Is Not Enough, The (Apted,
US/GB)

2000 (January to September): 11/NA
Alien Fury: Countdown to Invasion
(Hedden)
Chain of Command (Terlesky,
FR/US)
Crackerjack 3 (Simandl, CA)
Fail Safe (Frears, TVM)
Frozen Inferno, The (Martinez, V)
Godzilla 2000: Millennium
(Ōkawara, JA '99) a.k.a. *Gojira
2000: mireniamu*
Intrepid (Putch)

On the Beach (Mulcahy, TVM)
Roswell: The Aliens Attack (Turner,
CA, TVM)
Space Cowboys (Eastwood)
Straight Shooter (Bohn, GR)

Not Yet Released, in Production, or in Development, as of September 2000:

2000: NA/NA
Class of Nuke 'Em High IV
Godzilla x Megaguilas (Tezuka, JA)
a.k.a. *Gojira tai Megagirasu;
scheduled release date: December
16, 2000*

2001: NA/NA
Incredible Shrinking Man, The
(Segal)
Spider-Man (Raimi) a.k.a. *Spiderman*
Sum of All Fears, The (Robinson)

2002: NA/NA
Mad Max IV (Miller)
True Lies 2 (Cameron)
Terminator 3 (Scott)

MISC (unconfirmed or otherwise not previously included films)
Funeral Racket (Misumi, JA
'68/'70) a.k.a. *Tomuraishi-tachi*
(Rarely seen film. Discrepancies in
reference books; some suggest an
atomic weapon is detonated in
the conclusion.)
Hiroshima 28 (Lung, 1974, HK)
Nuclear Baby, The (Iranian, late
1980s early 1990s); (nuclear
weapon kills only Salman
Rushdie)
Fatherland (Menaul, 1994, TVM)
Soldier (Anderson, 1998)
Thirteen Guys (Donoldso, 2000)
X-Men (Singer, 2000; vague refer-
ences to film, or characters, as
"Children of the Atom")
Z for Zacchariah (Pappas, 2000,
US/CZ); probable remake of
1984 film, based on a novel of
the same name)

INDEX